Teaching American Studies

Teaching American Studies

State of the Classroom as State of the Field

EDITED BY
ELIZABETH DUCLOS-ORSELLO,
JOSEPH ENTIN, AND REBECCA HILL

WITH A FOREWORD BY
RODERICK A. FERGUSON
AND AN AFTERWORD BY
KANDICE CHUH

UNIVERSITY PRESS OF KANSAS

Published by the University Press of Kansas (Lawrence, Kansas 66045), which was organized by the Kansas Board of Regents and is operated and funded by Emporia State University, Fort Hays State University, Kansas State University, Pittsburg State University, the University of Kansas, and Wichita State University.

Library of Congress Cataloging-in-Publication Data

Names: Duclos-Orsello, Elizabeth Ann, editor. | Entin, Joseph B., editor. | Hill, Rebecca Nell, 1969– editor. | Ferguson, Roderick A., writer of foreword. | Chuh, Kandice, 1968– writer of afterword.
Title: Teaching American studies : state of the classroom as state of the field / editors, Elizabeth Duclos-Orsello, Joseph Entin, Rebecca Hill ; foreword by Roderick A. Ferguson ; afterword by Kandice Chuh.
Description: Lawrence, Kansas : University Press of Kansas, 2021. | Includes bibliographical references and index.
Identifiers: LCCN 2020048515
ISBN 9780700632367 (cloth)
ISBN 9780700632374 (paperback)
ISBN 9780700632381 (epub)
Subjects: LCSH: Teaching—Methodology. | United States—Study and teaching.
Classification: LCC E175.8 .T4117 2021 | DDC 973/.071—dc23
LC record available at https://lccn.loc.gov/2020048515.

British Library Cataloguing-in-Publication Data is available.

Printed in the United States of America

10 9 8 7 6 5 4 3 2 1

The paper used in this publication is acid free and meets the minimum requirements of the American National Standard for Permanence of Paper for Printed Library Materials Z39.48–1992.

To all of our students and all of our teachers

Contents

Foreword

Teaching American Studies: State of the Classroom as State of the Field might also be considered an observation about the state of this nation; its insights reach beyond the confines of any particular field. Indeed, the editors and contributors to this essential volume address the ways that the interdisciplinary classroom in general, and the American Studies classroom in particular, is ground zero for the culture wars.

The volume itself is born out of the epistemic transformations within American Studies. We can think here of the field's move from an interdiscipline designed to bolster US exceptionalism, its subsequent transformation via the emergence of the New Left, and its rearticulation as a location for issues concerning migration, prison expansion, transphobia, heteropatriarchy, ableism, settler colonialism, racial violence, and so on. These epistemic shifts have also brought countless minoritized scholars to the field, making American Studies one of the most diverse sites of intellectual engagement within the American academy.

Reflecting that dynamism and diversity, *Teaching American Studies* points to the constant dialogue between "the classroom" and "the street." Witness, for instance, the discourse marshaled by Black Lives Matter protesters, and you will hear a language honed in American Studies, gender studies, queer studies, Black studies, Native American studies, disability studies, and ethnic studies—the very fields represented in the national meetings of the American Studies Association. In many ways, the protests around racism and state violence in the summer of 2020 prove the real-world importance and relevance of interdisciplinarity, testifying to the power that those fields can claim over the disciplines.

In addition to providing a context for the insurgency of subjugated knowledges and communities, fields like American Studies have also been the targets of conservative backlash. New and exciting curricular developments have been demeaned as the gathering of veritable mobs bent on suppressing democratic exchanges on college campuses. In many ways, though, this hysterical response proves what the editors and contributors of this volume already know. The conservative histrionics about left-wing takeovers of universities—however misguided—point to the potential of the progressive classroom to effect personal and social change. We might recall here the 1971 warning that former Supreme Court justice Lewis F. Powell issued to the conservative US Chamber of Commerce in his secret memo, popularly known as the "Powell Memorandum." Worried in particular about the classroom as the site for developing critiques of capitalism, he said about professors who engaged such critiques, "Such faculty members need not be in a majority. They are often personally attractive and magnetic; they are stimulating teachers, and their controversy attracts student following."[1] In our present moment, the interdisciplinary classroom has emerged as the object of fears like the ones that Powell had, fears that are not really about indoctrination—despite claims to the contrary—but fears having to do with training students to name and contest the operations of power.

In the spirit of this type of education, *Teaching American Studies* captures a defining element of truly interdisciplinary formations—their insistence on rigorous social observation, a rigor that requires those formations to constantly reorient themselves. Indeed, with this volume we are treated to powerful recommendations about how to be in the world at the granular level of classroom instruction. This volume will help inform instructors about the best ways to utilize the unsettled and dynamic nature of American Studies so that its classrooms can respond to an everchanging social world, a responsiveness that is the only mechanism we have for resisting the intellectual calcification that kills so many disciplines.

Roderick A. Ferguson

NOTE

1. Lewis F. Powell Jr., "The Memo," 1971, *Powell Memorandum: Attack On American Free Enterprise System,* 13, https://scholarlycommons.law.wlu.edu/powellmemo/1.

Acknowledgments

❖ ❖ ❖ ❖ ❖ ❖ ❖

We, Liz, Joseph, and Rebecca, are grateful to the staff at the University Press of Kansas, who have been enthusiastic champions of this project from the first tentative conversation about it at a conference book fair. To have moved from signed contract to tangible book during the pandemic year was a gift. Our thanks especially to Bethany Mowry, who understood the contribution this book would make to the field of American Studies and who shepherded it brilliantly, and to Colin Tripp, whose technical acumen made this production a smooth process. We are also grateful to the very helpful readers of this manuscript for the University Press of Kansas: Glenn Hendler, Shelley Streeby, and Julia Mickenberg. We were aided by both Salem State University and Kennesaw State University, which provided key funds that allowed us to complete the final document on time at a moment when time was of the essence. We thank them for seeing the value in this volume. Finally, we are indebted to our contributors, who took on the task to reveal both pedagogical successes and failures in order to offer a way forward to the field. Collectively, you have offered us more than we could have imagined, and your patience and good humor throughout this process were inspired examples of collegiality and collaboration.

REBECCA

My first acknowledgment is to coeditors Liz and Joseph, whose patience, organization, and intelligence made this book a reality. When I first started thinking about the many conversations with friends that have influenced my teaching, I realized again how much teaching consumes our day-to-day lives as academics. It is impossible to thank all of you individually, but in addition to the people who participated in panels on teaching at the ASA, whose work was the inspiration for this project, there are a few individuals who made specific contributions to my thinking about teaching American Studies. At Kennesaw State, I benefited from monthly conversations with colleagues about teaching, and especially from frequent discussions with Robbie Lieberman. Laura Davis's lessons in online teaching in the spring and summer of 2019 provided the foundation to my own online classes. Coteaching with Kathyrn Walkiewicz in 2014 helped me reimagine the American Studies graduate "theory" course. Mandy McGrew, who is both a graduate of KSU's American Studies MA and a teacher in our program now, has consistently helped me gain perspective. Further back, I learned from a group of exceptional teachers whose risk-taking and creativity in the classroom continue to inform my own practice, most especially Randee Haven-O'Donnell, Houston Roberson, Henry Abelove, Michael W. Harris, Vera Schwarz, Ron Schatz, Jill Morawski, Paula Rabinowitz, David Noble, Gail Noble, Maria Damon, David Roediger, and Douglas Hartmann. Finally, I want to thank my husband, Warner A. Belanger III, for his kindness and patience. He's been both a teacher and a student during our history together, and his experiences in an online MLIS program helped me realize that teaching well online was possible. He has listened to me complain about teaching for the entire thirteen years that we've been together, starting with that first date across from BMCC when I showed up aggravated at a student who had "sassed" me in class. Since then, he's seen me at my most annoyed and impatient and always managed to be supportive of me AND my students, understanding that conflicts in the classroom are part of the real life of education, not the missteps of bad teachers or bad students.

LIZ

My work in American Studies can not be separated from the linked work of teaching and learning. As such, my gratitude runs wide and deep. First and foremost, my thanks to Joseph and Rebecca for being amazing partners and coeditors on our book's journey. From our first chat over coffee, this has been a joy of a project. Thank you also to the American Studies Association and the European Association of American Studies, for creating space and opportunity for my unorthodox requests about conference sessions centering the scholarship of teaching and learning as field-making work. And thank you to my fellow scholar-educator-activists in the American Studies universe who joined in these endeavors. Bringing such conversations into "scholarly" spaces helped spark the ideas that fuel this volume. I owe much to the educators who shaped me (including one of this book's contributors) during my formative student days and to all of my talented colleagues (at Salem State University and elsewhere in the world of K-12 and higher ed) who have shared their teaching strategies and offered constructive feedback on my own. My thanks, too, to my mentors and colleagues at the many museums and social service organizations I've worked in and with over the years; their ways of transforming lives and minds outside of any classroom-proper have profoundly influenced my pedagogy. Most critically I am indebted to the students I have been honored to teach at Salem State and numerous other institutions in the United States, Europe, and Africa. They have helped me hone my craft, revise and improve the Salem State American Studies program, and become more acutely aware of the symbiotic relationship between "learner" and "educator." Finally, thank you to my family: My five siblings are all educators in formal or informal settings. I have had the luxury of discussing teaching for years and I thank them for their tutelage. To my husband, Chase, for affirming my work over two decades even though it is far removed from his own. And to my son, Luca, who was born on the cusp of my transition from primarily student to primarily teacher and is now launching his own college journey, thank you. You inspire me in all I do.

JOSEPH

I'm grateful to so many people who helped make my work on this volume possible and rewarding. First and foremost, to Liz and Rebecca for inviting me into this collaborative adventure and for being such clear-eyed, astute, and patient coeditors. It's been an honor and a pleasure to do this with you. Thanks are also due to many colleagues and comrades who have shaped my own thinking about teaching and American Studies: to everyone associated with the American Studies program and the Listening Project at Brooklyn College; to everyone on the *Radical Teacher* editorial board; to the extensive community of American Studies teachers and scholars around the United States and the world from whom I have learned about teaching and our shared field over the years, and whose work has inspired me; to fellow members of the Brooklyn College Professional Staff Congress Executive Committee, who are some of the most committed and compassionate teachers I know; to Jeanne Theoharis and Alan Aja, whose dedication to CUNY students continues to be a model for me; and to all the Brooklyn College students who have taken classes with me over the years: teaching and learning from you has been the great thrill of my professional life. Finally, thanks to everyone in my immediate and extended family, and especially to Sophie, Miriam, and Rachel, who give me hope and provide crucial inspiration for my own pedagogical work.

Introduction

How Pedagogical Practice Defines American Studies

ELIZABETH DUCLOS-ORSELLO,
JOSEPH ENTIN, AND REBECCA HILL

❖ ❖ ❖ ❖ ❖ ❖ ❖

Between the fall of 2016 and the summer of 2019, the *Chronicle of Higher Education* published thirty-three articles discussing the term "snowflake" and another thirty using the term "coddled" to describe college students in the United States. These terms have become common in the ongoing debate about politics on college campuses that reached its peak following a wave of student activism that surged after protests against police killings of Black men in Ferguson, Baltimore, and New York in the summer and fall of 2014. From feature articles in liberal magazines such as *Vox,* the *New Republic,* and the *Atlantic* to conservative denunciations at the *American Conservative* and *National Review,* stories about left-wing students have become fodder for news coverage far beyond the confines of campuses themselves. Much of this news coverage begins with dramatic anecdotes about student protests against particular classes, policies, or speakers. Often, these stories implicate not just young protestors but also professors deemed responsible for indoctrinating the offending students with political arguments that critics describe as irrational, censorious, infantile, or uncivil. Indeed, on September 17, 2020, the US president himself decried the "left-wing indoctrination" in schools and universities, including "critical race theory" and the *New York Times*'s 1619 Project, which together, he contended, "teach our children that we were founded on the principle of oppression, not freedom."[1] This larger conversation is unavoidable by anyone teaching in an American university or teaching about American culture outside the United States. American Studies departments and programs are often at the center of the local versions of the same conversation as it unfolds among administrators, faculty, and students.

The conversation is not a new one for the field. While some of the first American Studies programs in US universities were founded with government funding with the expectation that they would, through an affirmative elaboration of the "American character," help advance the cultural Cold War, many leading scholars of American Studies' first generation were public opponents of McCarthyism and champions of academic boundary shifting, proclaiming, as Leo Marx and Henry Nash Smith did in the mid-1960s, that they opposed attempts to bring the scientific method to the humanities.[2] By the 1970s, the American Studies Association's radical caucus sought to bring American Studies departments and publications closer to the ideals of the New Left, the feminist movement, and the ethnic studies movement. American Studies scholars, including some contributors to this collection, saw the project of the field as part of a broader progressive effort to remake universities into radical democratic spaces of learning.[3] In the 1990s, at the time of the last wave of the academic culture wars, American Studies announced itself as a champion of multicultural education and called for American Studies curricula to cast off American exceptionalism, become transnational, explicitly connect academic and community-based work, and consider the relationship between the field's history and US imperialism.[4]

Today, the conversation in American Studies scholarship and institution building is again part of academic conflict. In 2014, Professor Stephen Salaita was terminated from his job at the University of Illinois over tweets criticizing Israel during the attack on Gaza in 2013, an event that happened at the same time that the American Studies Association voted to join the cultural and academic boycott of Israel. The current discussion of academic politics has moved from a concern with the "civility" of faculty on social media to what Jeffrey Sachs describes as a "moral panic" about left-wing students suppressing the speech of fellow students and even professors.[5] As we completed work on this collection in the summer of 2020 in the midst of the COVID-19 pandemic, we were witnessing a new wave of social protest led by young people against anti-Black racism, police brutality, and economic austerity, along with a fresh wave of reaction. Particularly as protests have led to the removal of Confederate statues across the country, as well as monuments to Theodore Roosevelt outside the Museum of Natural History in New York City and conquistador Juan de Oñate in Albuquerque, New Mexico, an accusing finger is again pointed at progressive education.[6]

This current wave of protest and reaction, like earlier ones, affects how and what we teach, our attitudes about teaching, and our expectations of students we meet in the classroom. As Sachs argues, the ongoing coverage of a "free speech crisis" has occurred in the midst of the largest number of political firings of left-wing or liberal professors in a twenty-year period. In addition, the economic crisis precipitated by the coronavirus pandemic has generated economic retrenchment at colleges and universities across the country, making the positions of many higher education instructors, especially adjuncts, even more precarious.

This collection began with a simple goal in mind—to provide concrete resources to faculty teaching American Studies. By the time we began putting the collection together, we realized that our collection could also provide a more general intervention because much of what our contributors describe has to do with effective ways to teach about race, gender, sexuality, power, and other charged topics in a moment of political polarization and intense public scrutiny of universities. Because we asked contributors to describe student reactions and responses to classroom assignments, *Teaching American Studies* provides a view of the campus free-speech wars and related shifts in higher education through case studies of actual students in actual classrooms. How are our students confronting "controversial," "challenging" topics in our courses? How are instructors addressing the emotional, as well as intellectual, responses that our students bring to the classroom and the often difficult social and historical materials that are at the heart of American Studies classes? How must the field be remade or altered *in* the classroom to serve the realities of the students sitting there? How are instructors moving beyond "inclusivity" and "diversity" and "multiculturalism" to develop new strategies and approaches for reaching students, across a wide range of institutional contexts? In asking these questions, and situating our book within the contemporary culture wars, we acknowledge the public nature of teaching. Given the number of classes and the number of students we have taught, it is likely that what we do in our classrooms represents American Studies to a larger group of people than any of our published scholarly work. As the contributors to *Teaching American Studies* answer these questions in their descriptions and analyses of teaching practice, this collection presents the state of the field from the point of view of the classroom. Indeed, we contend the classroom, which we understand capaciously to exist in any space of collective teaching and learning inside or outside formal educational institutions, is the best site to understand the public work that American Studies is doing in the world today. It is there, in our teaching—in large part because that is where most American Studies practitioners devote most of their time and energy and where the issues, approaches, and claims of American Studies are taken up in diverse ways by students—that we come to see what American Studies really looks, sounds, and feels like.

The editors work at institutions where teaching is the primary activity that all faculty perform. All of us also work in some connection with American Studies programs, after having undergone training in American Studies as graduate students. Yet despite our training, as we encountered each other at meetings and conference panels over the years at the national conferences of the American Studies Association (ASA), we found that we were not the only people struggling with such basic teaching questions as "How do we teach the introduction to American Studies?" and "How do we teach the controversial issues of social and political injustice at the heart of our field to a heterogeneous body of students?" These have been difficult questions because of American Studies' historic resistance to self-definition, disciplinarity, and codification. Further, we wondered, how can the way we teach American Studies respond to our institutional locations and the preparedness and expectations of our students? How do we teach American Studies in the context of growing public contestation over the meanings of "America" itself as well as assaults on higher education funding and academic speech and freedom? This project began in conversations about questions like these, in sessions on teaching American Studies, and in discussions over breakfast at the annual meetings for American Studies department chairs and program directors. While Liz and Rebecca were members of that committee, a rules change by the association's national committee encouraged more panels about teaching and administration by allowing people participating on such panels to appear on two panels at the annual meeting. By 2016, the national conference had enough panels on pedagogy that a person could attend at least two such panels per day.

One panel would often inspire another, and a rich discussion grew up among those who appeared on and attended them. Following a long airport conversation about terminal MA programs, for example, Rebecca and Paul Lauter organized one such panel at the 2011 conference, "Teaching the Introduction to American Studies," with presentations by Phil Deloria, Betsy Esch, and Erika Doss. The panel drew a standing room–only crowd, and audience members, including Glenn Hendler, Julie Sze, David Roediger, and Udo Hebel all engaged in a stimulating discussion with both panelists and other attendees. The following year, under Liz's leadership and based on both her own struggles coordinating a small undergraduate concentration and her discussions with scholar-educators from across the world, the programs and centers committee organized a unique, well-attended interactive poster session where faculty engaged in animated one-on-one discussions sharing descriptions and practical advice on "the best class I ever taught," including work by Sarah Hentges and Paul Croce, who both have pieces in this collection. Independently of the programs and centers committee, Julie Sze, who contributes to this collection, organized a panel on teaching the introduction to American Studies in 2014, and in 2016 edited a forum on American Studies pedagogy for *American Quarterly.* Liz and international colleagues, including contributor Ingrid Gessner, also offered a pedagogy-focused panel at the 2018 European American Studies Association conference. As this growing interest in promoting discussions of teaching at the American Studies continued, Joseph, who had been part of the *Radical Teacher* editorial collective since 1997, was wrestling with similar questions as the newly appointed director of a small American Studies program at Brooklyn College, CUNY.

It was in the context of these discussions of teaching at annual conferences that Joseph, Liz, and Rebecca began to discuss what would become this collection of essays on teaching American Studies. Our original goal in the project was simple: to provide a resource for those teaching everywhere, whether they are graduate students embarking on their first class as an "instructor of record" or experienced classroom teachers reworking old courses or teaching new ones. We were especially interested in detailed descriptions of interdisciplinary assignments that people created, and we began collecting essays by reaching out to all of those who had participated in panels and forums that we had organized, or that we had attended or seen, on the ASA and international American Studies programs during the years between 2010 and 2018. While it is impossible to represent the full scope of American Studies teaching in a volume such as this, we tried to reach out to instructors in a wide range of subfields, in both university and nonuniversity contexts, who are at varied stages of their careers.

Liz and Rebecca both served as chairs of the programs and centers committee, and as part of our work, we began to gather information on American Studies programs. As we collected more and more data about these programs, we began to look outside the boundaries of the ASA itself in thinking about the needs of American Studies program faculty. The most important finding in a large survey that Liz and her committee cochair Lorraine Cox conducted in 2013 was that the vast majority of American Studies programs are built on undergraduate majors. In subsequent conversations and emails with program directors and chairs, we frequently heard that there was a need for more resources for American Studies faculty teaching in new programs, in small programs, and in programs where faculty teaching American Studies may be "borrowed" from traditional disciplines and departments, without much experience of American Studies as a field. For example, all three of us have directed American Studies programs at regional public universities where few of the faculty have a formal background in American Studies. Few faculty in our programs read American Studies journals or attended American Studies conferences. Often borrowed from traditional departments, they did not have funding to attend multiple conferences in a year even if they might have wanted to go. While students often joke that they have to learn to answer the question "What is American Studies?" they might be surprised to find out that faculty teaching American Studies are asking the same question when they are developing classes. We often fielded questions about how to teach the history of the field, along with questions about what should be included in American Studies methods class. As expectations for course development changed to include mandated learning objectives and rubrics, we also had to figure out the answer to "How can American Studies courses be explained using current models of assessment?" Being able to answer such questions has become increasingly important as administrators and state policy makers question, or even attack, the value of the humanities more generally.

While many of the questions that we have about teaching may seem prosaic and far from the wide-ranging questions we like to think about in our research, they also are crucial to thinking about how our field as a whole works in the context of contemporary university life. More significantly, we are interested in asking how teaching American Studies to undergraduates can in fact be informed by and contribute to the theoretical and conceptual questions being asked by scholars teaching in American Studies. This is crucial because, as we have come to realize, our classrooms are the place where American Studies takes its most tangible public form. It was in 2011 at a session on teaching in the introduction to American Studies that Rebecca began asking the question: "What if American Studies is defined not so much in the pages of the most cutting-edge publications, but through what happens in our classrooms?" In this volume, we have asked others to think about that question by writing essays about teaching American Studies in a way that uses a classroom activity or a particular course to reflect on the state of the field in American Studies.

We had two goals with this question. One was instrumental: we wanted to produce a book that could provide a useful how-to guide for faculty who might be new to, or unfamiliar with, American Studies and who were going into classrooms to teach the field. For that reason, we wanted the most practical "nuts and bolts" lessons possible. What was the assignment? How did students respond? How did the instructors adjust it? The second thing we hoped to produce in this collection was an impression of the field as it exists from the point of view of students and teachers. What primary and secondary texts, and what theoretical challenges and issues, do faculty use to organize their teaching? How does the teaching we do respond to our institutional and educational contexts? Addressing these questions would, of course, address important publications in American Studies and how to teach them. Essays in this collection comment on teaching Anne Moody, Octavia Butler, the widely used collection *Keywords for American Cultural Studies,* and any number of books that American Studies faculty find useful for engaging new students in the field. But the essays are also about dancing, eating, and walking around a campus to view statues and gravestones. They are about teaching during the era of Donald Trump, of Black Lives Matter, about giving up authority in the classroom, about teaching in the South, in New England, in the Midwest, and for ten-minute intervals at a cooking school in New Jersey.

Every few years, *American Quarterly* may feature an article that attempts to define the field. Graduate students are often required to read Gene Wise's essay on paradigm dramas in American Studies. More recently, Phil Deloria and Alexander I. Olson's *American Studies: A User's Guide* offers a history of the field through the archives of the American Studies Association and presents American Studies' current preoccupations through a series of what they call "academic mix tapes." People find themselves in American Studies classrooms in a variety of circumstances. They may have a traditional disciplinary background and be assigned to teach in, or be in a job that includes an opportunity to teach in, an American studies program. As program directors who make schedules and design curriculum, the three of us often consult with faculty who are teaching American Studies for the first time and don't find a great many resources for what makes a course an American Studies course. And many people who are trained in American Studies may not ultimately wind up teaching in American Studies programs, either in graduate school or afterward. Thus, rather than having to face the question "How do you teach the introduction to American Studies?" they might be wondering "Is there a way I can use my interdisciplinary training in a US history survey?" While they may intuitively bring American Studies approaches into their classrooms, it is often difficult to find a way to do so. After spending years in a graduate program learning interdisciplinary approaches and scholarship, in their postgraduate life they may feel they must rediscipline themselves in order to successfully teach history, literature surveys, or composition classes. In this phenomenon that Phil Deloria described in his 2008 presidential address as "Interdisciplinarity 1.5," the teaching lives of American Studies PhDs often involve efforts to bring American Studies in through the side door.[7] Does American Studies training give us any particular advantages when designing disciplinary courses? To what extent can we do so inside the confines of a disciplinary department curriculum, especially when we are junior or contingent faculty? By including essays about specific assignments as well as essays about entire courses, we are hoping to provide suggestions to new teaching faculty who want to preserve the value of their American Studies or other interdisciplinary degree through creative teaching in the wide variety of institutions and departmental settings wherever they land after graduate school. Recognizing these institutional realities, we believe this book will be useful for teachers in and also *beyond* American Studies—to everyone in humanities and social sciences who is feeling under siege, who is looking for innovative strategies to rejuvenate and inspire their pedagogical practice. How do we deal with the neoliberal expectations that classes and majors lead directly to waiting careers and high-paying jobs? Classroom teachers in a wide variety of contexts in this collection describe and reflect on classroom-level work that transforms student lives and demonstrate what we in the humanities and social sciences have to offer.

Teaching American Studies at the graduate level in an American Studies department presents challenges even for the long-time American Studies professional. Rebecca's own experience directing a brand-new terminal MA program in American Studies after a ten-year period of history teaching reacquainted her with the field's long-time conversations about itself. In a freshly minted program, where the habits and patterns are not set yet, it was both exciting and daunting to consider such basic questions as whether it was even worth teaching the old history of the field. Critical responses to Deloria's presidential address from Jack Halberstam and Nikhil Singh also showed that the questions were not resolved among American Studies scholars.[8] Could our students accept arguments against seeking consensus on the very purpose of the field? In this collection of essays, we want to provoke the field's practitioners to think about this same unsettled—and ongoing—debate, from the perspective of the classroom and the experiences of students. Resisting the impulse to teach through conventional disciplinary frames, or letting students know that American Studies lacks consensus about key analytic and methodological questions, may keep things interesting and keep potential open for creative work by students, but it also threatens to undermine the field's coherence, and even its existence, in the face of simultaneous demands from institutional leaders and anxious students who are taught to view their degrees instrumentally.

In a climate where STEM and even social scientific rigor are used to cast doubt on a variety of "studies" programs as "soft" fields based on ideological demands, the pressure to justify our curricular choices becomes ever more intense. Such concerns were part of the impetus for an ASA Working Paper series coedited by Liz in 2015 that focused on how to position American Studies within the landscape of twenty-first-century higher education.[9] Our call to scholars produced a confidence-inspiring response to that pressure. Essays in this collection demonstrate the wide applicability of American Studies across academic disciplines and the relationship of American Studies approaches to skills building, whether related to public presentation, visual and graphic arts, or work with nonprofit organizations.

The civic and "public" work of universities is central to the work many of us are called to do. Since the 1990s, scholars and activists on many campuses and in organizations such as Campus Compact, Imagining America, and beyond have been challenging the notion that authority and knowledge resides exclusively within the academy. They have been advocating for and working with educators not only to break down divisions between classroom and community but also to radically reimagine what knowledge looks like, where it is located, and how social change happens. Some of the essays here engage directly with these discourses, pushing our notion of the sites and purposes of American Studies education in new directions. These issues are taken up in a material way in the essays that follow—particularly Friedensohn's essay about teaching at a culinary arts program and Duclos-Orsello's essay (coauthored with three partners from a social service nonprofit), which centers the issues of equity, power dynamics, and shared authority when doing "engaged" teaching.[10]

WHAT HAPPENS WHEN WE DEFINE AMERICAN STUDIES BY WHAT WE TEACH?

As we began reading early drafts of essays, we realized our project could be more than a useful collection of assignment ideas for new teachers. The essays here still provide that, but they also intentionally seek to define the state of the field of American Studies from the perspective of the classroom teacher. In the contemporary neoliberal academy, we are often told to increase the "public engagement" and community involvement in our programs. In private colleges, this instruction seems logical; how can private colleges open the gates between their elite campuses and surrounding communities? Some of the essays in this collection address this question directly in a traditional classroom context, such as Paul Lauter's essay about teaching in a terminal MA program at Trinity College in Connecticut. In public universities, the command to "engage the public" becomes more vexed, suggesting in a way that what happens in public university classrooms is not already public work. Our premise in defining the state of the classroom as a state of the field is partly about recognizing that what happens in public university classrooms is itself a public activity, more public than the publication of articles in specialized journals, and certainly more public than partnerships or "sponsored research" projects for corporate entities. And yet, "public" institutions are still situated within geographic communities that do not always benefit from or coexist as equal partners in the decision-making surrounding university policy, expansion, or retrenchment. In addition, while universities have become central to political conflict in the United States, what happens day to day in our classrooms is a subject of public discussion, including, but not exclusive to, decontextualized videos and screenshots that make their way through internet news pipelines into television headlines and state legislative hearings.[11] Not all the essays in this collection come from courses taught in public universities, but the majority do. Schools whose classroom practices are described here include Salem State, Kennesaw State, UC Davis, the City University of New York, the University of Illinois, the University of New Hampshire, and others. One contributor teaches at a public high school. We start with the premise that teaching is the primary public face of our practice. Together, the essays in this volume test that premise and explore the ways it plays out in a range of classroom and institutional settings.

A number of the essays directly address the impact of political polarization on what happens in our classrooms. Megan Bayles and Julie

Sze, for example, describe teaching the introduction to American Studies in the age of Trump, when the "grievance narrative" of right-wing students meets contemporary American Studies scholarship in classes they had taken when anticipating a course in "Patriotism 101." In contrast, Wendy Kozol, who teaches in a Comparative American Studies program at Oberlin, where progressive students have become the center of right-wing hand-wringing, addresses the complexity of real student conversations about "cultural appropriation" in a more nuanced way than can be seen in the glib pronouncements of magazine articles about coddled adolescents. In fact, the essays in this collection suggest that rather than coddling students, American Studies classes disrupt student expectations of classroom learning through blending disciplinary methods and presentation styles. Often, as Stanley Thangaraj notes in his description of an assignment to use the visual arts to explain theoretical concepts, and as Rebecca Hill explains in her discussion of her students' public presentations of posters on selected American Studies keywords, students can be anxious about the prospect of these kinds of projects but then produce fantastic and interesting results beyond what they would do on more traditional tests or term papers.

One of the benefits of having a field that is in a constant state of flux and reinvention is that it creates space for, and an openness to, modes of pedagogical experimentation, both on the part of faculty and quite often by students. The essays in this collection highlight a number of inventive, even unorthodox, pedagogical approaches and creative assignments, as students and faculty alike adapted what might otherwise seem to be a liability—disciplinary uncertainty—into an asset. In this way, the essays present a picture of American Studies as it exists today: a location for pedagogical innovation that strives to create inclusive classroom spaces where students do not just read or hear but experience and share in the development of the critical insights of American Studies scholarship.

Each three- to five-thousand-word essay in this collection responds in some way to the following prompt: *Bring us into your classroom and your practice. Offer specific, concrete details about your teaching and your students' learning. Draw the line between theorizing and educating. Be willing to share challenges and difficulties and what you learned from them.* The resulting relatively short essays are organized around specific classroom discussions, encounters, assignments, and challenges. They are theoretical and offer ideas that can travel, but they are always grounded in specifics. And, critically, they are grounded in a range of classroom/teaching locations: from the general education classroom at a regional state university to graduate courses at a variety of institutions and from a STEM-focused campus to a learning space outside of a formal university setting at all. We have organized the essays into five parts. The first part, "Behind the Syllabus," includes essays describing planning and changes to entire courses. The second part, "Unpacking the Familiar, Introducing the New," includes essays focusing on experiences of teaching key texts. Part three, "Individual Assignments," contains detailed discussions of individual assignments. Part four, "Movements and/in the Classroom," presents case studies of student responses related to larger social movements. The fifth part, "American Studies Outside," contains examples of classes and assignments that take students and instructors outside traditional classroom boundaries.

Critical to our project is the diversity of contributors and case studies they offer. *Teaching American Studies'* contributors reflect the racial, ethnic, gender, and institutional variation that makes up the American Studies community as a whole. The students they teach do the same. In every essay, theory and practice merge, each informing and challenging the other, rewriting and revising American Studies in the process. In each essay, too, educators lay bare their challenges, struggles, uncertainties, and failures. This intentional focus is to bring to the "pedagogy" arena an honest look at the messiness and sometimes impossible tasks at the heart of teaching and learning. This is not a set of idealized case studies; here are living, breathing educators and students struggling together to do and learn and teach this thing called "American Studies" wherever that work is being done.

NOTES

1. Michael Crowley, "Trump Calls for 'Patriotic Education,' to Defend American History from the Left," *New York Times*, September 17, 2020, https://www.nytimes.com/2020/09/17/us/politics/trump-patriotic-education.html.

2. Leo Marx, "American Studies—A Defense of an Unscientific Method," *New Literary History* 1, no. 1 (October 1969): 75–90; Henry Nash Smith, "Can American Studies Develop a Method?" *American Quarterly* 9, no. 2, pt. 2 (Summer 1957): 197–208.

3. Philip J. Deloria and Alexander I. Olson, *American Studies: A User's Guide* (Oakland: University of California Press, 2017); Allen F. Davis, "The Politics of American Studies," *American Quarterly* 42, no. 3 (September 1990): 353–374.

4. George Lipsitz, *American Studies in a Moment of Danger* (Minneapolis: University of Minnesota Press, 2001); Amy Kaplan, "Violent Belongings and the Question of Empire Today, Presidential Address to the American Studies Association, Hartford Connecticut, Oct 17, 2003," *American Quarterly* 56, no. 1

(2004); Shelley Fisher-Fishkin, "Crossroads of Culture: The Transnational Turn in American Studies, Presidential Address to the American Studies Association November 12, 2004," *American Quarterly* 57, no. 1 (March 2005): 17–57; Amy Kaplan and Donald E. Pease, eds., *Cultures of United States Imperialism* (Durham, NC: Duke University Press, 1994).

5. Jeffrey Sachs, "There Is No Free Speech Crisis: The Right's New Moral Panic Is Largely Imaginary," *Salon*, May 1, 2018, https://www.salon.com/2018/05/01/there-is-no-campus-free-speech-crisis-the-rights-new-moral-panic-is-largely-imaginary/.

6. David Harsanyi, "The Year Zero," *National Review*, June 26, 2020, https://www.nationalreview.com/2020/06/2020-year-zero/.

7. Philip Deloria, "Broadway and Main: Crossroads, Ghost Roads, and Paths to an American Studies Future," *American Quarterly* 61, no. 1 (March 2009): 1–25.

8. Nikhil Singh, "Disciplining American Studies? A Response to the Presidential Address," *American Quarterly* 61, no. 1 (March 2009): 27–32; and J. Halberstam, "Beyond Broadway and Main: A Response to the Presidential Address," *American Quarterly* 61, no. 1 (March 2009): 33–38.

9. American Studies Association, 2014–15 Working Paper Series, Elizabeth Duclos-Orsello and Karen Leong, eds., accessed June 29, 2020, https://www.theasa.net/resources/institutional-support/working-papers.

10. Some of the key texts are Nancy Cantor, *Transforming America: The University as a Public Good* (Foreseeable Futures #3), Imagining America, 2003, accessed December 23, 2020, https://imaginingamerica.org/nancy-cantor-transforming-america-the-university-as-public-good; David Scobey, *Civic Engagement and the Copernican Moment* (Foreseeable Futures #11), Imagining America, 2011, accessed December 23, 2020, https://imaginingamerica.org/david-scobey-civic-engagement-and-the-copernican-moment; Randy Martin, "Linked Fates and Futures: Communities and Campuses as Equitable Partners," *PUBLIC* 1, issue 1+2 (2013), accessed December 23, 2020, https://public.imaginingamerica.org/blog/article/linked-fates-and-futures-communities-and-campuses-as-equitable-partners/; Campus Compact at www.compact.org.

11. Anita Levy, "State of the Profession: Targeted Harassment Faculty Report Back," *Academe*, January–February 2018, https://www.aaup.org/article/state-profession-targeted-harassment%E2%80%94faculty-report-back#.XWaXzehKjcs; Statement on "Targeted Online Harassment of Faculty," AAUP updates, AAUP Updates, January 31, 2017, https://www.aaup.org/news/targeted-online-harassment-faculty#.XWaYM-hKjcs.

PART I

Behind the Syllabus

Planning and Transforming Whole Courses

1

Course Objectives

On Resisting Solutions to the "Race Problem" in the Southern STEM Classroom

NIHAD M. FAROOQ

❖ ❖ ❖ ❖ ❖ ❖ ❖ ❖ ❖ ❖ ❖ ❖ ❖ ❖ ❖

I teach American Studies at Georgia Tech, an engineering school—where I landed fresh out of a very humanities-centered graduate program over a decade ago. At the end of my first semester of teaching there, I received a most curious and instructive course evaluation, for a course I taught called Virtual Subjects: Cultural Camouflage and the Construction of Race in American Culture, which was a class that moved historically from Ellen Craft to Brandon Teena.[1] A student noted that while they enjoyed the course material very much, they wished I had considered "one aspect" of "the race problem" that we might have spent the semester "solving," so that we would have felt, by the end of term, that we had "fixed" something—a very STEM-focused response, indeed. I now use this anecdote at the start of each semester to help students think about why a solutions-oriented model is not an effective way of examining race, and why the framing of questions about race "as a problem we can solve"—even as we accept its status as a constructed fiction—will be challenged throughout the course. My contribution to this collection comes from that experience and the conjoined pedagogical and research philosophy it helped me carve very early in my own career.

For from the tight parameters of this space—a college of liberal arts tucked inside a southern engineering institute—I have had to grapple with two seemingly distinct yet surprisingly intertwined questions from my peers elsewhere: (1) What does it mean to teach American Studies in the South? (2) What does it mean to teach race and literary studies at a STEM school? The first of these has its own historical urgency but has not been as perplexing to answer. American Studies, after all, *is* race studies, and always has been, so to begin and grow my scholarship here in the South, in the heart of a city that is still very much central to American racial discourse, has been, in many ways, incredibly powerful—it is a site of real privilege and possibility. And for my students at Georgia Tech—a STEM school located in the heart of midtown Atlanta—the work of American Studies and/as race studies is both a much-needed oasis and a reminder of where and who they *really* are, outside the GT bubble.

Yet that's the part of my southern American Studies story that puts me in a position of alterity to the rest of the field—it's not the *southern* part that has been a challenge to explain, but the *tech* part. To do this work at an engineering school has required a willful act of both undisciplining my students about their preconceived understandings of science, history, and the political work of literary and cultural studies and, in a way, redisciplining myself so that *I* fit more squarely in the field of literary studies (I do this somewhat reluctantly, as my own work is deeply invested in the permeability of manufactured boundaries between disciplines).

Ironically, then, and in part *because* of my research work in the areas of culture and science, I find it necessary to situate myself even more firmly in a shrinking corner of our institute that stresses the importance of history, context, and reading, all the while working in a larger space in which the neoliberal fantasy of corporate-sponsored or financially backed innovation is pushed forward as the only kind of creativity that matters, and where this wholesale immersion in an abstract, utopian future of techno-creativity, often at the expense of vital critique and analysis, belies the very struggle of the communities that would ostensibly be served by, for example, its "smart city" technologies or "the internet of things."

But let me return to the importance of *undisciplining*, which is, somewhat uncoincidentally, the title of my first monograph and the driving force behind my early years of research, which was also clearly shaped by my experience at a southern technological institute. In *Undisciplined* I argue that nineteenth-century scientific travel—as a project that merged a study of the diversifying natural and cultural spaces of the Atlantic world with the strict social order of the metropole—reflected and responded to debates about science, race, and personhood through the travel narratives and field notes of scientists and ethnographers and their encounters with indigenous and diasporic persons. The book follows, as it progresses, a new generation of racialized subjects who stepped out from behind the lens of observation to become observers and writers themselves, performing the inherent interdisciplinarity and codependence of scientific and humanistic inquiry.[2]

Yet, even as I write and teach about the importance of this philosophy of undisciplining, I have found myself reluctantly forced to *rediscipline* myself—to stake a firm and exceptional territorial claim as a humanities scholar—in order to be visible at a STEM school. In such an environment, in which the humanities are viewed primarily in "elective" terms and where the relevance of historical humanities is questioned at every turn, it has been extremely important for me to foreground my own work as both routed through and rooted in the nineteenth century in order to convey the inextricability of history and the present; the intertwining of slavery and contemporary understandings of race, racism, and resistance; and of course, the ways humanistic inquiry has both shaped and been shaped by the culture of scientific discourse, then and now.

Drawing from the lessons I learned about students' desire for a more telos-driven pedagogy in that early-career course on passing, I began mapping classes that deconstructed the "solutions-based" model by actually deploying it. For example, in a course called Science, Technology, and Race, I brought the humanities and sciences together by demonstrating how science has functioned in certain historical moments *as* fiction, and how it has functioned in other moments to *dispel* fictional myths about humans or to create alternative myths that would empower instead of disenfranchise. I did this specifically through an examination of the constructions and reconfigurations of narratives about race.

After all, the very discourse of racial construction in the Americas *was* the original science fiction narrative, creating and transforming a socially expedient category intended to justify enslavement into a biological category that could prove inherent, genetic differences based on inconsistent, superficial identifying markers such as skin color, hair texture, and/or facial features. Thomas Jefferson, in his 1781 *Notes on the State of Virginia*, issued just such a call to scientists, by putting forth his "suspicion only" that "the blacks are inferior to the whites in the endowments both of body and mind." This difference, according to Jefferson, was not simply a product of circumstance or environment but was, he suspected, something deeper and more innate. But he left it to science to take up the charge by stating that this suspicion had "never yet been viewed" as a subject "of natural history." By intimating that such a subject might be worth exploring, Jefferson subtly asked scientists for a creation myth, and the field delivered one.[3] By the 1850s, Jefferson's suspicion had been transformed into an assertion that there was an irrevocable, scientific difference between people. Slavery ended in the United States soon after this, but the rationalization for slavery had been impressed into the fabric of western culture through the lens of western scientific narrative (even as the scientific *findings* of practitioners such as Charles Darwin and even Louis Agassiz—albeit against his hopes—continued to refute such narratives).[4]

Helping students understand how ideologies of racial difference were solidified through manipulated scientific narratives is vital to helping them understand the difficulties of a "solutions-based" model for the "race problem." If such fictional findings, and the birth of pseudoscientific theories (such as eugenics) created to prop them up, could be used to justify the many horrifying acts of enslavement, colonialism, and genocide throughout history, and were also used to boost a kind of fervent nationalism and nativism, how could we work to undo them? For students who already understood the power of science, the power of storytelling now became a mirror to that paradigm as well. When theories as inclusive and nonhierarchical as Darwin's could be taken out of context and twisted in a manner that justified the exploitation and degradation of other people, how might we now, in the present, work together to extricate them?

Well, with stories, of course. Alternative ones. As I moved to the contemporary era in the second half of the course, I was able to show students how scientific narrative was later wielded to try to solve the very problems it had once been commissioned to create. Marginalized groups began to take ownership of the scientific tools and the voices that once made *them* the objects of study: We read stories by those who took up narratives of science fiction and fantasy for themselves, not as a genre that helped to justify their enslavement and eradication but rather as a genre that might hold the potential for their liberation. We looked, for example, to films such as musician and poet Sun Ra's 1974 *Space Is the Place*, in which a new colony of African Americans is created in outer space, teleported over through music. It's a Garveyite message, but instead of advocating that his people go *back* to an Africa that has not been *home* for centuries, Sun Ra advocates, instead, a move forward, in time, in music, to a new, yet-undiscovered space of the future. The Afrofuturist view of an elsewhere—across geographic and historical space—is one that Tech students always love to imagine, not only because it mirrors some of their work and study in other parts of the university, from human-computer interaction to aerospace engineering, but because it allows them to imagine worldbuilding in a more inclusive manner. By examining the history of race through science fiction and fantasy, students were able to understand the way that science has evolved throughout political history—once defining and empowering a racist logic of superiority that tried, in vain, to ground itself in empirical logic, and later, in more contemporary configurations, allowing us to attach mythical significance to everyday events, encounters, and spaces. These contemporary science fiction narratives, then, give readers the possibility to be heroes, to imagine alternative futures, and eventually to implement positive change in our own lives and in the lives of others, by perceiving that things are more than what they seem and that the power to shape destiny in a manner that is inclusive, collective, and positive lies in our own hands.[5]

Yet, this trajectory—from the nowhere of Jefferson's empty hypothesis to the elsewhere of Sun Ra's Afrofuturism—still plagued me as a circular one that debunked one solutionist model simply to land on a more heroic version of it. Students perhaps entered the course with a better introduction to the complicity of science in creating "the race problem," but I feared they also left the course with a naively celebratory sense that scientific endeavor had redeemed itself through a different kind of fiction for the contemporary era—the science fiction that had created the false category of race had now launched it into an Afrofuturist elsewhere. Somewhere between individual erasure and collective escape, the persistent struggle of everyday life and the intractability of the racial from our cultural present had been lost. We had moved from discomfort to outrage to the celebratory no-place of utopian fantasy. So I reorganized again.

This time, I shaped a new class, Global Networks, that emphasized the interdependence between those marked by racial parameters and those who marked them. Specifically, I demonstrated to students the power of social networks, from the era of Atlantic slavery to the present moment, in helping us to understand how infrastructures of antiracist resistance—however loosely formed—could work to slowly dismantle systems of control from within. This strategy still applied the familiar language of technocracy in which students were well steeped but then used it to undermine the logic of order, programmability, and tidy resolution with which they typically associated it, replacing it instead with an emphasis on the necessary perpetuity of struggle—of fugitivity, of marronage—as ideologies of resistance that demand movement.[6] I also knew we needed a broader, cross-disciplinary lens to understand what scholars such as Denise Ferreira da Silva and others have defined as an "analytics of raciality"—one that aims not to transcend or obliterate the logic of racial difference but rather to prioritize the productive centrality of the racial in the construction of globality.[7]

The course thus brought together many disciplines—the human sciences, ethnography, literature, and theories of technology—to examine the construction of global theories about race, asking students to grapple more carefully with the evolution of these discourses and their role in continually shaping our understanding of persons and/as information. In other words, not *how do we move beyond the stifling parameters of race, or escape beyond it?* but rather *how do we deploy it to fight racism in our daily present?*

Now, literary scholars such as Paul Gilroy have long called for a reprioritization of networks, of "routes" over "roots," when considering the African diaspora. Reconfiguring students' understanding of the racial in this routed way helped them understand how networked collectives—of shared information, of bodies traveling along escape routes, of rumors that inspired bodies that could not move—forged disparate yet powerful communities of resistance.[8]

Through this emphasis on routes, I was also able to suggest a further expansion of Gilroy's concepts of diasporic dispersal and the resulting "underground" it enabled, as a vast network of fleeting, ephemeral encounters that draws its very strength from transience, instability, and precarity. Such a consideration allowed us to move beyond the static space of captivity and into the whispers of revolution and resistance, of movements that spread through anxious and hopeful ears across the Atlantic and that could not, and still cannot in today's even more dispersed and distributed networks, be contained.

The movement of information and rumor followed the increased movement of bodies through the Americas, as I showed students through our historical sweep in the course. From the growth of technology like the cotton gin to the rise of military interventions like those in Saint-Domingue, industrial and political shifts led to demographic shifts in the southern Americas that encouraged communication and contact within and across varied Atlantic spaces from the close of the eighteenth century onward.

But how, exactly, did—and do—networks operate across varied temporalities, affiliations, and experiences to create unified structures of organization and revolt, from the Atlantic world to today's coalitions, from the Arab Spring to #BlackLivesMatter? How do captive or scattered populations construct *social* networks out of isolation and precarity? We turned first to literature for the answer, examining, for example, the alliance between slaves Cora and Caesar in Colson Whitehead's 2016 *Underground Railroad*, which develops not through friendship or long-standing kinship, but through a hushed seed whisper-planted in Cora's ear—"I'm going back North. Soon. Running away. I want you to come"—by a stranger recently transplanted to the Randall plantation from Virginia.[9]

Whitehead builds on these shifting, migratory alliances throughout the novel and also helps us to understand that the struggle for liberation is perpetual, persistent—a foundational ontology of the American experience. In following Cora's struggle to "settle" into the notion of freedom as "a community of laborers striving for something lovely and rare," we are also prompted to think of Keeanga-Yahmatta Taylor's current provocation that it is "within the struggles for the basic rights of existence that people learn to . . . strategize, and build movements and organizations. It is the struggle itself that can compel people to push for more." In her powerful work, *From #BlackLivesMatter to Black Liberation*, Taylor reminds us that this daily struggle is the wellspring of any movement—labor, alliance, revolution.[10]

Such narratives of fugitivity and marronage, from the nineteenth century to the present, help students trace the development of migratory alliances through the spread of information itself, from coachman to conductor, pulpit to tavern, attorney to officer, and even crossing over from slave catchers to fugitives, ICE agents to refugees.

These acts of disruption, whether temporary or permanent, help us to think about slave and refugee temporality as resistant to fixity and situatedness in the same way that information flows are resistant. For example, the presumed erasure of space and time for slaves boarded onto European sailing vessels—the social death of which Orlando Patterson has famously written, and the birth of a necropolitics that emerges from it, as Achille Mbembe has discussed—opened the possibility of a new model of *becoming* that was inherently mobile, resistant, and political.[11] By shifting the focus of my course—from disciplinary and disciplining spaces to the interdisciplinary *process* of networked ontologies like fugitivity and marronage—I was able to emphasize both the mediated quality of race (i.e., in which one is property in one state and person in another) as well as the productive centrality of the racial in the construction of globality.

Networks, in such situations, then, are not quite synonymous with a traditional "collective" that moves in unison toward a common goal, like revolutionaries or protestors who meet and move in concert. A network, in fact, often gathers its constitutive strength from anonymity and separation. Network elements may be interconnected by a common node (the slave or refugee), but networks do not, by nature, have intentionality. They may have potential outcomes (such as freedom, recapture, or deportation), but they often move—like fugitive bodies—in a nonlinear relay through potential adversaries as well as collaborators, in an elaborate network of information exchange and clandestine movement.

While I do not intend to draw a direct or simplistic link in the course between nineteenth-century networks and today's complicated network structure, which is as complicit in empowering the neoliberal order as it is in challenging it, the liberatory parallels in this long arc are well worth tracing, especially those that build solidarity across vast distances. As Johnetta Elzie, a key leader in the Ferguson Black Lives Matter movement, observes: "Thanks to Twitter, I have been able to see photos of Gaza the week before, and feel connected to the people there on an emotional level. I never thought Ferguson, this little part of Greater St. Louis, would become Gaza."[12]

Taken together, the actions of a network, however aggregate, anonymous, or distributed, can stand as a collective act of refusal, working, as Judith Butler and others have argued in a different context, to dismantle "regulatory power" from the inside. In the contemporary case of prisons, as Butler, Michelle Alexander, Ruth Wilson Gilmore, and others have explained, which "depend upon the successful regulation of human acts and movements," even small acts of refusal, such as the hunger strike, the labor strike, the implementation of clandestine modes of communication, can begin to chip away at the functional capacity of the institution, turning a space of confinement into a platform for opposition—the public square, or in the case of Cora and others like her, the plantation space, turned inside-out. Perhaps "the confined body does not always have the freedom to move," Butler attests, "but [it] can . . . still make use of its confinement to express resistance."[13]

The force of this resistance is intensified, then, through an understanding of the "accelerating precarity" of the bodies who assemble, who demand, who are in need. By recognizing precarity not as an identity but as a shared social, historic, and economic condition, and by asserting a "plural existence" against it, the disenfranchised lay claim to their rights—using the collective force of their condition to overturn it.[14]

For us, today, this means, again, as Taylor reminds us, building "networks and alliances with Latinos on immigrant rights, with Arabs and Muslims against Islamophobia, with Native organizations that fight for self-determination within the United States."[15] Of course, collective action cannot always overturn long-standing conditions of vulnerability and disenfranchisement, as the continued struggle for Black freedom itself proves. But the significance of collective opposition and collective demand can be, as Butler, Taylor, and others encourage, the first step toward "enact[ing] the world we wish to see, [by] . . . refus[ing] the one that is doing us in."[16] This struggle is as close to a solutionist model as I can provide for students, for it is perpetuity and continuity that is vital to my pedagogy. In this sense, my classroom is never a finite space but a true incubator, an aperture through which we learn to concentrate and sharpen our focus for the world outside.

Examining the fields of literature and science through the lens of slavery and race is vital to my work, as it allows me to demonstrate the ways in which racial history is not in opposition to science and technology but constitutive of the way these fields developed from the nineteenth century onward. Yet the significance of race in my pedagogical framing is not simply a matter of research focus, of personal experience, or of a political philosophy I utilize as a tool to sharpen students' understanding of interdisciplinarity or to undiscipline their solutionist tendencies. Rather, it is essential to my pedagogy because race is about the paramount importance of refusal—of oppression, of received narratives, of disciplines, and yes, of institutional logic. In this sense, my focus is less on the definition of race itself than on the capacious spirit of fugitivity, as Fred Moten and others have theorized it—a concept that is not simply about escape or a *running from* but about a search and a desire "for the outside," for the margins, a refusal of the very notion of the university as a regulating and proscribing force. In that sense, the classroom will always remain a challenging space for the scholar of race and humanities in the twenty-first century.[17]

For what I hope to map for students is their role in continuing this legacy of fugitivity and movement by carving out their own spaces of work and study—an "undercommons" that is deliberately and necessarily outside the space of the academy, as Fred Moten and Stefano Harney discuss in the close of their book on this topic. Like them, I want my students to leave my classroom "committed to the idea that study is what you do with other people. It's talking and walking around with other people, working, dancing, suffering, some irreducible convergence of all three, held under the name of speculative practice. . . . The point of calling it 'study' is to mark that the incessant and irreversible intellectuality of these activities is already present."[18]

Finally, this leaves us with the larger question of the role of the institution in race work, regardless of its primary focus as STEM, liberal arts, or otherwise. If the goal of the undercommons is to move to the edge, the margins, the outside of disciplinary parameters, then am I stranding students in the same utopian elsewhere that had left me so dissatisfied with the close of the Science, Technology, and Race course? Can we foster the work of the undercommons from within the space of the institution? Can the master's tools indeed destroy the master's house? Is Bhabian mimicry the response to Lorde's lament?[19]

Roderick Ferguson recalls Frederick Jackson Turner's turn-of-the-century understanding of the American university as "an imperial site ready to discover and name new frontiers" that it might "incorporate," one that could, in Turner's words, "create tendencies" and "direct them." Turner imagined the university as a new frontier for colonial expansion, writing that "in place of old frontiers of wilderness, there are new frontiers of unwon fields of science, fruitful for the needs of the race; there are frontiers of better social domains yet unexplored." But as Ferguson adds, "even Turner could not have imagined that minority difference would become one of the fields that the academy and other dominant institutions would attempt to win over."[20]

And well into the twentieth century, in those "hegemonic complexes of official or state-recognized liberal antiracisms that emerged after WWII," as Jodi Melamed has argued—from the acclaim and study of best-selling protest novels to the progressive, solutions-oriented disciplines of sociology and literary studies—and as Ferguson has once again brilliantly unpacked through his reading of Ralph Ellison's unpublished chapter of *Invisible Man* in *Aberrations in Black*, in which African American Professor Woodridge angrily tears apart the pages of a protest novel, calling it the "dirty shuck literature they drop to soil our hearts and minds," these projects and institutions have all worked to determine "the limits of social possibility in the United States and within fields of US global intervention."[21]

Whither, then, the real transformative *work* of fugitivity, of racial education, of diversity, at the institutional level? Not diversity as a word connoting the "happy point" of intersectionality, as Sara Ahmed critiques, in which difference is obscured and disappeared in the name of neutrality or empty celebration,[22] but diversity as resistance, as praxis, as performativity, as all the scholars cited and mentioned thus far have encouraged and implored? The answer, I think, lies in the persistence, the necessity, the vitality of the question—a race-radical education depends on the prioritization of diversity work as a *central* and *permanent* project of university education, not marginal and contingent, not a problem or a policy issue that must be addressed and solved but a question of deep and significant urgency that must remain so: not as some unhealing wound or as empty rhetoric but as a vital, consistent, and persistent organizing principle around which our teaching, our research, our advocacy, our learning, our joy, and our resistance must circle, always.

But we must be careful in our insistence on resistance, too. For by engaging with the racial only through narratives of resistance, emancipation, or some collective convergence that amounts to disappearance—in other words, through the eventual obliteration of the racial—we fail to reckon with the priority of the racial in the construction of a global ontology.

As theorists Denise Ferreira da Silva and Andrew Weheliye, among others, have argued, we must be careful not to fall into the historicist and universalizing trap of transparency that seeks to disavow the racial as a critical category in the name of a *new* politics of self-determination (which is, in fact, just a propping up of the same western subjectivity that has been complicit in the subjugation and erasure of racial others all along). This politics of self-determination continues to assert itself, only this time in a seemingly benevolent wish to "obliterate" racial difference and solve "the race problem," the source of so much strife and violence, in a universalizing gesture of erasure masked as welcome. Da Silva rejects this recursive brand of politics, and offers, as stated earlier, an "analytics of raciality" that prioritizes the role of the racial in today's global ontologies. Weheliye similarly asks us to consider, in defining racial assemblages, "what different modalities of the human come to light if we do not take the liberalist human figure of Man as the master-subject but focus on how humanity has been imagined and lived by those subjects excluded from this domain?"[23]

Diversity, through this lens, becomes our primary and most powerful weapon—or "tool" is perhaps a better, more collaborative word—as educators, in challenging institutional imperialism, in supporting those who are further silenced by its empty gestures of inclusivity and transparency, and in performing, as bell hooks has herself so beautifully insisted, a truly transformative pedagogy. For as Wendy Chun has elegantly argued, a reconfiguration of "race as technology" allows us to "shift the focus from the *what* of race to the *how* of race, from *knowing* race to *doing* race."[24] It also collapses the manufactured distance between disciplinary practices such as biology, engineering, art, and culture, which are part of the same technological apparatus of making, unmaking, and becoming. It is through this shift in focus from disciplinary and disciplining *spaces* to an interdisciplinary *process* that emphasizes the productive centrality of race in both the construction of and resistance to the neoliberal global order that we might truly engage in a radical politics of difference—regardless of our geographic location, our thematic or educational focus, or the financial priorities of our institutions.

NOTES

1. William Craft and Ellen Craft, *Running a Thousand Miles for Freedom* (Athens: University of Georgia Press, 1999); John Gregory Dunne, "The Humboldt Murders," *New Yorker*, January 13, 1997, 45–62.

2. Nihad M. Farooq, *Undisciplined: Science, Ethnography, and Personhood in the Americas, 1830–1940* (New York: New York University Press, 2016).

3. Thomas Jefferson, *Notes on the State of Virginia* (Philadelphia: Prichard and Hall, 1787), 153. See also Christine Herbes-Sommers, Llewellyn M. Smith, and Tracy Heather Strain, *Race: The Power of an Illusion*, directed by Christine Herbes-Sommers, Tracy Heather Strain, Llewellyn Smith (San Francisco: California Newsreel, 2003), VHS.

4. See Charles R. Darwin, *On the Origin of Species by Means of Natural Selection, or the Preservation of Favoured Races in the Struggle for Life* (1859; London: John Murray, 1860); Charles R. Darwin, *The Descent of Man and Selection in Relation to Sex*, 2nd ed. (1871; London: John Murray, 1882); Edward Lurie, *Louis Agassiz: A Life in Science* (Baltimore: Johns Hopkins University Press, 1988); Christoph Irmscher, *Louis Agassiz: Creator of American Science* (Boston: Harcourt, 2013); and Josiah Clark Nott and George Robins Gliddon, *Types of Mankind: or, Ethnological Researches, Based upon the Ancient Monuments, Paintings, Sculptures, and Crania of Race, and upon Their Natural, Geographical, Philological and Biblical History; Illustrated by Selections from the Inedited Papers of Samuel George Morton . . . and by Additional Contributions from Prof. L. Agassiz, LL.D., W. Usher, M.D., and Prof. H.S. Paterson* (Philadelphia: Lippincott, Grambo, 1854).

5. Marcus Garvey, *The Philosophy and Opinions of Marcus Garvey, or Africa for the Africans*, vols. 1 and 2 ([1923 and 1925]; Dover, MA: Majority, 1986); Sun Ra and Joshua Smith, *Space Is the Place*, directed by John Coney (1974; San Fran-

cisco: Dilexi Series/Harte Recordings, 2015), DVD; Ytasha L. Womack, *Afrofuturism: The World of Black Sci-Fi and Fantasy Culture* (Chicago: Lawrence Hill, 2013); Reynaldo Anderson and Charles E. Jones, eds., *Afrofuturism 2.0: The Rise of Astro-Blackness* (Lanham, MD: Lexington, 2016); Alondra Nelson, ed., "Afrofuturism," special issue, *Social Text* 20, no. 2 (71) (Summer 2002); Sheree R. Thomas, ed., *Dark Matter: A Century of Speculative Fiction from the African Diaspora* (New York: Aspect, 2000).

6. Fred Moten, "The Case of Blackness," *Criticism* 50, no. 2 (Spring 2008): 177–218; Tina M. Campt, "Black Feminist Futures and the Practice of Fugitivity," Helen Pond McIntyre '48 Lecture held at the Barnard Center for Research on Women, October 7, 2014, http://bcrw.barnard.edu/videos/tina-campt-black-feminist-futures-and-the-practice-of-fugitivity; Saidiya Hartman, *Lose Your Mother: A Journey along the Atlantic Slave Route* (New York: Farrar, Strauss, & Giroux, 2007).

7. Denise Ferreira da Silva, *Toward a Global Idea of Race* (Minneapolis: University of Minnesota Press, 2007); Neil Roberts, *Freedom as Marronage* (Chicago: University of Chicago Press, 2015).

8. Paul Gilroy, *The Black Atlantic: Modernity and Double Consciousness* (Cambridge, MA: Harvard University Press, 1993).

9. Colson Whitehead, *The Underground Railroad* (New York: Doubleday, 2016), 26. See also Nihad M. Farooq, "'A Useful Delusion': Valentine Farm and the Flight for Freedom," *Utopian Studies* 30, no. 1 (2019): 87–110.

10. Whitehead, *Underground Railroad*, 272; Keeanga-Yamahtta Taylor, *From #Black Lives Matter to Black Liberation* (Chicago: Haymarket, 2016), 216–217.

11. Orlando Patterson, *Slavery and Social Death: A Comparative Study* (Cambridge, MA: Harvard University Press, 1982); Achille Mbembe, "Necropolitics," trans. Libby Meintjes, *Public Culture* 15, no. 1 (Winter 2003): 11–40.

12. Johnetta Elzie, "When I Close My Eyes at Night, I See People Running from Tear Gas," *Ebony*, September 8, 2014, https://www.ebony.com/news/ferguson-forward-when-i-close-my-eyes-at-night-i-see-people-running-from-tear-ga/#axzz3FTUHgnS1.

13. Judith Butler, *Notes toward a Performative Theory of Assembly* (Cambridge, MA: Harvard University Press, 2015), 136; Ruth Wilson Gilmore, *Golden Gulag: Prisons, Surplus, Crisis, and Opposition in Globalizing California* (Berkeley: University of California Press, 2007); Michelle Alexander, *The New Jim Crow: Mass Incarceration in the Age of Colorblindness* (New York: New Press, 2010).

14. Butler, *Notes*, 10, 16.

15. Taylor, *From #Black Lives Matter*, 186.

16. Butler, *Notes*, 153.

17. Fred Moten, *The Universal Machine* (Durham, NC: Duke University Press, 2018), 131.

18. Fred Moten and Stefano Harney, *The Undercommons: Fugitive Planning and Black Study* (New York: Minor Compositions, 2013), 110.

19. Homi K. Bhabha, *The Location of Culture* (New York: Routledge, 1994).

20. Roderick Ferguson, *The Reorder of Things: The University and Its Pedagogies of Minority Difference* (Minneapolis: University of Minnesota Press, 2012), 229.

21. Jodi Melamed, *Represent and Destroy: Rationalizing Violence in the New Ra-*

cial Capitalism (Minneapolis: University of Minnesota Press, 2011), xv; Ralph Ellison, unpublished draft of "Woodridge" episode chapter of *Invisible Man* (1952), cited in Roderick Ferguson, *Aberrations in Black: Toward a Queer of Color Critique* (Minneapolis: University of Minnesota Press, 2003), 54.

22. Sara Ahmed, *On Being Included: Racism and Diversity in Institutional Life* (Durham, NC: Duke University Press, 2012), 14.

23. Da Silva, *Global Idea of Race*, xix; Alexander G. Weheliye, *Habeas Viscus: Racializing Assemblages, Biopolitics, and Black Feminist Theories of the Human* (Durham, NC: Duke University Press, 2014), 8.

24. bell hooks, *Teaching to Transgress: Education as the Practice of Freedom* (New York: Routledge, 1994); Wendy Hui Kyong Chun, "Race and/as Technology, or How to Do Things to Race," in *Race after the Internet*, ed. Lisa Nakamura and Peter A. Chow-White (New York: Routledge, 2012), 38.

2

Teaching an Introductory Master's Degree Course

PAUL LAUTER

❖ ❖ ❖ ❖ ❖ ❖ ❖ ❖ ❖ ❖ ❖ ❖ ❖ ❖ ❖

When, late in the last century, I began teaching the introductory graduate course in American Studies at Trinity College, I had a number of constraints as well as some distinctive opportunities. First, my students were mainly adults—in their late twenties or thirties and up. Most already had jobs. They taught or would teach in secondary school—usually history or English; they worked in museums or as lawyers or social workers. They viewed our MA program not as a step on the pathway to a PhD, certainly not in American Studies. Rather, they shared the teacher's mantra: "What shall I do on Monday?" They often hoped to derive from our classes material that might be helpful in their own work. That gave a practical dimension to discussions, often reflected in the subjects they chose for their course papers, such as "Differing Viewpoints about the Extent of Hartford's Gang Violence."

Their choices were also, of course, swayed by my own developing interests, particularly in film and cultural studies. During those years, I published *From Walden Pond to Jurassic Park* (2001), and I had begun teaching undergraduate courses involving fiction and film. Many graduate students found my favorite formula—"why this thing, in this way, at this time?"—handy. They used it to frame course papers on television series or films that interested them, such as *Battlestar Galactica* ("Why it worked in 2003 and not in 1978") or *Monsters vs. Aliens* (the cultural work it performed for—or with—one of my student's children). I realized that the course had to change in response to student concerns and altered areas of faculty interest, apart from my own in film. For example, a new concentration in "museums and communities" needed to be included in the introductory course. But what else might demand a presence? Given such factors, I always shaped the course somewhat differently over the dozen or so years I taught it.

I was happy with the practical approach to cultural issues my students began to develop. But I was also invested in seeing them learn to deploy theoretical terms like "hegemony," "ideology," and even "gender," which were mostly new to their intellectual vocabulary. I thought they ought to have a handle on the language they would find in readings from the field. In this respect, the course might serve as a kind of preface to the large book of American Studies. Even though my students were not PhD candidates, I wanted a rich curriculum for them, not unlike well-designed introductions to doctoral programs about which I'd inquired during the 1990s. I sought to bring the field to the students, rather than the students to the field. That probably was not a wise choice. It's obviously important to start with where one's students are, what their prior education and political experience entails, and where they might be headed. Many of my students came from limited undergraduate backgrounds, mostly not in American Studies. While I hoped they had read American "classics," such as *Walden*, Frederick Douglass, Melville's fiction, Emily Dickinson's poetry, I didn't expect them to arrive with a body of common knowledge. Nor did they come to our program with a common agenda; for some, the degree itself was more important than the subject matter of the anomalous field, American Studies.

Personally, I found the history of our discipline interesting in itself; moreover, I thought it could help reveal significant features of the social and cultural surround both of the field's earlier incarnation and of our own intellectual moment. "Always historicize," I said. But was it worthwhile historicizing the American Studies of the twentieth century? Could that help students keep pace with a rapidly changing discipline increasingly unlike the one in which I had been brought up? Did a focus on our history turn American Studies into an object of antiquarian scholarship? Did that approach help them in the work in which they were already engaged? Such questions were always a presence in my planning, as they remain in this essay.

I particularly wanted my students to experience *some* of the challenges of advanced graduate study. The first reading assignment in the 2009 iteration of the course was this:

(Some of) What We Mean When We Say We Do American Studies

Paul Lauter, "Dinosaur Culture," in *From Walden Pond to Jurassic Park: Activism, Culture, and American Studies* (Durham, NC: Duke University Press, 2001), 99–115. (So you'll know where I'm coming from.)

Ana Maria Manzanas Calvo, "Contested Passages: Migrants and Borders in the Río Grande and the Mediterranean Sea," *South Atlantic Quarterly* 105 (Fall 2006): 807–823.

Jane Tompkins, "'Indians': Textualism, Morality, and the Problem of History," *Critical Inquiry* 13 (1986): 101–119.

William Truettner, "Ideology and Image: Justifying Westward Expansion," in *The West as America,* edited by William Truettner (Washington, DC: Smithsonian, 1991), 27–53.

T. J. Jackson Lears, "The Concept of Cultural Hegemony: Problems and Possibilities," *American Historical Review* 90 (1985): 567–593.

C. L. Barney Dews, "Gender Tragedies: East Texas Cockfighting and *Hamlet,*" *Journal of Men's Studies* 2 (February 1994): 253–267.

That was, as students complained, a heavy load. Yes, but it served many purposes: first, as a warning to students who approached the program as a casual avocation. More important, it quickly demonstrated some of the ways in which American Studies addresses contemporary political issues, such as migration, borders, imperial expansion, and the construction of ideologies. The readings introduced students to the variety of American Studies "texts," film and other visual media, legal and journalistic materials, as well as personal experiences. They offered a taste of some theoretical issues that would recur in the course: for example, the meanings of culture, hegemony, and ideology and the problems presented by poststructuralism and point of view in arriving at conclusive understandings of events and values. Finally, the readings provoked discussion about the "we" in the assignment title: who were those doing what they may or may not have named "American Studies," what differences did they bring to our classroom, was it an advantage to be "American" to do this work?

My students particularly appreciated the essays by Tompkins and Dews, primarily I think because both open with stories about the authors' lives that their articles are dedicated to understanding. Tompkins begins thus: "When I was growing up in New York City, my parents used to take me to an event in Inwood Park at which Indians—real American Indians dressed in feathers and blankets—could be seen and touched by children like me. This event was always a disappointment."[1]

Similarly, the Dews article begins with his memories of the cockfighting to which his family took him: "I remember limp necks and the lifeless swaying heads of beautiful birds as they were carried by their feet to barrels for burning. I remember perfect drops of blood left behind in the sand. I remember the many colored feathers shining in the sun. I was told not to cry, not to remember these things. We always remember what we're told to forget."[2]

For many students, learning involved looking at an event that has deeply affected their life and trying to figure out why it happened as it happened and what that might mean. Of course, autobiography is not the only way to learn, but it certainly offers a powerful mode of education and one with which I was quite sympathetic.

The Lears article, by contrast, seemed constructed not from experience—it didn't seem to "explain" anything my students needed to have explained—but from a world of mostly unfamiliar texts. It begins: "Twenty years ago the Italian communist Antonio Gramsci was rarely discussed outside his native land; now he has become an intellectual cause célèbre and in some quarters a cult hero." "Really?" my students asked. Lears goes on to mention Raymond Williams, Clifford Geertz, Herbert Gutman, C. Wright Mills, among many others—writers with whom most of my students were unfamiliar. This is not to say that they shouldn't be. Part of my rationale for including this tough piece was to introduce students to the world in which Lears participates, a world in which the unaccustomed term "cultural hegemony" has a significant resonance.

I am not suggesting that the Tompkins and Dews articles lack theory or complexity. Quite the contrary: a major point of Tompkins's article, for example, was to examine the problem of indeterminacy fostered by poststructuralist theory in conclusions about values. The Lears article also raised a basic pedagogical issue: where does one start? That is, how do you provide students—especially those like mine emerging from modest undergraduate backgrounds—with entry to that unfamiliar textual world? A term a week (this week it's "hegemony")? A single three-hour class devoted to terminology? Leave them to sink or swim? I tended in good pragmatic style to get at them as we got to them.

I came to think that the problem was not so much the unfamiliar lingo of a changing discipline but alterations in what issues American Studies was seen as illuminating. So I figured that it made sense to begin with the history of the discipline itself and of its early practitioners: Perry Miller, Henry Nash Smith, Leo Marx, and others from the Myth and Symbol school. Myth and Symbol, dominant when I first encountered American Studies, seemed to me to remain interesting both for the questions it asked and for those it failed to ask. I had the students read important selections from the "founders"—"forefathers," if you will—and then contemporary critiques (sometimes by the writer himself) that called into question the premises implicit in that work. Early in the course I paired Perry Miller's influential "Preface" to *Errand into the Wilderness* with Amy Kaplan's brilliant analysis of it in "'Left Alone with America': The Absence of Empire in the Study of American Culture."[3] Predictably, my students sympathized with Miller's personal narrative about unloading drums of oil in Central Africa and were suspicious of Kaplan's revelation of the implications of Miller's starting point for American Studies. The Puritan "errand into the wilderness" provided Miller with a coherent "beginning"; whereas for him, Kaplan argues, Virginia

> would obstruct coherence for reasons other than the insignificance of the white settlers and their lack of an articulate body of expression, as Miller claims. Beginning with Jamestown would evoke a counternarrative of migration to that of the Puritans: the forced migration of Africans on slave ships, and the unarticulated expression of another historical trajectory. . . . Jamestown is incoherent as a beginning, because it would resonate with Miller's immediate setting in Africa to initiate an alternative narrative of beginnings in slavery, in the triangle of Europe, America, and Africa, not the neat dyad of the errand into the wilderness.[4]

"Isn't she really saying he's a racist?" one student memorably protested. I tried to deflect attention from Miller's psychology and toward the implications of his narrative for the early shape of American Studies. Students usually weren't persuaded.

But the discussion led us to apply Jameson's rubric—"always historicize"—to the three moments with which we were dealing. First, the pre–*Brown v. Board* world of 1953, which helped form what Miller would consider important—or even visible. That conversation helped us reflect on why, in 2008 or 2009 (as Obama was elected and took office), our discussion about Kaplan's 1993 essay (as the US invaded Iraq) focused on race, whereas her subtitle, "The Absence of Empire in the Study of American Culture," expressed her focus on imperialism. Examining Miller in this way enabled us to understand how what we designated as "American Studies" was not fixed by history into a particular profile but like other cultural phenomena was historically rooted in the starting points particular scholars in particular circumstances at particular times might recognize as significant.

We approached the frontier in a similar fashion:

Conceptions of the "Frontier"

Frederick Jackson Turner, "The Significance of the Frontier in American History," in *The Frontier in American History* (New York: Henry Holt, 1921), 1–38.

Henry Nash Smith, *Virgin Land: The American West as Symbol and Myth* (Cambridge, MA: Harvard University Press, 1971),vii–xii, 3–34, 44–80, 112–144, 184–194, 201–230, 250–260.

Henry Nash Smith, "Symbol and Idea in *Virgin Land*," in *Ideology and Classic American Literature*, edited by Sacvan Bercovitch and Myra Jehlen (Cambridge: Cambridge University Press, 1986), 21–35.

Alan Trachtenberg, "Myth, History, and Literature in *Virgin Land*," *Prospects* 3 (1977): 125–133.

Annette Kolodny, *The Lay of the Land: Metaphor As Experience and History in American Life and Letters* (Chapel Hill: University of North Carolina Press, 1975), 3–29, 52–70, 138–160.

In this class, seldom successful until I totally altered it, I tried to address some of the ways in which the Myth and Symbol school underwrote American exceptionalism with all of its imperialist baggage. We needed to ask: What issues is American Studies designed to illuminate? The problematic of traditional disciplines usually seemed obvious: What *did* happen in the fall of 1928? (History). How does buying and selling peanuts work? (Economics). How do groups of people create and modify rules that enable them to live together? (Politics). But what of American Studies? Is its inescapable assumption that American history and culture are unique, exceptional, and therefore need to be studied as a distinctive enterprise? The 2016 presidential election illustrated that such American exceptionalism remains a powerful political idea.[5] Even though American Studies activists have tried to deconstruct it, did American exceptionalism also provide the fundamental premise underlying the field from its first beginnings?

In any event, most of my students took it for granted. I thought, mistakenly, that the exceptionalism debate was dead and buried with Ronald Reagan. Besides, deeply absorbed in Gloria Anzaldúa, I was more interested in reconfiguring the traditional conception of the "frontier" as "border." "La Frontera," after all, was a live political as well as cultural concept, whereas the "frontier"—even reprised by JFK—remained ancient history. Not surprisingly, then, this unit proved contentious—even after I revised it. Turner, whose ideas my students seem to have imbibed with their kindergarten milk and cookies, seemed to them to provide a lucid justification of exceptionalism, which Smith properly elaborated. Was my disbelief in exceptionalism un-American? American exceptionalism came, at times, to feel like an article of faith, which I might as well have been burning up with the Book of Common Prayer they could find in Trinity's elegant chapel.

Smith's work also raised questions about the place of high and popular culture in American Studies. "Culture" was one of those troubling terms, especially for students who had been English majors. Trained to read novels and poems closely and not inclined to respect popular texts such as dime novels or *Jurassic Park*, they seemed to feel, as Smith usually did, that our classrooms should continue to focus on "high" culture, literary writers. But in accord with the strategy of cultural studies, American Studies increasingly examined a variety of artifacts of the society whatever their origins and standing. I, of course, had shifted my view, as the title of my 2001 book, *From Walden Pond to Jurassic Park*, asserted. The frontier turned out to be too conflicted a ground on which to address these questions of high, mass, and popular culture. I therefore designed a different unit involving essays by Dwight Macdonald, Lawrence Levine, and Janice Radway, and a piece of my own on cold war culture.[6] These readings better enabled us to discuss varied objects of study as well as the institutions, like book clubs and museums, which have shaped how Americans understand culture.

Dealing with the "frontier," I also had wanted to explore the central role gender played in shaping our forefathers' ideas about such myths and symbols. The texts in question, we all saw, focused almost exclusively on men. Why had they *not* considered female experience of the frontier? More generally, what had American Studies *not* been asking? Was it the main function of this discipline to examine the identity category of male, white, Protestant? Smith had himself nicely reappraised his own impeccable title and its implications as, of course, had Annette Kolodny. Again, this frontier assignment did not provide the best context to approach gender. I eventually decided to create a separate unit, pairing Kolodny with Joan Scott's important 1986 article on gender as a category of analysis and articles such as Rebecca Walsh's "Sugar, Sex, and Empire" on Sarah Orne Jewett's "The Foreigner" and the Spanish-

American war.[7] These readings better enabled us to examine one more of the field's difficult terms, "gender." Looking at what Myth and Symbol did led usefully into what it did not do and therefore to better understanding of the ongoing changes in American Studies.

At this point, generally well into the term, I always faced a dilemma: Do we plunge into the other central category of identity, race? Or do we follow the historical, if abortive, transition of American Studies from myths and symbols to corporate culture and class? My students, almost all white, were as anxious to study race as they had been to examine gender. Class, the traditional third identity category, proved to be puzzling—and occasionally embarrassing, since enrolling in a program at Trinity represented for some a step across some ambiguous class line.

My approach to race differed significantly from the highly theorized analyses of post–Black Lives Matter American Studies. My students needed knowledge of historical landmarks beyond *Plessy v. Ferguson* and Emmett Till, a handle on what they had never called "racial formation," and a way of systematically rethinking racism as a social rather than a psychological category. For the last, they found Micaela di Leonardo's "White Lies, Black Myths"[8] and George Lipsitz's "The Possessive Investment in Whiteness"[9] particularly useful. Both demonstrate in the vivid detail my students wisely prized how laws, policies, and social norms that seem not at all racially inflected in practice advantage white people and subvert the economic and political positions of people of color. For many students this was not new news, though the particularities cited in these articles surprised many. Di Leonardo's piece, which examines New Haven, just down the road, and which begins with her rape by a Black man, proved particularly effective in demonstrating the racial impact of local decisions having to do with, for example, city planning.

These articles led us to a big question: what is this thing called "race"? Combining a historical and a sociological approach offered helpful answers to that question—and also provided students with some insights to differing methodologies. Barbara Jeanne Fields's "Slavery, Race and Ideology in the United States of America" (1990) argues that race as a way of categorizing people as inferior came into being only during the revolutionary period. It became necessary, to quote Fields, following "the incorporation of Africans and their descendants into a polity and society in which they lacked rights that others not only took for granted, but claimed as a matter of self-evident natural law."[10] In a nation that asserted that "all men are created equal," some men were plainly "more equal" than others. How to explain? Race, as Fields brilliantly argues, explains that anomaly.

But then, what is meant by "race"? Doesn't the meaning or the framework of "race" change over time? Michael Omi and Howard Winant argue in *Racial Formation in the United States* (1994) that race exists as a signifier of inequality, the actual content of which alters in relation to the character of social and political forces. Their analysis and their history differ from those of Fields: they claim that representations of the "conquest of America . . . first in religious terms, but soon enough in scientific and political ones, initiated modern racial awareness."[11] My students found this clash of cogent but conflicting analyses stimulating. I also used readings by Milton Gordon and Stephen Steinberg to illustrate how explanations of Jewish "success" in the new world differed.[12] In this case, students rapidly came to see that Gordon was often inaccurate, in both analysis and prediction. This assignment proved useful for undercutting students' tendency to accept opinion and long-accepted "common sense," like that offered by Gordon, as truthful. And it helped them gain confidence in their own negative responses to his ideas.

Omi and Winant also challenge mainstream discussions of race as a "problem" to be solved by policy adjustments or by forms of "social engineering" and "state management." What needs to be understood, they argue, is "how groups become racially identified, how racial identities and meanings changed over time . . . [and] how racial conflicts shape the American polity and society."[13] They focus on "racial projects," like social movements, including civil rights and Black Power activities of the 1950s and 1960s, and Black Lives Matter today, as well as post–*Brown v. Board* reactionary "massive resistance" to integration and today's dog-whistle racism. Omi and Winant challenged us to translate their abstractions into the particulars of my mostly white students' lived experience.

Related readings helped address that problem. In my course, I used James Baldwin's *The Fire Next Time* sometimes, Richard Wright's "The Ethics of Living Jim Crow" usually, and W. E. B. Du Bois's *The Souls of Black Folks* always. I insisted on Du Bois's *Souls* because I had not found it on a number of the introductory PhD syllabi I had consulted in planning my own; perhaps the instructors assumed that students would have read it, along with Thoreau's *Walden* and Franklin's *Autobiography*, as undergraduates. Perhaps. Today, we have a larger library from which to choose—from Ta-Nehisi Coates to the many individual, often local, accounts emerging from Black Lives Matter. However one feels concerning Du Bois's ideas about "double consciousness," the "talented tenth," or the propaganda functions of art, he remains a towering figure among American intellectuals and activists. *Souls* is a paradigmatic

American Studies text like no other. Most of my students had never studied it intensively—or at all. It remained throughout my time with the course one of the works I always had students read.

Du Bois's work also provided me with a means to move from the analysis of race to the understudied issue of class. Two of Du Bois's lesser-read essays from *Darkwater: Voices from Within the Veil*, "The Souls of White Folks" and "Of Work and Wealth," clearly articulated his critique of early-twentieth-century socialists' racial blindness.

> Yesterday we righted one great mistake when we realized that the ownership of the laborer did not tend to increase production. . . . Today we are challenging another ownership,—the ownership of materials which go to make the goods we need. . . . Today, therefore, we are challenging this ownership; we are demanding general consent as to what materials shall be privately owned and as to how materials shall be used.[14]

Du Bois's basic statement from a century ago of socialist ideology remains clear. But he always goes further than the economics of socialism: "What we must decide sometime is who are to be considered 'men.'" Not, he argues, under the present dispensation, all human beings:

> In the teaching of my classes I was not willing to stop with showing that this was unfair,—indeed I did not have to do this. They knew through bitter experience its rank injustice, because they were black. What I had to show was that no real reorganization of industry could be permanently made with the majority of mankind left out. These disinherited darker peoples must either share in the future industrial democracy or overturn the world.[15]

Classes involving essays from *Darkwater* took off into disputatious terrain, aka "socialism." Normally, I kept our eyes fixed to the texts. But here—and I would imagine now post-Bernie, even more so—that seemed intolerable. I preferred to let them argue the politics so clearly set before them on Du Bois's page.

When I was teaching this course, two impediments to examining class always arose in our path: first, "class" seemed quickly to be assimilated into a category of identity, akin to gender or race—especially for my largely middle-class students. But thinking of class as a matter of identity proved confusing—and often also embarrassing for students from working-class origins. As an identity category, "class" might aid them in explaining their residual loyalties to family and community and their confusion about where their master's degrees might be taking them. But it was not terribly helpful in understanding the dynamics of power that helped separate working-class men, in particular, from the elitism that Hillary Clinton came to represent for them. Talking about what it meant to *be* working class did not engage the political differences even then reshaping party alignments.

Also, the common wisdom, to which my students had been heavily exposed, had it that discussing socialism—to which any developed class analysis inevitably led—meant wasting our time on a long-failed project of merely historical curiosity. I tried various ways—none altogether satisfying—of confronting the problems of class-as-identity and socialism-as-history. Du Bois's *Darkwater* was one. But I was pushing uphill against the resident ideology of American institutions, including universities; even the best of my readings could not fully compensate for the intellectual biases considered wisdom at the time.

Alan Trachtenberg's *The Incorporation of America* (1982) and Richard Ohmann's *Selling Culture* (1996) provided different approaches to the central issues of class. Trachtenberg's own work illustrates the transition from Myth and Symbol to corporate power in American Studies thinking. In his *Brooklyn Bridge: Fact and Symbol* (1965), he moves away from symbolic statements toward a new emphasis on the material factors that shape culture. During the period in which I was teaching this introduction—before Occupy, before Bernie—*The Incorporation of America* led to a useful examination of the impact of corporate dominance on American culture and society.[16]

Ohmann's book extends this approach to capitalism and culture. Using details derived from magazines of that period to dramatize cultural changes—including how the covers and advertisements of *Harper's* compared with those of *Munsey's* and how the magazines' content was designed to address differing audiences—Ohmann lays out the significant alterations occurring in the cultural landscape between about 1880 and 1910. He uses the concept of hegemony, with which we had earlier struggled, to trace the emergence of consumer capitalism as the dominant organizational form of modern America. And he shows how that quintessential expression of consumer capitalism, the marketplace and the advertising essential to it, functioned to produce consumption adequate to sustaining the enormous productive capacities of American industry. His portrait of these popular magazines helped students grasp how advertising underwrites the functioning of radio, then TV, and the internet today.

Ohmann's brilliant but underused book demystifies the processes of historical change—one *can* to some useful degree track causality. It suggests how the concept of hegemony can be used to understand the dynamics of more recent developments, including social media, of commanding interest to students. And—so valuably here—it reintroduces the explanatory power of class analysis to the concerns of American Studies and of social movements more generally. That is, I saw in it a precursor of the intellectual and political dynamic, made manifest in the 2016 election campaign, that has eroded the dominance of capitalist ideology by placing not only class issues but socialism (!) on our agendas.

My course stayed close to the dialectic between politics and culture. I believe the excitement of American Studies lies precisely in that region where culture and politics shape and reshape one another. We devoted much time to Paul A. DiMaggio's articles on the interactions between wealth and cultural institutions such as the Boston Symphony Orchestra and the Museum of Fine Arts.[17] Likewise, we studied Eva Cockcroft's examination of how Cold War art critics deployed abstract expressionism to promote American beliefs and power during the postwar period.[18] It seemed to me important to challenge the notion that culture constituted a nonpolitical domain of leisure. Rather, I wanted the students to see the multiple ways in which culture helped constitute the hegemonic domain in which they lived and struggled.

Looking back at the course and trying to assess what it might offer to other faculty and students now, I wish to return to the fundamental error in my planning I mentioned at the outset. Before I started the course, I asked a number of friends which books and articles they taught in what I took to be comparable courses in graduate departments. I did not consider, as I should have, the differences implicit in thinking of a graduate course in American Studies as preparation for a professional vocation, as distinct from an approach to everyday life in the United States of America or to teaching about that in a secondary school or elementary classroom. The differences are not absolute, but they are real. My readings also differ strikingly from those one would assemble on the basis of articles in *American Quarterly* over the last few years. At its best, *AQ* provides a view of the cutting edges of the field. So, I think, did many of the readings I assigned a couple of decades back. But things change. Many students now bring to the classroom knowledge and political practice that instructors, other students, and older readings might not engage. One needs, then, to design curricula sufficiently open to enable such resources to flourish together with the touchstones of a field always in flux and, like its titular subject, never finished.

NOTES

1. Jane Tompkins, "'Indians': Textualism, Morality, and the Problem of History," *Critical Inquiry* 13 (1986): 101.
2. C. L. Barney Dews, "Gender Tragedies: East Texas Cockfighting and *Hamlet*," *Journal of Men's Studies* 2 (February 1994): 253.
3. In Amy Kaplan and Donald Pease, eds., *Cultures of United States Imperialism* (Durham, NC: Duke University Press, 1993), 3–21.
4. Amy Kaplan, "'Left Alone with America': The Absence of Empire in the Study of American Culture," in *Cultures of United States Imperialism*, 7–8.
5. For a striking instance, see Hillary Clinton, "I Still Believe in American Exceptionalism," accessed August 6, 2016, http://www.cbsnews.com/videos/hillary-clinton-i-still-believe-in-american-exceptionalism.
6. Dwight Macdonald, "A Theory of Mass Culture," *Diogenes* 1, no. 3 (Summer 1953): 1–17; Lawrence W. Levine, "William Shakespeare and the American People: A Study in Cultural Transformation," in *The Unpredictable Past: Explorations in American Cultural History* (New York: Oxford, 1993), 139–171; Janice Radway, "The Scandal of the Middlebrow: The Book-of-the-Month Club, Class Fracture, and Cultural Authority," *South Atlantic Quarterly* 89 (Fall 1990): 703–736; Paul Lauter, "Cold War Culture," in *From Walden Pond to Jurassic Park: Activism, Culture, and American Studies* (Durham, NC: Duke University Press, 2001), 234–249.
7. Rebecca Walsh, "Sugar, Sex, and Empire: Sarah Orne Jewett's 'The Foreigner' and the Spanish-American War," in *A Concise Companion to American Studies*, ed. John Carlos Rowe (Boston: Wiley-Blackwell, 2010), 303–319.
8. "White Lies, Black Myths: Rape, Race and the Black 'Underclass,'" in *The Gender/Sexuality Reader: Culture, History, Political Economy*, ed. Roger N. Lancaster and Micaela di Leonardo (New York: Routledge, 1997), 53–70.
9. "The Possessive Investment in Whiteness," with Comments, *American Quarterly* 47 (September 1995): 369–466.
10. Barbara Jeanne Fields, "Slavery, Race and Ideology in the United States of America," *New Left Review* no. 181 (1990): 95–118, quote on 106.
11. Michael Omi and Howard Winant, *Racial Formation in the United States* (New York: Routledge, 1994), 62.
12. Milton Gordon, *Assimilation in American Life* (New York: Oxford, 1964); Stephen Steinberg, *The Ethnic Myth* (Boston: Beacon, 1989).
13. Omi and Winant, *Racial Formation*, 3.
14. W. E. B. Du Bois, *Darkwater: Voices from Within the Veil* (1920; New York: Schocken, 1969), 100.
15. Du Bois, *Darkwater*, 101, 102.
16. Alan Trachtenberg, *The Incorporation of America: Culture and Society in the Gilded Age* (New York: Hill and Wang, 1982), and *Brooklyn Bridge: Fact and Symbol* (Chicago: University of Chicago Press, 1965)—frustratingly, these books were

sporadically unavailable; Richard Ohmann, *Selling Culture: Magazines, Markets and Class at the Turn of the Century* (London: Verso, 1996).

17. Paul J. DiMaggio, "Cultural Entrepreneurship in Nineteenth-Century Boston," in *Nonprofit Enterprise in the Arts: Studies in Mission and Constraint* (New York: Oxford, 1986), 41–61; and "Cultural Entrepreneurship in Nineteenth-Century Boston, part II: The Classification and Framing of American Art," *Media, Culture and Society* 4 (1982): 303–322.

18. Eva Cockcroft, "Abstract Expressionism: Weapon of the Cold War," *Art-Forum* 12, no. 10 (June 1974): 39–41.

3

Teaching the Medical Other

Thinking beyond Assumptions through the History of Midwifery

PAUL J. CROCE

After teaching an American Studies course with a section on midwifery, I ran into a course veteran and asked him how it had been sitting with him. As with much of American Studies, my courses challenge mainstream assumptions, with stories of raucous politics before our own polarized times and descriptions of the agency of African Americans despite persistent racism. I was curious to hear a student's view.

This student focused on our inquiries into midwifery as practiced before and after the rise of scientific medicine. He said the course was hard. Was he referring to the old-school language of the early-republic midwife we studied or our coverage of scientific evaluations of birth experiences alongside the changing support for midwifery? No. It was consideration of alternatives that had prompted him to rethink a previously easy choice. Along with most contemporary Americans, including me before study of medical history, he had simply assumed that giving birth meant going to the hospital under the care of a scientifically trained OB/GYN (obstetrician-gynecologist). Straying from this norm has seemed as archaic as the words of the traditional midwife. It was an American Studies moment. Alternative ways of thinking became for him, as psychologist and philosopher William James would say, a "genuine option," with choices replacing assumptions. Here was a tangible expression of the "constant state of flux and reinvention" in teaching American Studies, which is at once challenging and an asset.[1]

A TOPICAL APPROACH TO AMERICAN STUDIES AT STETSON UNIVERSITY

This discussion of midwifery is just one part of my course, American Cultural Traditions, at Stetson University in Florida.[2] The course explores multiple topics in American culture, with some privileging of local examples. The course has two main purposes: to provide an overview of what makes the United States tick and to challenge student assumptions about American culture.

In addition to midwifery, my class discusses the following:

1. Contested presidential elections through study of fierce ideological and procedural contests in the elections of 1800 and 2000, including the postcampaign campaign for the close 2000 Florida vote;
2. Moments in Florida history, including US expansion and the strategic retreats of the Seminole Nation, and accounts of Zora Neale Hurston gathering African American folklore in her hometown of Eatonville, Florida, recently revived with the Zora! Festival since 1990;
3. Evangelical religion in the nineteenth-century reformist revivalism of Charles Grandison Finney, and the pietistic and mostly conservative evangelicals gaining strength since the 1960s, with interviews of local street preachers; and
4. African American responses to injustices through focus on the vigilante destruction of the town of Rosewood, Florida, in 1923 and calls for remembering African American history from Malcolm X to the 1994 Florida reparations for the Rosewood tragedy.

In addition to teaching knowledge and skills, American Studies courses extend "the tradition of progressive education," as Jay Mechling, Robert Merideth, and David Wilson declared in 1973, by encouraging "resocialization," empowering students with "not only adaptation to the world but transformation of it."[3] The field's institutionalized anti-institutionalism has enabled attention to social "Others" without power by questioning assumptions pronounced by mainstream authorities and routinely circulating in mass culture. The open inquiry enables students to develop their own views.

Midwifery once was the only birthing practice; when modern hospitals and professional doctors gained authority, midwifery was severely marginalized; it has revived recently. As late as 1940, midwives attended about 20 percent of American births; by 1989, that number had declined to under 4 percent, only to rise to almost 10 percent today.[4] According to mainstream narratives, midwifery is a simplistic folk practice, readily displaced by scientific medicine, whose techniques and understanding of anatomy and physiology finally made childbirth safe. The unspoken story line that everyone "knows" emerged in student interviews on birthing experiences. In my class, we start by discussing what students already know about birth. This practice enables me to meet students from within their own experiences for enriching examination of debates between doctors and midwives. Because American Studies is untethered to disciplines and debates, it can actually clear the field for raising questions about conventional assumptions, making students' "own experience . . . problematic," as Mechling, Merideth, and Wilson envision.[5] As my former student spoke bluntly, that's hard, even as the stories go down easy. One student's parents insisted they would have "no midwives—only hospital births," and they were glad in his own case because he was "born with breathing complications." Another student reported that when she was born, her mother had "never considered midwifery" because she trusted doctors and "wanted drugs." This student was born by vaginal birth after (prior) cesarean section (VBAC), and the birth went smoothly. These stories highlight the students' support for mainstream medicine, with expertise and technology to deal with complications and to lessen the pain of labor and delivery.[6]

In my course, I explain to students that human birth includes an anatomical design challenge, expressed flippantly by comparing pregnancy and delivery to building a boat in a basement then trying to get it out. Biological adaptation has addressed two contrasting needs, for gestation long enough to enable newborn viability but not so long that a large baby could no longer emerge safely. Human babies at term have heads so large that they create the most difficult moments of delivery, yet are so small and helpless that they need constant care, in striking contrast with other newborn mammals, ready to move on their own within hours or days. Students' own experiences with helpless babies confirm the importance and challenges of our topic.

While mainstream medicine brings physiological, technological, and pharmacological expertise for dealing with these challenges, midwifery emphasizes experiential and intuitive skills, with more personal interaction. The choice now facing that course veteran reflects the possibilities that emerge when cultural study opens alternatives.

SETTING UP COURSE DISCUSSIONS ABOUT MIDWIFERY

A story from Walt Disney's *101 Dalmatians* (1961) addresses a question that students may have thought but have never asked about their male professor teaching about birth practices, and this serves as another opportunity to address cultural assumptions. In the movie, while dog mother, Perdita, gives birth in a closed room, with human women birth attendants (but no doctor), dog father, Pongo, and his male human companion wait anxiously in the next room. In this course, I open the metaphorical door to the birth room; while of course I have no experience of giving birth, I do share witnessing the birth of my own children.[7] Along with my lived experience (including limitations), I bring research in the history of medicine to approach students as fellow inquirers, for all to gain deeper understanding of American culture, even on topics distant from our own lives. Stepping from cartoon story to historical studies and personal accounts, I and the students, women and men, work together for improved understanding of birth experiences and possibilities beyond mainstream assumptions. As we dig deeper, I serve as assumption-challenging consultant for hearing out students, and I provide further questions for enlarging and deepening inquiries: What attracted diverse expectant mothers to midwifery, and what repelled them? Did midwifery decline from its own shortcomings, from the superiority of other medical practices, or from nonmedical factors? How did midwifery evolve as scientific authority increased, and how has the role of birthing mothers and their intimate partners also evolved?

Midwifery before Students' Own Experiences: The Early Republic

In my class, Laurel Thatcher Ulrich supplies the opening stories, with *A Midwife's Tale*, along with segments of the *American Experience* film of the same name. These texts depict the life and work of Martha Ballard (1735–1812), who practiced midwifery in frontier Maine from at least 1785 until her death. Ulrich generates drama by turning her evidence building and inference making into treasure hunts about the likely thoughts and feelings of the actual woman on the lived side of the diary. For example, in August 1787, Ballard attended the death of a child from "canker rash" (scarlet fever), reporting "how Distressing [the] Case" of the "poor mother." Ulrich infers that this "burst of emotion" compared to Ballard's usual "literary reserve" reveals her deep feelings, since ex-

Figure 3.1. Starting in the eighteenth century and accelerating in the late nineteenth century, the obstetric revolution in childbirth, emphasizing anatomical knowledge and laboratory study, encouraged the discrediting of midwifery as a traditional and even primitive folk practice. These advances in scientific medicine led to the loss of women's roles in support of pregnancy and birth and to the increased influence of men with training in science and with high social standing in hospitals. Isaac Cruikshank, "A Man-Mid-Wife," 1793, courtesy of the Wellcome Library, Wellcome Images no. L0018481.

actly eighteen years earlier her own daughter had been born during another deadly epidemic. This tangible expression of Ballard's heart, Ulrich reports, "gave me chills," and students showed vicarious excitement on witnessing a historical character leap off the archival page.[8]

The film adds still more drama by visually depicting everyday life in rural Hallowell, Maine. As one student observed, "just living was hard work," in summary of Ballard constantly making healing remedies and attending to the sick and pregnant, while also cooking meals, organizing home life, and seizing moments of household comfort and enjoyment. With the film displaying our best understanding of life two centuries ago, the book serves as the lyrics while the film supplies the music, so to speak, for student understanding. Ulrich recognized that "other things come into play" when "dramatizing" a book: how much did this health-care provider touch her patients and "what did she sound like?" She frankly admitted, "I didn't know." Students express surprise at an authority figure showing limitations, which provides a good opportunity to show a historian at work, with "tension between what we can know and what we can't."[9]

Ballard's record, in attending about one thousand births with the loss of no mothers and only a few children, is in keeping with the assessment of historians Richard and Dorothy Wertz: Even before the addition of "new knowledge of birth practices, . . . American midwives were not a persistent peril." While mostly female midwives steadily attended births, male scientific elites hoped for more enlightened practices. Looking at midwifery in Ballard's time shows the incremental process of transition from midwifery to scientific medicine. In fact, the traditional and modern medical practices actually reinforced each other. During Ballard's time, new anatomical knowledge of the organs of birth both enhanced and lent a new medical significance to the midwife's "traditional 'touch'" for surmising the quality of each birth experience and estimating timing. Midwives continued to practice, including for most births in Hollowell, well into the next century. Meanwhile, a surging number of men in the early to middle nineteenth century added midwifery skills to scientific knowledge for retention of traditional skills, while women receded from public spheres. The vivid stories of Ballard's successes "normalized" midwifery, as one student reported, at least for two centuries ago.[10]

Midwifery in Students' Own Time

The course explores the "obstetric revolution" starting in the eighteenth century (with roots earlier and accelerations ever since), which brought trends toward institutional management of births, with doctors claiming authority based on empirical knowledge of female and fetal anatomy and physiology, along with increasingly sophisticated pharmacological, technological, and surgical innovations. The turn to hospital births capped these trends, which "became a flood," in the words of the Wertzes. These changes brought improvements in efficiency, safety, and comfort along with an increasingly passive role for the delivering mother and less attention to the relation of mother with child or other family members.[11]

These contexts prepare students for reading *Midwifery and Childbirth in America* by nurse-midwife and epidemiologist Judith Pence Rooks, which tracks the evolution of midwifery to its modern complementary relation with scientific medicine. By the end of the twentieth century, 90 percent of American midwives were certified nurse-midwives (CNMs) or licensed midwives (LMs). The remaining 10 percent have gone by many names, as often happens with work less structured; these traditional birth attendants, granny midwives, or doulas develop their skills in apprenticeship with experienced colleagues. Rooks emphasizes the need to make use of doctors and hospitals when medically indicated, but in most cases, the differences in their medical outcomes are "not statistically significant."[12]

Midwifery's persistence and adaptation to scientific medicine prepares students for the presentation by Karen Kennedy, LM, who vividly displays her experiential familiarity with birthing and each distinctive case. Just as Rooks reports, Kennedy also insists on the need for "gatekeeping" in cases that call for medical intervention. She readily affirms, "I have a good working relation with the doctors and hospitals" in her central Florida practice. All students show eagerness to meet Kennedy, who offers frank reports that "I don't manage births" the way doctors do, and "I have fewer cesareans," meaning cesarean sections or C-sections, the surgical removal of the baby when natural birthing runs into problems. She has indeed transferred 8 percent of her patients to doctors among more than one thousand babies delivered. Some students approach her with cautious curiosity; others embrace her work wholeheartedly, with dramatic reversal from utter disregard of midwifery to eager acceptance; still others respond with fear because she is not a doctor. Her fee is about one-third what doctors charge (and those doctor costs can double or triple with C-sections), and her work includes more in-person contact during pregnancy. Even students skeptical of the medical care of midwifery warm to this side of her work; as one student observed, "an increasing use [of] . . . midwives could save the US billions of dollars."[13] For students who had felt "a taboo about midwives," personal contact with a working professional midwife made the practice seem less arcane or weird; as one student said vividly, "I realize it's not so crunchy."[14]

STUDENTS CONSIDERING MIDWIFERY

Evaluation of the ability of scientific medicine to gain persuasive intellectual authority since the nineteenth century is a central part of American Studies' attention to the way segments of culture gain power and influence. The affiliation of medicine with science increased its ability to understand the parts directing actions of the whole. In particular, technological improvements enabled transition from clinical focus on organs as a basis for evaluating health to laboratory study of still-smaller cells. By contrast, midwifery attends to the experience of whole persons. This too is a kind of empiricism, an experiential empiricism, an idea foreign to many students, based on the laboratory empiricism of their science classes. This perspective itself has a history, as shown by the nineteenth-century supporters of scientific medicine who called the work of midwives and other nonmainstream healers "senseless empiricism" because it lacked laboratory support.[15]

American Studies has a history of questioning established authorities; a major assumption that this course challenges is one common to many students and to most Americans in general—the cultural authority of science. Even as most scientists approach their field as a path of constant correction, enthusiasts for science who adopted the name "positivism" promote science as the only positive knowledge. This outlook took on militant forms with doctors' "war of extermination against . . . midwifery" as a "pestiferous remnant" of prescientific practices, in the words of a New York obstetrician in 1898, even as others called midwifery a "necessary evil" for patients in poor urban and remote rural areas, according to a 1928 study.[16] Enthusiasm for science is not recently so aggressive, but it still encourages confidence among most Americans. Students generally greet these contexts as a revelation: confidence in scientific medicine, embedded in their own views, emerged at a particular time, promoted by particular intellectual and cultural elites, whose advocacy of objective scientific truths coincided with their social interests.

Students read stories about how twentieth-century midwifery endured in segments of society with limited resources and minimal educational opportunities related to other social structures they have learned about in the course. Reliance on practical knowledge even became a point of pride in many nonwhite, immigrant, and poor communities whose own traditions include great respect for midwives and deep suspicion of male doctors attending the intimacies of birth. Voter registration activists in the 1960s South often turned first to midwives to gain community trust.[17] Students respond to these accounts based on their views of contemporary multiculturalism, with liberals showing sympathy for subaltern practices, while conservatives (ironically) insist on the value of science for support of (liberal) cultural progress.

Obstetric medicine has gained strength based on its science and also because its practices suit mass culture, with institutionalized experts employing technological sophistication to manage large numbers of people. Student stories illustrate some of the problems emerging on these large scales. For example, one student reported that her mother appreciated the benefits of personal care from the experience of a "great uncle from Mexico who was a midwife," but was persuaded by her own husband to seek a hospital birth, where she received two doses of Pitocin (a drug to encourage labor), seven epidurals (an anesthesia) that "kept missing," then a C-section with a catheter left inside. Her mother offered a polite response to a challenge faced by many large institutions based on the specializations that have emerged with the abundance of professional knowledge: "The doctors needed better communication." Institutionalized settings also brought tacit disincentives for patients to take responsibility for their own well-being, with many assuming doctors and devices are the active agents.[18] These assessments generate fault lines in students' minds between the power of scientific help and the significance of personal responsibility.

The tensions that students experience serve as a step toward the American Studies goal of raising questions about assumptions, with the history of childbirth opening choices for healthcare and childbirth. Modern professional birthing practices are powerful and especially important for the minority of births with problems, but these achievements bring trade-offs, which encourage students to hear out medical alternatives. We also study the specifics of medical birth in the United States relative to the rest of the world. The rate of surgical intervention in US births is 33 percent, two to three times the World Health Organization's medical recommendations, with these high numbers spurred by threats of malpractice against doctors. But the urge for medical action is often encouraged by a reinforcing loop of medical actions. In a healthy natural birth, if a mother's anatomical processes slow or stop, midwives encourage gentle body movements or mental relaxation. By contrast, possible problems prompt doctors to intervene, often with Pitocin. But induced contractions have mild-to-severe impacts on the vigor of mother and baby, which can encourage turns to surgical interruption of the birthing process. Doctors sometimes prescribe Pitocin to suit their own schedules; one student reported that this attitude made "my mother [feel] unimportant." Similarly, tests such as fetal monitoring have the advantage of detecting some problems early but tend to prompt interventions even when they turn out to be unnecessary.[19] Many students notice that midwifery can mitigate these pharmacological, legal, and social problems within modern medicine.

In a hospital, full of sick people, pregnancy is "treated like [a] sickness," as one student observed, and another realized that she had never considered that "hospitals treat births like an illness." Midwives approach giving birth as a natural part of life, rather than treating pregnancy as a condition that needs correction, while another student noticed that midwifery "lets nature take its course . . . as much as possible." Although the strict identification of labor and delivery with illness does not hold, as another student pointed out, the strains of birthing require recovery as with sickness. These moments of awareness show students noticing the choices for childbirth that the course illuminates. The impulse to correct nature's ways has roots in views of women as deviations from male norms, with pregnancy being the most dramatic aspect of female difference. Also, the impulse to intervene reflects the history of mainstream medical distrust in natural processes, which in turn is based on some truly cruel natural results. One student reported the tragedy of her grandmother's death in childbirth; her own mother was glad for medical improvements on nature's ways. These comments show why nineteenth-century doctors called alternatives to scientific practices "nature-trusting heresies."[20] Most midwives support medical interventions in risky cases, as with class guest Kennedy's commitment to gatekeeping, but generally, midwives remain nature trusting, listening to patients reporting bodily feelings as clinical indicators in each distinctive case.

The contrast between midwifery's emphasis on personal accounts and the mainstream treatment of these clinical reports as mere anecdotal asides compared to objective technological data generates serious debates in class, based on deep values questions, with students displaying their own assumptions about professional authority and their degree of concern about safety and comfort. Recently, the American Medical Association defended the primacy of doctors for managing births with interventions ready, because "an apparently uncomplicated pregnancy or delivery can quickly become very complicated."[21]

Scientific medicine has also provided a succession of powerful anesthetics to address the notorious pains of childbirth. These were most popular in the 1910s to 1950s, when standard practice meant pregnant woman would enter a hospital, be given twilight sleep leaving her completely unconscious, and wake with a baby who had been removed from her body by forceps or surgery. Many women demanded drugs to avoid pain, and doctors welcomed the ability to control the process. However, since the 1980s, the most common childbirth anesthesia has been the epidural, which reduces pain while the mother remains conscious.[22]

Recently, celebrities have provided publicity for new medical practices in choosing "designer births," with pain relief for the mothers, transfer of agency to top-flight professionals, and even elective early cesareans before the last weeks of pregnancy, when the sheer size of the near-term fetus can leave a women's midsection distended. "You don't have to be a star to appreciate pain-free care," as one student observed. She supported hospital births along with her mother, who enthused about her hospital experience—she actually enjoyed it. The pull of modern medical care is sometimes matched by a push away from midwifery, such as with another student who reported that his grandmother had three midwife births, which predisposed his own mother to try it, but she "had a bad experience" and did not trust midwifery.[23]

By contrast, midwives remain skeptical about the need to allow fear of troubles in some cases guide the norms for all. They promise an embrace of difficulties as part of the extraordinary experiences of bringing forth a new life while standing ready to seek mainstream medical care in the few cases that need it. Recognizing that the experience of labor is aptly named, they seek natural ways to reduce discomfort rather than artificial ways to avoid pain. The very difficulties, they propose, are part of the process of bonding mother with baby. In her class presentation, Kennedy insists on the vital importance of this first contact, which contributes to her skepticism about overuse of drugs during labor: "Why intrude on that natural high by getting mother and child stoned?"—this brought a lot of student smiles. Reduced pain and limits on awareness also bring reduced ability for mothers to engage in the birthing process in pushing the fetus, or for the process to function robustly, thus making surgical intervention more likely; as one student reported for his mother's first birth, the epidural worked well, but for the second, it "did not take," which led to a C-section. Some proponents of natural births even promise "orgasmic births," initiated by sexual intercourse and itself on a par with sexual experiences. Students ask many "values questions" on hearing these propositions and accounts. The course presentation of the contrasting approaches of doctors and midwives from their own respective points of view enables students to make their own choices. Some students confirm their trust in scientific medicine, while others are drawn to serious consideration of midwifery both for conservative support of personal responsibility and for liberal ideas of women's agency. On childbirth pain, student views differ, with echoes of two approaches to feminism: for female empowerment in the emotive and spiritual depths of birth, or for women's equality with freedom from birth's burdens. One student summarized the contrasting choices concisely between a midwife's "empathy [and] the professional expertise of medicine."[24]

Doctors have not always been antagonistic to midwives. Even as mainstream medicine was most hostile to midwifery in the 1920s to 1930s, modern medical interventions often increased mother mortality compared with most midwifery care. A 1933 report therefore urged professional doctors to "accept the midwife as . . . an ally." In recent years, they have moved toward still more cooperation, as illustrated in a student story about a provider "between midwifery and gynecology." This doctor's training in both fields was most welcome to the student's friend because her baby was in breech position, with the head not in the proper position. Although this complication usually leads to a C-section, her doctor used midwifery skills to "massage her belly to move the baby" until a vaginal birth became possible. Throughout the experience, she had "no loss of faith in modern medicine," even as she appreciated the addition of alternative skills. This example is in keeping with the 94 percent of midwife-attended births now in mainstream medical centers; and many hospitals include rooms resembling homey birth centers. As mainstream medicine has recognized problems with specialization, midwives serve as generalists complementing the work of OB/GYNs with nutrition counseling, parenting education, and reproductive health visits before and after births, all work that can prevent problems.[25]

Students readily acknowledge that our inquiries into midwifery challenge their assumptions—and that is the American Studies point, for encouraging consideration of different views. James uses the elegant oxymoron "sentiment of rationality" to describe the grounding of assumptions in temperaments, traditions, and emotions, which shape our rational commitments.[26] Ironically, despite the empirical research and rational arguments of mainstream medicine, most students, like most citizens in general, adopt its perspectives as articles of faith.

Sharing stories in American Cultural Traditions about midwives past and present summons up questions about science and tradition, expertise and women's agency, and even personal attitudes toward safety and pain, enabling students to discover their own views of these medical "Others" with support from their professor as a pedagogical midwife in the evolution of their thinking. We join other American Studies classrooms in "bothering" students by challenging their prior assumptions.

NOTES

1. William James, *The Will to Believe* (1897), in *The Works of William James*, Frederick Burkhardt et al., eds. (Cambridge, MA: Harvard University Press, 1979), 14; "Introduction," this volume, 11.

2. On Stetson University, see http://www.stetson.edu/home/, and on its American Studies Program, http://www.stetson.edu/artsci/american-studies/.

3. Jay Mechling, Robert Merideth, and David Wilson, "American Culture Studies: The Discipline and the Curriculum," *American Quarterly* 25 (1973): 378, and *Morning Work: A Trialogue on Issues of Knowledge and Freedom in Doing American Culture Studies* (Bolinas, CA: Connections, 1979), ix. Before the turn in the early 1970s away from consensus scholarship, "politically engaged scholarship" was central to early American Studies, and its interdisciplinary focus was "hospitable to issues of diversity"; Elaine Tyler May, "The Radical Roots of American Studies," *American Quarterly* 48 (1996): 182; and Linda Kerber, "Diversity and the Transformation of American Studies," *American Quarterly* 41 (1989): 420. Also see Michael Denning, *The Cultural Front: The Laboring of American Culture in the Twentieth Century* (London: Verso, 1997); and George Lipsitz, "Sent for You Yesterday, Here You Come Today: American Studies Scholarship and the New Social Movements," *Cultural Critique* 40 (1998): 203–225, who emphasize the roots of American Studies in scholars of the 1930s–1950s, with focus on figures and groups excluded from consensus culture and its benefits. Since the 1960s, American Studies has become more explicit in approaching the study of American life as a form of "culture therapy" for raising awareness about power differentials; see Gene Wise, "'Paradigm Dramas' in American Studies: A Cultural and Institutional History of the Movement," *American Quarterly* 31 (1979): 293–337; and Matthias Oppermann, *American Studies in Dialogue: Radical Reconstructions between Curriculum and Cultural Critique* (New York: Campus Verlag, 2010), 21–23.

4. "Essential Facts about Midwives," American College of Nurse-Midwives,

updated February 2016, http://www.midwife.org/default.aspx?bid=308; and Ina May Gaskin, *Birth Matters: A Midwife's Manifesta* (New York: Seven Stories, 2011). See also William Rothstein, *American Physicians in the Nineteenth Century: From Sects to Science* (Baltimore: Johns Hopkins University Press, 1992); and Bert Hansen, *Picturing Medical Progress from Pasteur to Polio: A History of Mass Media Images and Popular Attitudes in America* (New Brunswick, NJ: Rutgers University Press, 2009).

5. Mechling, Merideth, and Wilson, "American Culture Studies," 380.

6. Alex Altland and Haley Farman, Interview Reports on Birth Experiences, AMST301, American Cultural Traditions course, Stetson University, March 18, 2019.

7. Bill Peet from a story by Dodie Smith, *101 Dalmatians*, directed by Wolfgang Reitherman et al. (Walt Disney Productions, 1961). Richard Reed, in *Birthing Fathers: The Transformation of Mean in American Rites of Birth* (New Brunswick: Rutgers University Press, 2005), identifies a "new fatherhood" emerging in recent decades, with men "invited into the [birth] chamber," as a step toward their increasing "nurturing role" (4).

8. Laurel Thatcher Ulrich, *A Midwife's Tale: The Life of Martha Ballard, Based on Her Diary, 1785–1812* (New York: Vintage, 1990), 43; "A Midwife's Tale," directed by Richard P. Rogers, *American Experience* (PBS, 1998).

9. Kendall Couture, Interview Report, March 11, 2019; Randall Stephens, "The Importance of Studying Ordinary Lives: An Interview with Lauren Thatcher Ulrich," *Historically Speaking* 10 (2009): 10. Ulrich exhibits what Oppermann calls "adaptive expertise," with "risk-taking under conditions of uncertainty" (*American Studies in Dialogue*, 210).

10. Richard Wertz and Dorothy Wertz, *Lying-In: A History of Childbirth in America* (New York: Free Press, 1977), 11 and 31–32; Judy Barrett Litoff, *American Midwives, 1860 to the Present* (Westport, CT: Greenwood, 1978), 7–13 and 21; and Dylan Croup, Interview Report, March 18, 2019. Jane Donegan, in *Women and Men Midwives: Medicine, Morality, and Misogyny in Early America* (Westport, CT: Greenwood, 1978), points out that while women were denied training, men adopted midwifery skills both as physicians and as male-midwives (120, 133–135).

11. Wertz and Wertz, *Lying-In*, 133; Ulrich, *Midwife's Tale*, 27–34.

12. Charlotte Borst, *Catching Babies: The Professionalization of Childbirth, 1870–1920* (Cambridge, MA: Harvard University Press, 1995), 3, 6–7; Judith Pence Rooks, *Midwifery and Childbirth in America* (Philadelphia: Temple University Press, 1997), 370 and 365–392.

13. Karen Kennedy, "Trusting the Process, Supporting the Birth," presentation in AMST301, American Cultural Traditions course, March 13, 2019; David Brandhorst, Seminar commentary, March 23, 2020.

14. Kennedy, "Trusting the Process"; and Kelly Jenks, Interview Report, March 18, 2019. See Selma Taffel, "Midwife and Out-of-Hospital Deliveries," *National Vital Statistics System* series 21, no. 40 (1984): 4; and Sally Curtin and Melissa Park, "Trends in the Attendant, Place, and Timing of Births, and in the Use of Obstetric Interventions: United States, 1989–97," *National Vital Statistics Reports* 47 (1999): 7. There are limited historical statistics on midwifery,

largely because of its diverse local and individualized practices; the field lacks "a formal, unvarying body of belief"; Wertz and Wertz, *Lying-In*, 11. Robbie Davis-Floyd describes the compromises between experiential and scientific practices in the emergence of CM professionals; "Qualified Commodification: The Creation of the Certified Professional Midwife," in *Mainstreaming Midwives: The Politics of Change*, ed. Robbie Davis-Floyd and Christine Barbara Johnson, 163–201 (New York: Routledge, 2006). Kennedy's practice, Agape Midwifery Service, is based in Daytona Beach, Florida, https://www.facebook.com/AgapeBirthAndWellnessCenter.

15. Ulrich, *A Midwife's Tale*, 53; Mary Lay, *The Rhetoric of Midwifery: Gender, Knowledge, and Power* (New Brunswick, NJ: Rutgers University Press, 2000), 172; John Harley Warner, *The Therapeutic Perspective: Medical Practice, Knowledge, and Identity in America, 1820–1885* (Cambridge, MA: Harvard University Press, 1986), 44; Donald Caton, *What a Blessing She Had Chloroform: The Medical and Social Response to the Pain of Childbirth from 1800 to the Present* (New Haven, CT: Yale University Press, 1999), 48; Paul Croce, *Young William James Thinking* (Baltimore: Johns Hopkins University Press, 2018), 90, and "James and Medicine: Reckoning with Experience," in *Oxford Handbook of William James*, ed. Alexander Klein (New York: Oxford, 2021).

16. Charles Cashdollar, *The Transformation of Theology, 1830–1890: Positivism and Protestant Thought in Britain and America* (Princeton, NJ: Princeton University Press, 1989); Litoff, *American Midwives*, 23 and 75. Irvine Loudon, in *Death in Childbirth: An International Study of Maternal Care and Maternal Mortality, 1800–1950* (Oxford: Clarendon, 1992), argues that "the intemperate attacks on midwives by obstetricians [in the 1920s–1930s] were ill-considered, unjust, and had a lasting effect. They laid the foundations of the deep and unjustified prejudice against midwives in the USA which persists to the present day" (326).

17. Litoff, *American Midwives*, 29; Rooks, *Midwifery and Childbirth in America*, 17–33; Martin Berger, *Freedom Now!: Forgotten Photographs of the Civil Rights Struggle* (Berkeley: University of California Press, 2013), 92.

18. Geneva Alpert, Interview Report, March 18, 2019; Charles E. Rosenberg, *The Care of Strangers: The Rise of America's Hospital System* (Baltimore: Johns Hopkins University Press, 1995); David Rothman, "The Doctor as Stranger," in *Strangers at the Bedside: A History of How Law and Bioethics Transformed Medical Decision Making* (New York: Basic, 1991).

19. *Oxorn-Foote Human Labor and Birth*, 6th ed., ed. Glenn Posner et al. (New York: McGraw-Hill, 2013), 180; Curtin and Park, "Trends in the Attendant, Place, and Timing of Births," 4; and Cassandra Concilio, Seminar commentary, March 23, 2020. Despite the added information it provides, electronic fetal monitoring, widespread since the 1970s, has not brought a reduction in C-sections or a significant change in neonatal outcomes; see Michael Greene, "Obstetricians Still Await a Deus ex Machina," *New England Journal of Medicine* 335 (2006): 2247–2248.

20. Tyler Clark and Lili Simonetti, Seminar commentaries, March 23, 2020; Jordan Toth and Madi Russell, Interview Reports, March 18, 2019; Warner, "'The Nature-Trusting Heresy': American Physicians and the Concept of the Healing Power of Nature in the 1850s and 1860s," *Perspectives in American History* 11 (1977–78): 291–324.

21. Litoff, *American Midwives*, 22; American Medical Association House of Delegates Resolution 205 (A-08) on Home Deliveries, April 2008, https://www.ftc.gov/system/files/documents/public_comments/2014/03/00041-88892.pdf.

22. Jacqueline H. Wolf, *Deliver Me from Pain: Anesthesia and Birth in America* (Baltimore: Johns Hopkins University Press, 2009); Judith Walzer Leavitt, "Birthing and Anesthesia: The Debate Over Twilight Sleep" *Signs* 6 (1980): 147–164; and Caton, *What a Blessing She Had Chloroform*, 28.

23. Michaela Sellaro and Doug Cardone, Interview Reports, March 18, 2019.

24. Kennedy, "Trusting the Process"; Thomas Bryant and Thomas Kilger, Interview Reports, March 11, 2019; Laura Shanley, *Unassisted Childbirth*, 3rd ed. (Westport, CT: Bergin and Garvey, n.d.), and see "Orgasmic Childbirth," accessed November 13, 2020, http://www.unassistedchildbirth.com/your-sensual-self/orgasmic-childbirth/.

25. Report from the New York City Public Health Committee and New York Academy of Medicine (1933), quoted in Loudon, *Death in Childbirth*, 528; Parker Lewin, Interview Report, March 18, 2019; and "Essential Facts about Midwives."

26. William James, "The Sentiment of Rationality" (1879), in *Essays in Philosophy* in *The Works of William James*, 1978, 33.

4

Always the Good Guys

Latinx Studies and the Myth of American Exceptionalism

GUILLERMO AVILA-SAAVEDRA

It seemed like a good place to start. Highly symbolic, still relevant, and easy to find on a map, the Panama Canal appeared to be an ideal site to begin a conversation about American interventions in Latin America. It was only the third week of Intro to Latinx Studies and was the first time I was teaching the course. I recognized that pedagogically I was in uncharted waters. Still, I was convinced that the Panama Canal was a safe departure point for what I had planned to be a three-week module for students to learn about the painful history of American interventions in Latin America and put the immigration waves that gave birth to Latinx as an American ethnic group in their proper historical and political context. A couple of days in advance I had posted to our class virtual platform a brief reading about the history of the canal. The succinct review included the following fragment:

> In 1901 engineer Philippe Jean Bunau-Varilla pitched the idea of the Panama Canal to U.S. President Theodore Roosevelt who was willing to pay the engineer's price if Colombia, of which Panama was a province, relinquished control of the canal. When Colombia refused Bunau-Varilla supported Panamanian revolutionaries and persuaded the U.S. to intervene. The presence of American gunboats was enough to make Colombia give in.[1]

The "liberated" province became the Republic of Panama and a staunch ally of the United States to this day. However, in class discussion, it was as if the above fragment had not registered at all. When asked to comment on the reading, students referred to the canal as a "technological feat," as "an American contribution," and some even expressed surprise at the notion that America does not currently control and operate the canal. Pressed to comment on the specific element of American intervention, students were more likely to romanticize history, imagining the United States had come to support Panamanian liberation from a tyrannical Colombian regime. Some insinuated that President Carter had betrayed the United States for having negotiated the treaty that eventually returned ownership of the canal to Panama. Students were also eager to embrace an "ends justify the means" approach. At the end of the day, wasn't the canal a gift from America to the world?

I was caught off guard but not entirely surprised by the students' resistance to challenging America's essential virtuousness. Having taught several semesters of American Mass Media & Race, I had come to learn that in order to address white privilege and systemic racism, I had to find a way for students to distinguish racial and ethnic identities from the process of racialization and along the way challenge enduring American myths such as meritocracy and Manifest Destiny. In a media studies course, understood broadly as "the academic investigation of the mass media from perspectives such as sociology, psychology, history, semiotics, and critical discourse analysis," I had multiple strategies available to accomplish my pedagogical goals.[2] Discourse analysis, framing and narrative analysis, and critical examination of representational practices—all of which the students expected—allowed me to bring the students to the realization that racial categories are socially constructed according to a hierarchy of social power.

Intro to Latinx Studies was a different animal altogether. I am teaching at a midsize public university in the Northeast with a very diverse student body but with dwindling resources and ever-increasing enrollment minimums. The first attempt to offer the course was cut by the administration due to low enrollment. I am teaching outside of my academic department as part of an interdisciplinary project to create a Latinx studies minor modeled in the tradition of ethnic studies and housed under the larger umbrella of American Studies. This discipline inside a discipline approach makes sense if we understand American Studies' paradigms to include "analyses and celebrations of regionalism and the laboring of American culture; the study of myths, images and symbols; social science inquiries and investigations; cultural studies critiques; an efflorescence of post structural, postcolonial and queer theories" that respond to "lived social experience."[3] Although at this point it sounds almost repetitive to say that American Studies requires an interdisciplinary approach, it remains a fact that the project as defined above cannot be fully realized without borrowing from history, literature, and sociology, to name a few. In this chapter, I recount how my Intro to Latinx Studies students' reluctance to challenge American exceptionalism required me to reassess the focus of the course, my pedagogical goals, and the means to achieve them. Reporting from my classroom, I detail my own realization of how embracing a media studies approach to pedagogy helped me transform and improve my students' understanding of the long and complicated hemispheric histories and their impact on the current lived experiences of Latinx people in the United States. This required not only a major revision to the syllabus that gave more prominence to the topic of American interventionism but also the constant recalibration of assignments and classroom activities.

I decided I would start by teaching them about the history of American interventions in Latin America and its related sociological phenomena of immigration, racialization, and assimilation. After establishing the Monroe Doctrine and the Roosevelt Corollary as the political foundation for American foreign policy in Latin America as well as FDR's Good Neighbor policy as the more contemporary incarnation of the same philosophy, I decided to challenge my students' faith in American inherent goodness by providing them with a detailed chronology of US interventions in Latin America. I posted to our course virtual platform policy papers that outlined official American foreign policy priorities,[4] journalistic accounts of American intervention,[5] and a striking infographic that detailed more than fifty American military interventions in Latin America since 1946 authorized by all presidents from Eisenhower to Obama and that introduced the Western Hemisphere Institute for Security Cooperation (formerly known as the School of the Americas) as a "training school for Latin American soldiers that has been producing assassins, death squad leaders and human rights abusers for dirty work in Latin America since 1946."[6]

This new approach, admittedly less gentle than the Panama Canal introduction, proved more successful at engaging students in meaningful classroom discussion. Still, many students preferred to focus on the failure of the education system at not including these events in their history lessons, rather than on the intent or consequence of the acts themselves. Of particular concern was the inclusion of Barack

Obama among the perpetrators, since many students deeply admire the former president.

I believe that the students' reaction has two explanations. On the one hand, it is a reflection of American individualism. It insulates their ignorance from any guilt or shame by placing the blame on bad schools and bad teachers. On the other hand, it shields their patriotism from self-scrutiny. It is one thing to be critical of the education system; it is another thing to be critical of the American system. Sensing potential for breaching those defenses, I decided to further explore the lack-of-awareness angle and devised a simple assignment. The prompt I gave students read:

> Decades of US interventions in Latin America have left lasting consequences in the region and have contributed to the waves of immigration to this country. However, most Americans are unaware of these events and often refuse to believe they happened in the first place. In the attached map choose one of the more than 50 cases of American military intervention in Latin America. Then conduct an informal survey asking friends, family members, professors, and even random strangers if or how much they know about or remember such event. Share the findings of your survey and offer your own thoughts on the results.

Students chose a diverse sample of events to survey. A few students who identify as Latinx chose examples of American interventions in the countries their parents or grandparents came from. The reports of their informal surveys were consistent. Representative statements include: "For such large casualties, it astounded me that no one I asked had ever heard of this. Granted, everyone I asked had been born after 1964, but still, I feel as though people should have heard of this," and "When asking other Brazilians about this event nobody knew about it, but being fair most of them grew up in America." Students correctly identified the lack of awareness as problematic, but they were still discussing each event in isolation from each other. My assignment had checked the interdisciplinary box of American ethnic studies by bringing history and political science into the curriculum, but it had failed at identifying the "contradictions between the national culture's bright promises and its bitter betrayals" as they provide the necessary context to understand the lived Latinx experience in America.[7] My frustration with the shortcomings of the assignment forced me to reassess my role and reposition myself pedagogically. I was aware that media studies is an integral part of American Studies scholarship and pedagogy, yet somehow despite my training I had failed to embrace the fact. I needed to reassess my approach to Latinx studies and work through a pedagogical hurdle by fully embracing the breadth of the field.

AN EXPANSIVE VIEW OF LATINX STUDIES

Individual and cultural identities take shape at the intersection of numerous social locations, including but not limited to gender, race, ethnicity, nationality, and linguistic ability, and are sites of constant struggle and renegotiation. Hardly ever is there a consensus on who has the right to claim membership into an identity category, the criteria to determine the boundaries between identities, or even the labels used to group individuals into social classifications. The instability of a single, all-inclusive social identity for Americans of Latin American descent is currently in full display as those who claim a Hispanic or Latino/Latina or more recently a Latinx identity openly challenge each other on the meaning of those labels, their ability to include or exclude, and more importantly their potential impact on social and political change. This open conversation on self-identification takes place in the context of a state invested in preserving the marginalized status of Americans of Latin American descent and much of the prevailing status quo.

Combining paradigms from American Studies and ethnic studies, Latinx studies is an examination of the interdependent relationship among the dynamics of identity, social status, and political agency in a historically marginalized but growing segment of the American population. Latin American studies contributes solely from the perspective of the region's relationship with the United States by examining the history of political instability, slow economic growth, and inequality by questioning the role of American influence, intervention, and exploitation. To fully understand Latinx as an American ethnic group it is necessary to put Latin American immigration in a broad cultural context, challenging hegemonic narratives and confronting the random and arbitrary nature of citizenship and national borders and the rights they bestow or deny.

This broader cultural context includes the examination of the systems of symbolic representation that through the framing of particular narratives, the silencing of histories, and the active validation of national myths justify the othering of Latinx Americans and the lower social status they occupy. Despite the ubiquity of the mass media in every aspect of life in America, media studies as an academic field is not well understood and its legitimacy is often suspect.

Media studies is uniquely positioned to contribute to American Studies' interdisciplinary project of a critical analysis of race, ethnicity, racialization, and intersectionality with a focus on the identities, experiences, and perspectives of Latinx people in the United States. The evolution of identity labels and the debates on a real or imagined collective identity for Latinx Americans are set in motion by myths and narratives deeply embedded in American culture. In contemporary America, the most prominent discursive space where myths and cultural values are reinforced, negotiated, and reimagined is the mass media, with their representational practices and conventions that bestow or deny visibility and legitimacy. The pedagogical challenges I experienced teaching Latinx studies also presented an opportunity to utilize media deconstruction skills as a tool to challenge myths and narratives, which is central to the American Studies project.

DECONSTRUCTING AMERICAN EXCEPTIONALISM IN THE MEDIA

The social function of myths is widely established. Myths are an inescapable element of any nation's efforts to shape its past. Arguably, the line that separates the mythification of the past and academic history in the United States has been blurry more often than not. The mythification of the American narrative has had a visible, lasting impact on the design and execution of foreign policy. A young but rich and powerful nation adopted in freedom and democracy a new religion that was intended to replace previous imperial powers. The result has been an imperialistic philosophy implemented by both overt and covert interventions.

It is evident that literature and the mass media, especially film and television, have contributed to the fabrication and survival of the myth of American exceptionalism, positioning the United States, in both the domestic and international realms, as the rich and powerful relative, firm but above all fair when mediating disputes. The brave and industrious pioneer and the noble cowboy who shoots with incredible precision that established the myths of individualism and manifested destiny transmuted in the global context into the soldier, the politician, the diplomat, the missionary, and a host of characters in various genres, including children's animation and science fiction. When the situation becomes untenable in the novel or the movie, an American icon appears to save the day. To challenge the myth of American exceptionalism is to expose the explicit and implicit ways the mass media sustain the narrative of American virtuousness.

All media messages are made or constructed by people. One of the most important media literacy skills is deconstruction—closely examining and "taking apart" media messages to understand how they work. Deconstructing a media message can help us understand who created the message and who is intended to receive it. It can expose points of view, values, and biases. It can also uncover hidden meanings—intended or unintended. The seminal example of deconstruction of American imperialism in the media that is read in Latinx and Latin American studies is Ariel Dorfman's *How to Read Donald Duck,* originally published in Spanish as *Para leer al Pato Donald*.[8] The Marxist critique of the analysis lost currency after the translator of the original work into English argued that the illustrators themselves despised Disney's model of exploitation: "I saw many of the stories not as *justifications* of imperialist adventure but as *satires* upon it, in which the imperialist Duckburgers come off looking as foolish as—and far meaner than—the innocent Third World natives."[9] However, the enduring legacy of "How to Read Donald Duck" is not the Marxist analysis but rather how Disney's representational practices portrayed the American project and American identity for domestic and international audiences. With that perspective, the redeeming qualities Kunzle identified do not undermine but rather reinforce the mythical construct of America on a global scale: mean (when needed) to protect innocent (but weak) Third World natives.

For my "Media Deconstruction of the American Exceptionalism Myth" assignment, I borrowed from an American Media & Race project where I had previously asked students to

> analyze the representation of a non-human character in a media text. Your task will be to report how the character has been *racialized.* To do so, you will need to deconstruct the media codes and conventions used in the character's representation and portrayal. Note that the media text you select doesn't have to be "about race." In fact, deconstruction is often more effective when the media message's cultural meaning is not explicit.

In my American Media & Race course, this assignment had been successful in helping students not only to understand the arbitrary nature of racial categories but also to realize that whiteness is also a social construct. Key to the success of this assignment was the "non-human character" requirement.

To introduce my Latinx studies student to the concept and process of media deconstruction, I guided them through an in-class analysis of a media text they could easily relate to. I chose *Kim Possible*, an animated series that ran on Disney Channel from 2002 to 2007, because it clearly generated interest and excitement. Kim Possible is a "teenage girl tasked with fighting crime on a regular basis while coping with everyday issues commonly associated with adolescence. The majority of Kim's missions involve her traveling to various destinations around the world to rescue citizens from harm and fight a variety of enemies and villains."[10]

Beforehand, I had posted to our class virtual platform links to a few episodes available on YouTube. In class we discussed the program by addressing the four core concepts of media analysis: media texts are constructed, media texts follow rules and conventions, media texts are polysemic, and media texts embed or omit values and points of view (see Critical Analysis of Media Texts). Students quickly made connections to our ongoing conversation on American imperialism and interventions. Kim was constructed to embody hegemonic Americanness, which is to say a white, suburban, middle-class experience. The constant juxtaposition of global crisis with Kim's adolescent concerns made clear that her point of view alone drove the narrative. Goofy villains were portrayed in formulaic ways, thick foreign accents included, which explained why they were constantly defeated by a teenager. In sum, Kim Possible embodied the myth of the exceptional American individual. The main breakthrough of this exercise was that students started to speculate how, given Disney's global reach, Kim Possible could be understood by audiences around the world.

CRITICAL ANALYSIS OF MEDIA TEXTS (FILM OR TV)

Core Concepts and Key Questions
All Messages Are Constructed

1. What kind of "text" is it? How similar or different is it to others of the same genre?
2. What choices were made in the construction of the narrative?
3. What choices were made that might have been made differently?
4. Who are the creators of the media text? What do they represent?

Media Messages Are Constructed Following Rules and Conventions

1. What do you notice about the way the message is constructed?
2. How is the story told visually? What are people doing?
3. Are there any symbols? Visual metaphors?
4. What's the emotional appeal? Persuasive devices used?
5. Are there different rules used for white characters and characters of color?

Different Audiences Read Different Meaning from the Same Media Text

1. How close is this portrayal to your experience?
2. What did you learn about yourself from experiencing the media text?
3. What did you learn from other people's response? From their experience of life?
4. How many other interpretations could there be? How could we hear about them?
5. Are there coded messages that may influence how audiences identify racial categories?
6. Are other viewpoints just as valid as mine?
7. How can you explain the different responses?

Media Embed or Omit Values and Points of View from Media Messages

1. What kinds of behaviors/consequences are depicted?
2. What type of person is the watcher invited to identify with?
3. What ideas or values are being "sold" to us in this message?
4. What political ideas are communicated in the message? Cultural ideas?
5. What judgments or statements are made about how we treat other people?
6. What ideas or perspectives are left out? How would you find what's missing?
7. Are voices and perspectives of people of color included in the narrative? How?

MASTERS OF THE UNIVERSE AND THE EXCEPTIONAL AMERICAN NATION

For their individual assignment, I asked students to write a media analysis of *He-Man and the Masters of the Universe*, an American animated show based on a toy line that ran very successfully through first-run syndication between 1983 and 1985.[11] The story set in an undetermined time places human and nonhuman characters in the fictional planet of Eternia. This basic saga set human-looking Prince Adam and his alter ego He-Man to defend Eternia from the evil Skeletor.[12] Eternia is also populated by numerous "races" or "peoples," some humanlike and some not, exhibiting diverse cultural practices, languages, and degrees of development. In a clear feudal system, the peoples of Eternia provided services and goods for the kingdom in exchange for protection from Skeletor. I chose this program for two main reasons: its fantastical setting without explicit or easily identifiable national and racial identities and students' lack of familiarity with the show, which protected their analysis from preconceived assumptions. In particular I asked students to pay attention to and deconstruct the relationship between He-Man and the various races or peoples that inhabit Eternia. The goal of this assignment was for students to uncover the myth of American exceptionalism hidden in harmless children's entertainment and understand the role media play in providing an unquestionable justification for American interventions in Latin America and around the world. The precise instructions I gave students were:

1. Become familiar with the mythology of the show by reading its Wikipedia entry and watching the episode "The Beginning" on YouTube.
2. Choose one or two of the peoples that inhabit Eternia (your choices may be limited by the episodes you find available on YouTube).
3. Analyze the relationship between He-Man/Adam and the other characters with special attention to dynamics of power, wealth, might, and authority.
4. Deconstruct the potential interpretations of the show and its characters by Americans of different ethnicities and by foreign audiences.

In their analyses, students invariably came to the conclusion that Adam/He-Man was American. When asked to describe him in everyday language, students used expressions ranging from "frat boy" to "football player" and even "cornfed boy." While the evil Skeletor sparked little interest in the students, the Cold War being a lost reference on them, the peoples of Eternia intrigued them deeply. While no specific nationality could be attached to any group, as a student put it bluntly, "they're not American, they're not European." Students found many endearing qualities among the peoples of Eternia. The Widgets are "short and funny and act like little children," the Tree People are "brave and stoic," and the Kulataks are "huge but docile like Big Foot." For the specific issue of relationships of power and authority, a student used the "good cop, bad cop" analogy, pointing out the duplicity of the He-Man/Prince Adam character. From that insight it was easy for me to draw an analogy to American soft and hard imperialism, diplomacy and military interventions. Many students noted how grateful the peoples of Eternia were for He-Man's protection, evidenced by several episodes where they welcomed He-Man and his entourage with flowers, feasts, and parades. In class, I explained to students how in March 2003, just before the invasion of Iraq, Vice President Cheney said to NBC that "from the standpoint of the Iraqi people, my belief is we will, in fact, be greeted as liberators."[13] Students laughed, recognizing how those words could describe He-Man entering a village of Eternia after defeating Skeletor. This almost comical connection between the media text and a very real, very consequential event proved critical to underscore the power of American mythology. As a student wrote, "I'll never watch a cartoon the same way again."

DISCUSSION

My report from the classroom is that American Studies is both a vibrant and an urgent field. From my vantage point, its vitality is evidenced by the level of student engagement and the dedication of several of my colleagues to expand the curriculum even with inadequate institutional support. Its urgency is made clear by the field's broad and inclusive focus to examine what it means to be American from the intersection of race, ethnicity, class, gender, all layers of identity, in ways that connect directly with the cause for social justice. In institutions like mine that lack an American Studies department, the significance of the discipline may be obscured even though students enroll in multiple courses that examine the core questions of the American Studies project. My experience of teaching Intro to Latinx Studies was challenging, rewarding, and revelatory. In a personal way, it confirmed the centrality of media studies and reaffirmed the potential of interdisciplinary pedagogy. The insight gained and shared by my students showed me that the myths and narratives that define Americanness are dynamic. I cannot think of a more impactful teaching environment. However, I do not want to come across as naively optimistic. We must become better, louder advocates of the vitality and urgency we experience in the classroom in the face of declining funding for public higher education and misinformed, sometimes hostile public opinion.

NOTES

1. Richard G. Bohem, *World Geography and Culture* (New York: Glencoe/McGraw-Hill, 2007).

2. "Media Studies," Oxford Reference, accessed November 14, 2020, https://www.oxfordreference.com/page/mediastudies/media-studies.

3. George Lipsitz, "What Is American Studies?," ASA White Paper Series, American Studies Association, April 2015, www.theasa.net/sites/default/files/What_is_American_Studies.pdf.

4. Abraham F. Lowenthal, "Latin America in US Foreign Policy: Changing Interests, Priorities and Policies," Plataforma Democrática, accessed September 25, 2020, http://plataformademocratica.org/Arquivos/Latin%20America%20in%20US%20Foreign%20Policy.pdf.

5. Luigi Morris, "The US Interventions in Latin America," Left Voice, December 31, 2018, https://www.leftvoice.org/the-u-s-interventions-in-latin-america.

6. School of the Americas Watch, "Half a Century of US Interventions," accessed November 14, 2020, https://i.imgur.com/scLiyv2.jpg.

7. Lipsitz, "What Is American Studies?"

8. Ariel Dorfman and Armand Mattelart, *How to Read Donald Duck: Imperialist Ideology in the Disney Comic*, trans. David Kunzle (Amsterdam: International General, 1975), and *Para leer al pato Donald* (Buenos Aires: Siglo XXI Editores, 1971).

9. David Kunzle, "The Parts That Got Left Out of the Donald Duck Book, or: How Karl Marx Prevailed over Carl Barks," *ImageTexT: Interdisciplinary Comics Studies* 6, no. 2 (2012), http://imagetext.english.ufl.edu/archives/v6_2/kunzle/.

10. Wikipedia, s.v. "*Kim Possible*," last modified November 13, 2020, 10:52, https://en.wikipedia.org/wiki/Kim_Possible.

11. Wikipedia, s.v. "*He-Man and the Masters of the Universe*," last modified November 12, 2020, 14:16, https://en.wikipedia.org/wiki/He-Man_and_the_Masters_of_the_Universe.

12. "Eternia," Wiki Grayskull: The He-Man and She-Ra Wiki, accessed November 14, 2020, https://he-man.fandom.com/wiki/Eternia.

13. Reuters Staff, "FACTBOX: Iraq War, the Notable Quotes," Reuters, March 11, 2008, https://www.reuters.com/article/us-iraq-war-quotes/factbox-iraq-war-the-notable-quotes-idUSL2127625200803111.

PART II

Unpacking the Familiar, Introducing the New

Teaching Key Texts and Terms

5

When an Old Assignment Becomes New Again

Teaching Benedict Anderson's Imagined Communities *in the Age of #BlackLivesMatter*

CATHERINE MCNICOL STOCK

When he published his now classic analysis of nationalism, *Imagined Communities*, Benedict Anderson did not see Colin Kaepernick coming. In 1983 Anderson was interested in the unexpected spread of nationalism across the globe, even in communist countries. While he acknowledged that internal conflicts and inequalities existed within nations, understanding the complexities of such lived realities was not his primary focus.[1] He aimed to demonstrate that the nation, hardly the "ancient" structure that patriots consider it to be, was instead a modern construction that came about in the wake of specific historical processes, amplified by the increased power of the bourgeoisie. In its full expression, the nation was "imagined" by its members to be a "deep horizontal comradeship" among people who would never know or meet each other but who would nevertheless willingly give their lives for it.[2] When San Francisco Giants quarterback Colin Kaepernick took a knee during the playing of the national anthem at the start of the 2016 NFL season, his action seemed to my students to mark new understandings of identity, new rejections of the concepts that determined national identity, even new imagined communities themselves. In an interview before the game, Kaepernick explained: "I am not going to stand up to show pride in a flag for a country that oppresses black people and people of color. . . . There are bodies in the street and people . . . are getting away with murder."[3] Kaepernick was not imagining that he belonged to any community in the United States other than the one people of color had built for themselves in the face of genocidal white supremacy.

The events that inspired Kaepernick's protest—and countless others in the years since 2013—drastically altered my students' responses to a paper about Anderson's ideas that I had assigned for more than two decades. I was unprepared for their shift in thinking. In my teaching and research, I had long sought to connect social and cultural theory to the real events in American life, past and present, private and public. Even so, I had not expected one series of events—however momentous—to change the conversation in my class so quickly. In reading the new responses to Anderson—initially written by students of color and LGBTQ students, but increasingly by white, heterosexual, and cisgender students as well—I learned that while I might be able to assign the same book and the same essay for many years, it would not in fact *be* the same book or the same essay assignment for my students. Doing my job meant reading the book through their eyes and responding in kind: revising the paper topic, rescheduling the week it was introduced, and rethinking student discussion about it. It might even mean that I needed to abandon the assignment altogether, or at the very least to engage with the book's complexities with renewed vigor. In short, it could not be the same book for me either.

In 1995, when I first assigned *Imagined Communities* in the capstone seminar for the American Studies major at Connecticut College, my goal was relatively straightforward—and so was the assignment itself. I wanted these seniors, while it was still early in the term, to read an important cultural theorist and grapple with his challenging ideas and prose style. I also wanted them to think about the United States in transnational perspective. But most of all, I wanted them to use interdisciplinary methods to show how everyday icons of nation—flags, coins, anthems, memorials, war photography, kindergarten pageants about "Pilgrims and Indians"—were powerful communicators of national identity. To do so, I asked them to choose an object or an image that they felt illustrated "American-ness" and "write an essay explaining how and why it does this." Looking back, the assignment shared much with the 1950s Myth and Symbol approach in American Studies, in that it accepted the basic concept that certain icons could stand in for nations, and its challenges were primarily in adopting methodologies like that of Susan Sontag to do so. Examples that worked well, I told them, included well-known photographs like Neil Armstrong planting the American flag on the moon. My only caution was to avoid items that were "too huge" to discuss in detail in a five-to-seven-page paper. Instead of McDonald's, then, they should consider writing about a Big Mac or just the Golden Arches symbol.[4]

In this straightforward conceptualization, the assignment was genuinely successful—so successful for so many years that I did nothing to alter it. Most of the time students made creative choices, did intensive research, effectively used interdisciplinary methods, and drew conclusions through deep engagement and critical thinking. For example, Ray Hawkins argued that an image taken in 2009 of a US Marine in Fallujah, Iraq, handing candy to a small boy confirmed Anderson's idea that the limits of nation are constantly being reinforced in order to renew and redefine the bonds of the imagined. He wrote:

> Ultimately, the photograph confirms our sense of belonging in our own community, while simultaneously distancing the "other." It says that we, the United States of America, have existed and will continue to exist as a unified, morally praiseworthy entity. Whether the enemy is Nazi Germany, global communism, or simply "terror," we have a right to defend our way of life the way we see fit, whatever the cost. Saddam Hussein, Osama [Bin Laden], the Taliban . . . these names are simply details.[5]

But I see now that even papers as engaging as Hawkins's were not as robust as they could have been. Their authors thought critically about the United States—but they were largely *uncritical* of Anderson. They had not done the paper incorrectly; I had not asked them to evaluate Anderson's basic premise—that nation is a social construction and an imagined community. I had only asked them to illustrate how everyday images or objects communicated nation to us, helped us to "think" the nation, in Anderson's terms. As a result, when I criticized a paper in those years (read: decades), it was when an individual student had not engaged deeply enough with the object or image to draw a nuanced insight into national identity in the United States. For example, I suggested to one student who had written about a thirty-pack of Budweiser that he might have been able to critique American culture more deeply had he mentioned that thirty cans of beer was a lot of beer.

The first sign that I might have to reconsider the assignment much more fundamentally came from the right. It was not often that I had a confident, vocal conservative in the class, but in 2006 I did. Bobby Brooks was not only the president of his class but also president of the Connecticut College Republican Party. He was not just surprised by Anderson's thesis, he was appalled, even offended, by it. How dare Anderson say the nation was invented and subsequently imagined? How dare he say that those who gave their lives in the military gave them for "limited imaginings?"[6] Far from *illustrating* Anderson's argument that "nationalism is not the awakening of nations to self-consciousness; it *invents* nations where they do not exist," Brooks argued that Joe Rosenthal's iconic 1945 photo of marines raising the American flag on Mount Suribachi fully *contradicted* it.[7] "It is difficult to conceive," he wrote, "that had someone asked [marines] Michael Strank or John Bradley how they felt about America at that moment, that they would have responded by admitting that the United States was little more than a figment of their imaginations."[8] Instead of inventions, the image showed that nations "are better characterized as organized, tangible structures built and defended by the sacrifice and toil of the members." The photo itself, he concludes, shows that America is not just the idea of a "'shining city upon a hill'" in Reagan's words but a real thing "'built on rocks stronger than oceans'"—even if those rocks and oceans were a world away.[9] For Brooks, then, the idea that nation was "limited" made heroes seem foolish and their deaths pointless, conclusions that themselves felt un-American at the very least.

I did not concur with Brooks, but that was not the point. His passionate defense of nation as more real than imagined made me consider the possibility that other students in the class also disagreed with Anderson and that I had not asked for critique as much as methodological flourish in their work. This revelation marked my first—albeit tiny—adjustment to the assignment. I did not write a new paper topic. But beginning in 2007, I talked about Brooks's paper and encouraged students with more conservative views to try to take Anderson on. Brooks's paper did not prepare me for the storm of criticism that would come in later years from students of color and others on the left, however. It did not prepare me for students like Randsel Brannum, who, in 2016, took Anderson's own words and turned them over to identify a new reality: "People not only die in the name of nationalism but nationals are killed for the sustenance of their nation."[10]

At this point in the story, some personal and institutional context is needed. I am a white woman, and Connecticut College is a historically white college, at its founding for women only. The cost of attendance is very high, and, as is often the case at selective liberal arts colleges, many students come from affluent, majority-white communities. In my twenty-five years of teaching there, the administration has made intermittent strides toward "diversifying" the faculty, the student body, and the curriculum. In the past five years, however, student and faculty activists have begun to ask for more, much more, than to be included. Like others around the country, Connecticut College students of color and their allies have demanded access to power, a full interrogation of the relationship between power and knowledge, and an institutional commitment to their right to speak and to be safe from both macro- and microaggressions.

For reasons both local and national, these questions and demands took center stage during the 2014–2015 academic year. In August 2014, a faculty member posted to his Facebook page comments that many in the community found racist and hateful. The posts, combined with a slow response to them by the administration and a subsequent series of racist, anti-Semitic, and Islamophobic incidents on campus, created an institutional crisis that continued into the fall of 2015. Meanwhile, the killings of Trayvon Martin, Michael Brown, Eric Garner, Tamir Rice, and many others by white police or other citizens filled national headlines and campus conversation. One thing was clear: the "Connecticut College bubble" was nothing like a bubble: the issues faced by students of color, Jewish students, Muslim students, and LGBTQ students on campus were exactly those faced by nonmajority Americans as a whole.

The first paper I received that focused on an "alternative" imagined community within the United States was written before these incidents, in the fall of 2013. For that reason and many others, I now see the courage it took to write. In 2013 Jannette Rivera expressed her view in the title itself: "An Alternative Black Nation in the U.S.A." Rivera argued that African Americans had adapted the traditional symbols of nation to carve out an alternative nation for themselves. She used the famous Frederick Douglass speech "What to the Slave Is the Fourth of July?" to demonstrate the historic "evidence of the origins of alternative, national consciousness among the black community."[11] For Rivera, "a Black nation within America manifested after slaves were freed" but nevertheless was rejected by white Americans. She advanced her thesis to the present day by arguing that the ongoing celebration of Juneteenth and the use of the Black national anthem, "Lift Every Voice and Sing," by

African Americans also advanced a separate Black nation within the United States. With systemic inequality in the twenty-first century, she concluded, this idea of a separate Black nation within the United States is stronger than ever. "Blacks still cannot completely enjoy the freedoms and luxuries of white America," so why not create a "nation" of their own?[12]

Rivera might have been the first student to apply Anderson's concepts to Black America, but she certainly wasn't the last.[13] By the spring of 2015, events on campus and in the world at large had usurped discussion of conventional course content in most American Studies classrooms. In my senior seminar, I saw that suddenly more students of color found in the Anderson paper an opportunity to write about their feelings of alienation from the American "community." "Black hands are threatening," Bria Sawyer wrote in her spring 2015 paper. She focused on two images: the 1968 Black Power protest from the Mexico City Olympics and a CNN image of congressional staffers protesting on Capitol Hill for the nonindictments of white police officers in the deaths of Michael Brown and Eric Garner in December 2014. "If your hands aren't the 'right' color while grabbing for your wallet in your pants pocket as you are being frisked by the police—black hands can be a threat," she wrote.[14] Likewise that spring, Jae Majors wondered how a nation could be imagined when what was really required to belong was something much more concrete: a Social Security card.[15]

These first passionate counterarguments, along with the circumstances on campus and beyond, forced me to see that it was time—high time—to change the paper assignment. First, I saw that it would no longer do to ask students to simply "illustrate" Anderson's views through the framework of a unified Americanness. My challenge to them in the revised paper topic was, as before, to find an image or an object that represents America or Americanness in some way, but then to write an essay "explaining how it does or does not illustrate Anderson's point of view." What intervention did their primary source make into his theory? Does the image or object amplify his view, challenge it, contextualize it, contradict it, or do something else entirely? After all, this is what scholars do when they work with primary sources—they ask what difference, if any, these new materials make when put in conversation with the conventional knowledge in their fields.[16]

More importantly, I realized that the assignment offered a new opportunity for community building and peer-to-peer learning in the classroom. In the past, the papers were individual efforts: a student wrote a paper, a student turned in the paper, I read the paper, I returned the paper. So individualized was this process in fact that the day the papers were due was traditionally a day *off* from class. Going forward, I aimed to create a common effort at understanding. We began together the week before the papers were due, when I brought in examples of items that would work well (Neil Armstrong on the moon again, but also King on the Edmund Pettis bridge) and asked the class to evaluate whether the images reflected Anderson's thinking about how nation functioned and was expressed. The next week, when the papers were due, we used the class time for individual presentations of the students' own choices and theses, once we had established firmly that the classroom was a confidential space and that respect for everyone's ideas was paramount. I asked all those students whose papers fundamentally agreed with Anderson to take a turn explaining why. Then those students whose papers refuted Anderson, for whatever reason, did the same. These were not easy discussions. Indeed, they were at times the most contentious discussions of the term. But they were also fascinating and revealing—and more than once they went beyond the official end of class time.

Within this new context of critical thinking and discussion, students from many different backgrounds began to find the fault lines in Anderson's ideas, some of which went to issues that Anderson himself in 1983 considered fundamental to his thesis. On the most basic level, for example, many students asked if Anderson's ideas really withstood the test of time. Was his idea about the power of print capitalism still relevant in the era of the internet? Did he fully acknowledge how new information organizations like Google and new corporations like Disney could shape knowledge? Had expensive experiences shared on social media become a new kind of vernacular language—a "vernacular of the elite"?[17]

But students have penned the most searing critiques of Anderson by focusing on a single sentence—a sentence that is at once critical to Anderson's thesis and literally unfathomable to many students: "Finally, it is imagined as a *community*, because, regardless of the actual inequality and exploitation that may prevail in each, the nation is always conceived as a deep, horizontal comradeship."[18] Student after student problematized each word of the sentence—and especially the seemingly least important. How could any sentence that defined nation and acknowledged the reality of social inequality begin with the word *regardless?* They read this sentence to be dismissive, even obliterating of real inequality and exploitation, finding the sentence made no sense at all. Without that sentence was it possible that the book's thesis made no sense at all? And if the book's thesis made no sense at all, what were we doing reading it in the first place?

Five papers from 2015–2016 and 2016–2017 exemplify so many others that, as a collective, revealed that Americans' consent to the idea of nation, "regardless of inequalities," is beginning to crack. In his paper, "Comradeship across Time and Borders," David Barrera Garcia compared two images: one of a man standing in front of tanks in Tiananmen Square, the other of a woman protesting the police killing of Sylville Smith by standing up to a police barricade in Milwaukee. Not only does he show that protest requires the courage of maintaining the vertical in the face of the overwhelming power of horizontality, but he also shows that across nations and time, protesters often share more in common with each other than they do with citizens of their own nation: "It's not nation or national pride that connects these individuals; rather, they can find commonality in facing similar struggles against the oppressive structures of their separate nations."[19] David refuted Anderson's argument that "such palpable inequalities can be put aside in order to unite the nation." What both images demonstrate, he concludes, is that "imagined communities do not put aside the injustices and inequality in times of need, but instead help to promote them through violent repression."[20]

For Wesley Chabrasz, "The Soiling of Old Glory," the famous image of a white man appearing to use the American flag to impale an African American attorney during the Boston busing riots in 1976, revealed that America is not imagined "regardless" of social inequity and racism but through it and by it and because of it. He concedes that Anderson understands that race was a factor in creating nation in the New World but inherently disagrees with Anderson's contention in a later chapter that racism is caused by class division not nationalism.[21] As Anderson might put it: "White Americans defined themselves as Americans by defining themselves specifically as not black, and it is this historical definition of citizenship that prevailed in the United States for so long that makes 'The Soiling of Old Glory' about more than just nationalism, or violence, or even just race."[22] The flag, a symbol for the nation, was in fact a weapon, used that day and every day to enforce injustice.

A deeper understanding of the reach of history in the New World also informed Lysandra Saldana's contention that Anderson did not grapple with the inescapable facts of the killing of indigenous people by the state and its connection to nationalism. This genocide, she argues, paved the way for a national history based on a false concept of horizontal comradery that perpetuates the "knowledge" of the erasure of indigeneity even while survivors maintain their communities and resist American hegemony. Among the best known representations of this dynamic is John Gast's "American Progress," which shows native people feeling the oncoming nation with nowhere to go except the edge of the painting itself and oblivion. "This painting," Saldana wrote, "is very symbolic of two conflicting realities—on the left indigenous nations exist but are forced into disappearance, while on the right . . . the engineering of a new nation of progress is brought by white settlers."[23] Reading Anderson's understanding of America as similar to that in the painting, she argues that not only does the existence of indigenous people after attempts at genocide reveal Anderson's acceptance of erasure, but indigenous peoples also threaten his notion of a nation as fully "sovereign."[24]

In this same vein, Gil Mejia argues that if Anderson in his use of "regardless" can brush aside inequality—even genocide—with the stroke of a pen, so can the rest of white people holding power. In the United States, Mejia writes, whether deliberately or not, "institutions operate under orders of white supremacy because it enforces and insists upon a social, moral, and personal psychology that manipulates self-understanding." For the assignment, Mejia looked at two headlines and photographs of men who made the news—for very different reasons—and argued that the mass media privileges white people, making horizontal comradeship impossible because it "insists and depends on a belief that black Americans are culturally and socially incompatible." The headline "Theater Shooting Suspect Was Brilliant Science Student" paired with a clean-cut image of mass murderer James Holmes is one example of how the media portrays white suspects and killers as better people than Black victims of police violence, Mejia argues. Compare that with a headline reading "Michael Brown Struggled with Officer before Shooting" and an "intimidating" picture of the eighteen-year-old Black man who was killed by a white police officer in Ferguson, Missouri, in 2014; the report not only suggests that Brown "is to blame for his own death because of his alleged struggle with the officer," but it becomes one piece of the "assassination of the Black character [that] sets in order a violent cycle . . . in which Black lives continue to be disregarded and disposable."[25]

Finally, while Anderson argues that people fight and die for their nations, sometimes people also kill for their nations, Randsel Brannum writes in 2016. Brannum uses Hurricane Katrina as a focal point to argue that Anderson's analysis "completely disregards nationalism as a lived experience for marginalized and oppressed peoples."[26] Using a photograph of a Black man clinging to a car in the middle of a flooded landscape, taken about six days after Katrina tore through New Orleans, Brannum writes: "His solitude and his skin (are) a statement to the way in which Black Americans were left alone with few governmental resources during the hurricane."[27] Along with this image, Brannum uses stills from Beyoncé's music video "Formation," in which the singer lies on a New Orleans police car in the middle of a flood, eventually drowning as the water covers her and the car. The video "calls attention to the fact that people not only die in the name of nationalism but nationals are killed for the sustenance of their nation," Brannum writes. The drowning imagery symbolizes Black death "due to systematic neglect, poor building materials, and inattention to communities." The police car is a more obvious symbol: "For many people, the police are a civilizing force that helps keep order and organization in the nation state, while for many Black Americans the police are a danger who target black communities."[28]

In the spring of 2017, during our discussion of the class papers, a few students reached a conclusion I had—once again—not expected. The ideals of Americanness they associated with Anderson did not simply reflect racism in our society, they promoted them. Thus reading him in class reinforced what they read as a false and dangerous knowledge.[29] By asserting his ability to know and understand experiences he could not possibly know or understand, wasn't Anderson simply creating knowledge that fostered the cycle of oppression? Likewise, weren't we doing the same thing every day we studiously "evaluated" his views? Even writing a paper forced students to engage with ideas that threatened their very existence as individuals and collective members of religious, ethnic, and gender-queer groups—that assumed their experiences could be categorized as "regardless"—that they could be erased. They wondered aloud if someday soon, one of my students would refuse to write the paper. They suggested instead that I consider refusing to assign it.

CONCLUSION

For the time being, an essay in which students evaluate Anderson's *Imagined Communities* is still on my syllabus. I am newly hopeful that the idea of nation as the most powerful concept through which people see the world and for which they are willing to die is more relevant than ever. Even so, I cannot promise it will be there to stay. I can promise, however, that I will take seriously my students' lived experiences and perspectives in creating my goals for my classes and all my assignments.

Many of us have had assignments or readings we have held on to year after year because they "work" or because they seem important for some other reason—or perhaps because it's just too much work to make a change. But my experience teaching Anderson for nearly a quarter-century has shown me that in fact, it is not possible to teach the "same" book year after year. Is Anderson's text the same now as it was when he published it? Yes. When I first started to assign it? Yes. But don't I, as a professor and human, bring a "different self" to the book the second or twenty-fifth time I read it? If so, I should also bear in mind that each group of students is unique, with different minds and insights than in years past. Over time, they become a different generation of students who have grown up in and come to see a different world. For all these reasons, even if the text is identical, a book is never the same; it can never be the same, one year to the next. If we are practicing our craft in the ways American Studies allows, perhaps even requires, our approaches to teaching it must change, too. In my case, that means that I will continue to evaluate and change my approach to teaching *Imagined Communities*—even if that means never assigning it again.

NOTES

Thanks to all the students in AMS 465 who have tried their hand at this paper assignment. There were far too many fascinating and provocative essays to include here, especially those written by the class of 2020, after I had completed this essay. I am mindful in particular of ideas presented in papers or in class discussion by Brian Belisle, Kate Campbell, Leah Swinson, Emily Ryan, Lili Lan Visgilio, Justin Mendillo, Grace Pearlman, Grace Finley, Bettina Weiss, Clay Lenahan, Sarah Haddad, Kelsey Millward, Amelia DeFrancis, Hanna Bobrowicz, Emma Walsh, Ali Harris, Cameron Segal, Elyse King-Guffey, Anna DiGravio, and Kayla Johnson. Thanks also to the many students who granted me permission to reread their papers, to quote from them if needed, and to use their names. All your papers helped me to form my ideas and, along the way, remember each of you fondly.

1. Benedict Anderson, *Imagined Communities: Reflections on the Origins and Spread of Nationalism* (London: Verso, 1983), 1. In the preface to the second edition in 1991, Anderson comments further on his purpose for writing the book; see xi. The book was reissued in 2006 as well.

2. Anderson, *Imagined Communities*, 7.

3. As quoted in Steve Wyche, "Kaepernick Explains Why He Sat during National Anthem," NFL.com, August 27, 2016, http://www.nfl.com/news/story

/oap3000000691077/article/colin-kaepernick-explains-why-he-sat-during-national-anthem.

4. The full text of the original assignment reflects that I was not yet interested in making Anderson the focus of the paper. It allowed students to engage a different cultural theorist, and even leave out Anderson altogether. Later his ideas would become the focus of the paper:

> Please choose one object, image, symbol, event, or photograph that represents America or American-ness in some way and write an essay explaining how and why it does this. Avoid "huge" objects—like all of the McDonalds or Nike corporations, and focus on a smaller more manageable ones, like the Golden Arches or the swoosh. Think about how Barthes deconstructs objects, Sontag examines images, and Anderson understands nationality as an "imaginary" construction. You must directly and explicitly incorporate the analyses of two of these three theorists in your paper. You should research your object (its history, for example) and provide what you have learned in a fully-documented background section. Please include a bibliography of any citations you have used or any other works you have consulted. [5–7]

5. Ray Hawkins, "Confirming National Identity: Al-Faedal and the War on Terror," February 20, 2013, 7–8, 123. Unpublished manuscript in author's possession. Permission granted for use March 24, 2017.

6. Anderson, *Imagined Communities*, 7.

7. Anderson, *Imagined Communities*, 6.

8. Bobby Brooks, "Image of America: The Iwo Jima Flag Raising," n.d. [2006], 4. Unpublished manuscript in the author's possession. Permission for use granted June 11, 2017.

9. Ronald Reagan, "Farewell Address to the Nation," January 11, 1989, as quoted in Brooks, "Image of America," 5.

10. Randsel Brannum, "What Happened at New Orleans?: Marginality, Nationalism, and Inclusion," n.d. [2016], 6. Unpublished manuscript in the author's possession. Permission for use granted November 8, 2016.

11. Jannette Rivera, "An Alternate Black Nation in the U.S.A.," October 9, 2013, 2. Unpublished manscript in author's possession. Permission for use granted March 23, 2017.

12. Rivera, "An Alternate Black Nation," 7.

13. Rivera was more in line with more recent scholars, such as Melani McAlister and Alicia Schmidt Camacho, who have introduced ideas of pan-African or pan-national "imaginaries." See Melani McAlister, *Epic Encounters: Culture, Media, and U.S. Interests in the Middle East since 1945* (Berkeley: University of California Press, 2005); Alicia Schmidt Camacho, *Migrant Imaginaries: Latino Cultural Politics in the U.S-Mexico Borderlands* (New York: New York University Press, 2008).

14. Bria Sawyer, "'Put Your Hands Where I Can See 'Em': American Symbolism of Protest by Black Hands," February 25, 2015, 1. Unpublished manuscript in the author's possession. Permission for use granted March 23, 2017.

15. Jae Majors, "An Imagined America," n.d. [2015]. Unpublished manuscript in the author's possession. Permission for use granted March 24, 2017.

16. The full text of the assignment from 2016 read

> Anderson argues that ideas of nationalism, indeed nations themselves, are "imaginary communities." And yet, as he admits, these imaginings are powerful enough to cause men (and now women) to die in their names. Moreover, he believes that the power of the nation is based in its concept of shared experience, simultaneity, and horizontal comradeship. Please choose one object, image, symbol, event, or photograph that represents America or American-ness in some way and write an essay explaining how it does or does not illustrate Anderson's point of view. Does your chosen image or object amplify his view? Challenge it? Contextualize it? Contradict it? Something else?

17. The term "vernacular of the elite" comes from Clay Lenahan, "Maggie and Eloise at the Plaza," n.d., unpublished manuscript in the author's possession; permission for use granted November 4, 2016.

18. Anderson, *Imagined Communities*, 7.

19. David Garcia Barrera, "Comradeship across Time and Borders," September 28, 2016, 3. Unpublished manuscript in the author's possession. Permission for use granted April 3, 2017. What David did not discuss is that in fact Anderson, as he argues in chapters on official nationalism, was himself banned from Indonesia through such repression.

20. Garcia Barrera, "Comradeship across Time and Borders,"5.

21. Anderson, *Imagined Communities*, 149.

22. Wesley Chrabasz, "Representations of Nationalism: The Soiling of Old Glory," n.d. [2016], 7–8. Unpublished manuscript in the author's possession. Permission for use granted March 23, 2017.

23. Lysandra Saldana, "Beyond the Essence of American Nationalism," February 22, 2017, n.p. Unpublished manuscript in the author's possession. Permission for use granted June 10, 2017.

24. Saldana, "Beyond the Essence," n.p.

25. Gil Mejia, "Building Characters: A Life or Death Issue," February 22, 2017, n.p. Unpublished mss in the author's possession. Permission for use granted June 10, 2017.

26. Brannum, "What Happened at New Orleans?," 7.

27. Brannum, 4.

28. Brannum, 6.

29. In a follow-up email, Gil Mejia explained:

> Anderson is also a subject of the hegemonic project. The way he understands shared experience is informed by what experiences matter, whose experiences matter, and what mediates those experiences. (I of course see this through the context of America) I see how Anderson is used to support American exceptionalism in talking about how we overcome, how our experience of freedom is unique to the world, and how improvement here is

different than anywhere else. But who is overcoming and what? who is living free and at what expense? For whom is America improving? Anderson's VERY limited existential experience itself disproves his shared experience argument.

Mejia to Stock, June 12, 2017.

6

Coalition Time in the American Studies Classroom

RICHARD T. RODRÍGUEZ

If there is one text that regularly makes its way onto my syllabi, it is the speech cum essay "Coalition Politics: Turning the Century," by Bernice Johnson Reagon, founding member of both the Student Non-violent Coordinating Committee (SNCC) and the all-Black female a cappella ensemble Sweet Honey in the Rock. Whether for my class on The Queer 1980s or Queer of Color Cultural Critique, Reagon's piece usefully assists in contextualizing the rise of women of color feminism and the concept of intersectionality. In addition, the essay allows students to consider the historical antecedents of terms and concepts that figure prominently in their own personal lives and political inclinations. Yet the essay is not always embraced as one might assume. Indeed, over the years that I've taught the piece, students at times resist many of Reagon's claims as either accommodationist, shortsighted, or outdated. Taking their arguments seriously, I ask that as they challenge the points Reagon makes on which they don't agree, they must also interrogate their own ideas, which they often assume to be unflawed. While this has often led to heated class sessions, it has also proved beneficial for students to think critically about how they grasp material from earlier historical moments as well as what they assume to be true in their present conceptualization of activist politics.

In this chapter, I will signal the key moments in "Coalition Politics" that have not only generated debate for the sake of argument but occasioned critical conversations prompting transformative results. Preferring to see the American Studies classroom as a potential space for democratic exchange rather than a hierarchical top-down exchange of knowledge, I engage with Reagon's essay to advance a pedagogical approach informed by dialectical thinking. In many ways, the essay serves as a blueprint for ascertaining the classroom, as English literary critic Raymond Williams declares of culture, as "a whole way of life."[1] That is, instead of accepting the information transmitted in the classroom as either right or wrong (akin to Williams's divergence from reading culture as either high or low), the critical tenets of "Coalition Politics"—through the multilayered analytic consideration it elicits—open up the classroom onto an even greater social scale for perceiving the complexities of communal interaction.

I first read Reagon's essay as an undergraduate at the University of California, Berkeley—a moment when coalition politics assembled many of my peers of color whose activism took shape in the form of occupying administrative buildings to demand increased funding for ethnic studies and student-initiated journals created by women and men of color with the titles, respectively, *Smell This* and *In Your Face*. But it wasn't until I began writing my doctoral dissertation that I reread "Coalition Politics" on the recommendation of my advisor.[2] My dissertation focused on the rise of Chicano cultural nationalism in the late 1960s and its intimate connection with the discourse of the family for unifying Mexican American communities for social justice. According to my advisor, Reagon's piece was an important resource for assessing the potential for and limitation of nationalist discourse. And he was absolutely correct. Fittingly, "Coalition Politics" nicely aligned with then-recent scholarship in Black British cultural studies debating ethnic absolutism, antiessentialist, and anti-antiessentialist cultural politics.[3]

Not only did Reagon's essay supply me with an illuminating position on cultural nationalism from a Black feminist perspective, but it also provided a way out of the impasse such a perspective invariably tenders. Furthermore, the essay made clear the meaning and function of women of color feminism. That is, rather than depend on predetermined or essentialist individual and group identities to mobilize collective action, "women of color feminism" instead requires the adoption of shared political objectives to form coalitions comprised of sometimes seemingly unlikely affiliates united for working toward similar goals. Conveying this in the classroom, however, is not always easy.

In the present moment, when activist discourse is constantly invented and reinvented, conversant with emergent political formations and breaking with those of the past, the materials that had a profound impact on earlier generations (mine included) of students may not carry the same weight they once did. As made clear not only by my students but by encounters with those active on social media, it's clear that certain terms and concepts from earlier historical moments do not always translate smoothly for recent situations. At times they feel outdated or in need of revision or outright abandonment. One such term, I've learned, is "coalition." On more than one occasion, students have told me that the word reeks of reformist politics and lacks the urgency for a radical sense of solidarity. Even the term "solidarity," I've often been told, is impossible to achieve if certain manifestations of oppression are not prioritized. Yet while this dissent manifests alongside reading and teaching "Coalition Politics," it does not render the essay irrelevant. Regarding a song she writes as a declaration of camaraderie with Vietnam (riddled as it is with clichés about Vietnamese people that make even her cringe in retrospect), Reagon maintains: "If in the future, somebody is gonna use that song I sang, they're gonna have to strip it or at least shift it. I'm glad the principle is there for others to build on."[4] This is how I ask my students to approach Reagon's essay, despite whatever feelings they may harbor about the word "coalition."

While the terms "nationalism" and "cultural nationalism" seem to hold less value for more recent generations of students (at times, nationalism is simply understood as synonymous with the nation-state), there is still a way that a focus on racial or ethnic particularity resonates in an interconnected fashion to nationalism as described in "Coalition Politics." Like Paul Gilroy, who understands nationalism as a double-edged sword that, even in its antiestablishment and anti–nation-state articulations, always runs the risk of upholding "ethnic absolutism," Reagon pulls the curtain back on what a singular political focus often reveals.[5] As she argues, nationalism can be "nurturing, but it is also nationalism. At a certain stage nationalism is crucial to a people if you are going to ever impact as a group in your own interest. Nationalism at another point becomes reactionary because it is totally inadequate for surviving the world with many people."[6]

When I ask students how nationalism might operate in their everyday lives, some reference their ties to campus centers such as Chicano student programs, African student programs, and the LGBT resource center. Affirming how their connections to these centers might be read in a similar fashion to Reagon when she writes, "I don't start nothing except with Black people," students more often than not discuss how their affiliation with those centers is or is not exclusive.[7] That is, while some students declare their association with one center as "like home" or "like my community back home," others at times claim two or all three of the aforementioned centers. Seizing on such declarations allows me to explain how coalition politics for Reagon works. Indeed, Reagon's starting point with Black people refuses to manifest as an endpoint. And rather than lavish praise on the students in the latter group and admonish those in the former, I ask them to relate Reagon's discussion of "nurturing space" to their particular situation. But before they respond to my request, I read aloud the following passage:

> Sometimes you get comfortable in your little barred room, and you decide you in fact are going to live there and carry out all of your stuff there. And you gonna take care of everything that needs to be taken care of in the barred room. If you're white and in the barred room and if everybody's white, one of the first things you try to take care of is making sure that people don't think that the barred room is a racist barred room. So you begin to talk about racism and the first thing you do is say, "Well, maybe we better open the door and let some Black folks in the barred room." Then you think, "Well, how we gonna figure out whether they're X's or not?" Because there's nothing in the room but X's.[8]

Explaining the utmost need to disprove accusations of a "racist barred room," the white X's will seek out potential Black members, but only if their politics match those in the barred room. As Reagon succinctly puts it, they "don't really want Black folks," they "are just looking for [themselves] with a little color to it."[9]

So while a "barred room" for "white X's" is unquestionably distinct from a space like Chicano Student Programs, given that the latter functions as a reprieve from the former, often predominantly "white X," space of the university, it nonetheless exists as a safe space designed for those who identify with, or hold an approximate connection to, the category "Chicano."[10] Yet Reagon, I insist, wants us to grasp the limits of such space in fostering solidarity with those who are not like "us." As she makes clear in her article, such spaces are ultimately provisional given that beyond the barred room or the student center, safe space in general does not extend beyond its designated perimeter, nor does it always travel with us. For Reagon, then, it becomes necessary to ascertain the limits of aligning only with those who think (or look or act) like us if the overall goal is progressive action for our respective communities.

Using the example of Black Lives Matter, I explain the importance of Latinx communities speaking up and taking action against systemic racism against African Americans just as it's important for African Americans to take a stand against the perpetual anti-immigrant rhetoric directed at Latinx communities. As Reagon tells us, "Coalition work is not done in your home. Coalition work has to be done in the streets. And it is some of the most dangerous work you can do. And you shouldn't look for comfort. Some people will come to a coalition and they rate the success of the coalition on whether or not they feel good when they get there." On the refusal of confusing "home" and "coalition," Reagon insists that those aiming to conflate the two are "not looking for a coalition; they're looking for a home! . . . In a coalition you have to give, and it is different from your home. You can't stay there all the time." Yet what about those—students included—who regard coalition as always falling short of its intended goal, an illusory entreaty that clouds the aspirations of specific struggles?[11]

The last time I taught Reagon's essay, I had the fortuitous opportunity to bring in an op-ed piece published in the *Los Angeles Times* by Nadra Widatalla titled "The Term 'People of Color' Erases Black People. Let's Retire It" (2019). For Widatalla, interracial and ethnic solidarity is indeed important. But, she argues, "the reality is that not all 'people of color' suffer equally from the effects of institutional racism." Citing alarming statistics on the number of Black people (especially women) promoted in the workplace and the rates of parental incarceration for Black children in the United States, Widatalla reasons that

> parsing the implications of these differences, instead of flattening them, is what it means to be "intersectional," an important but widely misunderstood concept—even by the liberals who use it most. Intersectionality is not about building the biggest interracial team possible. It's about catering to the individual needs of different communities to make sure no one is left behind.
>
> The idea of different groups of minorities working together to fight racism of all sorts is fantastic, but any effort that sees the struggles of all minorities as a single movement is actually harmful. Black women, for example, are a minority within a minority—and we're being left behind. Rectifying that means the work of inclusivity has to go beyond being friendly to "women of color." Perhaps the best place to start is to retire that term altogether.[12]

I argue that the call to "retire" (and how exactly one might do this poses a serious challenge) "people of color" or "women of color" rests on that what Widatalla endeavors to resist: an "effort that sees the struggles of all minorities as a single movement."[13] Arguably an activist whom Reagon identifies as seeking to "prioritize the cutting line of the struggle," Widatalla, as many students argue, seems incapable of understanding that coalition does not necessitate the discarding of specific struggles nor flatting them.

In her essay "La Guera" from the classic anthology *This Bridge Called My Back: Writings by Radical Women of Color*, Chicana lesbian poet and playwright Cherríe Moraga cautions against not only the lateral ordering of oppressions but also the failure to recognize the differences marking those oppressions:

> In this country, lesbianism is a poverty—as is being brown, as is being a woman, as is being just plain poor. The danger lies in ranking the oppressions. The danger lies in failing to acknowledge the specificity of the oppression. The danger lies in attempting to deal with oppression purely from a theoretical base. Without an emotional, heartfelt grappling with the source of our own oppression, without naming the enemy within ourselves and outside of us, no authentic, non-hierarchical connection among oppressed groups can take place.[14]

Moraga, I would argue, adds a necessary dimension to Reagon's essay in raising the stakes of coalition by compelling us to "name the enemy within ourselves and outside of us" in order to work toward "authentic" and "non-hierarchal" connections with those relatedly oppressed. This is not unlike the ongoing struggle of Latinx and Black communities to unlearn anti-Black racism and anti-immigrant sentiment to fully grasp the parallel and intertwined histories of Black and Brown racial subordination in the United States.

In a recent speech delivered in Oakland, California, at a "Black/Brown Unity" rally following the tragic murder of George Floyd at the hands of a Minneapolis police officer, long-time activist Angela Y. Davis recounted how during her historic trial in San José, the local Chicanx community took to the streets to rally in support of her release from prison. Davis recalled how there were few African Americans residing in the South Bay city, and were it not for her Mexican American allies, the local outcry for her freedom would not have been as pronounced. As a grad student, I frequently commuted with Professor Davis from Oakland to Santa Cruz. During one of our many conversations, she recalled her dear friend Victoria Mercado, a Chicana from San José who worked tirelessly on the Free Angela campaign and who was pivotal in rallying the Chicanx community. At this particular moment, it is advantageous not only to remember but to learn from the rich history of Black and Latinx coalition work in the United States, as well as the other coalitional possibilities. As coalition politics permeate Reagon's activist inclinations as detailed in her essay, I want my students to similarly embrace the importance of establishing bonds with those heretofore unrecognized fellow travelers also walking the road toward social justice.

Even if students find little value in collective organizing and mobilization under the banner of "coalition politics," any refusal to work with others outside the barred rooms we inevitably find ourselves in at some point or another runs the risk of embracing and living in the polarization and division that the recent dominant culture—what might very well be called Trumpism—thrives on. In addition, the recent tendency in some academic and activist quarters to consign certain terms and concepts ("coalition," "multiculturalism," etc.) to the dustbin of liberal or neoliberal bankruptcy often offers no alternatives except the reliance on libertarian anarchism, since utopian models (including Marxism) are rendered inadequate at best and irrelevant at worst. Incapable of offering a viable way out, such dismissals result in the most minimal of solidarity struggles, often confined to elitist quarters of the university.

At a recent department faculty retreat, an extended discussion about curriculum revision turned to an adamant declaration on the part of many colleagues that our job was not to train our students for jobs. Reading this declaration as an understandable refusal of the recent refashioning of higher education as a neoliberal enclave, such a position nonetheless forecloses the possibility of seeing the classroom as a space that may indeed part with the structural dictates of the institution by offering information that not only translates into securing employment (as if that is necessarily a bad thing) but is advantageous for shifting the terms of how we relate to one another as individuals and communities in the world within and beyond the university. Like Williams's notion of culture as "a whole way of life," one might very well see the university as the high culture incapable of always eclipsing the "low" value of knowledge production in the classroom and its cultural capital beyond it. Recalling José Esteban Muñoz's embrace of pedagogy's queer utopian potentiality (2009) and Roderick Ferguson's provocation to always move beyond a one-dimensional assessment of queer (2018), Bernice Johnson Reagon's "Coalition Politics" heeds the call—as commanded recently on social media and T-shirts—to "Cite Black Women!" while also learning from them on how to work together in alliance.[15]

NOTES

1. Raymond Williams, *Culture and Society, 1750–1950* (New York: Columbia University Press, 1958), 29.

2. For a history of *Smell This*, see Ruxana Meer, Rhacel Parreñas, and Catherine Ramirez, "*Smell This*: Undergraduate Women of Color Constructing Our 'Homeplace,'" *Inscriptions* 7 (1994), https://culturalstudies.ucsc.edu/inscriptions/volume-7/ruxana-meer-rhacel-parrenas-catherine-ramirez/.

3. See Paul Gilroy, "Nationalism, History and Ethnic Absolutism," *History Workshop* 30 (Autumn 1990): 114–120; Gilroy, *Small Acts: Thoughts on the Politics of Black Cultures* (London: Serpent's Tail, 1994); Stuart Hall, "Old and New Identities, Old and New Ethnicities," in *Stuart Hall: Essential Essays*, vol. 2, ed. David Morley ([1990] Durham, NC: Duke University Press, 2019), 63–82; and Kobena Mercer, *Welcome to the Jungle: New Positions in Black Cultural Studies* (New York: Routledge, 1994).

4. Bernice Johnson Reagon, "Coalition Politics: Turning the Century," in *Home Girls: A Black Feminist Anthology*, ed. Barbara Smith (New York: Kitchen Table-Women of Color), 353.

5. Gilroy, "Nationalism, History and Ethnic Absolutism," 115.

6. Reagon, "Coalition Politics," 345.

7. Reagon, 351.

8. Reagon, 345–346.

9. Reagon, 346.

10. This, however, is not always a given. Many Central American students, for example, might not feel welcome in a distinctly marked "Chicano" space, nor may Chicanx students who refuse the masculinist "o" in Chicano.

11. Reagon, "Coalition Politics," 346.

12. Nadra Widatalla, "Op-Ed: The Term 'People of Color' Erases Black People. Let's Retire It," *Los Angeles Times*, April 28, 2019.

13. Widatalla, "Op-Ed."

14. Cherríe Moraga, "La Guera," in *This Bridge Called My Back: Writings by Radical Women of Color*, ed. Cherríe Moraga and Gloria E. Anzaldúa, 27–34 (New York: Kitchen Table/Women of Color, 1983), 29.

15. See José Esteban Muñoz, *Cruising Utopia: The Then and There of Queer Futurity* (New York: New York University Press, 2009); and Roderick A. Ferguson, *One-Dimensional Queer* (Cambridge: Polity, 2019).

7

Teaching American Studies One Word at a Time

LINDA STEWART

In her essay "Dialect" in *Keywords for American Cultural Studies,* Shelley Fisher Fishkin discusses American authors' subversive use of dialect writing. She concludes, "'Dialect,' as it turns out, in the hands of sly and talented artists and astute and sensitive critics may do cultural work that is a good deal more complicated than we may have thought."[1] Like artists, educators in American Studies classrooms can also engage in this cultural work. Fishkin continues: "U.S. English is a dynamic amalgam of a range of varieties of speech and writing" found in "literary experiments" such as Gloria Anzaldua's "code-switching blend of poetry and nonfiction."[2] This same "dynamic amalgam" exists in the spoken words and complex identities of our students in American Studies classrooms, offering the space to subvert received notions of what it means to be "American" by taking a linguistic approach that focuses on dialect.

In my American Studies classes at Kennesaw State University, I've engaged students with assignments and activities that ask them to think about the relationship between vocabulary acquisition and identity, whether in conversations about colloquial dialects, about the rigors of academic language, or about terms like "political correctness." The editors of *Keywords for American Cultural Studies* urge their readers to make "something new" from their keywords project, which by its very nature is incomplete.[3] As I reflect on the activities in my "American Identities" course—the discussions, readings, popular culture analysis, and artifact narrative assignment—that I describe here, I am beginning to think my students were actually initiating their own keywords projects—one word at a time.

John McWhorter, a prolific author and professor of linguistics and American Studies at Columbia, complicates simple definitions of dialect. He states, "The very fact that 'language' and 'dialect' persist as separate concepts implies that linguists can make tidy distinctions for speech varieties worldwide. But in fact, there is no objective difference between the two: Any attempt you make to impose that kind of order on reality falls apart in the face of real evidence."[4] This crucial assertion denies any simple hierarchy represented in language trees depicting dialects as subordinate to languages. When introducing students to the concept of dialect, dictionary definitions provide a starting place for understanding dialect: "a regional variety of language distinguished by features of vocabulary, grammar, and pronunciation from other regional varieties and constituting together with them a single language."[5]

FROM THE START

To establish community and a welcoming environment in my AMST undergraduate classes, I introduce the concept of dialect with an interactive map, "22 Maps That Show How Americans Speak English Totally Differently from One Another."[6] The students and I walk through the map together, talking about the lexical variations, for example, different regional vocabulary. Not only does the activity engage the students, but the focus on words is an attempt to prepare students for welcoming diverse experiences as we note that there isn't one correct "American" pronunciation or dialect. While this activity gives students a chance to share their backgrounds, we also address language encounters with humor, something I have learned over the years is essential in the early days of the semester. For example, many students have moved to a new region in the United States and experienced misunderstandings about the name for a soft drink: pop, tonic, coke, or soda. The shared activity is a starting point for acknowledging diverse, but similar, experiences with languages or dialects. According to John Rickford, the author of *Spoken Soul: The Story of Black English*, linguists give "primary attention to speech rather than writing" and they "use the term dialect as a neutral term to refer to the systematic usage of a group of speakers—those in a particular region or social class."[7] My main goal in beginning with this map activity is to establish that, according to Rickford, "everyone speaks a dialect—at least one" and that no one dialect is *better* than the other, unless we assign meaning or preferences to different dialects.[8]

While that claim is true, it may not be the lived experiences of our students. John McWhorter explains in his chapter "It's Complicated . . . The Real Story about Black English Grammar" that trying to convince Americans that Black English and "the speech of Appalachian whites" are not lesser forms of Standard English hasn't worked because of the deficit-based contexts in which these dialects or languages are approached.[9] Using compelling examples, McWhorter argues that to change perceptions, "Black English must be introduced via a collection of ways in which it is *more complex than Standard English,* not less. People respect complexity."[10] While no one dialect or language is necessarily "better," they have different levels of complexity, and all have (or should have) legitimacy.

Years ago, one of my students whose writing assignments demonstrated she was clearly engaged in our course never participated in class discussions. When I privately asked her why, she explained that she was embarrassed to speak because her accent was so strong. She lived in a rural North Georgia town and she felt her accent would affect how other students viewed her. While McWhorter rightly asserts, "Americans have trouble comprehending that *any* vernacular way of speaking is legitimate language,"[11] students in American Studies classes deserve to know that Black English, for example, is a complex and sophisticated language.

One word that provokes student discussion early in the semester is the contraction y'all: the handy fix for the gap in the English language representing the second person plural. Despite the regional alternatives, "youse guys" or "yinz" in various parts of the United States, I explain my preference for "y'all" over the supposedly universal and unfortunately ubiquitous "you guys," which surprises students who hear my Midwestern accent. It's an opportunity to share a personal story about moving to the South and wanting to use "y'all" because it's more inclusive and casual but feeling like that word was not an authentic part of my personal lexicon. In fact, at one point, I felt the need to ask permission from my Southern students to borrow this Southernism for my own. Common student observations about "y'all" include the assertion that it should be used only in certain circumstances or that it sounds "dumb" or "friendly." This initial conversation about "y'all" generates multiple opportunities to discuss meaning, place, identity, class, gender, race, region, and more. Thus, we begin our semester-long inquiry by establishing an inclusive environment that acknowledges both our commonalities and our diversities, while emphasizing the mobility of language across the world, in our own vocabularies, and in American Studies.

Identity and Language

Further complicating this cultural work of dialect is the intricately related concept of identity, the subject of Carla Kaplan's chapter in *Keywords*. Kaplan describes personal and social identities, identity politics, and the tensions between binary identity theories. She argues, "Identity is neither something we possess nor something that defines us, but is instead an *unending* linguistic process of becoming."[12] To understand identity is to be aware of dialect. The fluidity of dialect mirrors the fluidity of identity. Neither is a fixed, singular, easily defined concept. However, students new to American Studies courses who themselves are in the process of becoming may initially understand both concepts as rigid and discrete concepts. Asking students to attend to the "dynamic amalgam" of words, dialect, and their own evolving personal lexicon is a means to involve students in the complex and changing "cultural work" required in American Studies.[13]

At my university, the American Studies program offers an American Identities course, an undergraduate general education course often populated by traditional-age first-year students. The textbook, *American Identities: An Introductory Textbook*, edited by Lois Rudnick, is supplemented with alphabetic, visual, and digital texts and media. Most of the courses are reading- and discussion-based and include a range of writing assignments and presentations. Teaching an introductory general education American Studies course requires an approach that capitalizes on students' prior learning and establishes personal relevance to encourage student motivation and to provoke their curiosity. By taking a linguistic approach through dialect to *American Identities*, I have found that starting small, word by word, leads us to big ideas—the dynamic and complicated cultural and intellectual work that Fishkin and Kaplan describe. My goals, along with the stated course goals, are to engage students in activities that increase their awareness of self and others, to enhance their understanding of the role of language in constructing our personal and social identities, and ultimately to complicate what it means to be "American." To that end, one classroom activity invited students to record new words they encountered and to consider whether they would resist or welcome these words into their own lexicon. Next, they shared the reasoning for their decisions with their peers, which raised questions around language appropriation, insider-outsider language, and more. Subsequently, this reflective word study became the groundwork for a more formal assignment that asked students to observe, research, and analyze community formation and identity (see appendix).

SPOKEN WORDS, EMBODIED LEARNING

Whether the course is an American Studies class that explicitly addresses identity as a theme or an upper-level methods course, students are thinking about identity formation, often through the lens of rhetoric, linguistics, and language. When we examine words, vocabulary acquisition, and a student's personal lexicon, the focus is on speech—a spoken dialect, a willingness to say a word, how we talk—to diverse audiences. But the words we speak cannot be separated from our physical selves or the places we inhabit or the people who surround us. The study of an innovative area of composition studies—"embodied rhetorics"—adds another dimension to how students acquire and use unfamiliar words in American Studies.[14] In her book *Yoga Minds, Writing Bodies*, Christy Wenger leans on D. J. Haraway's research and an extended profile of the author Nancy Mairs to explain an integrated and embodied approach to language. She quotes Nancy Mairs: "I always write, consciously, as a body." Mairs wrote of her experiences "from the seat of a wheelchair" in *Waist-High in the World*.[15] When we write or when we speak, we are speaking in place—from a wheelchair, behind a lectern, in a circle of students. And each one of our students speaks not only as a budding scholar but through their body. I ask the students: What does a new word feel like in their mouth? Do they cringe when they use it, afraid they may be misusing or mispronouncing it? What does it signify when a student tries on a new word and it doesn't "fit" in a particular audience or a specific place? Those questions provoke discussions and raise awareness about the relationship between language and identity. As Wenger explains, embodied rhetorics "embodies self-reflexivity, or the ways the body is an anchor of our self-awareness and can be used as a tool of executing and monitoring this reflexive-reflective attention."[16] If we are to ask our students (and ourselves) to be aware of and engage in the cultural work necessary for American Studies, shouldn't we be asking them to consider the body as "an anchor of our self-awareness" as we consider the relationship between language and identity?[17]

These interwoven concepts of dialect, identity, and embodiment are the frameworks for asking students to pay attention to how we make and use words. This tripartite approach inductively allows students to consider the words they commonly use, the words they are acquiring informally and formally in college, and the influence of their various audiences who may be assigning meaning to how and what they are saying. Because one of "the most important characteristic[s] determining student learning is prior knowledge,"[18] word study builds upon students' current vocabularies while increasing awareness of the significance of language in American studies as they encounter new terms and concepts.

WORDS MATTER; WORDS MOVE

In researching the development of graduate students, Nyquist and Sprague concentrated on graduate student teaching assistants' talk, in which they discovered the students' beliefs and the communities in which they participated. They observe: "Growth is not a matter of unfolding according to some preprogrammed plan; it occurs with other people in conversation and joint action. We borrow each other's words and phrases. In time they become our own, and with them ideas and beliefs from the social world become internalized, and then become part of our action and identity."[19] Similar to graduate students, undergraduates are borrowing and reconstructing language as they borrow words, phrases, ideas, and beliefs that transform their identities. Calling attention to students' current word usage and asking them to intentionally consider what words they choose to acquire in their own personal lexicon as student-scholars invites them to interrogate the "struggles and inequalities hidden under the established order" of academic discourse.[20] As they acquire new vocabularies, they become aware of discourses that Michel de Certeau describes as "a practice of the order constructed by others" to find a "space for maneuvers of unequal forces."[21] In other words, they become more conscious of their language practices and how they might "subvert ascriptions [that] are placed onto individuals and groups by others."[22]

But learning academic language is not the only new linguistic and self-making activity students do in college. First-year college students also find this "space for maneuvers" as prolific creators of slang phrases that play with the "established order" on college campuses.[23] In her book, *Slang & Sociability: In-Group Language among College Students*, Connie Eble states, "It is also possible that recent generations of college students are creating, appropriating, and using more slang than their counterparts did a century ago."[24] She illustrates how slang is not a marginalized form of the language but a way students create community through language use. Eble avers, "College students put more of their time and youthful spiritedness in figuring out who they are in relationship to others . . . and what they will and will not tolerate than in trying to figure out their textbooks, lectures, and professors."[25] Building upon this undergraduate propensity for language formation is one way of establishing common ground in the American Studies classroom in preparation for some of the difficult conversations that emerge during the semester.

READINGS AND DISCUSSIONS

As in most undergraduate classes, one challenge is helping students read more carefully and critically. When reading a multicultural text in an American Studies class, students often encounter terms, language, or concepts that are unfamiliar and challenging. In this course, students read the introduction and the first chapter from Gloria Anzaldúa's multigenre *Borderlands/La Frontera*.[26] In the past, I found that the discussions about this text were too superficial and that I failed to interest students in this seminal text. In my view, students did not satisfactorily grapple with the complexity of Anzaldúa's style or arguments, and I was seeking a better way to help students encounter her multilingual text, walk around in it, and discover they were surrounded by an intoxicating landscape. For homework in an honors AMST course, I asked students to identify and make a list of unfamiliar words, locate definitions, and decide which words or terms they would like to claim for their own personal lexicon, that is, words they routinely and comfortably use, as a means to get them to connect to the reading.

In our next meeting, students carried the class discussion. Each student offered their understanding of the words selected from Anzaldúa's *Borderlands*. I prompted them: What do the words mean to the author? To them? Please explain their rationale for selecting specific words to add to their lexicon, and most importantly, explore how this act connects to the history and themes in the reading. This approach was intended "to clear conceptual space" for students to find their own way into the reading.[27] This inductive and learner-centered approach to a reading discussion opened up Anzaldúa's text in ways I had not imagined. The discussion moved organically from one student to another, since often their borrowed words or terms were similar to another student's selection. Students analyzed and discussed the text to try to negotiate their understandings of Anzaldúa's concepts. One of the bilingual students from South America took the lead, since she understood the text in a way that monolingual students did not. She read aloud some of the passages in Spanish with a fluency and beauty that caught everyone's attention. And together with her English-speaking classmates, they puzzled out the meanings of some of Anzaldua's poetry, prose, and claims. In hindsight, however, I missed the most important step—metacognition—asking students to reflect upon this student-led, communal, and multilingual construction of the text.

Teachers of American Studies have their own unique goals and assignments when reading *Borderlands*, but letting the students lead the way one word at a time into this encounter with a dense, multilingual text is an approach that aligns with Anzaldúa's message of language as resistance to existing systems of power or oppression—and perhaps the "tyranny" of instructor-led reading discussions. In fact, were I to use this approach to teach *Borderlands/La Frontera: The New Mestiza* again, we would begin with the chapter "How to Tame a Wild Tongue," which more explicitly addresses the fluidity of language, power, borders, and identity. We discussed some of the goals for our reading discussion: to call their attention to language as a form of resistance, meaning making, and the construction of personal and collective identities. Asking students to decide whether to add Anzaldúa's terminology to their own personal lexicon complicates the notion of borrowing (or appropriating) the language and culture of others and invites them to think about the relationship between their dialect and identity. This work resonates with the ideas of Mooney and Evans in their book *Language, Society, and Power: An Introduction*. They write:

> The value of exploring this linguistic diversity, the way languages divide the world differently, is that it reminds us that linguistic signs are neither natural nor stable. . . . We need to remember that our own division of reality is worth consideration. In a sense, we need to treat our own language as a foreign language, and examine the relationships between signs. In doing so, we can come to an appreciation of the representation of reality that language performs.[28]

POPULAR CULTURE ANALYSIS AND POLITICAL CORRECTNESS

Taking a linguistic approach to an American Studies class also works well when bringing in current debates in popular culture, where much of the discussion of language revolves around criticisms of "political correctness" or "language policing." My approach to the relationship between language and identity helps explain the larger issues behind battles over words. For example, the controversy over author Chimimanda Adichie's comments about transgender women highlighted the tension between language and identity:

> Had I said, "a cis woman is a cis woman, and a trans woman is a trans woman," I don't think I would get all the crap that I'm getting, but that's actually really what I was saying. But because "cis" is not a part of my vocabulary—it just isn't—it really becomes about language and the reason I find that troubling is to insist that you have to speak in a certain way and use certain expressions, otherwise we cannot have a conversation, can close up debate. And if we can't have conversations, we can't have progress.[29]

While Adichie attributes the "transgender row" to a dispute about "language orthodoxy," many still disagree. As one of my colleagues points out: "I think it's more than words, which is where she took it—it has to do with her wanting to say that transwomen and cis women have different experiences, and that transwomen once experienced male privilege. This is something that many trans activists find to be an unacceptable idea entirely."[30]

Adichie's comments provide the basis for a complicated conversation about gender, language, lived experiences, and "political correctness" in American discourse or what might be considered as a type of language reform. Our students often use the term "political correctness" freely and sometimes with disdain, so to circumvent their resistance, I ask students to consider the mobility of vocabulary about gender. We research organizational statements about gender equality and newspaper-style books. After these discussions about gender and language, it's helpful to measure student understandings and perspectives via a "minute paper," a brief anonymous response to a question prompt. Gathering their responses and reporting back to the students in the following class period on any patterns, inaccuracies, or insights that emerged in their feedback gives voice to those who may have been reluctant to participate in the class discussion.

ARTIFACT NARRATIVE ASSIGNMENT AND REFLECTION

I also incorporate a focus on word study and development of a personal lexicon into my artifact narrative assignment. Different iterations of this assignment are popular in our American Studies general education classes. I take a metonymic approach to the artifact narrative, in which the artifact represents both a personal and a public meaning, so as to encourage students to research the significance of the artifact to the writer and to the culture at large. Examples might include a wedding ring, a concert pin, a photograph, a letter, and more. Students are asked to identify artifacts that act as an entry point to recovering their memories and telling their individual, family, or American stories. This assignment also asks that they locate a personal artifact that is both meaningful to and representative of them and American culture and history. Through prewriting activities, reading discussions, peer feedback, and research, students compose a narrative essay that explores the personal and public relevance of their artifact within the context of American identities. As students begin their personal narratives, I ask them to pay attention to their word choices and to be willing to adapt academic vocabulary into their developing personal lexicon. When they write about the intersections between the personal and the public, they must seek words to represent both spheres, engaging and experimenting in the cultural work Fishkin describes.

Nash explains the model of the scholarly personal narrative, or SPN: "The SPN becomes a sustained exploration of one's own narrative experience of a particular question or problem that has broader social significance. . . . Also the story you tell is constantly compared to relevant theory that confirms and challenges your narrative."[31] This narrative strategy has been used at the graduate level, but it is also relevant for first-year undergraduate students, and the creation of a growing lexicon of academic terms is central to the students' incorporation of theory into the narrative of personal experience. In this way, like the *Borderlands* activity, the artifact assignment encourages students to build upon their familiar vocabulary while integrating new concepts, language/s, and themes from their readings in American Studies.

❖ ❖ ❖

The most productive way to encourage students to fully realize the tensions and links between these concepts of dialect, identity, or "American" is to prompt them to critically reflect often and deeply about their learning. Asking students to examine their underlying assumptions, articulate challenging ideas, and intentionally develop their personal lexicon is best achieved when teachers model it. Stephen Brookfield states, "When it comes to students' learning how to practice this skill it seems they constantly look to us to see what the process looks like. . . . So before we ask students to unearth and research their assumptions, we must show how we're attempting to do the same thing."[32] Being transparent about my own mistaken assumptions or language choices and encouraging students to do so as well is a way to model how we learn about ourselves, others, and American Studies. If there is anything I have learned from my students, it is to plan opportunities for critical reflection throughout the semester not only to reinforce learning but also to encourage students to embrace Kaplan's description of identity as "an *unending* linguistic process of becoming."[33] This mutable and empowering conceptualization of identity calls for intentional and frequent reflection to inspire future actions or activism by American Studies teachers and students alike.

APPENDIX: AMST 1102—ASSIGNMENT TWO

American Communities Summary and Report (100 points/20% of grade)

"Identity formation is a lifelong endeavor that includes discovery of the new, recovery of the old, forgotten, or appropriated, and synthesis of the old and new" (Rudnick 10).

I. DESCRIPTION

For Assignment Two, you will identify an existing community on our KSU campus and **attend one of their events, activities, or exhibits** (e.g., art galleries, museums, or public art). An event might be a lecture, performance, film night, conference, protest, presentation, meeting, discussion, and more. The community you choose might be a student group, an academic department event, an interest group, or campus-community collaboration. The community might be formally created, sanctioned by the university, or organically formed at KSU. Your report essay might include the community that sponsors the event or the community that is the subject of their event. It does not have to include both communities.

Keep in mind that our inquiry is driven by a curiosity about a community formation, word study, and identity. Pay attention to how language functions to create, define, or reimagine a community. What languages, dialects, or terminology do community insiders share?

II. GUIDING QUESTIONS

You may use the following divisions to organize your report essay.

A. *General Background*

1. What type of community or community-sponsored event/exhibit is this?
2. How did it form, whom does it serve, and what is its purpose?
3. What are the rituals, practices, patterns, or languages that establish and sustain this community?

B. *Community and American Identity*

1. In what ways does this community demonstrate "American" values, beliefs, structures, or identity/ies?
2. How is this community connected or related to other "American" communities?
3. How do the concepts in our readings apply to this community and its practices?

C. *Individual and Group Identity*

1. What is your relationship to this community?
2. How would you define or describe this community?
3. What were your perceptions before attending the event/exhibit?
4. How did your understanding of this community expand or deepen after observing, attending, or researching it?
5. How does your "American" identity resist or affirm, conflict or align with, this community? What is the vernacular, slang, or insider terminology of this community?
6. What are some of the tensions between their language, beliefs, values, or knowledge and yours?
7. What questions remain?

III. REQUIREMENTS

Four–five pages, 11–12 pt. font. Hard copy due at the beginning of class.

- Participate in all process activities.
- Informal classroom presentation.
- Connect community observation with concepts from the readings.
- Explicitly address "American Identity" and our focus on language.
- Integrate at least 5 sources (one of which is the observation). The additional 4 sources should be from our course readings.
- Optional, but encouraged: You may include an image/images or additional research in your report essay.

IV. RESOURCES

See separate handout for a list of possible events or exhibits to get you started.

V. RUBRIC:

Grade Summary (Rubric): 100 points total

Content: This report essay describes an "American" community roundly from many angles, noting the writer's relationship to this community or its members. The report includes a discussion of how this community is "American" and what features contribute to its collective identity. This report addresses some of the essential questions posed about "American" community formation included in this assignment. Independent thinking is valued. 40 points/________.

Outside sources: The report essay includes information from observations of the community event, connections to concepts in the course readings, and supplementary independent research (optional). 30 points/__________.

Includes 5 supplementary sources total, which includes the observation. You may embed original images as well, e.g., photographs.

Organization: Clear summary of the event, analysis of the community event, and discussion of the writer's relationship to the community related to identity. Material is in the most effective order. Relevant integration of outside sources. 10 points/__________.

Editing/proofreading/documentation: 10 points/___________.

MLA documentation. Carefully arranged, edited, and proofread.

Participation: 10 points/_________.

Participate fully in all activities involved in developing this paper.

Points Available: 100 **Points Earned: ______/100**

NOTES

1. Shelley Fisher Fishkin, "Dialect," in *Keywords for American Cultural Studies*, ed. Bruce Burgett and Glenn Hendler (New York: New York University Press, 2010), 81.

2. Fishkin, "Dialect," 81.

3. Bruce Burgett and Glenn Hendler, "Introduction," in *Keywords for American Cultural Studies*, 6.

4. John H. McWhorter, "What's a Language, Anyway?," *Atlantic*, January 19, 2016, https://www.theatlantic.com/international/archive/2016/01/difference-between-language-dialect/424704/.

5. Merriam-Webster.com, s.v. dialect.

6. Walter Hickey, "22 Maps That Show How Americans Speak English Totally Differently from One Another," *Business Insider*, June 5, 2013, https://www.businessinsider.com/22-maps-that-show-the-deepest-linguistic-conflicts-in-america-2013-6.

7. John R. Rickford, "How Linguists Approach the Study of Language and Dialect," 1, in "[Rickford's] Papers Available Online," Stanford University, accessed June 6, 2017, http://web.stanford.edu/~rickford/papers/.

8. Rickford, "How Linguists Approach," 1.

9. John H. McWhorter, *Talking Back, Talking Black* (New York: Bellevue Literary, 2017), 27.

10. McWhorter, *Talking Back*, 36, 37.

11. John H. McWhorter, quoted in Vinson Cunningham, "The Case for Black English," *New Yorker*, May 15, 2017, https://www.newyorker.com/magazine/2017/05/15/the-case-for-black-english.

12. Carla Kaplan, "Identity," in *Keywords for American Cultural Studies*, 125.

13. Fishkin, "Dialect," 81.

14. Christy Wenger, *Yoga Minds, Writing Bodies: Contemplative Writing Pedagogy* (Anderson, SC: Parlor, 2015), 33.

15. Wenger, *Yoga Minds*, 34.

16. Wenger, 35.

17. Wenger, 35.

18. Marilla D. Svinicki and Wilbert J. McKeachie, *McKeachie's Teaching Tips: Strategies, Research, and Theory for College and University Teachers*, 14th ed. (Belmont, CA: Wadsworth, Cengage Learning, 2014), 24.

19. Jody Nyquist and Jo Sprague, "Thinking Developmentally about TAs," in *The Professional Development of Graduate Teaching Assistants*, ed. Michele Marincovick, and Jack Prostko, and Frederic Stout (Boston: Stanford University, 1998), 68.

20. Michel de Certeau, *The Practice of Everyday Life* (Berkeley: University of California Press, 1984), 18.

21. Certeau, *The Practice of Everyday Life*, 18.

22. Kaplan, "Identity," 126.

23. Kaplan, 126.

24. Connie Eble, *Slang and Sociability: In-group Language among College Students* (Chapel Hill: University of North Carolina Press, 1996), 141, consulted online.

25. Eble, *Slang and Sociability*, 141.

26. Gloria Anzaldúa, *Borderlands/ La Frontera: The New Mestiza*, 2nd ed. (Minneapolis: Aunt Lute, 1999).

27. Burgett and Hendler, "Introduction," 6.

28. Annabelle Mooney and Betsey Evans, *Language, Society and Power: An Introduction*, 4th ed. (New York: Routledge, 2011), 39.

29. David Smith, "Chimamanda Ngozi Adichie on Transgender Row: 'I Have Nothing to Apologise For,'" *Guardian*, last modified March 21, 2017, https://www.theguardian.com/books/2017/mar/21/chimamanda-ngozi-adichie-nothing-to-apologise-for-transgender-women.

30. Rebecca Hill, email message to author, June 21, 2017.

31. Stephen D. Brookfield, *Becoming a Critically Reflective Teacher*, 2nd ed. (San Francisco: Jossey-Bass, 2017), 181.

32. Brookfield, *Becoming a Critically Reflective Teacher*, 88.

33. Kaplan, "Identity," 125.

8

Our "Positive Obsession"

Teaching Interdisciplinary American Studies through Octavia Butler's Life and Work

SARAH HENTGES

Octavia Butler's work was made for American Studies. Her speculative fiction, science fiction, dystopia, and essays provide a critical interrogation of American culture, power, identity, ideology, politics, institutions, and communities. Her characters—primarily Black women at the center of a diverse cast of characters—embody generations of America's oppressed. An American success story and a humble hero, Butler continues to inspire activists, writers, students, teachers, and diverse readers more than a decade after her death.[1] Here, I illuminate the myriad ways that Butler's work can be used in a variety of classrooms—in composition courses and in American literature survey courses as well as in interdisciplinary American Studies and women's and gender studies courses—to teach American Studies. Butler's work provides a palatable example of multicultural America, especially in Maine, where many of my white students have not even met a Black person before they go to college, and in Denmark, where I found that Southern Black culture was the focus of African American literature and culture. Butler's work challenges the definitions of "diversity" that most institutions embrace and calls for a critical, intersectional approach to "diversity" that goes beyond inclusion of "multicultural" characters. As Collins and Bilge argue, "intersectionality is a way of understanding the complexity in the world, in people, and in human experience." Butler's work helps to illuminate this complexity, and students can use intersectionality, for instance, as an "analytical tool to solve problems that they or others around them face."[2]

In short, Octavia Butler's work models American Studies' critical interdisciplinarity and inspires a development of oppositional consciousness that speaks to American culture and politics past, present, and future. As Beth Barila notes, "in order to shift the dominant oppressive paradigm, the voices on the margin need to provide the lens—either by centering them or by disrupting the entire center/margin paradigm." This centering and disruption are at the heart of American Studies. Further, she argues, "The kind of oppositional consciousness . . . that can occur when dominant voices are decentered and marginalized perspectives are featured, offers us a critical literacy into how power works and strategies for how to *respond rather than react*."[3] Through Butler's speculative fiction, students begin to see the ways in which power operates and often feel empowered to work toward social justice.

My students know that I am obsessed with Octavia Butler. It isn't difficult to figure out. When we discuss these works, I share my passion with my students. We read her short essay, originally published in *Essence Magazine*, where Butler writes about the driving and defining idea of "positive obsession." She explains, "I saw positive obsession as a way of aiming yourself, your life, at your chosen target. Decide what you want. Aim high. Go for it."[4] Positive obsession is about more than a goal and hard work; it's the kind of boundless passion that many of us devote to our life's work. Butler writes: "I couldn't stop. Positive obsession is about not being able to stop just because you're afraid and full of doubts. Positive obsession is dangerous. It's about not being able to stop at all."[5] Many of my students have hard lives, and they have to take a kind of "positive obsession" approach to their education. Their lives resemble some of the struggles that mark dystopic fiction—in and beyond Butler's stories. My students deal with poverty, hunger, homelessness, absent parents, mental and physical illness, addiction, abuse, and more. Many are first-generation college students, single parents, working parents, caregivers to their ailing parents. Students identify with Butler's life and work as well as with the worlds she creates.

I teach Butler's work like she lived and wrote—with a "positive obsession." My status as a fan of Octavia Butler's work stems from a love of her stories but also of her body of work and its cultural value. I am a fan because Butler's body of work centers women—and Black women, specifically—in the world of science fiction, a space where they are often absent. I am a fan because everything I love about American Studies—namely, the way in which it challenges the "truths" of our country—is reflected in Butler's stories. Even if students love science fiction, few have ever read Butler and some have not even heard of her. Making Butler worthy of fandom makes students pay attention. I gush my love of Butler all over my students, but she can hardly be considered a "single author" in the context of any classroom or American Studies program. Butler is a touchstone, a figurehead, a conduit. She connects the past, present, and future, and she makes connections to other authors, movements, ideas, and contexts.

Since Butler is a writer with big ideas, her stories often span several books, making her work difficult to incorporate. Octavia Butler's collection of short stories *Bloodchild and Other Stories* is useful since the stories are short and accessible. Not only does it contain several diverse short stories, but it also includes two essays about writing, and each story includes an afterword that provides further context. The other books I use regularly in classes are Butler's dystopian Parables series: *Parable of the Sower* and *Parable of the Talents*. Both can be used as stand-alone texts, but together they are more powerful. In fact, most of Butler's books could be taught as stand-alone books. For instance, *Wild Seed* is an interesting study of gender and power dynamics as well as early American settlement, *Mind of My Mind* provides a context for considering mental illness and urban communities, and *Kindred* provides contexts for discussing the messy realities of slavery. Finally, Butler's work could certainly be taught as a single-author course where students not only would have the opportunity to read a significant portion of Butler's original texts but also could consider the rich body of theory and praxis that the work has inspired.[6]

In all of my classes, students are required to "respond rather than react" by completing "action" projects that take ideas from class into the world beyond the classroom. Students produce art projects, write creatively, and create social justice initiatives inspired by Butler's work. Further, since many of my students want to be writers, Butler's idea of positive obsession is also an inspiring formula regarding how to become a writer. We read what she writes about being a writer, and students can see an example of someone who beat the odds.

INTERDISCIPLINARY AMERICAN STUDIES IN ENGLISH CLASSROOMS

Because Butler's work is fiction—short stories and novels—English classrooms are the most logical spaces for teaching Octavia Butler, and I have used pieces of Butler's work in English composition classes, American literature survey courses, and a literature course about young adult dystopia. In my American literature survey course, *Bloodchild* is the last book that we read in our "since 1900" course. Chronologically, Butler's work does not fit at the end. However, this placement allows us to think about the future of American literature while it asks us to also think about the future of America. Through the story "Speech Sounds," we consider language and communication. Through the story's characters, we consider the power of literacy and the ways in which our society would be impacted if language became inaccessible to the majority of the population. Through "The Morning, the Evening, and the Night" we consider power, gender, disease, and bioethics. I ask students to consider Butler's life and work through the lens of power and privilege, and we revisit conversations about Black and ethnic American writers as a part of the bigger picture of American literature. Butler's work extends our discussions of the American canon as narrow and whitewashed as well as our discussions of oppositional ideas and authors that disrupt this canon; it gives us hope for a different, more diverse future.

Even in these disciplinary spaces, interdisciplinary American Studies approaches are necessary to more fully understand any idea or piece of literature. This can be particularly powerful in composition courses, where students are learning rhetorical strategies that cross disciplines. In my ENG 101: College Writing classroom I used "The Morning, the Evening, and the Night" as an example of writing for the humanities related to our annual academic theme of bioethics. This bioethics theme at my university lent itself to talking about science, ethics, business, and other topics that are less often found in the humanities, and Butler's stories brought opportunities to make sense of complex ideas in relation to other kinds of texts. Students began to learn the value of interdisciplinary American Studies approaches to textual analysis. Initially, however, some students did not realize that they were reading fiction. A few were frightened by the "new" disease they were reading about and were relieved to find out that what they read was "just a story." This gave us the opportunity to also discuss the power of fiction and how fiction might also blur the lines of reality. What was it about this story that made it so believable?

While ENG 101 centers on rhetorical strategies, using Butler's work also provides a means to introduce critical race theory, bringing American Studies lenses into English composition. For one in-class group assignment, I asked students to compare and contrast writing from several different disciplinary approaches in order to better understand style and expectations as well as the conventions of argument that we had been practicing. Rebecca Skloot's *The Immortal Life of Henrietta Lacks* (the official book related to our academic theme) opened the door for thinking about race and privilege and storytelling, as well as science writing and popular journalistic writing. An article by Patricia A. King, "Race and Bioethics in the United States," gave a social science perspective and cultural critique as well as some historical context through the Tuskegee experiments. And Butler's story gave an example of creative writing and a context for considering the possible impacts of the realities that Skloot and King report and reflect on. The compendium of these works provided students with the opportunity to make connections and unpack, for instance, power and privilege. After this brief introduction to American Studies, American culture and history cannot be viewed in the same way.

After comparing and contrasting the writing styles and the ways in which each author dealt with bioethics, students better understood the different disciplinary modes of writing and interdisciplinary American Studies approaches. They were then assigned to write something that was different than the standard "college essay"—a blog, a letter, a short story, a poem, a piece of art (image + text)—with the only requirement being to use the bioethics theme and to write a short reflection on the text they produced. One student created a painting that illuminated the issues with reproductive policies and reflected the darkness of Butler's work. Another student wrote a stellar essay about transhumanism. I collected some of the best bioethics-themed work of students in my English and American Studies classes and created a bioethics zine to highlight this work. The five-by-seven booklet containing student art and writing was distributed on campus and shared with students' family and friends. This assignment not only opened students' minds to interdisciplinary American Studies approaches to topics like bioethics, but it also introduced them to Octavia Butler's work. It inspired them to try their own expression. It is this kind of inspiration from Butler—pursuing their own positive obsessions—that most resonates.

BIRTHING AMERICAN STUDIES FUTURES THROUGH BUTLER'S PROGENY

My "positive obsession" with Butler also led me to develop an online Girls on Fire: Gender, Culture, and Justice in YA Dystopia course that was cross-listed as American Studies, English, and women's and gender studies. I also taught this as a graduate-level course in Denmark. In the book that this class inspired, *Girls on Fire: Transformational Heroines in Young Adult Dystopian Literature,* I position Butler as the foremother of YA Dystopia and Lauren Olamina as the original Girl on Fire. Octavia Butler—through her body of work generally and her character of Lauren Olamina specifically—opened the door for women writers to create a body of YA dystopia with female protagonists that speaks to the challenges of the American present and the problems and possibilities inherent in our whitewashed American futures. The American conditions of dystopia—climate change, violence, ethnic/racial oppression, corruption—can be fully understood only through an interdisciplinary American Studies lens. In dystopia, these conditions are a realistic extension of our current world and reveal the textures of oppression and liberation that have shaped the United States. Butler's connections between the past, present, and future also give a richer template for dystopia as intersectional.

While Butler's work is not YA, *Parable of the Sower* focuses on fifteen-year-old Lauren Olamina as she comes of age and becomes a leader. This age is close to adulthood but also leaves room for growth. Lauren also navigates The Pox—conditions created by a confluence of social, political, and environmental catastrophes. She is a girl of color who creates a kind of religion and a following of people who work with her toward a better future. This is generally the description of every YA dystopia book, minus the religion and color. Butler's work provides a lens for YA dystopia that requires us to critically consider race, class, gender, sexuality, and ability in even the most whitewashed texts and to hold authors, characters, publishers, critics, and fans accountable to versions of the future that replicate narrow definitions of the present. Thus, students were able to see the ambiguous (assumed white) identities of several characters and speculate on the author's decision to obscure racialized characters. For instance, several popular and scholarly articles consider *The Hunger Games'* protagonist, Katniss, as a girl of color. Because we had already considered race in the context of an overtly Black protagonist, students were less likely to consider Katniss as white and more willing to entertain possibilities of her otherness.

Students not only were able to reflect upon choices made by authors and the business of publishing, they also had to confront their own biases. In the second-whitest state in the nation, as well as in Denmark, many students read Lauren Olamina as white. We had robust discussions about how Butler presents her character and why and how students misread her race, even when they had a book that featured a girl of color on the cover. Some students assumed that the picture on the cover was of a different character. Some thought that Butler was being subtle about the character's race in the first part of the novel in order to draw readers in. Some students realized that they read Lauren Olamina as white because they are white and they are enacting their white privilege in their reading. As a result, they shifted their reading lens. And once students learned more about Octavia Butler, they had to rethink the novel and its place in our course. Students were able to recognize how fundamental Butler's work is to a critical understanding of the YA books and female protagonists that we read through the lens of Lauren Olamina.

With a conscious consideration of race and intersectional identity begun through Butler's book, when students were asked to make connections with current events, several of them reflected on the struggles over indigenous rights and the Dakota Pipeline protests through books like *Shadows Cast by Stars*. When we focused more explicitly on gender and sexuality, they critiqued social constructions of race and gender—and the possibilities of polyamorous love—through books like *The Summer Prince*. When we turned our attention to the environment (and our academic theme of climate change) they considered the impact of environmental racism and catastrophe through *Orleans*.[7] In all of these books, the protagonist is a girl of color, and our foundation in Butler's work helped students to be able to "respond rather than react." Considering a variety of YA dystopia texts, students also put ideas into action through projects and reflected on the impact they were able to make in their worlds. They became Girls on Fire.[8] For instance, one student created an activist art project that she submitted to an art contest in Detroit. With some inspiration from the idea of Butler's fictional Earthseed, she designed and assembled a variety of seed packets with quotes from the Hunger Games. In these packets were a variety of seeds so that no matter where they were scattered, something would grow. Another student created a series of paintings that she saw as a way of processing her trauma and remaking herself as a Girl on Fire.

OPPOSITIONAL INTERDISCIPLINARY AMERICAN STUDIES

When working with Butler's texts, students are engaged, connected, and empowered. In no other class was this more true than in an experimental "cluster" course that I team-taught with two other faculty members and one group of fourteen students. My part of this course was Culture, Consciousness, and Community, and after reading a variety of theories on these topics, we applied what we had learned by considering *Parable of the Talents*. Students in this class had not read *Parable of the Sower*; I chose to use *Talents* not only because we could consider only one novel in our reading load, but also because this second book more explicitly engages with ideas of culture, consciousness, and community as well as contemporary political trends toward fascism and religious zealotry. For instance, we read several pieces considering intentional communities, and Olamina builds two kinds of intentional communities—the physical community of Earthseed as well as the "transcendent community" that defies physical place.[9] Students discussed these versions of community in relation to the physical and virtual communities we created in our class.[10]

Students were also able to better understand racial politics in, and beyond, Maine. For instance, despite the lack of racial diversity in Maine, most students find that while Butler is writing about race, she is also writing about the diverse whole of America. She does not rely on simple stereotypes; instead, she paints complex characters. In both Parable books, Olamina describes the diversity of her group of nascent Earthseed followers and celebrates the fact that her group is so mixed. One of my students insisted that calling his family member "mixed" was not a racist sentiment; it was simply the reality of being both Black and white. We discussed the ways in which an understanding of race has evolved in the United States and how the ways we understand race in Maine are shaped by the demographics of our state.

In addition to illuminating race, Butler also speaks directly to the challenges that Olamina faces as a girl and a woman in a violent society. For all of my female students, this is a reality they also face. At one point in each of the Parables books, Olamina disguises herself as a man in order to be safer and more respected. Students were able to consider the dangers of being a Black woman under threat of the corrupt and failing power structure, present and future. Through these discussions, they were also better able to understand their own oppression as well as their relative privilege. Students also had plenty of opportunities to think about America as bigger than their little corner of Maine, but their economic struggles resonated with the characters who struggled to survive in the future. For instance, in Maine, many students live in the contrast between "Vacationland" and rural poverty. Food insecurity, for instance, is a documented problem for the majority of our students. In order to survive impoverished winters, many of them find employment catering to the rich who flock to Maine during the summer. Butler's work helps to bring intersectional awareness to our conversations about students' identities and lives as well as the larger structures and institutions of America.

In my cluster course students had even more opportunity to explore racial and cultural difference. We considered this book not only after reading a ton of theory, but also after taking a class trip to Nicaragua, where students learned more about the global politics of aid, water, and food as well as the particular dynamics of revolution and American politics in Nicaragua. The comparative power of American Studies was woven through a variety of theories and activities. Through service work, students directly served a population that was already "making do" with much less than we have in the United States.[11] They made connections with many of the people in Nicaragua while they learned about another language and culture. One student was invited to share his indigenous American traditions of drumming and chanting with a group of Nicaraguan musicians whose indigenous traditions, we learned, are also American. When the musicians called, "*Viva America,*" we remembered that America is bigger than the country we are privileged to live in.

Reading *Parable of the Talents* in this course was an exercise in revolution. Students brought what they had learned in theory and action to our conversations of this dark novel. And suddenly, a new philosophy/religion/belief system like Earthseed seemed possible. A new America seemed possible. Not only could they see the need for multifaceted change, they could also see many possible ways to make change happen. And they knew that they were part of what Robin D. G. Kelley calls the "new wretched"—the multicultural working classes that comprise America's oppressed.[12] Students created a toolbox (from construction paper and markers) of the American Studies theories and methods that they had learned about and displayed their work—the toolbox, photo/essay/memoir books, presentations, and art projects—at a public exhibit. The multidimensional power that students found in American Studies was made more real through Butler's fiction.[13]

One student in this cluster class had a very difficult time with *Parable of the Talents*. As a survivor of a cult, she was particularly struck by the cultish aspects of Olamina's vision and behavior. She had seen these tactics in action, and she wondered whether it mattered if the message is "God is change" (the premise of Olamina's Earthseed) or "God is love" (as the cult of her youth claimed). We had some heated debates. It wasn't until she read *Parable of the Sower* in my cultural criticism and theory class that she began to be able to reconcile the "Shaper" Olamina of *Parables* with the adolescent Lauren Olamina of *Sower*. She was able to see the context of family and culture that made Olamina who she was, and she tacitly agreed that while Olamina's methods were similar to many cult leaders', there was a difference between Olamina's manipulations in her fictional context and those of infamous cult leaders in our real world.

Being able to continue our discussion of Butler's work over the course of several American Studies classes, with several overlapping students, was a luxury at a university that offers only a minor in American Studies and a self-designed interdisciplinary major. Because of limitations of time and budget, I have not been able to replicate the experience of these clustered courses. Several students cite this experience as transformational, and they changed or honed their major course of study as a result of this curricular experience. One continued on to a PhD in American Cultural Studies, one to law school, and one into a master's degree in art therapy. All of these students see American Studies as being responsible for developing their oppositional consciousness and enabling them to "respond rather than react."

Butler's work provides a model for a plethora of ideas and theories from American Studies, and students can talk about the issues of the present through the lens of the future. What I have not detailed here—because I have yet to have the opportunity to teach it—is the possibility and potential of teaching an American Studies course focused exclusively on Octavia Butler's work. Years ago, I taught a course about Maya Angelou, and students flocked to this course. They were fans of this inspirational figure and jumped at the opportunity to dig deeper. One student who signed up for this course, and swiftly dropped it once he saw my syllabus, told me that he thought this was going to be a "read and write about it course." He had no interest in the projects (like writing a children's book or creating and writing about a favorite dish to share at a Welcome Table potluck) or the contextualization of Angelou's work through Black history or feminism. An Octavia Butler course would have similar challenges, since her novels connect to patterns of historical oppression as well as contemporary politics. In the course's asking students to "respond rather than react," action projects and contemporary connections would be foundational. Further, Butler does not have the same kind of fan base as Maya Angelou. However, teaching Butler through interdisciplinary American Studies makes fans.

Teaching Octavia Butler also makes conscious citizens, engaged writers, and social justice warriors. In a course focused on Butler's rich body of work, students would consider not only the few works that I outline here but also her Patternmaster fantasy/science fiction series and her Xenogenesis series, which includes an alien species with a third gender. Butler's novels and short stories span dystopia, speculative fiction, science fiction, and fantasy, and we could consider the connections between slavery past and present in *Kindred,* the subversion of vampire myths in *Bloodchild,* and the possibilities of life on other planets in *Survivor.* Alone, these works provide more than enough material to comprise an American Studies course. But more than these fictional works, a course on Butler would include the works that her fiction has inspired, such as *Octavia's Brood: Science Fiction from Social Justice Movements,* a collection of fiction written by social justice activists, and *Emergent Strategy: Shaping Change, Changing Worlds,* a "radical self-help, society-help, and planet-help" book inspired by Octavia Butler's ideas about change. In addition to analysis, students could write creatively, filling in the holes left by Butler's untimely death or imagining alternate endings. Students could imagine how these works could be adapted for stage or screen and what would be lost and gained in these alternative formats. Students could write their own theories of change and apply the interdisciplinary, intersectional theories they learn about to real-world problems. They could develop their own positive obsessions, in and out of academia.

Teaching interdisciplinary, intersectional American Studies is a challenge that is aided by the richness of Butler's work. The power of the stories, the power of the ideas behind her stories, the hope that undergirds each story, speaks to students and challenges them to see their lives and their educations in empowering ways. Oppositional consciousness grows from Butler's ideas through discussion and writing, as well as action and application projects. Students are inspired by what Butler achieved in her life as well as the ideas that she plays with in her texts. My "positive obsession" influences students' passions, and Butler's work raises consciousness in ways that other works cannot. In turn, Butler's works give American Studies pedagogy a resonance of theory in action—American Studies theory plays out through the power of stories that speak to the past and present as well as to the future.

NOTES

1. For instance, see adrienne maree brown and Walidah Imarisha, *Octavia's Brood: Science Fiction Stories from Social Justice Movements* (Chico, CA: AK, 2015).

2. Patricia Hill Collins and Sirma Bilge, *Intersectionality*, Key Concepts series (Cambridge: Polity, 2016), 25, 2.

3. Beth Barila, "Introduction: What's the Link between Feminism and Yoga?," in *Yoga, the Body, and Embodied Social Change: An Intersectional Feminist Analysis*, ed. Beth Berila, Melanie Klein, and Chelsea Jackson Roberts (Lanham, MD: Lexington, 2016), 5, my emphasis.

4. Octavia E. Butler, *Bloodchild and Other Stories* (New York: Seven Stories, 1996), 129.

5. Butler, *Bloodchild*, 133.

6. In my coedited book, *Teaching Girls on Fire: Essays on Dystopian Young Adult Literature in the Classroom*, Bryan Yazell writes about teaching a course devoted to the works of Octavia Butler.

7. Catherine Knutsson, *Shadows Cast by Stars* (New York: Atheneum, 2012); Alaya Dawn Johnson, *The Summer Prince* (New York: Levine-Scholastic, 2013); Sherri L. Smith, *Orleans* (New York: Penguin, 2013).

8. I detail my curriculum and pedagogy in my article in SIGNAL. I also more extensively develop approaches to teaching YA dystopia in my book *Girls on Fire*, which includes a number of quotes from students' work. Both pieces include charts that detail assignments and other key aspects from young adult dystopian texts. Sarah Hentges, "This Class Is on Fire! (and Online): Teaching YA Dystopia and the Girl on Fire Through Themes, Contexts, and Action," *SIGNAL Journal* 39, no. 1 (Fall 2015/Winter 2016): 41–53, and *Girls on Fire: Transformative Heroines in Young Adult Dystopian Fiction* (Jefferson, NC: McFarland, 2018).

9. One of the theory pieces we read was a chapter from Joy James's book *Shadowboxing: Black Feminist Politics* where she writes about segregated communities and transcendent communities. I further develop this idea in *Girls on Fire*.

10. Several students in this cluster course were simultaneously enrolled in my Race, Class, Gender, and Sexuality in American Culture course, where we also apply the theories of the course—in this case, intersectional feminism—to *Parable of the Talents*. Considering this novel in two classes with complementary theories helped to further illuminate our discussions in both classes.

11. One piece students read was my essay "*Rasquachsimo*: A Theory, Method and Pedagogy for Hip-Hop Intersections," *Words, Beats, & Life: The Global Journal of Hip-Hop Culture* 5, no. 1 (2013): 38–49, about *rasquachismo*, a term from Chicano studies that considers art and aesthetics that draw from the limited resources at hand.

12. Robin D. G. Kelley, *Freedom Dreams: The Black Radical Imagination* (Boston: Beacon, 2003).

13. Several students took my course Cultural Criticism and Theory: The Arts

of Social Change the following fall, where we worked with the annual academic theme of revolution and read *Parable of the Sower*. We continued to build on ideas developed in this cluster class, considering, for instance, Gene Sharp's *From Dictatorship to Democracy*, and students created a piece of theory, a piece of cultural criticism, and an action project that modeled an "art" of social change.

PART III

Individual Assignments

Challenges, Adjustments, and Innovations

9

Teaching Theory in American Studies

Efforts at Unsettling Home in Three Assignments

REBECCA HILL

One of the more difficult things about teaching American Studies is the centrality of theory to our field. Not only do we use a lot of theory, but because people approach American Studies from so many different disciplinary angles and subfields, we could fit a wide range of disciplinary theories under our umbrella. Finally, the ideological aspects of theory also often provoke students to reject specific theories or theory in general. In this chapter, I'm going to analyze some failures and successes I've had in my attempts to navigate these difficulties. Whether teaching graduates or undergraduates, my general philosophy has been that the best way to develop a real critical understanding of theory is to attempt to apply it, rather than simply to summarize a set of terms. I also believe that regardless of student level, a good assignment will be difficult enough that students are challenged and learn something but not so difficult that only a few students can pull it off. I've tried to implement these general principles in a modified review essay assignment for first-year MA students, a presentation assignment for upper-level undergraduates, and a final paper assignment for the same undergraduates.

I always build my classes around the assignments I'm giving, going back to my early training as a teacher in a composition and rhetoric program at the University of Minnesota that encouraged the reverse engineering of a syllabus through the outcomes students are expected to achieve, while incrementally building from one assignment to the next. In teaching the introduction to the field of American Studies for both undergraduates and graduates, I hope that by the end of the semester, students will produce work that, in the words of one of our program outcomes, "distinguishes between, evaluates, and applies major theories and concepts. Accurately summarizes relevant scholarly work." However, an excessive focus on final products can cause us to miss the value of the process that students go through as they work through these assignments. At times, my efforts to create particular learning processes don't end up with the outcomes I want, and yet students' less formal descriptions of what they are learning often surpass the final written products they turn in. As Walter Benjamin once wrote, "The work is the death mask of its conception."[1]

I teach at Kennesaw State University, a large regional state university with about thirty-five thousand students in the Northern Atlanta suburbs that has recently been designated an "R2." The school has grown dramatically in both numbers and diversity since it was founded as a community college in 1963. Located in historically conservative Cobb County, in a town that famously requires that all residents own a personal firearm, Kennesaw State has long held a reputation as a "white flight" university for metro Atlantans who are afraid to go "downtown" for school at Georgia Tech or Georgia State.[2] However, as the city of Atlanta has gentrified, the nearby suburbs have diversified. Cobb County, which sent Newt Gingrich to the House in 1979, is now over 40 percent Black and Latinx, went to Hillary Clinton by a slight majority in 2016, and elected Rep. Lucy McBath (D) to the House on a gun-control platform in the 2018 midterms.[3] In addition, as a nearly open-admissions campus, Kennesaw has a history of being a commuter campus with a significant portion of "nontraditional," older students, as well as many first-generation college students. But this is changing. In the last ten years, Kennesaw has increased its on-campus housing and started a football team, bringing more "traditional" students to campus and creating a more active residence life culture. The current student population is about 55 percent white, 21 percent African American, 9.6 percent Latinx, and 5 percent Asian, with another 4.5 percent of students identifying as multiracial, and only 2 percent international students.[4] This population is relatively close to that of the town of Kennesaw, which is now 62 percent white, 25 percent African American, and 13 percent

Latinx. That the university demographics are changing with the suburban population makes sense, as 95 percent of Kennesaw's students are in-state, mostly from the cluster of counties immediately surrounding Kennesaw: Cobb, Cherokee, Gwinett, Bartow, and North Fulton.[5] Combining students from North Georgia counties that are 70–90 percent white and vote over 70 percent Republican with students from diversifying edge-cities, Kennesaw's campus is increasingly sharply ideologically divided, with groups such as Turning Point USA and Young Americans for Freedom on campus at the same time as a growing Young Democratic Socialists of America chapter, a Pride Alliance with strong participation of trans students, and a number of popular classes in African and African diaspora studies, Latinx studies, and gender and women's studies. Because American Studies courses don't appear in the catalog as connected to these programs—although we are housed in the same department—our undergraduate courses usually have a mix of students who take our courses with the expectation of learning about diversity and students who expect that they will be taking a course that reinforces notions of American greatness. Our graduate students also come from a wide range, including KSU graduates from the popular gender and women's studies minor, history majors who want to stay in Kennesaw, working adults seeking professional advancement or intellectual stimulation, and local high school and middle-school teachers, along with a handful of out-of-state students specifically seeking an MA in American Studies.

This mix of students in a beginning graduate "theory" course can be challenging, as some students expect everyone in the class to share their own ethical commitments to specific theories, such as intersectionality as learned in women's studies, while other students are less familiar with learning "theory" in general and are just trying to puzzle their way through difficult texts. It's easy to feel in the moment as if you are pleasing no one. However, the one thing that I did right from the beginning, and that could get these students talking to each other, was to always ask students to imagine the application of theories we were discussing to specific examples in the classroom discussion. This often goes well, with plenty of "a ha!" moments and deep thinking. It could be as simple as getting students to talk about Benjamin's concept of "aura" by asking them why people take photos of the Mona Lisa in the Louvre but don't do this with a poster of the Mona Lisa in a dorm room. However, I did not ask them to apply theories to a concrete example in formal writing until the final paper of the semester. Initially, I required students to write three review essays comparing concepts in the assigned readings, which had to be turned in on the day those theories would be discussed—why? Because this is what I had done when I was a graduate student! Here is an example of one of those questions, essentially a "compare/contrast" paper:

> Take one or two of the essays from the "Whiteness: Redux or Redefined" forum along with the *Keywords* essay on " Whiteness" and Nell Painter's *New York Times* op-ed piece, and explain how these recent works engage in dialogue with, extend, respond to, differ from, and/or revise the understanding of whiteness as explained in Roediger's *Wages of Whiteness.* What concepts or ideas do you see in any of the works that draw concepts or ideas from the much earlier work of W. E. B. Du Bois? Are these discussions of whiteness different from the way that race is usually discussed in media and politics? What do you see as the strengths and weaknesses of these arguments, and how might they be potentially useful or problematic if adopted by scholars, activists, or the general public?

Students often did well but described the process of writing as difficult and boring. There were about seven different review essays to choose from over the course of the semester, and they could pick any three that appealed to them, so students turned in papers on different subjects, on different days. Some wrote on feminist theory, and some wrote on myth and symbol, for example. Students got to the end of the semester having written about only a small number of theories that we had discussed in the class, and then replicating that analysis in a final paper applying the same theories to a concrete text or event. Students hated turning in papers before having the opportunity to discuss very difficult readings in class, even as my goal in creating that process was to get students to experience grappling with the ideas on their own before getting an authoritative "read" on them. After tweaking these writing assignments over a period of five years, I finally decided to restructure them entirely. I scrapped the final paper and created four short-paper assignments that would come at the end of each of four "units" (critical race theory; myth and symbol to postcolonialism; critical theory and British cultural studies; discourse analysis and affect theory). Students now turn in their papers on the same day, and they all write about all the theories, after a unit on a group of theories has "wrapped up." In each of these short papers, they must use a combination of related theoretical writings to interpret a single popular culture text or current event of their choice. Since I made that change to each review essay question, the students have become more engaged with the writing. The new timing of the assignments also reduces the individualist emphasis of textual grappling before class in favor of encouraging students to draw from the more collaborative experience of class discussions in writing their papers. The essay question looks like this:

> In their introduction to the 2014 *American Quarterly* forum on whiteness, Cynthia Young and Grace Hong write that rather than being over, whiteness has been "redefined" or "reconsolidated" (1072). In your paper, use David Roediger's book *Wages of Whiteness,* W. E. B. Du Bois's *Souls of Black Folk,* and one of the essays from the *American Quarterly* forum *to analyze an example from current events or contemporary popular culture in order to discuss how the ways in which scholars think about or define race has changed over time.* In your paper, be sure to explain how the different authors define race or "whiteness" and compare and contrast their analyses. How do later authors build on, adjust, or change analyses of earlier authors, and how do these changes reflect the way these authors might read the text you chose? (For example, how does Roediger build on Du Bois? How does Singh build on Roediger?) Through the application of the three academic texts to your chosen popular text, explain the strengths and weaknesses of the different approaches. How do these three ways of thinking about or analyzing race help you (or others) to understand how race functions in society?

When this works well, it not only helps students learn new theories but also helps them think about how they might shift their own standard interpretations of everyday life, unsettling the frameworks they got comfortable with as undergraduates or as professionals. This application of theory to the study of everyday life and popular culture also seems to me to fit the overarching mission of American Studies. Students have used Foucault to analyze a middle school's discourse about their restless child, Habermas to explain political YouTube, Jonathan Fiske to describe their "resistant" appreciation of Captain America, and descriptions of SEC football games to explore affect theory. I no longer get complaints about these papers being boring to write. One student commented sardonically after my most recent online seminar, "I [said I] enjoyed applying theory to 'stupid examples' because [in] the last paper I wrote about cultural studies I was astounded by the absurdity of using Adorno and Horkheimer to analyze the whole episode of Belle Delphine selling her bathwater online."[6]

TEACHING THEORY TO UNDERGRADUATES

This experience with beginning graduate students helped me in my efforts to teach theory to upper-level undergraduates. I started teaching our core undergraduate Principles and Methods of American Studies course in 2016. I have now taught that course four times. The two linked assignments from that course that most involve theory are a midterm presentation using the *Keywords for American Cultural Studies* and the final project, which requires students to do independent interdisciplinary research to write about a specific place where they experience "America."[7] To my surprise, the keyword assignment has been almost wildly successful every time I've taught it. Each time I've assigned the presentation, the students and I have been a little unsure about how it will go. It began in a format deeply connected to real-time face-to-face interaction: a poster session. I assigned students to create posters based on individual keywords from the *Keywords for American Cultural Studies* book and connect them to two assigned course readings and a specific place that would also be the foundation for their final paper. They were then to present their posters to their classmates and to passersby in the atrium of the humanities and social sciences building at KSU. The elements that make this assignment work are the tight structure requiring the application of a theoretical concept to concrete examples, a limited choice of readings, and the choice to write about a place that had meaning to the student. Because they had to address the course readings, they couldn't avoid addressing course issues, but because they had to apply those readings to a specific place that they were familiar with, they were less likely to describe those readings in a rote and distant way. The first year, I made it optional to present in the atrium, and the students opted to stay in the classroom, presenting only to me and to each other. In our small group of seven students, three chose Miranda Josephs's essay on "Community," and while it was fascinating to see different takes on a single word, I saw the problem. Still, what they did remained striking. One student, concerned about the impact a new stadium would have in displacing his own community, used Josephs's essay to write about both his own community and the new corporate community inside the stadium itself.

The second time I taught the course, I required that students pick a word that was not already on the syllabus and that another student had not chosen. The twelve students in that class chose words such as "fashion," "technology," "dialect," and "digital." I did not give them a choice about the public presentation but booked the atrium and held the class there on the appointed day in the semester. There was as buzz of excitement in the room as they presented their posters to each other and passersby. The mood was jovial and supportive. The poster assignment clearly advantaged students with strong design and drafting skills, but the others more than made up for less elegant posters with in-depth discussion of each of the poster's sections during the hour of presentation in the atrium. Those presentations got better over the course of the hour, as students had to practice the presentation numerous times, as new people came by to see their poster. However, I noticed that on this group of posters, which I could evaluate later as texts, many did not address a *Keywords* essay itself, but in following the requirement to define the term in their own words they abandoned the text and avoided the interesting ways that the *Keywords* book makes them consider changing uses of words. The third time I taught the course was in an asynchronous online class. I was worried about how this assignment would make the transition, but it turned out to be easy. Instead of a poster, students did online presentations using PowerPoint with voice-over, or writing a script in the notes section if they had problems using the voice-over tool. We lost the dynamic and interactive buzz of the face-to-face session, but I assigned interaction within the framework of the class by assigning students to work with partners for a draft workshop and for a final presentation Q&A.

I also required that students discuss the central themes of the *Keywords* essay they had chosen in their presentations before giving their own definition of the word. One difficulty with the *Keywords* book in this context is that the essays intentionally describe each word's changing usage, refusing to provide a simple definition. Students accustomed to finding the answers quickly sometimes light upon the first definition given in the essay, pulling quotations without enough context. But most students drew unexpected and interesting connections among course readings and extended these to the place they chose for their American place. Taryn Tragesser, for example, used the word "normal" to connect to assigned readings about Salvadoran teenagers fleeing from gang violence on the train known as "The Beast"; an episode of *This American Life* about a man who grew up in an Italian American family without knowing that his biological father was African American until he reached adulthood; and finally the chapter of David Roediger's book, *How Race Survived U.S. History*, about how Central and Eastern Europeans "became white" to assimilate to US norms. In her presentation, "normal" had to do with the goals of assimilation to a local culture, whether that was a culture of white supremacy or a situation where violence had become an omnipresent reality. Tragresser's presentation showed how the requirement to connect the keyword to more than one course reading caused students to think about multiple applications of a concept and to identify underlying similarities in ostensibly disparate situations.

What is this if not applying a theory—but without putting it in so many words? Because it was a presentation, they did not have to write long paragraphs justifying their connections, but they were able to make a quick connection by using a single quotation or scene from the reading. Then they were able to talk about how they saw this connection, whether in real-time responses in face-to-face poster sessions or in written discussion posts in responses to classmates' questions in the online Q&A assignment. In her response to a question from a classmate, Tragesser explained, "When things go against the majority in society, we think it's abnormal, but it's really not." Not having to fill a paragraph or page quota seemed to free students from the rote characteristics of college papers, giving them a greater sense of ownership over their projects despite the fairly rigid requirements of the assignment. The final way that Taryn used the word "normal" was in her application of the word to Central Park, which she had chosen as her American place. She pointed out that norms are situational: it might be normal for people to play music or do yoga in the middle of a park, but it would be less normal if done on an urban street. In this case, the different requirements of the assignment required students to do some thinking about abstract concepts in direct application. Students made diverse and engaging connections between their keywords, places, and course readings, and when a few students chose the same word, they enjoyed seeing the very different "takes" from other students. The asynchronous online Q&A assignment first paired students with a partner in a brainstorming exercise before their presentations were due and then paired them with the same partners as well as a second new partner for the Q&A on the finished presentations. I intentionally paired students who had chosen the same word, so that they could see how differently—and how still interestingly and "correctly"—the other student had applied the same keyword. Another student who used the word "normal" in his paper was Asad Siddiqui, who chose a local mall as his place. In his presentation, he pointed out the many messages being sent to people in the mall about how they could fit into society and be "normal," providing "a prime opportunity for companies to define what is and is not normal to wear, to eat, consume, think, and even do." Picking up on the end of McRuer's keyword essay, Taryn asked Asad during the last Q&A, "How do you think abnormal helps define what normal is in our society? And do you think abnormality is becoming normal in today's world? We are obsessed with being unique and standing out from the norm, so is abnormal the new normal?"

Because of the large number of students in the online class, I did not restrict them to choosing words that others were not using, but I kept the requirement that the word they chose not be one that was on the syllabus. While the online session did not have the spontaneous and fun quality of the class poster session in the atrium the year before, the online conversations about the presentations were in many cases more substantive, as were many of the presentations themselves. Students who responded to my survey about the assignment all had very positive things to say about it, and what they had to say is helpful for understanding why this assignment works, which includes the process as well as the product. The first reason that I believe this assignment works is that it is not a paper and that it includes classmates in the audience. It may also be because I did my own eight-to-ten-minute voice-over PowerPoint presentations for the students, including a model presentation following the assignment guidelines, so that the students would have a direct example. One of the students surveyed explained their experience this way: "Requiring me to talk about the keyword in a presentation encouraged me to bring my own expression to what I was learning rather than a traditional paper which usually I'm concerned about being academic, although it should also be about individual expression. It's different. It was more fun than an essay, I played the part of a professor, I felt like Professor Hill when she does her presentations" (survey 4).

The students who participated in my survey were unanimous in finding that the presentation format made the assignment more interesting than more typical assignments. Like this student, many students enjoyed the opportunity to speak more conversationally. I had worried that the technology itself would be a barrier, but the students said that the technology did not make the assignment harder, but did make it more interesting. One wrote, "I felt that the voiceover made it more personal and unique than a traditional paper" (survey 2). Another student said the assignment allowed them to be "more creative" (student 5). While the second student struggled with the keyword essay format itself, the guide to find a "takeaway" was helpful: "My keyword went all over the place so I was worried about how I was going to bring it all together for a short presentation. Once I realized I was just supposed to highlight what I took away from it then my presentation came together quickly and I actually enjoyed doing it" (survey 2).

I was especially surprised to read a student response on my survey that a student "loved this assignment and everything about it" and found that they learned a lot, had "very meaningful" interactions with other students in the class, and liked seeing other students' keyword presentations, writing: "I think it was a very nice touch to have us relate our 'American Place' to the readings from the semester. It allowed more insight to the points of view of the other students, when seeing what they chose to compare them to, than a simple description of their place would have done" (student 3).

Most importantly, talking about and sharing images of specific places gave the students more context for understanding each other in the disembodied and alienating online learning environment.

FROM KEYWORD TO AMERICAN PLACES: TOO LITTLE THEORY, TOO MUCH RESEARCH

The biggest problem I experienced with the online class wound up being with the final American Place essay. In his work on local history, Joseph Amato described the tension that already exists in this assignment, in which I simultaneously want students to apply theories about America writ large from the course and to practice interdisciplinary research on a specific locale. He writes:

> The local historian must learn to switch between two narratives of the countryside. The first is the story of the dominance of outside forces. The second is the story of unique local people and their singular experiences. As the first narrative destroys local history's integrity by rendering local places and events redundant microcosms of the world at large, overlooking the history of successful resistance, compromise, and even transformation of the countryside, so the second narrative produces eccentric histories that exclude the larger world.[8]

It was easier to break down the complexity of this task in the process of twice-weekly face-to-face classes than in an asynchronous online class, even if I created all kinds of online workshops for the students. In all four classes, some students produced well-researched and thoughtful essays that very clearly connected to concepts in the course while also analyzing the specifics of places. One student's paper on how three generations of her family have worked at Walmart still stands out as an exemplar in the discussion of a localized experience of American capitalism. Even when this assignment did not reach the outcomes I wanted though, students demonstrated more in the process of research than they did in the final paper. One student in a face-to-face class talked about discovering the low-income neighborhood near a popular local commercial district that she had chosen as her American Place in more detail than what she ultimately put into a final paper. Perhaps in seeking to meet the goals of what they think a final paper should be, students wiped out the more interesting ambivalence that I heard from them during class workshops. Other students treated their own place not as a microcosm of but as an antidote to the critical frameworks covered in class, using this space of the final paper to finally resist the idea that race continues to shape American life, or that a history of settler colonialism has any relevance for the present lives of North Georgians, or that free enterprise isn't an unalloyed good. This happens especially if students write about their most cherished spaces: churches, neighborhoods, and hometowns. A number of online students also lived on military bases and tended to write about them in glowing and exceptionalist terms, even if their responses to readings about American empire in the past had been more critical and complex. They could understand the concepts in general—but they didn't want to bring them home.

When the problem of "boosterism" came up in my face-to-face classes, I was able to sit in small-group workshop sessions with students, interacting directly around research questions and conclusions. If students wondered aloud about what to write about, I could encourage them to critically discuss their ideas both with me and with each other. I could help them find sources in real time. In that second face-to-face class, one student who wrote his paper about his own megachurch was shocked at the extent to which the church functioned as a business. A student who wrote his paper about Asheville, his favorite place to vacation, wound up learning all the downsides of a tourist economy when he went there and did some interviews with locals. In an asynchronous online class, it's much harder to get students to take the time to engage the complexity of this assignment, as they may concentrate research efforts into short, solitary bursts, never engaging in that process of even the forty minutes of interaction with classmates or me about the research in progress. Too often, they started by looking at the tourism board or the chamber of commerce, googling their way to narrative histories of their places and then lovingly describing the present day. Students who chose their place based on their interest in illustrating a keyword were less likely to do this than students who chose to write about a place that they loved.

The fourth time I taught the class, in fall 2020, I revised the assignment to require that students include at least three academic sources and two newspaper articles, engage two assigned course readings about a specific concept from class, and use census data. I also gave an early PowerPoint lecture on the concept of "microcosm," assigned documentaries analyzing places paired with relevant reading from *Keywords*, and had students practice discussions of themes in local places in discussion post assignments throughout the semester.[9] The students still had freedom to research the specifics of their places. The latest set of submissions showed clearer applications of course themes to student experience. One student even wrote about the struggles of precarious students striving to succeed at Kennesaw State itself, commenting on how marketing of universities as places of "limitless possibility" plays into familiar—and deceptive—American frontier mythology. There continue to be papers that do not engage course readings, and a few resist them. However, all the students who write these papers learn more about their places than they knew before and enjoy doing the research.

The ultimate challenge of this paper comes back to the ideological elements of theory and the way American Studies concepts may challenge the implicit theories that many of our students live by. If I ask students to think seriously about how the history of white supremacy might be present in their suburban cul-de-sac, how the military base that they live on is part of American empire, or how power and money operate within their dearly loved megachurches, I am asking them to do more than simply learn a theory by applying it to an amusing, if possibly "stupid example." The challenge is bigger than the academic problem of communicating abstract "theory." As teachers of American Studies, we can only encourage our students to do what we attempt to do in all our work, unsettle themselves in the place where they feel most "at home." We cannot determine what they will do in response, but we can continue to try to create processes to gently shake the certainty of the ground under their feet.

APPENDIX: KEYWORD ASSIGNMENT

Note: This is the structure of the keyword presentation assignment in an asynchronous online class. That class was built around Monday/Thursday discussion board posting assignments, and the keyword assignment, workshops, and responses all followed that pattern, with longer writing assignments due on Mondays and shorter assignments or "quick checks" due on Thursdays.

25% Keyword Presentation with Q&A: A PowerPoint or Google Slides presentation on one keyword from the *Keywords* book that was not one of the words assigned on the syllabus. In your presentation, you will summarize key points from the *Keywords* essay, define the keyword in your own words, connect your keyword to two different assigned course readings, and finally explain how your keyword can help explain something about your chosen place for the My American Place project. You are encouraged to do your presentation with a voice-over explanation, but this is not required. You can also provide the printed script to go with your PowerPoint slides. On the day when the keyword presentations are due, there will be an assignment on D2L to ask questions about other students' presentations, and you will need to answer your classmates' questions about your presentation.

Draft Workshop through Final Keyword Project

I. Keyword Project Workshop Part One (due online Monday)

Note: I assigned partners for each student by email. I gave feedback to every student on the discussion board.

1. Write 4–5 sentences explaining how this week's readings and the film *Shake the Dust* relate to the keyword "Globalization." Choose at least 1 specific example or big idea from each of the readings and the film that connect to specific ideas or themes in the keyword essay.

   And now, time to brainstorm and start working on your own keyword project.
2. Spend 30 minutes doing the following free-writing, either handwritten or typed.
   A. Write down some of the examples or ideas from course readings (any course readings from the entire semester so far) that are related to your keyword—this doesn't have to be in complete sentences.
   B. Think about a place that represents America to you—what is that place? It can be as small as a workplace or school, and as large as a city or town, but no bigger. What is that place?
   C. Connect your place and your keyword: Do you see any examples of how your keyword works in this place? Can your keyword help explain something that happened in this place or is still happening in this place? Is there some other connection between your keyword and your place? What is it?
3. **Post here: a photo or typed version of your free-writing in response to questions A, B, and C.**

4. **Post here: one or two paragraphs** explaining what you think are the most important ideas in the course readings related to your keyword, and the most interesting or important way that you can connect your chosen keyword to your place.

II. Keyword Draft Workshop Part Two (due online Thursday)
Read your partner's keyword brainstorming paragraph from Monday night. Ask them at least 2 questions to help them clarify and develop their ideas. Some suggested things you might want to think about as you read their paragraphs: Do they need to clarify any terms, not just the keyword, but any other terms? Do they need to explain historical events, facts, or other examples? Does their connection between their place and the keyword make sense to you? Is there anything they said that seems really interesting and could they emphasize this more?

III. Keyword Workshop Part Three (due the next Monday)
Read the questions you got from your partner and from me on your presentation brain-storming exercise. Write a couple of sentences about what you are doing to deepen or clarify your analysis.

IV. Projects Due
Note: Students had an opportunity to write a quick progress report on Thursday and ask me direct questions. The presentations were due the following Monday.

V. Q&A Assignment after Presentations Were Posted
Note: I assigned a new partner and asked students to also respond to the final presentation of their partner from the workshop they had done before.

Thursday:
Presentation Discussion Board as a Direct Reply to the Posted Presentation

1. Watch and/or listen to your old partner's keyword presentation and ask them a question about their presentation. If you are not sure what to ask, you can ask them to clarify something in the presentation, or explain it in more detail; you can ask them about another idea that occurs to you; or you can ask them more about their American place in relation to their keyword.
2. Watch and/or listen to your new partner's keyword presentation and ask them a question. If you are not sure what to ask, you can ask them to clarify something in the presentation, or explain it in more detail;

you can ask them about another idea that occurs to you; or you can ask them more about their American place in relation to their keyword.

3. Extra Credit: Watch and/or listen to one additional keyword presentation and ask the presenter a question or make a comment on something interesting or confusing about their presentation.

Monday, as part of final discussion assignment for that week: Presenters answer the questions from classmates

Answer the questions you got on your keyword presentation (please do this on the discussion board under your presentation, not on this discussion board).

NOTES

1. Walter Benjamin, "Post No Bills: The Writer's Technique in Thirteen Theses," in *Reflections: Essays, Aphorisms, Autobiographical Writings* (New York: Shocken, 1986,) 80–81.

2. Omar Jimenez, "In This American Town, Guns Are Required by Law," CNN, March 7, 2018, https://www.cnn.com/2018/03/06/us/kennesaw-georgia-gun-ownership/index.html. On the North Georgia suburbs, see Kevin Kruse, *White Flight: Atlanta the Making of Modern Conservatism* (Princeton, NJ: Princeton University Press, 2007).

3. Dante Chinni, Sally Bronston, and Matt Rivera, "As Cobb County Trends Blue, So Goes Georgia Statewide Politics," NBC News, March 10, 2019, https://www.nbcnews.com/politics/meet-the-press/cobb-county-trends-blue-so-goes-georgia-statewide-politics-n981051.

4. Kennesaw Office of Institutional Research, *2018–2019 Kennesaw State University Fact Book*, accessed June 19, 2020, https://ir.kennesaw.edu/publications/fact-book.php.

5. Kennesaw Office of Institutional Research, *2018–2019 Fact Book*; and US Census, "Quick Facts: Kennesaw City, Georgia," accessed May 23, 2021, https://www.census.gov/quickfacts/fact/table/kennesawcitygeorgia,mariettacitygeorgia,cobbcountygeorgia/PST045219.

6. Austin Wilson, email to author, April 17, 2020.

7. Bruce Burgett and Glenn Hendler, eds., *Keywords for American Cultural Studies*, 3rd ed. (New York: New York University Press, 2020). See this chapter's "Appendix: Keyword Assignment."

8. Joseph A. Amato, *Rethinking Home: A Case for Writing Local History* (Oakland, CA: University of California Press, 2002), 58.

9. For example, I had them watch a free online documentary *Plagues and Pleasures of the Salton Sea* and read the *Keywords* essay "Environment." *Plagues and Pleasures of the Salton Sea*, directed by Christ Metzler and Jeff Springer, KQUED, Truly, CA, 2006.

10

Reppin' American Studies

Asian Pacific Islander American Studies and Popular Culture as Pedagogy

STANLEY THANGARAJ

When teaching American Studies classes, one must stay attuned to the politics of representation, especially embedded within transnational, transhistorical circuits of popular culture. The site of representation is one key site for the negotiation, management, and consolidation of US empire, both domestically and globally.[1] Showcasing the multiplicity of representations of Asian Pacific Islander Americans through popular culture provides one venue to teach American Studies. In this instance, American Studies is Asian Pacific Islander American Studies. It is an investigation of Asian Pacific Islander America that simultaneously interrogates structural forces and everyday management of racial structures.

By inserting explicitly Asian Pacific Islander America and popular culture into the American Studies curriculum, the syllabus pulls together everyday practices of race, self, and meaning making that we take for granted while attending to ethnic communities who have often been omitted in the configuring of the United States through a hegemonic black-white racial binary. Thus, I will be providing a road map for how I teach Anthropology of Asian America. My teaching of

American Studies, as influenced by Lisa Lowe's *Intimacies of Four Continents*, is one that foregrounds an Asian American Studies curriculum by expanding the spatial, temporal, and organizing logic of US racial logics whereby race making is multiple, transnational, and simultaneous. To engage with such multiplicity and simultaneity, I introduce assignments in class that specifically engage with critical theories of race and indigeneity while engaging with longer histories that disrupt the simplistic, binary discussions of race and American citizenship.[2]

In this chapter, I will concurrently showcase both my nontraditional pedagogical assignments and my class syllabus. In the interdisciplinary tradition of American Studies, I begin with a coupling of history and critical theories of race through a comparative racializations frame to highlight the shifting, fluid, and contradictory nature of race in the United States and within Asian Pacific Islander America.[3] By first being given the foundations of Michael Omi and Howard Winant's theory of racial formation, students comprehend the fluidity and expansiveness of race in structuring US society.[4] In addition to giving students the theory of racial formation, I also assign the chapter on "racialized discourses" from David Theo Goldberg's *Racist Culture* so that students have an understanding of how race is articulated not just in large institutions and political structures but also in nefarious, everyday ways—such as through representations, discourses, and interpellations of Asians and Asian Pacific Islander Americans in every day media.[5]

Through a theoretical engagement with racial formations, students are then equipped to decipher the multiple ways that various cultural productions prove historically instrumental in the racial formations of "Yellow Peril" and "Hindoo" in early US history. In assignments using the seminal work of Sucheng Chan along with Jack Tchen and Dylan Yeats,[6] students grapple with immigration law and early Chinese labor as "racial projects."[7] By examining problematic cartoon depictions of Chinese men as a "threat" to the nation and white reproductive labor (miscegenation), students can comprehend the ways these racializations depended on class, ethnicity, and sexuality in order to secure the Chinese as "forever foreign."[8] I also introduce the work of Helen Jun, David Roediger, and Leslie Bow so that students can connect how whiteness, Blackness, and Chinese-ness were in tension and in relation to each other.[9] Additionally, with a historical context assembled through the scholarship of Fiona Ngo, Sarah Gualtieri, and Vivek Bald, students are able to decipher the "heterogeneity, hybridity, and multiplicity" within Asian America.[10] Through these readings, students are asked to theorize geographies of race that both include and exclude South Asians and communities from the Middle East, while assembling and consolidating normative whiteness and the parameters of national belonging as always in opposition to Chinese-ness.[11] Through the intentional unanchoring of American Studies and Asian Pacific Islander American Studies from simplistic cartographic understandings of Asia and race, we can expand our understanding of the racial formation of "Yellow Peril" in relation to the various popular cultural representations and racializations of South Asians as "Hindoo,"[12] the Japanese as internal enemies,[13] and the racialization of West Asian/Middle Eastern communities.[14]

While attending to the mainstream stereotypical representations of these communities, I assign chapters from Linda Espana-Maram, Fiona Ngo, Samuel Regalado, Ryan Reft, and Shalini Shankar so that Asian Pacific Islander American cultural production, leisure, resistance, and pleasure is also foregrounded.[15] With these readings, students are able to move beyond simplistic understandings of power and, more importantly, see how communities manage their racialization through struggle and pleasure. Through sport (boxing, baseball, basketball) and music (taxi halls), Asian American communities mediate their racialized marginalization by inverting the relationship between "race and ability" on the playing fields and leisure spaces.[16]

Students are required to turn in a nontraditional project: an art project on the readings on early Asian Americans and their leisure practices. They have to explain, translate, and depict the theoretical material and archival material through any artistic medium of their choice. A project of this sort has been used in my classes for many years and is inspired by the pedagogy of my father, M. Thomas Thangaraj. I had seen my father do this brilliantly in his class Different Images of Christ at Emory University, and I adopted it for all classes I teach. Through art, students can see the deep theoretical angles and possibilities without privileging the written paper as the only mode of theorization, knowledge production, and politics. With art as a major mode of expression and political activism, art must be instituted as a mandatory part of the American Studies curriculum to capture an expansive American social context in early Asian Pacific Islander American history.

When I first mention the art project, the looks of anxiety spread across the classroom like a tidal wave. Students do not take American Studies classes on Asian Pacific Islander America to then be asked to produce something artistic. In the case of my students at Vanderbilt University, their anxiety stemmed from this departure from the kinds of preparation they had in high school, where they mastered academic language. With their abundant resources gained in elite high schools, the art project disrupts their conception of academic work and training. Thus, the project forces them to think much more broadly about how to study and theorize in American Studies. I do not take their anxiety lightly, and I emphasize that art provides theoretical traction in ways that academic papers can never offer. Likewise, I suggest students meet me during office hours to discuss art projects and find a way to translate the readings to art. Furthermore, as students worry that they have little to no artistic talent, I assure them that I am not an artist. Rather, I emphasize that their grades are based on their investment and energy in translating the themes into works of art.

The art project is wide open to any sort of art, such as collages, paintings/drawings, poems, spoken word, dance performance, origami, musical/instrumental performance, and short movies. To my surprise, my own limited and naive understandings of art are challenged each time I assign this project. Students bring in such a wide assortment of projects that challenge how I had narrowly conceptualized "art." The examples of origami and Claymation are just two such examples of art and theory.

At the City College of New York, although a few of my students come from elite high schools, a large number of my students are working-class and attended public schools, and several had never written a research paper. While these working-class students of color and working-class white students express their doubt about their artistic abilities, they have responded in quite different ways than I had expected. For these students, the art project taps into a variety of their skills and talents that were previously not accounted for in the traditional classroom. In a way, the art project decenters traditional academic vocabulary and discourse by giving students other mediums to theorize. As a result, students have expressed a sense of joy in owning an empowered and sophisticated ability to theorize through various art mediums (especially painting and spoken word). Importantly, the project allows students to theorize outside the limitations of academic jargon, demonstrating their critical ability to theorize beyond just what the author of the monograph provided. Through such a project, students realize their own intellectual strengths and use the art project as one way to affirm and legitimate their other academic work. Plus, for students who have always engaged with artistic forms, even if not in the classroom, their art is a window in sophisticated theorization and deep engagement with the social world. Through such a realization, students come to the understanding that they can interpret and decode material in sophisticated ways that exceed the analysis offered in a book—they get to own and cherish their own analytic voice that often exceeds the epistemologies of the white and Western-oriented university.

Over the years, I have taught many monographs on Asian America in my classes, and the artistic projects have been spectacular. For Junaid Rana's *Terrifying Muslims* (2011), one of my students brought her harp and detailed the changing dynamics of the background music in Hollywood movies featuring the Middle East/West Asia. She played background music of the "Middle East" that had a slow and exotic tremble to it when it was meant to signify movies before the 1980s. The shift from exotic foreign-ness[17] to constant and ever-present danger[18] with the emergence of deep tones, faster pace, and non-Western rhythms in Hollywood movies about the Middle East conveyed to the class the multiple, shifting, and fluid racializations of the "Arab/Muslim/Middle Eastern/South Asian" in the American imaginary.[19] Through such a project as this, students attain skills in reading critically the realms of popular culture and its artistic manifestations. Thus, they are able to understand the importance of art in understanding American Studies as a site of creativity and critique. Furthermore, it emphasizes to students that art is a site of pleasure where one can craft understandings of power in the United States.

As we shift from the earlier waves of Asian Americans to the more contemporary phenomena, we look to interrogate the shifts from the racial formation of "Yellow Peril" and "Hindoo" to "model minority." In this instance, I foreground the work of Vijay Prashad (2000) and the relationship between immigration laws and US empire. Once students establish an understanding of the 1965 Hart-Cellar Act and the new interpellation as "Model Minorities" in response to Black and Brown activism for civil rights at the height of the Cold War with the USSR, we can then delve into ethnographic monographs dealing with the lives of Asian Pacific Islander Americans. Chapters from Andrea Louie's *Chineseness across Borders*, Pawan Dhingra's *Managing Multiculturalism*, and Martin Manalansan's *Global Divas* along with Gayatri Gopinath's *Impossible Desires* illustrate how negotiating Asian Pacific Islander American identity involves engaging, managing, challenging, and contesting the "model minority" moniker across various intersecting categories of difference.[20] In this case, their racialization as "model minority" exists with certain projections of gender, sexuality, and class. I couple this set of readings with Queer of Color Critique[21] and Queer Diasporic Critique[22] as a way to challenge the equivalences around sexuality and race. Instead of celebrating this racialization of "model minority," the chapters disrupt its ideological hold while illustrating the ways in which (cis) gender and (hetero)sexuality police the boundaries of Asian Pacific Islander America.

The last set of readings bring together masculinity, popular culture, and state violence to further interrogate the relationships between US empire, Asian Pacific Islanders, and popular culture. In this final section, the readings interject key theories on settler-colonialism, refugee status, and rising Islamophobia. Although these are not equivalent themes, they serve to address Asian Pacific Islander American "heterogeneity," "hybridity," and "multiplicity."[23] In this instance, we must not also fall prey to situating the historicity of Asian Pacific Islander America with the Chinese Exclusion Act of 1882 or the recent 1965 Hart-Cellar Act. If we center 1965 as a critical (Asian) American Studies moment, we will be dismissing and failing to account for the longer histories of US empire and various class histories within API communities.[24] We must articulate the settler-colonial histories and US imperialism in broader contexts. Instead of centering the violence done to First Nations/Native American communities as the only site of settler colonial violence, the readings and exercises used in this section of class readings extend the analysis of US empire outside our borders and outside the hegemonic reliance on Atlantic studies. Rather, by looking at Pacific Islander histories, we can decenter Atlantic passages and look at also the Pacific passages of US empire, race making, and Asian Pacific Islander stories.

Students come to know Pacific Islanders through rich ethnographic and critical geographies of Hawaii and Polynesian communities in Ty Tengan's and Laurel Mei-Singh's scholarship. With an explicit politics of indigeneity, students are asked to understand the simultaneous and contradictory representations of Hawaiian men as "lazy" and "dangerous," while Hawaiian women are positioned as "Hula girls." In Mei-Singh's beautiful work, we witness the ways in which tourism, the US military-industrial complex, and the occupation of land take place through discourses that position Hawaii as exotic, intimate, and open. Mei-Singh further complicates the picture by inserting the long history of the US military-industrial complex, the destruction of native lands, and the forced removal of natives.[25] I couple this important sociohistorical and macro-level analysis with the work of Ty Tengan. In Tengan's work, we are given access to the intimate space of the Hale Mua (men's house) for indigenous Hawaiians. Through a deep ethnography of the Hale Mua, we are privy to the ways through which indigenous masculinity is negotiated through the managing of the lost land, through ritualistic practices, creating longer historical forms of fraternity, storytelling, and providing support for each other. The storytelling, the warrior dances, and the informal infrastructures of support challenge the Hollywood renditions of Hawaiian indigenous identity as always barbaric. Counter to the mainstream depictions, in the Hale Mua, Tengan illuminates how indigenous masculinity and claims to land are also negotiated through popular culture.[26] Such a theoretical signpost also opens up a larger social justice frame, an expansive politics of solidarity, and potential for coalition building by linking up Asian Pacific Islander America with Native America and the politics of American Indian studies.

For this final section of class, students are required to produce their own popular cultural product—a YouTube video, a song, or a short film. The students form groups of four. For the reading that is due the day they present, the group must investigate both what aspects of representation and popular culture racialize working-class, Muslim, and/or Pacific Islander communities and how that is done. With the readings on Hawaii, students are required to engage with mainstream representations that are both limited and highly popular. For example, the "haka" has become so commonplace and a hegemonic marker of Pacific Islander masculinity. One can just look at sport and see how American football masculinity is negotiated by the University of Hawaii football team through such warrior dances, which depict indigenous masculinity as singular, innate, desirable, and threatening.

As a result, one part of the project involves presenting the negative racializations that are commonplace in US society of Pacific Islander communities. While providing such representations, the group must also engage critically with the reading and qualitative methods to construct their own popular culture platform. Students must insert within this popular culture text another alternative text that sustains and foregrounds the multiple, heterogenous voices of Pacific Islanders on the ground. The videos students produce provide a political nuance to everyday discourse. Accordingly, students produce videos or songs that fight back against the dominant stereotypic representations of these communities. While students have enjoyed this project in unexpected ways, I was surprised by some of the comments on the class evaluation forms. Several students highlighted this project and exclaimed that this project allowed them to master skills with various technological venues and virtual sites and learn to weave through various archival sources and secondary scholarly material. They commented how the project allowed them to master a skill that is helping them in the workplace and in other social spaces. These popular cultural products also serve as a very important part of their graduate school applications. For example, for *Native Man Remade*, one of the groups constructed a video that had Manoa playing alongside hula dancing women in the background. Against this background, the group created intimate ceremonies of men in the Hale Mua that incorporated critiques of settler-colonialism, while queering the space of national, diasporic, and communal normative masculinity.

A project such as this demands extensive group work and sets the stage for engaging in productive collaborative work. As the group works on their popular cultural product, they become cultural producers whose main goal is to provide informed, important, and radical disjuncture from the mainstream media narratives of Asian Pacific Islander American lives. By learning such processes of cultural production, students then "encode and decode" critically the nativist and media representations of other communities of color in the United States during a time of anti-Black racism, trans women of color death, and increasing xenophobia.[27] We have the beginnings of solidarity work and coalition building. Here we see one of the main benefits and goals for this kind of American Studies curriculum.

While these assignments further critical and multitextual engagement with American society and American Studies, these must also be coupled with the traditional academic learning methods: quizzes, exams, research papers, and extra-credit opportunities. Extra-credit opportunities constitute exactly the space where larger community involvement and service prove instrumental in materializing the political mission of American Studies as a site of community engagement and social justice praxis. The class experience must have a clear engagement with resources and Asian Pacific Islander America communities outside the classroom. I accomplish this through two methods: required and voluntary events.

The events I mention to students are usually lectures or performances highlighting the lives of people of color. Students write a page summarizing the event and critically analyzing it with the theories of race from class. By doing so, they use Asian Pacific Islander America as a foundational site for theorizing race across communities of color in US society. Activities like this can foster a greater engagement with the university and the local community. Such activities also facilitate types of critical scholarship that are not limited to textual analysis alone. Rather, such events push students to form a sense of community outside their classroom, and most often outside the university. When the site of learning is spread across society, students then open up to opportunities to work with, collaborate with, and serve communities of color through the work of Asian Pacific Islander America advocacy organizations and their partners in other communities of color.

The structure of my syllabus and the methods to teach American Studies are flexible. The assignments in the syllabus allow students to explore other parts of their own epistemologies and their own talents, skills, and gifts. One can use any of these assignments, a combination of a few, or all of them as a way to structure a class. These assignments all initially give students great anxiety. However, after completing them, the majority of them have shared how these assignments made them more analytical, creative, and engaged scholars. By instituting Asian America, popular culture, and representation as one way to teach American Studies, the pedagogical project will simultaneously put many communities of color in conversation with racial heteronormativity and racial homonormativity. Through such methods of complicating Asian Pacific Islander America, popular culture, and our understandings of US society, we can simultaneously create critically political spaces where new forms of solidarity and coalition building can take place in the classroom. Such moments of solidarity invoke the differential and different strands of race, gender, sexuality, class, ethnicity, and (dis)ability in the production of comparative racializations. Now more than ever we need an ethnic studies–informed American Studies in order to struggle for a kind of world where we foreground Asian American rights. Pacific Islander rights. Standing Rock, Black Lives Matter, and Trans Lives Matter.

NOTES

I am grateful to Rebecca Hill for inviting me so early on to contribute to this amazing project. Rebecca Hill, Joseph Entin, and Elizabeth Duclos-Orsello have been the most generous, patient, and engaging editors. I wish to also pay gratitude to many in Asian American Studies and American Studies who continue to teach, inspire, and energize me: Martin Manalansan, Junaid Rana, David Roediger, Nancy Abelmann, Mimi Nguyen, Fiona Ngo, Soo Ah Kwon, Jennifer Ho, Constancio R. Arnaldo Jr., Genevieve Clutario, Angie Reyes, Rod Ferguson, Lisa Lowe, Arthur Spears, Scott Brooks, Rich Milner, Rachel Buff, Chia Vang, Aarti Ratna, Daniel Burdsey, Pawan Dhingra, Nitasha Sharma, Tamara Bhalla, Katherine Chen, Cheryl Cooky, Jeffrey Montez de Oca, Arlene Torres, David Rubin, Rachel Endo, David Eng, Linda Espana-Maram, James Kim, Houston Baker and Charlotte Pierce-Baker, Shalini Shankar, Douglass Hartmann, Ben Carrington, Sarah Gualtieri, Evelyn Alsultany, Faith Kares, Laura Kina, Erica Rand, Arjun Shankar, Mariam Duranni, Shilpa Dave, Stephanie George,

Monisha Gupta, Lili Shi, Cathy Ma, Jan Padios, Daryl Maeda, Sonja Thomas, Christina B. Chin, Ana Ramos-Zayas, and Viraj Patel. My parents, M. Thomas Thangaraj and Cecelia Thangaraj, teach me about the world and how to be a responsible global citizen. Asher Brooks, my sweet little nephew, is always in my heart and I love our conversations. My wife, Alena Thangaraj, and my children, Jeya Evelyn Thangaraj and Louis Abraham Thangaraj, teach me every single day about how to care more, play more, love more, and engage more; I am very lucky to have them in my life.

1. Lucy Burns, *Puro Arte* (New York: New York University Press, 2012); Linda Espana-Maram, *Creating Masculinity in Los Angeles's Little Manila* (New York: Columbia University Press, 2006).

2. Lisa Lowe, *Intimacies of Four Continents* (Durham, NC: Duke University Press, 2015).

3. Grace Hong and Roderick A. Ferguson, eds., *Strange Affinities* (Durham, NC: Duke University Press, 2011).

4. Michael Omi and Howard Winant, *Racial Formation* (New York: Routledge, 1994)

5. David Theo Goldberg, *Racist Culture* (Boston: Blackwell, 1994.)

6. Sucheng Chan, *Asian Americans* (Woodbridge, CT: Twayne, 1991); Jack Tchen and Dylan Yeats, *Yellow Peril: An Archive of Anti-Asian Fear* (New York: Verso, 2014).

7. Omi and Winant, *Racial Formation*, 55.

8. Lowe, *Intimacies of Four Continents*, 5.

9. Helen Jun, *Race for Citizenship: Black Orientalism and Asian Uplift from Pre-Emancipation to Neoliberal America* (New York: New York University Press, 2011); David Roediger, *Towards the Abolition of Whiteness: Essays on Race, Politics, and Working Class History* (New York: Verso, 1994); Leslie Bow, *Partly Colored* (New York: New York University Press, 2010).

10. Lisa Lowe, *Immigrant Acts* (Durham, NC: Duke University Press, 1996), 63.

11. Fiona Ngo, *Imperial Blues* (Durham, NC: Duke University Press, 2014); Sarah Gualtieri, *Between Arab and White* (Berkeley: University of California Press, 2009); Vivek Bald, *Bengali Harlem* (Cambridge, MA: Harvard University Press, 2013).

12. See Stanley Thangaraj, *Desi Hoop Dreams* (New York: New York University Press, 2015).

13. See Ryan Reft, "From Perpetual Foreigner to Pacific Rim Entrepreneur: The U.S. Military, Asian Americans, and the Circuitous Path of Sport," and Christina Chin, "The Continued Legacy of Japanese American Youth Basketball Leagues," in *Asian American Sporting Cultures*, ed. Stanley Thangaraj, Constancio Arnaldo Jr., and Christina Chin (New York: New York University Press, 2016).

14. See Sunaina Marr Maira, *The 9/11 Generation: Youth, Rights, and Solidarity in the War on Terror* (New York: New York University Press, 2016); and Neda Maghbouleh, *The Limits of Whiteness: Iranian Americans and the Everyday Politics of Race* (Redwood City, CA: Stanford University Press, 2017).

15. Espana-Maram, *Creating Masculinity*; Ngo, *Imperial Blues*; Samuel Regalado, *Nikkei Baseball* (Urbana: University of Illinois Press, 2012); Reft, "From

Perpetual Foreigner to Pacific Rim Entrepreneur"; and Shalini Shankar, "Reflections on Sport Spectatorship and Immigrant Life," in *Asian American Sporting Cultures*.

16. Espana-Maram, *Creating Masculinity*, 88.

17. Amira Jarmakani, *An Imperialist Love Story* (New York: New York University Press, 2015).

18. Ahmed Afzal, *Lone Star Muslims* (New York: New York University Press, 2014); and Evelyn Alsultany, *The Arabs and Muslims in the Media* (New York: New York University Press, 2012).

19. Stanley Thangaraj, "Racing the Muslim: Strategies for Teaching Race and Ethnic Studies in the Education Curriculum," *Urban Education*, December 17, 2020, https://journals.sagepub.com/doi/10.1177/0042085920972449.

20. Andrea Louie, *Chineseness across Borders* (Durham, NC: Duke University Press, 2003); Pawan Dhingra, "Indian Americans and the 'Brain Sport' of Spelling Bees," in *Asian American Sporting Cultures*, ed. Stanley I. Thangaraj, Constancio R. Arnaldo, and Christina B. Chin (New York: New York University Press, 2016), 127–151; Martin Manalansan, *Global Divas* (Durham, NC: Duke University Press, 2003); Gayatri Gopinath, *Impossible Desires* (Durham, NC: Duke University Press, 2005).

21. E. Patrick Johnson, *Appropriating Blackness* (Durham, NC: Duke University Press, 2003); Roderick Ferguson, *Aberrations of Black* (Minneapolis: University of Minnesota Press, 2004); Chandan Reddy, *Freedom with Violence* (Durham, NC: Duke University Press, 2011).

22. Gopinath, *Impossible Desires*; Manalansan, *Global Divas*.

23. Lowe, *Immigrant Acts*, 67.

24. Eric Tang, *Unsettled* (Philadelphia: Temple University Press, 2015); Chia Youyee Vang, "Hmong Youth, American Football, and the Politics of Ethnic Tournaments," in *Asian American Sporting Cultures*.

25. Laurel Mei-Singh, "Carceral Conservationism: Contested Landscapes and Technologies of Dispossession at Ka'ena Point, Hawai'i," *American Quarterly* 68, no. 3 (2016): 695–721.

26. Ty Tengan, *Native Men Remade* (Durham, NC: Duke University Press, 2008).

27. Stuart Hall, "Encoding/Decoding," in *Media and Cultural Studies*, ed. Meenakshi Durham and Douglas Kellner (New York: Wiley-Blackwell, 2001).

11

"Mister, How Come We Never Learned This?"

Teaching American Studies in a High School Setting

DAVE DIPIETRO

One of the first units in my American Identities class focuses on family, housing, and wealth—visions of what family has traditionally been in American popular culture as well as the boundaries that have been created to police normative behavior and determine the "us and them" in the United States. Students read Stephanie Coontz's "What We Really Miss about the 1950s," pieces of Richard Rothstein's *The Color Law*, Judith Smith's *Visions of Belonging*, as well as Ta-Nehisi Coates's "The Case for Reparations."[1] Each day, I see students begin to look at their own neighborhoods and see the borders and barriers, both real and metaphoric, that separate them from their peers within the city. "Hey, is that why there is a highway cutting off East Somerville where a lot of El Salvadorans live?" asks one student, followed quickly by another: "Yeah, and I think you could say the same thing about Mystic Valley Parkway on the edge of the projects that separates it from Ten Hills." A third student excitedly exclaims, "That's right, and the redline stops in Alewife before it gets into the suburbs—the literal redline!" They are taking the scholarly and making it personal, mapping American Studies onto their neighborhoods and lives. After reading a section in Coates's piece about Clyde Ross, the Mississippi-to-Chicago transplant who fell victim to the predatory practice of "buying on contract," a student stops to raise her hand and ask, "Mister, how come we never learned this?" So much of my own education in American Studies in college classrooms was an "undoing" of what I understood about the past and society today. It is for this exact reason that offering American Studies programming at the high school level is so important: it allows us to introduce students to the perspectives and methods of American Studies as part of their formative education and worldview. In doing so, we also open the field to these students so they can contribute their experience and expertise to our understanding of what constitutes history and American Studies.

AMERICAN STUDIES AT SOMERVILLE HIGH SCHOOL

I teach an introduction to American Studies course called American Identities to twelfth-graders at Somerville High School in Somerville, Massachusetts. The course is a dual-enrollment program run in conjunction with the University of Massachusetts Boston's American Studies Department, a program of which I am a graduate. In the 1990s, UMB professors Lois Rudnick, Judith Smith, and Rachel Rubin developed the course and wrote the accompanying text of the same name. The aim of the class was to increase student engagement with the field by bridging the gap between national historical narratives and the community narratives that were the fabric of students' lives. They wanted students to see themselves as historical actors in the scholarship they confronted. As part of this project, the group also sought to broaden the opportunities the course provided by partnering with the secondary educators to offer the course to high school seniors. High schools would offer American Identities in partnership with UMB, and students could earn university credit at no charge.[2] In 2014, I approached Judith, Rachel, and the rest of the department there as an alum, and they excitedly brought Somerville on as a secondary partner site.

Somerville High School is a large urban school and the only public high school in the city. Somerville, a few train stops from downtown Boston, has approximately one hundred thousand residents and is very much a city struggling with the ramifications of an expanding urban ring and the impacts of gentrification and displacement. It's roughly 40 percent Latinx, 40 percent white, and 20 percent everyone else, with large El Salvadorian, Brazilian, Haitian, Nepalese, and Tibetan populations and immigrant groups, in addition to a historic white working class and an expanding white upper middle class. Almost 50 percent of students do not consider English as their first language, and 20 percent are enrolled as English language learners. In 2019, the state of Massachusetts designated 60 percent of Somerville High students as "high needs" and 40 percent "economically disadvantaged."[3] For these factors and many others, my classroom is without doubt the most diverse space that I have ever been a part of. Because the school serves a population of students who have often found themselves left out of the traditional history narratives, including many students who stand at the intersection of different cultural identities, it is a perfect location for American Studies. By contributing their work, ideas, and experiences, the students shape the classroom and what we learn about identity. An immigrant student who shares their perspective on how housing discrimination impacts their community, or how they feel as though they navigate two worlds as an American, is shaping and creating new narratives about American identity. Informed by scholarship, these students project American Studies through their own experiences, altering our understandings of both. In turn, they are empowered to bring that work out of the classroom setting and into the communities where they live. I have often heard from siblings and parents of students in my class that my student dominated the dinner table conversation with discussions about power, justice, and inequity. These are not lessons I can simply deliver; these are understandings we build together using American Studies as a guide.

The foundation of the course is built around *American Identities: An Introductory Textbook*, edited by Lois P. Rudnick, Judith E. Smith, and Rachel Lee Rubin. It excerpts several noted American Studies scholars, including Gwyn Kirk and Margo Okezwa Rey, Elaine Tyler May, Vine Deloria Jr., Kristen Luker, Lisa McGirr, Bennett Harrison and Barry Bluestone, John D'Emilio and Estelle Freedman, and Gloria Anzaldúa, in addition to a curated set of primary texts. The editors skillfully boil down each chapter into ten-to-twelve-page student-friendly excerpts with introductions that help students contextualize the work. Each chapter ends with thoughtful study questions that pull out main ideas and takeaways. For many of my students, this is the first time they encounter this type of scholarship or indeed even the word "scholar." It's a challenge for them in terms of both the book's intellectual gravity and also its academic language.

It is here that I think my role as a secondary educator comes into play. I see the course, taught to seniors, as both a moment for students to "try on" college and a practical preparation for them to be able to, well, actually *do* college the following year. Before students can wrestle with the scholarship, they must first wrestle with how to speak, think, and act in a college setting. As an educator, it is my role in these conversations to model scholarly discourse. In class I often ham up my own performance as scholar to expose students to this new world. In a high school with a wide range of diverse needs, there are many structures and routines I have to put into place to also model for students how to navigate the world of being a successful college student. Instead of a syllabus for the year, each unit gets its own reading schedule, with only about three to four weeks' worth of homework at a time. This eases them into managing a collegiate workload. We spend time doing background work on the traditional political and economic histories students may or may not have access to; I think it's important that I do not take for granted students' starting points of historical knowledge. I include direct instruction around both Tier 3 vocabulary (academic area–specific words like "interpolation" or "intersectionality") and Tier 2 vocabulary students will encounter in the readings (high-frequency complex and abstract vocabulary words like "hierarchical," "extricate," or "marginal"). To foster engagement, I add popular scholars, documentaries, and popular culture, particularly film and television, to every unit. I also provide students with predictable structures and assignments in class to help them focus their attention on accessing the texts without spending mental energy interpreting the task.

Our schedule has us meet four days a week for fifty-five-minute sessions, and each night students generally are responsible for a chapter of the *American Identities* book or a similar reading. As in all of my high-school classes, I follow a general outline for lesson planning using the BEAR lesson structure (build, engage, apply/explore, and reflect). Class is divided into four sections with clear distinctions between teacher and student active times, with an emphasis on the latter. A typical class begins with a build activator, or "do now" in secondary education terms, where students are asked to activate previous knowledge from the last class or the homework to help them ground themselves in the intellectual work. This is especially important because I think so often as teachers we forget that students are coming from chemistry and statistics classes to ours. Then, there is usually some kind of engagement or direct instruction from the front of the room—a slide or two of lecture, let's say, on who the Young Lords Party was, or perhaps a brief film clip from a documentary, or activity logistics, before students are asked to break into small groups to apply new knowledge or explore a text. Using a guided note structure like Cornell notes as a basis, students are given a focus question answerable by the text and asked to find evidence to answer and support it. I teach students to parse a reading into notes, section headers, and main ideas on the left of the page, and thoughts, comments, and quotes that respond to the question on the right of a page. I try to give students access to the thought process of a good collegiate student by using a "think aloud" strategy a lot. After reading a question, I model a healthy internal dialogue: "Okay, the question is asking about intersectionality, but I don't remember what that is. I am going to go back to my notes from yesterday and check before I raise my hand. Oh, I get it now, I know what to say." Each class concludes with some form of group reflection on the lesson's objective so I can assess student understanding, and then a sharing out with an emphasis on hearing a variety of student voices supported by a slew of teacher tricks that limit the same voices from dominating conversation.

The task of helping each student find their voice in my class is another essential goal of the course, so that each student who passes through my classroom has the tools to become a memorable face in a large college setting where professors and teaching assistants often see hundreds of students. One strategy that has been helpful in this endeavor is the implementation of "barn raising" discussions.[4]

The barn raising strategy deploys the metaphor of a collective barn raising as an event involving the entire community to construct something more than what one member could achieve on their own to get students to discuss in collaboration. Instead of debating, students frame out their own discussion questions in regard to a topic and pose them to their peers for discussion as a way of making meaning together as a group. I have found this to be a strategy that is nonconfrontational, and instead collaborative, and that creates greater access points for students, especially female students, who have typically been disenfranchised by traditional paradigms of debate and competition in education.[5] The teacher's role is to be note taker, which I do in live time on a shareable document students can *watch* and make edits or additions to throughout the discussion.

Additionally, while students are graded on their participation, before the discussion they work collaboratively to formulate the rubric themselves and then grade themselves on it at the end of each discussion based on their own perception of their participation. Included on each rubric is a checklist of "do's" and sentence starters the students can use to enter the conversation (see Appendix: Barn Raising Assignment).

Lastly, at the end of each unit are mini "bluebook" style essays that ask students to take the essential questions from the beginning of the unit and answer them in short, on-demand style essays. The goal is for students to synthesize the unit's readings into coherent arguments using the scholarship to make their points. Each of these essays is open-note, and students are given the questions in advance, as well as strategies and time to prepare for them in class. Each unit follows this same structure, and each daily activity creates opportunities for students to practice and play with their ideas before putting them together into writing.

This backward design is a common approach in secondary education that I think is often not a focal point of postsecondary education.[6] The goal of these structures and scaffolds is, of course, for students to increasingly need them less and less, to the point where students demonstrate increasing independence.[7] Put best by one of my seniors reflecting in May: "In September my barn raisings and bluebooks really stunk, but I think they are pretty good now." In demystifying these academic skills, we free students to engage in producing the work of American Studies; with these tools, students bring relevant personal experience and expertise to shape conversations about power, justice, and identity. In the process, they are made aware of their own agency in producing understanding of the world we live in.

THE FAMILY HISTORY PROJECT

This same process of scaffold, support, and empower comes into play in the students' final research papers, the Family History Project. For this project coming out of the Rudnick, Smith, and Rubin original course design, students write a family history spanning three generations, looking critically at their family experiences by applying American Studies frames to their own story.[8] The assignment asks students to think how people are driven by individual internal factors (dreams, desires, choices) as well external social, political, and cultural forces. The final product is a fifteen-to-twenty-five-page narrative essay written by students acting as both family historian and critical scholar making connections across time and place. This project requires students to balance many academic skills at once: they are historiographic researchers, interviewers and collectors of oral history, academic writers, and analytic historians who weave the personal into the historic. It is a lot to ask, especially for students in the midst of their first real college class. For precisely this reason, it is also a project that requires the craft of teaching at the forefront (see Appendix: Family History Project).

As a teacher looking at the entirety of this project, I see two major avenues of support that students need: scaffolding of the actual assignment and one-to-one coaching. The former is the culmination of all of the work of the craft that happens before you have the students in front of you and follows the same backward-design approach as unit planning. The scaffolding of any assignment begins with the educator asking themself, "What do I want students to know at the end of this assignment? What do I want them to show that they know?" In this assignment, the very first adjustment to practice that needs to be made is thinking about how to get students to practically create this twenty-five-page narrative, and the first step is breaking it down for them. The family history is written in three parts—one for each generation. Students turn in the assignment three times, getting feedback along the way, ultimately submitting a final draft at the end of the course. Each segment is only about six to eight pages and has its own steps and due dates so that students are able to focus on one generation and one family story at a time.

Within each of these three parts, the assignment is further broken down to help students manage each part of the whole. Each section begins with a timeline assignment, where students complete research on social, cultural, political, and economic histories for their time span and location. For example, if a student's grandparent was born in El Salvador in 1942, and the student's parent 1971, the student would have to conduct research on El Salvadoran culture and politics from 1942 to 1971, and then turn that research into a bullet-note timeline of events. I have found that students need instruction on how to complete the research for this type of assignment, and I have been very fortunate to have a wonderful research librarian who has come into class and taught students how to access our library databases and how to discern appropriate sources from inappropriate sources. We are privileged in Somerville to have access to one-to-one computer technology, a luxury not all public schools can afford. During the first section of the family history, we spend time in class researching together, much of it spent with me peering over students' shoulders and dramatically chiding them for using the Yahoo Answers "Soccer War explained" page. But much of it is also our librarian and me sitting with students and finding resources and thinking critically about which articles would be best, teaching students to look at the citations, the word counts, and even how to navigate the technology (Ctrl F with the year has been a very big hit in 2020).[9]

This is, however, ultimately a family history, and the timeline would be incomplete if it did not put these outside events into direct contact with the personal narrative. Students complete an interview assignment where they first develop questions, then conduct an interview that is transcribed into note form and added to their timelines. Again, students need to be taught how to conduct an interview, how to develop questions, and how to dig when their subjects reply "I don't remember." This requires direct instruction, coaching, and close monitoring of progress.

The completed timeline of family and outside events then acts as a scaffold and organizer for the writing process. After careful examination of a variety of models of student work from years gone by, students use the timeline to write a rough draft of their narrative. I, in turn, make fastidious edits on these drafts, commenting on word choice, asking questions, pointing out opportunities for connections or research, and suggesting moments for deeper analysis. As a final step, students turn this into a final draft of their first generation, which will ultimately get revised again and folded into the completed three-generation, twenty-five-page paper. Breaking down the larger assignment allows students to separate out the important skills required for each step of the process and allows them to wrestle with each of these skills one at a time. The first section we write takes a lot of class time, the second section less, and by the time they are writing their third section, it's entirely on their own. The goal of this type of scaffolding should be, by the end, to make it invisible to the eye through the gradual release of responsibility from teacher to student.[10]

While all of this planning helps students to do the work of the academic, they do not, however, help students with the difficult work that is doing scholarship on their own families. This requires coaching on a one-to-one basis that gives students flexibility and freedom to develop their best work. When overviewing the project on day one, I can usually read the anxiety on the faces of students as they start to think, "I don't think my family is going to work for this." Indeed, the questions I field the most from colleagues and fellow educators are these: "What if the student doesn't have a grandparent?" "Are you suggesting all students have to be/identify as American to take this class?" "What about students whose families don't match up with classic visions of American families?" All of these concerns are addressed through framing, flexibility, and coaching.

As mentioned earlier, the very first unit of our course looks to dismantle the idea that there ever was, or ever is, a singular narrative of what family looks like. Students begin the year doing coursework around traditional stereotypes about family construction and read scholars, such as Smith and Coontz, who work to explain where the myth of the traditional American family comes from and why it is indeed a myth. We look at what types of familiar constructions actually exist in this country, why some have been held up as examples, and why others have been cast out of the normative experience. From this framing point, we as a class contend that YES, you DO have an American identity if your family is here making up the fabric of this place, but NO, you do not have to identify with traditional connotations of Americanness, and that in writing the family history you are working out and actively claiming your family's place in our collective cultural reality.

This does not happen just through our readings and class discussion; it also requires a good deal of individual attention, flexibility, and coaching to get students to see where they fit and how to craft and reclaim the value of their own family experience. Like all successful endeavors in teaching, it requires knowing your students. At the onset of the assignment, I assign students a "pick your participants" homework, where they make initial decisions about whose lives they are exploring, usually a grandparent, parent, and themselves. I then conference with each of these students, many of whom a day ago were convinced that they had to drop out of the course because their family would not fit this project. There are students who come to me worried that their family was not in the United States during the grandparent and parent generation. I explain that this is not, in fact, an obstacle, but instead even more important, exciting, and interesting. We discuss themes and strategies for research and interviewing. We talk about the challenges of interviewing in immigrant communities, where individuals may be reluctant to tell their stories because of fears of status or experiences of trauma. To that end, there are also many students whose families have lived in the same triple-decker Somerville home for sixty years but fear interviewing family members because of trauma, or worry about talking to or about parents who are sources of trauma to the student or who have passed. There are many more students who come in simply reporting that they do not have grandparents, or they are adopted and can't research their biological family. To each of these questions, I respond with a variety of answers, each of which are tailored to the student's unique concern but express the same message, "It's okay. Your family can work for this project."

The objective of this project is for students to understand how both personal choices and outside factors influence people's lives; they do not have to consider grandma, mom, and themselves to do this. Is it easier to complete this assignment if your family fits this model? Yes. Is it required? No. Many students have chosen aunts, uncles, cousins, family friends, stepparents, pastors, and neighbors to complete this assignment. I have had students interview parents and family members to reconstruct a past about a grandparent they never met. They have found diaries, photographs, and personal records to achieve the same. They have chosen to skip their own story and in turn do a sibling. They have skipped a parent because of trauma, and they have also chosen to do a parent to process trauma. The most important thing I can do in these instances as an educator is meet the student where they are, talk to them, and be open, accommodating, and honest. For the vast majority of students, they ultimately find ways to select a grandparent, parent, and themselves to write a story that informs them not only of history and how history works but also of themselves.

The last area in which students really need coaching is not on the selection of family members but on the analysis of family members as historic actors—as figures who balance their own agency against the powerful forces of space, place, and culture. An often-expressed concern in conferences with students is that "my family just isn't interesting and doesn't connect at all to our society." I push students to consider what that means for our traditional narratives if they seem so distant from the stories our families tell, and ask them to consider what it means about our understanding of the past. I also encourage students to challenge this notion by becoming the family historian and reading the outside history into family histories they are recovering. I remember sitting with one student, who, despite being brilliant with an excellent internal timeline of US history, struggled a lot with academic writing and overall work production. We were going over his choices for interviewees, and he lamented that his family had no story to tell, that they didn't fit any part of the larger story in any remarkable way. I looked at his grandmother's birth year and asked him, "1929 right? Born in Tennessee? But your dad, he's born in 1958 in Detroit? Why did they move?" He replied that his grandpa got "some kind of factory job with cars." I asked him if his grandma would also identify as an African American and he replied "definitely." Looking at him, I said, "African American from Tennessee to Detroit in the 1950s to work in automanufacturing post World War II?" and I watched his face light up. "Wait, am I part of the great migration? Wait I am, right? My grandma didn't even say that! I am part of the great migration!" This is where coaching—teaching students to read between the lines of interviews to make the connections that their interview subjects will not—is essential. To teach the students to do the work of historians, this is a work that cannot only be intuited from the creation of assignments but must actively be cultivated through direct and individual instructional coaching and modeling. It is also coaching students to be the authors and owners of the historic narratives in our culture—to reclaim stories that have always been there but have not always fit into traditional frames of history. The course allows students to write history from below, to contribute their experiences to what stories are told and what we hold as sacred knowledge.

REFLECTIONS

The primary editor of *American Identities*, Lois Rudnick, tells a story in the teaching guide to *Identities* that goes something like this: after doing the family history, Rudnick asked students to raise their hand if they had trouble writing their family histories, finding enough historic context, finding good sources, conducting interviews, and feeling overall like they were able to fully capture a moment in time. All students raised their hands. She then asked them if they think the scholars and historians we have read this year felt the same way, and if that was true, what did it say about the validity of all our histories? Or what does it say about the value of the experience captured in their family histories versus the histories in the pages of so many high school textbooks? She ends with saying something about seeing the light bulbs going off over students' heads. In my experience in a twelfth-grade public high school classroom, this very much rings true. The Family History Project, and the American Identities course in general, first and foremost teaches students the currency of collegiate capital. They learn the skills and academic language to access intellectual college conversations on a level equal to their more affluent peers—in several reports from professors in my circle, at a much higher level. Additionally, in line with the themes of this book, it also engages them in the work of American Studies in reclaiming the narratives and histories of everyday people influenced by the culture that we inhabit. They tell stories that are about themselves but also about the world that we live in and that challenge stagnant or trite stereotypes about working communities, immigrant communities, communities of color, and many other communities and cultures of everyday life. From this unique vantage point, students taking this course are able to critically analyze the creation of modern identities in ways that traditional scholarship cannot, to see things simultaneously from the inside and the outside with authority. To bring American Studies to life in the classroom through teaching is not only to do the work of social justice, it is also to do the work of transforming the field.

APPENDIX: BARN RAISING ASSIGNMENT

Name: American Identities Homework

Barn Raising Discussion:
Unit 1 Social Location

Directions: In order to prepare for our Barn Raising Discussion, write 3 open-ended discussion questions you could ask about the texts below, using our thematic question as a guide. The best discussion questions are those that put the texts in conversation with each other, have no concrete or direct answer, and require evidence from the texts to answer. When you finish brainstorming your question, prepare for the discussion by reflecting in writing on the ONE question that you think is the best for open discussion.

Big Picture Thematic Question:
How does social location (micro, meso, and macro) impact identity?

Texts:

- *American Identities* Chapter 1: "Identities and Social Locations: Who Am I? Who Are My People?" (Gwyn Kirk and Margo Okazawa-Rey, 8–16).

PART 1: Draft Possible Barn Raising Questions

Brainstorm at least 3 open-ended questions below.

1.
2.
3.

PART 2: Write to Think

On a piece of lined notebook paper, brainstorm a response to your ***BEST*** *question in a well-written paragraph with a clear claim, evidence, and analysis. Be sure to quote, reference the text, and include page numbers in parenthesis if applicable.*

Discussion Starters and Sentence Stems

Overview:
In order to improve our ability to hold collegiate discussions, we are going to explicitly work on how to speak and respond in a seminar-style discussion. For this discussion each comment made MUST start with one of the sentence stems below (or a clear and appropriate variation). This will ensure that we keep our ideas and comments connected to each other. Everyone needs to speak and participate and be sure to use people's names when speaking.

I want to extend what _______________ said...
I want to challenge what _______________ said...
I want to support what _______________ said...
I want to respond to what _______________ said...
I want to connect back what _______________said...
I agree/disagree with what _______________ said...

American Identities *Discussion Checklist and Rubric*

- ❑ Everyone participates (speaking and actively listening).
- ❑ Active listening, eye contact, positive body language.
- ❑ Allow others to speak and share "air"—take turns speaking.
- ❑ Ask relevant questions and involve/engage others in the conversations.
- ❑ Spark conversation with open-ended responses.
- ❑ Support your argument with evidence and scholarship.
- ❑ Refute others' ideas respectfully.
- ❑ Respect others when they are speaking.
- ❑ Act as a leader—engage others in conversation.
- ❑ Be prepared.

1	2	3	4	5
Did not successfully participate in the discussion according to the checklist.	Met few if any of the discussion checklist measures.	Met a minimum number of items on the discussion checklist.	Satisfactorily participated in the discussion according to the checklist.	Excelled in the discussion according to the checklist. Over and above all-out rock star.

APPENDIX: FAMILY HISTORY PROJECT

Name: American Identities–FHP

Family History Project Project Overview

The culminating assignment in American Identities at UMASS Boston is the completion of a Family History Project (FHP) covering three generations of your own family history across the timeframe of the course from WWII to the present. The final project will consist of a timeline and a written narrative history for each of the generations you select to cover of your family—totaling 15–25 pages in length. The purpose of the timeline and the narrative family history is for you to demonstrate an understanding of the ways in which the three-generation history of your family is related to changing national, cultural, and local (community) events and trends. Throughout your family history, you will be answering the questions: "How was your family shaped from the outside?" (by political, economic, cultural, and social changes) and well as "How was your family shaped from the inside?" (by dreams and aspirations, religion/ethnic traditions/practices). In other words, you will work to identify each generation's specific social location based on their micro, meso, and macro layers of identity.

This narrative will be created in parts, and we will spend some class time researching, drafting, and writing these family histories. MOST of this assignment will be completed outside of class time. You will submit this assignment in parts broken down by each generation and have the opportunity to revise these parts before submitting the final copy for grading.

Each component will be worth 25% of your grades in the quarter in which it is due with the exception of Section III (see the table below). **FAILURE TO PASS IN A FAMILY HISTORY PROJECT THAT MEETS THE MINIMUM STANDARDS WILL RESULT IN FAILURE OF THE COURSE.**

Section I – 25% of Quarter 2
Section II – 25% of Quarter 3
Section III and Final Compiled Project – 50% of Quarter 4

FAMILY HISTORY PROJECT AT A GLANCE

Section/Generation	*Components*
Section I: ***Generation I***	1. Timeline of Events (1–2 Pages)
(Person Born 1940s–1960s)	2. Narrative History (4–6 Pages)
Section II: ***Generation II***	1. Timeline of Events (1–2 Pages)
(Person Born 1960s–1980s)	2. Narrative History (4–6 Pages)
Section III: ***Generation III***	1. Timeline of Events (1–2 Pages)
(Person Born 1980s–2000s)	2. Narrative History (4–6 Pages)
Final Project	
Combined Sections 1–3	1. Combined timelines (3–6 pages)
Generations 1–3	2. Combined Narrative History (12–18 pages)

TIMELINE SECTIONS (1–2 pages per section)

The purpose of the timeline is to show important moments in your family story chronologically and in historic context: for example, what was happening at the time when your grandfather entered the army, when your mother found her first job, when you entered high school? The timeline correlates the important dates and events of your family history with national and local (community) events, issues, movements, and the cultural productions that were important to your family and that we study in the course. Your timeline should read like a table or chart with columns for the categories as in the example below. I will provide a model worksheet to you digitally when we reach that step.

You will fill in the chart provided (or an approved alternative) chronologically, beginning at the lower end of the generational time period (ex: 1940) and going up to the upper limit for that generation (ex: 1960), including one or two events for each category that are most relevant to your family history. For example, if your grandparents were born during the time of the "Duck and Cover" PSA, that date/event should be on your chart. You do not have to include every year, but you must include those national, cultural, and social events relevant to the major turning points in your family history. International students and recent immigrants should use political, social, and cultural events and productions from their country of origin, although the latter can come from our course reading or other relevant material.

MODEL TIMELINE

Year(s)	*Family Events*	*National/International (Economic & Political) Events*	*Social/Cultural Events*
2001	David enters freshman year of HS at Lexington High School Fourth day of school David listens to World Trade Center attacks on radio broadcast during gym class David got fired from Ace Hardware for being accused (wrongly) of stealing	September 11: Multiple terrorist attacks on US soil War in Afghanistan begins America has strong foreign support/ approval	Airport security protocols change Profiling of Muslim Americans begins Relief concert for 9/11 victims held Wikipedia launched
2002	Text text text	Text text text	Text text text
2004	Text text text	Text text text	Text text text

HISTORICAL NARRATIVE SECTIONS (4–6 pages per section)

Using your timeline as a guide, each generation section will also include a written narrative history of your family's experience. Narrative history is written in summary form and should read like a story. Your historical narrative should focus on some of the key events and choices that altered the lives of each generation. Your job is not simply to recount the family chronology but to be the family historian—to find the connections between what happened to the family over time and the economic, political, social, and cultural events that most influenced the formation of your family, and to trace the changes over time. For example if your grandmother moved from Birmingham, Alabama, in 1949 to Detroit, Michigan, to look for work in the auto industry and to escape racism, this is likely connected to the great migration and the post-WWII economic boom. It's your job as the family historian to make the connections your family might not be able to explicitly draw. Try to give your narrative a motif: is there a theme (or are there themes) or experience(s) that unites or divides the generations? Coherence, imagination, and passion give life to "facts." At the end of your history, you should reflect back on the major changes and challenges faced by your family over time, and explain how their understanding of their American (or other national) identities have been shaped over time.

WORKS CITED PAGE SECTION (1–2 pages total)

The vast majority of your research will come from our two course texts *Out of Many* and *American Identities*. In some instances, independent research may be necessary to make these connections possible. Students whose families or who themselves are immigrants will need to supplement the assigned course reading with background research on the history of their family's country (I can help to guide this research). All research must be cited in a properly formatted MLA works cited page.

Family History Grading Rubric

Content & ORGANIZATION (80% of FHP Grade—80 Points)

Excellent (70–80 points): Fulfilled or exceeded all requirements of assignment • Well-organized narrative flow • chronological or thematic focus • biographical events situated within broader context in meaningful ways • events in timeline are included in narrative and vice versa • conclusion makes big picture observations about the three generations over time.

Good to Very Good (60–70 points): Fulfills requirements of assignment • generally well organized narrative that follows chronological or thematic focus • lapses in organization do not obstruct understanding • biographical events are generally but not always situated within broader context • connections to natural and cultural events are generally meaningful but may sometimes lack a substantive connection to life events • connections to national/cultural events are generally clear, but there may be the occasional lapse • With few exceptions, events in timeline included in narrative and vice versa • conclusion may make observations about generations while lacking big picture observations

Poor to Fair (50–60 points) : Did not fulfill all the requirements of the assignment • may be poorly organized and/or lapses in organization are frequent and may obstruct comprehension • generally biographical events are either not connected to national or cultural events, the connections are unclear, or not explained • may not have developed life events or included sufficient information about life events • numerous events in the narrative may be missing from the timeline or vice versa • may lack a conclusion or the conclusion does not make observations across the generations

Very Poor (Below 50 points): Did not fulfill the requirements of the assignment.

<u>Documentation of Sources (10% of FHP Grade—10 points)</u>

Excellent (9–10): Uses appropriate sources • internet sources are not over-represented and are appropriate for an academic project • used the in-class materials. *Out Of Many* (OOM) and *American Identities* (AI) whenever possible as a secondary source • sources are properly documented using in-text citations in the document • includes a properly formatted and complete list of works cited in the document • lack of use of OOM in any stage due to the narrative taking place abroad • use of secondary sources beyond OOM and AI

Good to Very Good (7–8): Internet sources may be over-represented although appropriate • generally used in-class materials when possible but may have relied excessively on internet sources for documentation rather than locating information in OOM • consistent use of in-text citations throughout the paper, although formatting may be inconsistent or incorrect • includes a full list of works cited • lapses in formatting works cited or in-text citations are either minor or few • lack of use of OOM and AI is due only to the narrative taking place abroad

Fair to Poor (6–7): May have relied excessively on internet sources • Internet source over-represented or inappropriate for academic use • largely failed to use OOM and AI or did not do so appropriately • if writing about the life of someone who lived outside the United States, failed to use appropriate secondary sources for determining relevant national and/or cultural events • in-text citation may be inconsistent or largely lacking• may lack a list of works cited or there are sources missing • formatting of sources may generally fail to follow proper guidelines

Very Poor (Below 5): May have failed to use in-text citations or used them rarely • works cited missing or incomplete • works cited may be incorrectly formatted • little if any use of OOM

<u>Mechanics (10% of FHP Grade—10 points)</u>

Excellent (9–10): Largely free of mechanical errors (e.g., grammar and spelling). Clear writing. Use of appropriate language.

Good to Very Good (7–8): Largely free of mechanical errors. May contain some awkward, unclear, or run-on sentences; have difficulty with paragraphing.

> ***Fair to Poor (6–7)***: May have a significant number mechanical errors, including spelling. May contain consistent and frequent errors in grammatical structure and/or word usage. Awkward, unclear, or run-on sentences are frequent or impede understanding.
>
> ***Very Poor (Below 5)***: Did not fulfill the requirements of the assignment

NOTES

1. Stephanie Coontz, "What We Really Miss about the 1950s," in *American Identities: An Introductory Textbook*, ed. Lois P. Rudnick, Judith E. Smith, and Rachel Rubin (Malden, MA: Blackwell, 2006), 17–28; Richard Rothstein, *The Color of Law: A Forgotten History of How Our Government Segregated America* (New York: Liveright, 2017); Judith E. Smith, *Visions of Belonging: Family Stories, Popular Culture, and Post War Democracy, 1940–1960* (New York: Columbia University Press, 2004); Ta-Nehisi Coates, "The Case for Reparations," in *We Were Eight Years in Power: An American Tragedy* (New York: Penguin Random House, 2017).

2. Lois P. Rudnick, Judith Smith, Rachel Rubin, Eric Goodson, and Carol Siriani, "Teaching American Identities: A University/Secondary School Collaboration," *American Quarterly* 54, no. 2 (2002): 255–277.

3. "School and District Profiles: Somerville," Massachusetts Department of Primary and Secondary Education, reported for 2018–2019, http://profiles.doe.mass.edu/general/general.aspx?topNavID=1&leftNavId=100&orgcode=02740000&orgtypecode=5.

4. Don McCormick and Michael Kahn, "Barn Raising: Collaborative Group Process in Seminar," *Exchange: The Organizational Behavior Teaching Journal* 7, no. 4 (December 1982): 16–20.

5. bell hooks, *Talking Back: Thinking Feminist, Thinking Black* (New York: Routledge, 2015), 35–41.

6. Grant Wiggins and Jay McTighe, *Understanding by Design* (Danvers, MA: Association for Supervision and Curriculum Development, 2005).

7. Nell K. Duke and P. David Pearson, "Effective Practices for Developing Reading Comprehension," in *What Research Has to Say about Reading Instruction*, 3rd ed., ed. Alan E. Farstrup and S. J. Samuels, 205–241 (Newark, DE: International Reading Association, 2002).

8. Rudnick et al., "Teaching American Identities."

9. Mary C. Waters and Reed Ueda with Helen B. Marrow, eds., *The New Americans: A Guide to Immigration since 1965* (Cambridge, MA: Harvard University Press, 2007). On Judy Smith's recommendation, I have found this source to be particularly helpful for students who have immigrant identities, as it catalogues and examines patterns of immigration from a great number of geographies.

10. Duke and Pearson, "Effective Practices."

12

Let This Seminar Be a Starting Point

Digital Storytelling and the African American Experience

KABRIA BAUMGARTNER

To know how much there is to know is the beginning
of learning to live.
—Dorothy West, *The Richer, the Poorer*

"What is motivating you to take this capstone seminar on African American culture and heritage in New England?" I asked the dozen students who greeted me on the first day of class at the University of New Hampshire. While a few students occasionally mentioned fulfilling a requirement or course scheduling, most students confessed that they were taking my course because their knowledge of African American culture was thin. "As someone who is interested in New England history, I don't know much about the African American experience in New England and I want to know more," one student revealed.[1] During that very first class, I highlighted these thoughtful responses, which signaled students' eagerness to learn and their recognition that there is much more to know. Moreover, themes such as race, place, and history were now on the table, and we would revisit them throughout the semester.

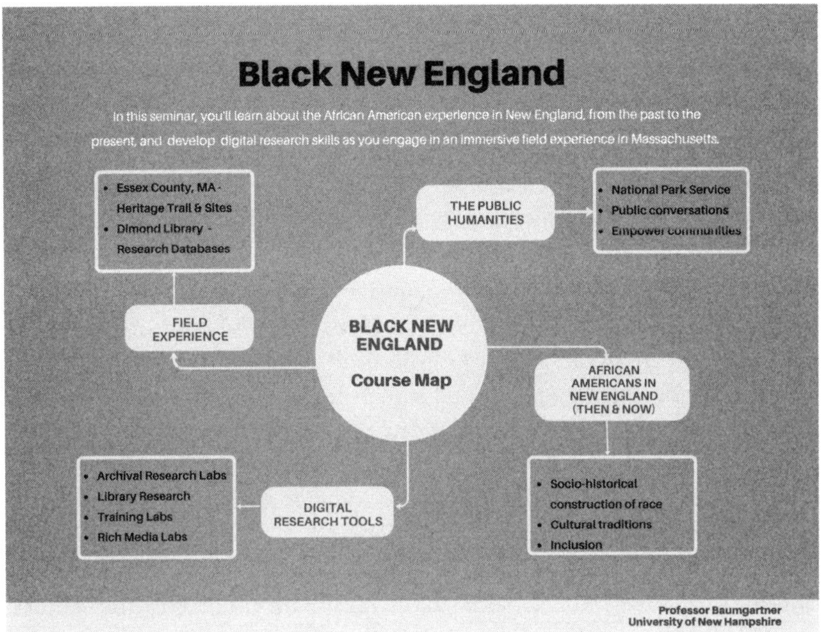

Figure 12.1. I generated this graphic, using Canva, to outline the major components of this seminar on African American culture and heritage in New England as well as to introduce rich multimedia web applications to students.

My overarching goal in this seminar was for students to learn to critically and thoughtfully engage in deeper conversations about race, racism, and African American heritage. To that end, I focused on developing students' content knowledge of the rich history of African Americans in New England and then helping them navigate and practice archival research and digital media. But what would the final project be that tied it all together? A presentation? A paper? It soon became clear to me that the best way to showcase students' energy, creativity, and newfound knowledge in this interdisciplinary seminar was through a digital storytelling video project. As neat as this plan was, challenges emerged, which actually opened up an opportunity for me to present a fuller picture of how the long history of race shapes our lives today. By the end of this seminar, students had gained direct, hands-on experience and skill building. More importantly, their experiences researching and writing prepared them to interrogate and examine local, regional, and debates about race and power.[2]

THE WHAT AND WHY OF DIGITAL STORYTELLING

Simply put, digital storytelling is the interactive art of telling a compelling story with rich multimedia such as audio, video, music, images, and text. These digital videos are typically three to five minutes long and have a strong narrative arc. The scholar Joe Lambert outlined seven elements of digital stories: point of view, dramatic question, emotional content, voice, soundtrack, pacing, and economy.[3]

Project-based digital storytelling videos have become increasingly common in foreign language, math, and literature classrooms, from middle school to college, as well as at cultural heritage sites.[4] Research indicates that digital storytelling projects allow students to be active participants in the learning process. It helps them build self-reliance, which aligns with the mission of many colleges and universities to educate students to become lifelong learners.

Digital storytelling is not new to American Studies either. The scholar Matthias Opperman maintains that digital storytelling in the American Studies classroom "provide[s] students with an alternative site to produce knowledge in the field," making them creators and producers of "alternative discourses."[5] Practically, students are also able to hone their critical analysis and reasoning skills and pull from multiple disciplines as they read, produce, and reflect. I turned to digital storytelling for these reasons and also because it emphasizes process, rather than product, which parallels how we ought to be teaching and learning about race. In other words, learning about race does not quite end. In fact, I want students to continue to ask questions about race, racial formations, and racism in the United States after they have left my seminar. Hence digital storytelling, *as a process*, encourages students to learn together while crafting their story, and their story then informs others, sparking deep reflection and engagement, similar to a feedback loop. The effective use of digital storytelling both in college classrooms and at cultural heritage sites prompted me to organize my seminar around it.

To better fit my seminar, I modified the digital storytelling video project in two ways. A three-minute video seemed too short, so I extended it to ten minutes, so that students would be challenged to sustain a controlling idea or premise. Second, the story in each video was loosely based on archival work about African American people, events, or traditions, as opposed to personal student reflections. Aside from these two changes, the project followed a straightforward roadmap, and I used a sequencing and scaffolding approach, moving from content and contextualizing African American history to planning and scripting, storyboarding, peer reviewing, revising, and then presenting. I reviewed the final project instructions with students early in the semester, answered some logistical questions, and introduced my research assistant, Sherard Harrington, who would be helping us.[6]

I structured this seminar so that students could familiarize themselves with the history and culture of African Americans in New England before learning the ins and outs of archival research and using digital tools. Given my training and expertise in the interdisciplinary fields of American Studies, African American Studies, and nineteenth-century US literature and history, I taught the course content. Then, I worked with librarians and archivists at my university to hold three cumulative archival research labs: the first provided a basic introduction to an archive; the second introduced students to archival materials and allowed them to practice their analytical skills; and the third focused on "smart searching," which covered how to search digital archives and find and use secondary source materials. Each of these ninety-minute labs included a short reading to anchor students' thoughts.[7] I also partnered with instructional technologists to lead three digital training workshops on using digital cameras and software like iMovie, Adobe Spark, and Canva. The hope was that, with content knowledge and training in archival research methods and digital tools, students would be ready to visit and conduct research at repositories. But the reality is that there were some challenges along the way.

THREE CHALLENGES (AND RESOLUTIONS)

My first challenge was trying to remedy my students' limited knowledge of African American literature and culture. Every semester comes with certain time constraints, but the fact that archival research and training in digital media were part of the seminar meant that I had even less time to explore key content. So I introduced topics that would be worth further archival exploration such as the history and legacy of Negro Election Day; the struggle for equal school rights in Massachusetts, New Hampshire, and Rhode Island; the radical abolition movement; African American family life and religious practices; and the work of African American artists and writers such as Edmonia Lewis, Allan Crite, Loïs Mailou Jones, Harriet Wilson, and Dorothy West. I realized that my approach to teaching this seminar did not have to be top-down, teacher to student, but rather students could build on what they had learned.

To resolve this first challenge, I asked students to complete a questionnaire identifying their interests in the broad fields of African American literature, culture, and history. Since this seminar was closely linked to a National Park Service and Organization of American Historians grant-funded project on African Americans in Essex County, Massachusetts, my research assistant, Sherard, and I located collections at selected repositories in Essex County that matched student interests. For the most part, this arrangement worked well, though the match between collections and student interests was not perfect.[8] For example, one student, John, indicated an interest in learning more about black churches. While a few Black churches exist in Essex County, their records are not readily accessible. Instead of researching Black churches, my student, John, found an equally exciting subject: Jacob Stroyer, a formerly enslaved African American man who migrated to Massachusetts, wrote his autobiography *My Life in the South* (1885), and became a preacher. These workarounds proved successful.

A subsequent challenge was helping students put their archival research skills into practice while working at a repository. None of my students could claim prior experience conducting archival research, and only two had ever visited a repository. I had anticipated that some students might be new to this, which is why I included a nuts-and-bolts guide for research in addition to the three labs. During the two-week research phase of the seminar, students worked independently at repositories, and they found themselves daunted by the very task of searching through folders and trying to make sense of letters, photographs, and other materials. Journaling was an ungraded assignment in this seminar, and in their journal entries, students admitted that they felt overwhelmed. What should they focus on? How do they form a story out of these disparate sources? What materials should they highlight in their videos and why? We had talked about pacing, goal setting, and managing expectations during our archival research labs, but there is nothing like firsthand experience. Periodic reminders to read the finding aid, take copious notes, or write down immediate responses to a document did not help much either.

What students needed was a space to reflect on the research experience itself. When we reconvened as a class after visiting repositories in Essex County, we talked through the joys and frustrations of doing archival research. For some students, the joys included the privilege of "looking at cool, old documents" and working with helpful archivists. The frustrations of archival research were "finding an excess of information that doesn't pertain to your specific area of research" and "not having enough time."[9] I, as an educator and researcher, acknowledged and validated these observations and responses. I mentioned that my own book on the educational narratives of African American girls and women in early nineteenth-century New England took about eight years to research and write. I described the days that I sat in a repository, looked through documents, and found next to nothing on the topic at hand. I stressed to my students that archival work is a research method, and they were doing it for the first time. "These repositories are free and open to the public; you can return, at any time. Let this seminar be a starting point," I added.

I also had to give my students some practical suggestions (sooner than I had planned), such as storyboarding, to guide them. All twelve of the advanced undergraduate students in this seminar had taken at least eight courses in US, British, and global literature; they had studied Shakespearean drama, sharpened their close reading skills, written analytical essays on novels and poetry, and so on. I asked my students to recall that previous knowledge. What makes a good story and why? What makes it memorable? Why do we even share stories? I worked with them in small groups and individually to answer these and other questions, and I helped them take their responses and place them on their storyboard.

As students prepared for peer review, another interesting challenge emerged: what do you do when you don't find any materials related to your area of research after visiting a repository? Most students found dozens of archival documents in their area of research, while a few students returned to class seemingly empty-handed. For example, one of my students, Evan, wrote about John Levy, an African American barber and abolitionist from Essex County, whose memoir *The Life and Adventures of John Levy* (1871) provided lots of context, as did a few documents available at Lawrence History Center in Massachusetts. Evan was in an enviable position as he worked to complete his video. In contrast, another student, Madi, explored the history of Negro Election Day, an eighteenth-century Black cultural festival, but her search at Phillips Library in Salem, Massachusetts, turned up only one source, a diary entry written by a white minister, William Bentley, commenting briefly on the festival. These divergent experiences provoked a great class discussion about whose stories are remembered, how documents are recorded, and how stories can be told even with a thin source base. I introduced several theoretical frameworks such as feminist standpoint theory, which rejects the idea of absolute objectivity; reading against the grain, which means reading deeply and critically for what is there and what is not;

and Saidiya Hartman's concept of critical fabulation, which relies on using historical context to speculate responsibly. I had not expected to share these frameworks and concepts, but students' inquiries provided an opportunity, which I think allayed some of their worries about not having enough material. Madi decided to reflect on the difficulty of locating materials about Negro Election Day and linked that to a broader discussion of history, power, and record keeping.

Despite these challenges, my students and I reached some great insights about archival work. For first-time or even seasoned researchers, digging in the archives can be daunting, frustrating, and time consuming. What we hope to find in a collection may never actually materialize, so we meditate on the stories that remain unrecoverable or we cleave to something else in a collection. One student reflected: "[I realized] that how we view history is based much on the work of archivists, power, privilege, and chance."[10] Archival practices centuries ago, which failed to catalog the experiences of African Americans and other people of color in any kind of systematic way, haunt us and complicate our ability to tell inclusive stories of the past. The optimist's view is that the changing practices within archival studies will mean that the stories of African Americans today will be shared and remembered for tomorrow.

THE DIGITAL STORYTELLING VIDEO PROJECTS

Once students began to work on their storyboard and video, they gained some confidence. One student realized that, in hindsight, archival research "was not as difficult as originally anticipated," because at the end of it all, little-known stories about the past would be disseminated.[11] In other words, certain stories could leave the confines of folders and boxes at a repository and be shared digitally with others, including peers, family, and the community.

My students' digital storytelling videos ranged in quality from decent to polished. I noticed that higher-quality videos often had a clear and well-developed story arc, featuring a variety of documents such as photographs, letters, and newspaper articles. Archival collections of at least one-quarter linear foot work better in a digital format compared to smaller collections with only a handful of documents or a collection with a single kind of source (e.g., only correspondence or receipts). In that sense, the digital format became somewhat limiting for those students who did not have rich multimedia to use, and their videos were consequently more static. Those students needed even stronger audio narration or a more precise central premise, which did not become apparent until after the video had been produced. Next time I teach this seminar, I will be sure to identify larger collections and encourage students to strategize before visiting a repository.

Two videos in particular were impressive in quality and production as well as subject matter. I highlight these videos because they extend the history of the African American experience beyond slavery and abolition. Maddy O'Leary, a graduating senior majoring in English, narrated the fascinating story of Allen Hinton, a formerly enslaved African American man from North Carolina who migrated to Andover, Massachusetts, in the late nineteenth century, where he and his wife, Mary, opened a successful ice cream business. Maddy spent hours sifting through the Hinton collection at the Andover Center for History and Culture and then zeroed in on a great story arc that both evoked the theme of triumph over hardship and also celebrated Black entrepreneurship. For Madelyn, the archival research experience and digital storytelling video project made her realize that "in the age of technology, it blew [her] mind how many stories haven't been seen and aren't known, especially about people of color."[12]

The second video, created by Christopher Craycraft, a graduating senior majoring in English teaching and Spanish, featured materials from the Sinclair Family Papers housed at the University of New Hampshire's Special Collections and Archives department. Clayton and Hazel Sinclair were an African American couple who opened Rock Rest, an inn located in Kittery Point, Maine, that was patronized by African American vacationers in the mid-twentieth century. This collection is vast, at six cubic feet, and Christopher carefully explored the finding aid and then spent lots of time leafing through specific folders to narrow down a slice of the Sinclairs' activism to spotlight in his video. He contextualized the story of African American travelers, discussing the problem of segregation, while also capturing African American leisure experiences. What I liked was that his approach offered a more holistic depiction of the African American experience; the struggle against racism and the desire for leisure were not mutually exclusive.

In terms of students learning about African American culture and heritage in New England, this seminar far exceeded my expectations. All students reported that that they had deepened their knowledge of African American cultural events like Negro Election Day, gained an appreciation of the African American literary tradition by reading Harriet Wilson's novel *Our Nig*, and familiarized themselves with the history and work of the Black Heritage Trail of New Hampshire, a nonprofit organization that aims to educate the public about the rich history of Black people in New Hampshire. My students impressed me with their thoughtfulness, openness, and hard work. In terms of skill building, this seminar hit the mark as students deepened their analytical reading, writing, and research skills. All students could now boast that they had visited *and* conducted research at a repository and learned new digital tools like AdobeSpark.

What I asked of my students in this capstone seminar was challenging, and they all stayed the course, which actually engendered new perspectives. One student reflected: "I know there is a rich African American history in New Hampshire that goes way back in time, and I better understand what it's like [for] African Americans in New Hampshire and the challenges that may come with it."[13] Another student's perception of the nineteenth-century North had shifted: "I learned that [African Americans] still had hardships. The north was not this racial safehaven [*sic*] we were taught it was when learning about the underground railroad."[14] This seminar yielded high student satisfaction, with an overall score of 4.91 out of 5.00 on student teaching evaluations, in part because it drew from an interdisciplinary knowledge base to contextualize the pressing issues in the United States now—like race and racism.

CONCLUSION

African American culture and heritage in New England too often remains on the periphery in a state like New Hampshire, which means that American Studies courses that engage race, gender, and other social identities are vital. Moreover, it is absolutely an enriching experience for undergraduate students to complete a capstone project that moves them through the research experience, from identifying a topic to evaluating secondary sources, finding and analyzing primary sources, and then presenting the final product. Digital storytelling with an archival research component further enhances the capstone experience as students gain hands-on skills and engage in student-generated conversations about race and power. One of my students explained, "I gained experience that I will be able to use later in life as well as a respect for those who do archival research for a living."[15] This comment captures exactly what I aim to show and remind students, namely how and why studying race and the African American experience is a relevant and meaningful process, not only for career prospects but also for intellectual and personal growth, lifelong learning, and civic engagement.

As Elizabeth Duclos-Orsello reminded me, when we as teachers in the field of American Studies "try to do many things in a capstone seminar—from interdisciplinary teaching, archival training, engaging with histories of race in the United States to developing digital media projects, the good advice, not just for students, but also for teachers is, to let this seminar be a starting point."[16]

APPENDIX: STUDENT RESPONSES ON THE JOYS AND FRUSTRATIONS OF ARCHIVAL RESEARCH

What were the challenges and frustrations of doing archival research?

- So much to look through—hard to find what I was looking for
- Lots and lots and lots to sift through to find what I really need
- Time consuming, felt like I might have missed things
- Not enough time and a lot of material
- Waiting to hear back from archivist if they are busy and that can take *forever*
- Hours of operation are limited
- Scheduling a visit in the middle of the week
- Difficult to decipher some of the handwritten documents
- Limitations, there are gaps and missing info
- Hard to choose what is/isn't important enough to take note of
- Finding an excess of information on your subject that doesn't pertain to your specific area of research
- Documents not organized (chewed through/dirty/mouse droppings)

What were the joys of doing archival research?

- Hands-on, direct w/ materials
- New and interesting form of research to me—hands-on and engaging
- Firsthand look into the period being researched
- So many options, you get to decide what to research
- Really cool old documents
- Looking at old things that are not considered significant or critically acclaimed
- Really interesting, lots of stuff to learn from, way better than a textbook
- Lots of information/facts to look at, it gives a good platform
- Lots of very fascinating info!
- Learning what a person was like through documents and artifacts that were present in their everyday lives
- Archivist was helpful, able to lead me in the right direction
- Archivist *so* helpful!

(continued on the next page)

(continued from the next page)

Note: After having visited repositories in Essex County, Massachusetts, students wrote these reflections on the whiteboard about their experiences.

NOTES

1. Anonymous student response on questionnaire, August 28, 2018.
2. I thank Elizabeth Duclos-Orsello for helping me articulate this point.
3. Joe Lambert, *Digital Storytelling Cookbook and Traveling Companion* (Berkeley, CA: Digital Diner, 2007), 9–19.
4. See, for instance, Martha E. Castañeda, "'I am proud that I did it and it's a piece of me': Digital Storytelling in the Foreign Language Classroom," *CALICO Journal* 30, no. 1 (2013): 44–62; Hannele Niemi, Shuanghong Niu, Marianna Vivitsou, and Baoping Li, "Digital Storytelling for Twenty-First-Century Competencies with Math Literacy and Student Engagement in China and Finland," *Contemporary Educational Technology* 9, no. 4 (2018): 331–353; and Akrivi Katifori, Fay Tsitou, Myrsini Pichou, Vassilis Kourtis, Evangelos Papoulias, Yannis Ioannidis, and Maria Roussou, "Exploring the Potential of Visually Rich Animated Digital Storytelling for Cultural Heritage: The Mobile Experience of the Athens University History Museum," in *Visual Computing for Cultural Heritage*, ed. Fotis Liarokapis, Athanasios Voulodimos, Nikolaos Doulamis, and Anastasios Doulamis (Switzerland: Springer International, 2020), 325–345.
5. Matthias Oppermann, "'Writing in 'that' other space"': Digital Storytelling and the Scholarship of Teaching in American Studies," *Amerikastudien/American Studies* 52, no. 3 (2007): 332 and 337.
6. Sherard Harrington is a doctoral candidate in the English Department at the University of New Hampshire. He studies queer theory, African American literature, and visual culture.
7. The assigned readings included Katherine E. Tirabassi, "Journeying into the Archives: Exploring the Pragmatic of Archival Research," in *Working in the Archives: Practical Research Methods of Rhetoric and Composition*, ed. Alexis E. Ramsey, Wendy B. Sharer, Barbara L'Eplattenier, and Lisa S. Mastrangelo (Carbondale: Southern Illinois University Press, 2010), 169–180; Wikipedia, s.v. "Archival research," last edited November 21, 2020, 17:49, https://en.wikipedia.org/wiki/Archival_research; and P. Gabrielle Foreman, "Introduction," in *Our Nig; or, Sketches from the Life of a Free Black*, ed. P. Gabrielle Foreman and Reginald H. Pitts (New York: Penguin, 2005), xxv–lv.
8. I did face another difficulty when one archivist became unresponsive. Fortunately, I had already anticipated this possibility and planned for a few students to conduct research in the Special Collections and Archives department at my university.
9. Student classroom board work, Fall Semester 2018. See appendix for complete list of student responses.
10. Anonymous student response, December 6, 2018.
11. Anonymous student response, December 6, 2018.

12. Maddy O'Leary response, December 2018.
13. Anonymous student responses, December 6, 2018.
14. Anonymous student responses, December 6, 2018.
15. Anonymous student response, December 6, 2018.
16. Conversation with Elizabeth Duclos-Orsello, June 22, 2020.

PART IV

Movements and/in the Classroom

Affect, Students, and Shifting Boundaries in American Studies

13

"Gonna Stomp Some Rump"

Embodied Learning and the Politics of Pleasure

WENDY KOZOL

Frustrated one day by the blank stares of forty-five students in Introduction to Comparative American Studies, I abruptly stopped class and insisted that they all stand up and dance to "The Wild Tchoupitoulas Gonna Stomp Some Rump," performed by the eponymous Mardi Gras Indians band.[1] Many students eagerly joined me, while others sat looking bemused, bored, or irritated. I called out these recalcitrant students and told them that I would not stop the music until everyone at least tried to dance. Fortunately for me, this last-ditch effort to engage them by asking them to move their bodies in ways that felt unfamiliar or even outlandish in the classroom led to a nuanced discussion about the benefits and risks of embodied learning.

Over the past several decades, embodied pedagogies have grown in popularity, not only in expected disciplines such as dance, drama, and kinesiology but also in more traditional fields such as mathematics.[2] Yet, as H. N. Wilcox notes, most practitioners of critical pedagogy have "by and large ignored the body's roles" in the teaching of power and inequality.[3] Or, as Anne Wagner and Riyad Shahjahan observe, the "mind-supremacist epistemology" of academia typically suppresses attention to the body, despite its presence in the classroom.[4] Recognizing "bodies as agents of knowledge production" can provoke an "epistemological and pedagogic shift" for both students and faculty that decenters Eurocentric ideals of rationality and disembodiment.[5] Importantly, feminist decolonizing interventions foreground race, class, gender, and sexuality as central to embodied forms of knowledge production.[6]

The turn to embodiment by feminist, critical race, and sexuality studies scholars has had a profound influence on American Studies scholarship in recent decades. (One has only to look at recent ASA conference programs or peruse new books in the field for evidence of this topic's prevalence.) It is less clear to me, however, how much this has translated into pedagogical practices. In my own experience in the Comparative American Studies Department (CAS) at Oberlin College, our commitment to teaching critical theoretical and historical perspectives on nation, nationalism, transnationalism, and globalization extends to considerations of the politics of inequality that shape classrooms. Oberlin is an elite private school where the majority of students are white and middle or upper class. Although the school's reputation attracts students who embrace a social justice worldview, cultural, racial, and socioeconomic privilege can be intimidating or even overwhelming for students of color and queer, dis/abled, trans, and first-generation students. In CAS, we strive to create learning communities in our classrooms that grapple with power dynamics between the instructor and students as well as between students. Yet, we faculty rarely discuss or develop embodied pedagogies.

As I argue below, American Studies classrooms like those at my institution would benefit from practices that connect analytical work to explorations of how bodies operate spatially and culturally both in and outside the academy. Greater attention to embodiment—corporeal movement as well as sensations and feelings—expands classroom spaces to include more varied ways of knowing and learning. Establishing learning communities that prioritize embodiment, education scholars argue, enables students to "come to understand how things relate to each other and to themselves."[7]

As valuable as embodied learning practices can be, alternative pedagogical practices are, of course, neither value-neutral nor uniquely positive.[8] Despite the critical perspective on structural inequalities that informs many embodied pedagogies, uninterrogated assumptions that embodiment can lead to recognition of another's humanness nonetheless risk essentializing the "body." Embodied learning, in other words, poses the pedagogical dilemma of how to incorporate movement, sensation, and feeling into one's teaching practice without perpetuating assumptions that bodily experiences transcend differences. Through an analysis of an impromptu class exercise, this essay explores both the value and the risks of embodied learning for critical American Studies pedagogies.

ENVIRONMENTAL VIOLENCE: UNIT DESIGN

Introduction to Comparative American Studies is the gateway class for CAS, a department that offers comparative and intersectional coursework on nation, nationalism, and transnationalism through studies of identities, communities, and institutional structures of power. Keywords such as settler colonialism, carceral state, agency, and social justice provide the structural framework for the introductory course. Environmental Violence: No Natural Disasters, a unit on environmental in/justice, pairs analyses of neoliberal capitalism and the racialization of space with expressive cultures of resistance to contextualize the destructiveness of Hurricane Katrina on the Gulf Coast. Students first read two critiques of the neoliberal political economy that contributed vastly to the devastating impacts of the storm. In his article on the "biopolitics of disposability," Henry Giroux argues that racialization was a determinative factor in enabling some populations to thrive while rendering others disposable both before and after Katrina. As he forcefully contends, the storm exposed the US government's "staggering indifference to human suffering."[9] Giroux's essay pairs well with George Lipsitz's incisive analysis of how the social warrant of competitive capitalism legitimized rapacious business practices in New Orleans at the expense of low-income African American communities.

For students with limited memories of Katrina, primary sources yield valuable reference points from which to understand the colossal failure of government agencies to meet the needs of marginalized communities. I therefore couple these scholarly articles with the documentary film *Trouble the Water* and *Salvage the Bones*, a novel by Jesmyn Ward. *Trouble the Water* features Kimberly Rivers Roberts, an aspiring rap artist who, along with her husband and neighbors, was trapped during the storm in the Ninth Ward, a district of New Orleans that suffered extraordinary damage when the levees broke. Unable to evacuate, Roberts videotaped their experience of living through Katrina, which serves as the core of the documentary directed by Carl Deal and Tia Lessin. Ward's brilliant novel, *Salvage the Bones*, recounts the days leading up to the impending storm for a poor African American girl and her family in an isolated town on the Gulf Coast with few resources and no state infrastructure to support them.[10]

Reading *Salvage the Bones* alongside *Trouble the Water* was an illuminating experience for students who had not encountered the scale of racial and economic inequality depicted in these texts. The accessibility and affective power of both the novel and the film provided vivid evidence of theoretical concepts that they had struggled with for much of the semester. Class discussion resulted in one of those rewarding pedagogical moments when previously alienating terms like the "biopolitics of disposability" became useful terms through which students developed analyses of the film and book.

DANCING IN THE CLASSROOM

Despite students' effective navigation between theoretical concepts and expressive culture, difficulties arose when I shifted the discussion from neoliberalism and biopolitics to cultural practices of resistance. Giroux ends his essay with a call for a pedagogy of hope, a pedagogy emergent in cultural practices that register politics as terrains of struggle.[11] Taking this point further, Lipsitz turns to New Orleans's musicians and other cultural practitioners who foster "alternative academies of knowledge," which he notes "cannot produce substantive realignments of political or economic power, but as repositories of collective memory, sites of radical solidarity, and sources of moral and political instruction, they hold enormous potential for the development of collective mobilization and struggle."[12] African American musicians and artists in New Orleans, he argues, foster community identification and resistance through articulations of shared suffering, desires, and joy. To complement this discussion, I showed the scene in *Trouble the Waters* when Roberts performs her original song, "I'm Amazing," which speaks of self-empowerment as she overcame experiences of sexual violence, drug addiction, and the early death of her mother from AIDS. First in small groups, then with the full class, students discussed her commentary on gender, sexual, and racial oppression. They remained skeptical, however, of my claim that Roberts's resistance came not only from the critique of power but also from joy and pleasure.

In an effort to visualize the relationship between disempowerment, pleasure, and resistance, I played a YouTube video of the Wild Tchoupitoulas performing their signature song during a Mardi Gras celebration.

The video augments Lipsitz's brief history of the Mardi Gras Indians, a tradition in New Orleans for over a century in which African Americans spend the year in community clubs making elaborate Indian costumes for Carnival. He astutely calls attention to the "seriousness that lies beneath the surface of the Indians' colorful handmade costumes."[13] I anticipated that students would readily grasp the seriousness that accompanies the buoyantly danceable music of "The Wild Tchoupitoulas Gonna Stomp Some Rump."

Instead, students were extremely reluctant to identify a politics of resistance in sites that appear "merely" pleasurable or just "make you feel good." Attempting to draw out this discussion, I asked student musicians in the class to explain why certain musical forms make you want to tap your foot and shake your hips, or "stomp some rump." A few tentatively explained how chords, beats, and other musical forms can evoke different feelings. In contrast to the early lively discussion, though, students continued to appear befuddled by my interest in the relations between affective pleasures and resistance. Seeking another way to get at this point, I encouraged students to talk about why they like to dance. Again, lukewarm answers constrained the discussion.

For me, the Wild Tchoupitoulas's visual and affective expressiveness seemed an accessible entry into analytical understandings of identity, agency, and community resistance. Throughout the semester, students engage with the concept of "politics," not just as institutional struggles for power but also as contestations in the everyday. I assumed that by this point they would recognize that expressive culture may not provide visible acts of defiance or resistance, nor have immediate impacts such as street protests or work stoppages, but can nurture resilience as well as envision alternative futures. Thus, students' reluctance to engage with the relationship between joy, power, and resistance took me by surprise.

In a moment of desperation facing a blank wall of silence, I asked everyone to stand and dance. Thinking about my own pleasures in dancing, I hoped students would connect their bodily experience to Lipsitz's arguments about the "seriousness" underneath the joyful energy of the music. Physical responsiveness to music can produce awareness that sensation, perception, and cognition are mutually constitutive, an awareness that can challenge Eurocentric educational practices that hierarchically privilege abstract or rationalist thought.[14] As they stood up to dance, some clearly began to connect their own delight in bodily movements with the politics of pleasure expressed in the video. Others, however, remained doubtful and uncomfortable.

In the subsequent discussion, students remarked on how strange it felt to dance in a classroom. Defamiliarizing the classroom space opened up a conversation about how conventional pedagogical practices privilege or exclude different kinds of knowledge. Dancing in a space not intended for such a purpose in turn led some to discuss the politics embedded in Mardi Gras Indians claiming the right to be on the street. One student observed that the largesse of the Indians' costumes seemed to reach out as if to touch the crowd, while others noted that the African American residents dancing alongside the performers fostered a communal space. From there, it became easier for students to grasp the argument about dancing as an empowering site of political resistance.

Observing the liveliness of this discussion, I came to realize that the earlier silence also resulted from a stagnation that had set in during our full class discussions. I typically began discussions by putting students in small groups, which usually resulted in noisy, energetic conversations. But when I called the class back together to share their ideas, as I did on this day, silence invariably resulted. Insistent questioning on my part typically led to contributions by the same students who always felt comfortable talking in a class. Comparing the by now routine silences of large group discussions with the vibrancy of the conversation after the dancing, I realized that the full-class discussion itself privileges rational and abstract thought. No longer the intimate and freewheeling space of small groups, the full class discussion reasserts an intimidating context that benefits those students most conversant in academic rhetorics.

While I still value the opportunity to bring diverse perspectives into full class discussions, I also now seek out pedagogical strategies that disrupt conventional academic spaces and/or push students out of their comfort zone. Doing so can be particularly beneficial for students from marginalized communities, for as Wilcox comments, "when educators value lived experiences and consciously cultivate trust and community, women and students of color are more likely to feel included and be engaged in the classroom."[15] Variation and innovation can create spaces and interactions that break down intimidating conditions for students marginalized from elite cultures and provide opportunities for different forms of knowledge production.

Unexpectedly, my impromptu exercise resulted in students' greater willingness to explore a breadth of perspectives. As Wilcox observes, "Students who do not participate in verbal discussions are sometimes the most engaged participants in embodied exercises."[16] Dancing in my class that day encouraged students to enjoy themselves, laugh, and make fun of their own awkwardness, while the expressiveness of the music fostered a sense of communal investment that opened up space for more students to take intellectual risks. In taking up those challenges, they garnered further insights into how expressive cultures can themselves be sites of risk taking and resistance.

DANCING AS CULTURAL APPROPRIATION

Students physically moving through the space of the classroom led to interactions with their own bodies and with each other that rarely occurs when sitting at their desks facing the lecturer. A fundamental benefit of embodied learning, Perry and Medina point out, is that defamiliarization asks students "to confront their assumptions regarding learning, their discipline, and their relationships to other learners."[17] They, along with other proponents of embodied learning pedagogies, insist that the objective is not to privilege individual learning experiences; rather, embodied learning practices situate students as "members of a learning community embedded in structural social relations."[18] Yet, attention to unequal structural relations between members of the class and in relation to the musical performance did not emerge in our discussion until a group of white students and students of color challenged the exercise as a form of cultural appropriation.

These students argued that for socioeconomically and racially privileged students and faculty to dance to "The Wild Tchoupitoulas" was a violent act of erasure of African American musical resistance to histories of slavery, segregation, and genocide. Recognizing the seriousness underneath the surface of masking for the performers and residents in the video, they insisted that privileged bodies in Oberlin dancing to the Wild Tchoupitoulas' music elided and appropriated the politics of this cultural practice.

Cultural appropriation has been in the spotlight on college campuses in recent years as students of color and white supporters have brought valuable attention to the pain caused by persistent adoption of cultural style, fashion, and music in dominant cultural spaces. These powerful critiques have exposed the range and depth of the pernicious ways in which cultural appropriation erases marginalized people's historical responses to oppression.

As valuable as this critique has been, it has also been challenged or undermined from two radically different quarters. One difficulty with the boundary-defining concept of appropriation is that, as much as it calls attention to historical and contemporary exercises of power, it can essentialize cultural formations in ways that disregard the fluidity and adaptability of cultures. This occurs most often when charges of appropriation function to police or regulate political identities and differences, a process that has taken hold in some quarters in Oberlin and on other campuses across the nation. When used in such a manner, such charges tend to uphold rigid boundaries around cultural identity rather than historicize the myriad ways in which cultures are mutable, fluid, and contested terrains.

Cultural appropriation has also become subject to the gaze of national media outlets, especially among conservative and far-right news bloggers. In fall 2015, for instance, Oberlin garnered national attention when Asian American students charged the dining service with cultural appropriation for serving "cheap imitations" of Asian food.[19] Media pundits often cherry-pick seemingly trivial protests such as the one at Oberlin, along with incidents at Pitzer and Hampshire and elsewhere, to denounce the tyranny of political correctness.[20] Such ridiculing attacks typically ignore the complexities of contestations on campuses and, in so doing, cause serious damage to our understandings of these politics.

In light of these heated debates about cultural appropriation, students calling out this exercise at first felt like an act of shaming for many of us, especially after the delight we had taken in moving our bodies and disrupting the decorum of class space. My initial defensive reaction was to reject this criticism as a policing strategy designed to claim the moral high ground, a reaction that stemmed from a sense of guilt that I should have paid more attention to the consequences of this exercise. Fortunately, I paused long enough to listen to the students' arguments, which offered more than a politically correct or knee-jerk response.

Importantly, students chafed against a contradiction at the heart of embodied learning practices that seek to use bodily experiences to connect students affectively to each other and distant others. For those of us entitled enough to be in the space of an elite college, they argued, attention to the body and the pleasure of dancing can presume a recognition of shared bodily experiences between the dancer and the disempowered community hailed through music, costumes, and dance. In claiming to feel in "our" bodies the pleasure of others speaking back to power, these students reminded the class, we can elide the very politics of African American resistance the exercise was intended to recognize. The assumption that moving our bodies or getting in touch with sensations, feelings, and muscle memories will connect us with others as "humans" risks essentializing embodiment.

In response, both white students and students of color who valued this moment of dancing defended pedagogical strategies that encourage students to recognize struggles and resistance for communities distant from themselves. At risk of deteriorating into naming and shaming, the discussion instead turned to a consideration of the value and risks of participating in cultures not one's own. They interrogated the heated language of appropriation, including questions about who "owns" or has rights to any cultural practice and what are the boundaries of belonging to a community. The robust discussion that ensued grappled with the benefits and limitations of embodied learning; in the process, they also explored some of the structural inequalities that existed between the students and between themselves and me.

Of note here, even as students examined problematic aspects of this exercise, neither they nor I considered the challenges of embodied learning for those in the class with diverse physical needs and abilities. This failure to attend to dis/ability should alert us further to the range of essentializing tendencies in embodied learning pedagogies.

CONCLUSION

Critics of student-centered pedagogical practices often claim that such practices devolve into solipsistic narratives unrelated to course content. In contrast, after dancing to the Wild Tchoupitoulas, students more readily connected their embodied experiences with theoretical concepts and histories of racial oppression and cultural resistance. Knowledge production through this bodily exercise facilitated analytical insights, in which students moved from attention to their own sensations to recognition of how cultural practices operate in places and times far removed from their own. Even more significant, dancing fostered a rich conversation about the value of embodied learning, how to study resistance, the risks of appropriation, and whether one can enjoy music outside of one's social position. As scholars increasingly attend to the politics of embodiment, this moment illustrates the potential for pedagogical pathways that can maneuver between analytical and experiential forms of knowledge.

Embodied learning offers American Studies additional pedagogical tools through which to interrogate structural and social relations of power and inequality. At the same time, we necessarily must reckon with the ways in which this pedagogy is inescapably riven with the very dynamics it aims to critique. Dance, for instance, encourages people to move their bodies in ways that have the capacity to facilitate recognition of diverse experiences, yet also risks apolitical assumptions about the embodied learner's ability to transcend differences and foster understanding and empathy. Rather than shy away from this valuable pedagogical practice, however, situating embodied learning within historical contexts can foster student interrogations about how power, inequality, and difference operate both in the classroom and beyond. In teaching American Studies, movement techniques provide a means through which to grapple with the complexities of bodies in space, place, and time, including a critique of the compelling pull of the "human."

NOTES

1. Steven Sacrob, "The Wild Tchoupitoulas Gonna Stomp Some Rump," posted January 21, 2012, YouTube video, https://www.youtube.com/watch?v=498LZARXzNo.

2. Anne E. Wagner and Riyad A. Shahjahan, "Centering Embodied Learning in Anti-Oppressive Pedagogy," *Teaching in Higher Education* 20, no. 3 (2015): 244–254.

3. H. N. Wilcox, "Embodied Ways of Knowing, Pedagogies, and Social Justice: Inclusive Science and Beyond," *NWSA Journal* 21, no. 2 (2009): 106.

4. Wagner and Shahjahan, "Centering Embodied Learning," 244.

5. Wagner and Shahjahan, 245; see also Wilcox, "Embodied Ways of Knowing," and Jennifer A. Tobin and Elizabeth J. Tisdell, "'I Know Down to My Ribs': A Narrative Research Study on the Embodied Adult Learning of Creative Writers," *Adult Education Quarterly* 65, no. 3 (2015): 216.

6. Wagner and Shahjahan; Wilcox.

7. Steven A. Stolz, "Embodied Learning," *Educational Philosophy and Theory* 47, no. 5 (2015): 484.

8. Wilcox, "Embodied Ways of Knowing," 106.

9. Henry Giroux, "Reading Hurricane Katrina: Race, Class, and the Biopolitics of Disposability," *College Literature* 33, no. 3 (2006): 174.

10. *Trouble the Water,* directed by Carl Deal and Tia Lessin (Elsewhere Films, 2008); Jesmyn Ward, *Salvage the Bones* (New York: Bloomsbury, 2011).

11. Giroux, "Reading Hurricane Katrina," 179.

12. George Lipsitz, "Learning from New Orleans: The Social Warrant of Hostile Privatism and Competitive Consumer Citizenship," *Cultural Anthropology* 21, no. 3 (2006): 462.

13. Lipsitz, "Learning from New Orleans," 462.

14. Wagner and Shahjahan, 246.

15. Wilcox, "Embodied Ways of Knowing," 117.

16. Wilcox, 117.

17. David J. Nguyen and Jay B. Larson, "Don't Forget about the Body: Explor-

ing the Curricular Possibilities of Embodied Pedagogy," *Innovations in Higher Education* 40 (2015): 338.

18. Wagner and Shahjahan, "Centering Embodied Learning," 246.

19. Conor Friedersdorf, "A Food Fight at Oberlin College," *Atlantic,* December 15, 2015, https://www.theatlantic.com/politics/archive/2015/12/the-food-fight-at-oberlin-college/421401/.

20. Scott Jaschik, "Dispute on Cultural Appropriation Leads to Assault Charges," *Inside Higher Ed,* March 20, 2017, https://www.insidehighered.com/news/2017/03/20/debates-cultural-appropriation-higher-education/.

14

Don't Look Away

The Bodies of American Studies

ADRIANA ESTILL

> 1,950 mile-long open wound
> dividing a *pueblo*, a culture, ...
> splits me splits me
> *me raja me raja*
> —Gloria Anzaldúa, *Borderland / La Frontera*

❖ ❖ ❖ ❖ ❖ ❖ ❖ ❖ ❖ ❖ ❖ ❖ ❖ ❖ ❖

In *Between the World and Me*, framed as a letter to his fifteen-year-old son, Ta-Nehisi Coates urges, "You must never look away from this. You must always remember that the sociology, the history, the economics, the graphs, the charts, the regressions all land, with great violence, upon the body."[1] Not looking away means, following Coates, making sure to remember the bodies screened by the academic production of knowledge, its histories, sociological tracts, literary treatments, remembering, indeed, Anzaldúa's body that screams *me raja me raja*—words that my students might be able to translate literally but oftentimes fail to feel. When I teach American Studies, I am teaching students to not look away.

Preparing students to do this work requires us to be pedagogically transparent about the effort that *looking at* the bodies of American Studies takes, particularly when doing this teaching and learning at historically white colleges and universities (HWCU).[2] Not looking away is emotionally demanding in ways that can throw into relief racialized, gendered, and sexual identities, resulting in an uneven affective burden. In this essay, I aim to interrupt the traditional expectations for academia that, as Coates details, tend to drape our bodies with statistics while warding off emotional understandings as irrational or irrelevant. I argue for our responsibility to surface, name, and develop the individual and collective emotional processes that inform and suffuse our students' educations, in a moment when American Studies bids us to reframe our knowledge of this nation-state through discussions of settler colonialism, slavery, and empire.

My interest in establishing and structuring classroom transparency around the emotional dimensions of learning has developed from years of responding to students' needs that surface after class time ends, whether they are processing discussion or reacting to a reading. I have listened to colleagues' oblique suggestions that students should learn how to take care of ("manage") their own emotional reactions; our jobs, they argue, are to expect students to practice inhabiting what we think of as "rational learning." I have wondered whether the comfort we take in rationality stems from the way it frees us, as teachers, from the responsibility for students tearing up in our offices. We like to think that our teaching and mentorship is absent of emotion except for a broad, equally applied ethics of care. But is cordoning off emotions and demanding neutrality really a stage for equitable learning? Looking around the room during a conversation about the movie *Twelve Years a Slave*, I observed the strong emotional responses of my students of color and first wondered, in line with broader societal discussions about resilience, how I could help them steel themselves against injury. However, chatting with individual students afterward, they pushed me to ask a better question: why were the white students so removed from emotion and so easily able to occupy the "rational," neutral mindset? Following their reminder to me that their emotion was an essential part of their learning, instead of continuing to buy into the desirability of rationality and neutrality as learning stances, I want to take a stand for the relevance of and need for what I call emotional pedagogies—the recognition that learning new material engages emotional processes, some individual, some collective. To continue to cordon off or ignore these processes means our classrooms will continue to produce unequal, racialized spaces of learning, particularly in the work we do in American Studies.

Because the neutral, rational classroom is the dominant model, not looking away requires pedagogical transparency about how knowledge is produced through, alongside, and with awareness of racial, gendered, and sexual politics. Placing themselves in relationship to their new understandings of the United States, students need time to confront the social practice of their emotional knowing—the way that their identity commitments position them as knowers in the classroom. What I discuss here has some relation to the current initiatives in inclusive teaching. Inclusive pedagogies aim to create spaces where students' feelings of fear, shame, or entitlement do not get "in the way" of learning.[3] But while inclusive pedagogies hone in on how an individual's emotions might keep them from risking fully in the quest of learning deeply, I argue that emotional pedagogies help us to name the affective responses that derive from collective subject positions as students find themselves confronting the ways in which their identities shape their relationship to US histories, narratives, and attachments.

In the following, I offer some suggestions for how to create pedagogical transparency around emotional epistemology in American Studies courses. They have been developed through my own experiences at a small liberal arts college. My overarching goal is to provide my students with a set of bridges that help provide them the skills and strength to not look away from the bodies. In using the term "bridge," I am invoking *This Bridge Called My Back*, my own introduction into affective learning and teaching a lifetime ago as a Chicana graduate student with a backpack full of impostor syndrome. Kate Rushin's introductory poem demands that everyone needs to "stretch or drown; evolve or die," be your own bridge, "mediate / [your] own weaknesses."[4] Students must engage fully and self-reflectively with these bridges; I cannot do all the work for them.[5]

COMING TO TERMS WITH THE EMOTIONS OF AMERICAN STUDIES

Discarding the exceptionalist narrative of the United States produces emotional narratives for students as they struggle to build new knowledge schema that can organize and make sense of the histories and stories they are asked to learn. It is not uncommon for my students to tell me that our class work is "depressing" or "a downer." I'm sure they are, in part, reacting to their preconceptions that American Studies will be a "'fun' class that allows them to watch movies, 'learn about America,' and fulfill university requirements," as Michael Mark Cohen and Grace Wang point out.[6] But because I agree with Wang that teaching the American Studies introduction should "provoke some cognitive dissonance" in our students as they reevaluate their ideal versions of the United States through and against American Studies critiques of the "structures of violence and inequity foundational to the nation,"[7] we need to recognize and build in ways to handle the fact that their cognitive dissonance has a profound emotional component that, when not acknowledged, can lead to a refusal to re-engage the course material.

It is not just the process of unlearning that provokes emotional learning. In order to live up to American Studies's "radical legacy" that invites us to "engage students in productive debates around racism, sexism, and social justice," we must recognize the fact that students find their footing in these conversations in affectively unequal ways.[8] Some students more than others feel interpellated and claimed by—and thus they feel differently—a topic like the ongoing physical and epistemic violence against people of color in the United States. Consider, too, that the traditional expectations of the college classroom means that they are often asked to do more work to "manage" their emotions while other students, with little sense of subjection through and within these histories, easily perform "rationality." Add to this that, as philosopher George Yancy reminds us, white bodies "are always already sanctioned as 'knowers' and are always already known as being at home within disciplinary matrixes of knowledge production," and we see that American Studies classrooms will lean toward racialized and gendered uneven emotional fields.[9] The unevenness risks reproducing some as "knowers" and others as "feelers," often along racial and other social identity lines. I won't forget the day an African American female student in my two-hundred-level Beauty and Race in the United States class spoke directly and firmly to her classmates, "You stay silent in discussion, worried that you might say the wrong thing and get push back, but every day that I do the readings for this class, what I learn hurts me."

Individual emotional engagements with our readings pervade the classroom, shaping the risks in thinking and discussion moves that students are able and willing to take, as the anecdote above makes clear. Some hesitate to enter a conversation knowing that they might hurt others; others hesitate because they don't want to get hurt. Both these hesitations—and, as faculty, our unwillingness to acknowledge the affective epistemological force of them—stall the work of the American

Studies classroom. In her work on indigenous feminist scholarship, Dian Million points out that "academia repetitively produces gatekeepers to our entry into important social discourses because we *feel* our histories as well as think them" (her emphasis).[10] From Million I want us to remember that those who feel the histories are also thinking them, are also knowing them. Those who are not feeling them, I would suggest, are not thinking them fully.

We owe it to our students to listen closely when they feel deeply. Many years ago, two events coincided at my college that have shaped my commitment to emotional pedagogies. In my own class, as we read Pedro Pietri's "Puerto Rican Obituary" out loud, some students flinched and I did not notice; a small delegation visited me later and pleaded with me to have a discussion in class about the word "spic" and how we had voiced it.[11] The word hurt them, and they did not know how to deal with how it made them feel. In two other classes—in the English and History Departments—the "n" word appeared, circulated, made waves. In response, several students organized a collective demand that resulted in a public forum in which faculty and students spoke about the pedagogical ethics of hearing, using, and/or reproducing the word. The juxtaposition of these conversations compelled me to think deeply about the cost of traditional learning practices that demand that students navigate material as if it were always, and for everyone equally, neutral and removed. Sitting in my office or in the forum, listening to students' pleas, I could tell that they were not asking for a reprieve from learning. Rather, they were asking us, the faculty, to pay attention to how the emotions that these words generated for them created obstacles to continued, significant learning in the classroom.

Over the years of teaching small discussion-based courses, I have developed explicit pedagogical strategies—bridges—to recognize the role of emotion in learning and to help students not look away and thus navigate the American Studies classroom.[12] This becomes particularly meaningful as we work to develop students' familiarity and practice with interdisciplinarity. Rebecca Hill suggests that American Studies interdisciplinarity is "the craft of shifting from one method to another, being able to stand between two conversations and listen well enough to pull them together, using methods that might contradict each other and finding ways to use the contradictions."[13] Interdisciplinarity ideally dislodges students' expectations for where and how knowledge is produced; I aim to interrupt students' expectations that literary/artistic texts produce feelings, not knowledge, and conversely that "academic" texts produce knowledge, but not feelings. Emotional pedagogies, then, are not just vital because of the content we teach and the ethical orientation of our analytics but because interdisciplinarity requires understanding the affective attachments to particular epistemologies in order to be able to listen well and navigate the contradictions.

Bridge One
Collective Affect: Getting Beyond "How Does This Make You Feel?"

The very privacy that makes the journal an effective tool at the individual level also makes it less useful for the kind of work that I think is important in highlighting the collectively generated and experienced affect of the classroom. Journals cordon off and individualize feelings instead of recognizing that they are culturally and socially produced, felt, and circulated. Lauren Berlant remarks that "by the time you've been in primary school for awhile, or whatever, you have feelings about citizenship, you have feelings about race, you have feelings about gender and sexuality. You've been trained to take on those objects as world-sustaining perspectives."[14] I want my students to move beyond how "this" makes "me" feel and consider their emotional training. Indeed, if they can see how what they understood as an individual response actually participates in larger structures of affective meaning and/or conflict, then they can better navigate questions of evidence, meaning, and relevance. For example, a student once started off a discussion of geographer Joseph Nevins's *Operation Gatekeeper* proclaiming that they were so angry; this led us into a conversation about why and how we might feel angry—whether because of histories we hadn't learned or histories that feel one-sided—and how to better engage the argument knowing how that anger oriented us.[15]

In the introductory course, I use two interventions to ground these lessons. During a lecture in the first week of the term, I introduce standpoint theory in a fairly broad way, asking students to think about how, as knowers and producers of knowledge, we can never be neutrally located. This serves as an invitation to reconsider the assumptions about research as "objective" and neutral and consider their own investments and attachments. On the very next slide, I show them Joanna Simpson's wheel diagram of intersectionality as a way for them to complicate and nuance identity within larger forces and structures.[16] I have found that standpoint epistemologies decenter some students and recenter others, helping them to confront the social practice of their emotional knowing—the way that their identity commitments position them as knowers in the classroom.

My approach approximates that of Karen Cardozo, who stresses the importance of introducing racial identity development schemas in American Studies classes: "Student emotions may appear supplemental or even disruptive rather than (as they really are) constitutive of learning. Yet although our courses are ostensibly 'about' economics, history, or literature, the race-related subject matter within them provokes both emotions and racial identity development."[17] Cardozo points out that "provocative race-related material generates emotional pressure: an explicit pedagogical strategy releases it so that classroom environment can remain a productive, reflective, and respectful one."[18] In my classroom, these brief introductions into standpoint epistemology (and thus into self-reflection of their own social identities) gives students language to acknowledge that the production of knowledge is fraught and differentiated; they no longer expect others to think and feel like them, and, to some degree, they start to see that feeling alienated, angry, or frustrated follows from their placement within social structures of race, class, gender, and sexuality. In the words of one student reflection, surfacing emotion in the classroom helped them "separate ideas from people" and stay engaged in the conversation.

Part of the work of helping students see collective affect is giving name to emotional currents that they do not yet want to own. In my work as a facilitator, we call this "reading the room," offering a thermometer that allows the collective to recognize emotion and work through it. In the classroom, a useful time and process to tackle this is through a midterm class evaluation. Often this quick evaluation simply offers a moment when I can further explain methods and approaches, for example, why we spend so much time in discussions rather than lectures. However, it also frequently generates students' frustrations, like the student who wrote, "I feel as if people are not fully expressing themselves, which can make it difficult to speak as openly as I would like about the issues we are addressing." This was too perfect of a complicated emotional comment to ignore; the student was silencing themselves because they perceived others as also silencing themselves, and they expected others to be open in order to facilitate their openness. In class we tackled this in a brief discussion—who had been taking risks? who felt like they had? what kind of inhibition was this comment skirting around?—with small groups prompted to tackle how to feel their way into making discussions happen.

Bridge Two
Deep Listening

The task of getting beyond the self (how I see the world and what I've been taught about the world) enables students to begin to listen deeply to all the stories that circulate in the class, both from readings and fellow students. In order to listen and read deeply, we need to consider what might keep us from reading deeply and how to move through those resistances, whether internal or external.

To begin this work, we read a section of Gloria Anzaldúa's *Borderlands / La Frontera* and so confront the limits of their reading abilities. My discussion questions center not just on questions of place-making and the borderlands but also on the readerly engagement with (or alienation from) the multilingual and multigenre nature of her work. In asking them to consider *why* she might choose to produce knowledge in ways that might be impossible for any single person to engage with fully, they must consider the emotional work of recognizing that their learning is partial, complicated by their subject position. I orient the discussion to flesh out what it means for them to continue listening/reading when confronted by their inevitable "failure," that is, the impossibility of full comprehension. Then, when they complete a midterm check-in for the communicative competence assignment—a term-long self-reflective set of tasks around reflecting on their speaking, listening, reading, and writing skills that I developed with my colleague Anita Chikkatur—students explicitly detail their listening goals.

The communicative competence assignment is multistaged. In the first week of term, they mark off goals for each area on a checklist that I provide. (This list primes them to think of these communication skills as non-binary and learned; they cannot focus on learning *all* of the skills as they can only choose three.) For the midterm assignment, they revisit their goals and check in: what practices/strategies are they working on to meet these goals? what obstacles might impede their progress? In other words, as they gauge their struggle to meet their goals, they're required *to reflect on why*.[19]

The sequence of self-reflective exercises provides me with opportunities to respond to their goals and help them adjust/refine if needed, but also to suggest possible strategies. I often get comments from them about the practical side of listening, whether it's struggles to take notes or odes to more sleep. But just as often their self-reflection leads them to comments like: "I learned to keep listening, even when I disagreed," "There were times I felt annoyed or frustrated with discussion, but I'm proud that I stayed in the discussion and didn't show my annoyance with my body language," "I thought I was good at listening, but it turns out I'm only good at it when I like what I'm hearing."

One day after class, three students stayed behind to talk to me. They were all buzzing and said, "Wow, that discussion was intense, and it did not feel good!" I had a sense of what moment in the discussion had put them on edge, but I also would bet that the majority of their classmates had not felt the tension at all. Learning to listen deeply means that some students get more attuned to these emotional fields that are not their own, leading to more attentive, productive conversations. Students can learn to recognize, name, and thus understand collective affect—the uneven but publicly generated and felt emotional processes of learning; as with any sort of learning, developing a nuanced vocabulary for naming new (or newly nuanced) concepts facilitates comprehension, use, and communication.

Bridge Three
Developing Language

In *How Emotions Are Made: The Secret Life of the Brain*, Lisa Feldman Barrett points out that emotions have no objective existence "out there" or "wired" into our brains; rather, we learn to name and nuance sensations we have about the world, bit by bit, brick by brick, word by word, in and through relationship with others.[20] "Emotions are very real creations of social reality, made possible by human brains in concert with other human brains," Barrett states.[21] For any of us who have worked to build our students' metacognitive skills over the last ten years, this understanding of emotion is familiar and the next steps should be clear: just as we help students recognize the ways in which they best learn (or don't learn) and how to adapt their learning processes, we also need to aid students in developing a full emotional vocabulary to further mediate their relationship to the content and process of learning and to their fellow students. Barrett calls this richer vocabulary "higher emotional granularity" and explains that "preciseness leads to efficiency," that is, having more complex and nuanced conceptual categories allows a person to experience, perceive, understand, and communicate emotions with greater facility.[22]

In order for students to begin to build attentiveness to the need for emotional vocabulary, first they must recognize the silences—the gaps in language and knowledge. I introduce the general matter of silences through an excerpt of Michel-Rolph Trouillot's "Silencing the Past: Power and the Production of History."[23] Because it is an introductory course, for most students, it is the first time they have thought about the ways in which archives are incomplete, and how some silences are produced through forgetting and others through willful refusals to listen and document. We then proceed to use Trouillot throughout the rest of the course, trying to become attentive to silences and imagining what it might look like (what sort of data/stories would we need?) to fill them.

The exercise of recognizing the limits of our knowledge sets up moments in which we can play with research questions (how would you ask this question? what archives would you need and how would you find/gather them? how would you read the archive?) but also often mark the gap between our learning goals and their learning expectations—their processing is cognitive (building new schema) but also emotional ("I thought I knew this! Wait, this [this finding; this silence; this history] isn't what I expected/wanted"). Together the students sketch out possible epistemologies as well as their struggle to inhabit them.

In a recent class, as they worked in groups for their final presentations, I could see the impact of these long-term conversations. Before they began their work, they filled out group contracts that asked them to detail expectations of each other as well as "key words/phrases to use when we feel the process isn't working." Groups differ on their degree of emotional granularity, particularly as it intersects with social identities, so while all five of the groups included "communicate" as part of their contract, only two connected that to an acknowledgment of how difference in backgrounds and experiences would complicate this desire to communicate well.

These forms also give them a chance to "have fun" (all five groups included this aim in their contracts!) with the key words/phrases. While a couple of the groups suggest straightforward language like "I'm confused about" or the imperative "be specific about problems" and "be direct," a couple create a secret language for the group (e.g., "peaches" = need to clarify; "plum" = I'm uncomfortable). Reading through these, I glimpse their languaging struggle in process. They had to name potential silences in order to fill out the form, but they also recognized that, in real-time conversation, they might need stone fruit to help them name their struggle to be in relationship to the group work.

Bridge Four
Vulnerable Spaces, Not Safe Spaces

While in small groups stone fruit can represent feelings of confusion or discomfort—both emotions that gesture directly at the failure or lack of language, the larger classroom space requires more work to make possible risk-taking. Fear of being called out and the way that "being wrong" gets amplified on social media means that many students stay silent while others speak with righteousness.[24] Both of these stances work against the good listening habits and ethics that I want my students to work on. The vulnerability we require in an American Studies classroom means we need to establish the classroom as a space that is fairly private and reasonably safe, by which I mean the risks they take in the classroom should stay in the classroom. This "Las Vegas" rule has been one that the students generate themselves to add to the classroom contract we set up in the first week of class.

A student-generated contract doesn't just work because it's student-generated. From the beginning of the term, I conduct the class reminding students that the "business" work matters. I take time at the top of every class to reiterate our class expectations of each other; we have regular check-ins to re-establish norms and diagnose problems. Taking it seriously means occasionally being willing to let go of the syllabus and the expected content in order to recalibrate the community.

In one class, a midterm check-in revealed that the Las Vegas rule had been broken. In their individual midterm feedback form, a student revealed that other students had been talking about what they said out of the classroom, with their name attached. The ensuant class discussion required time and ended up being a wide-ranging and necessarily emotional discussion of *why* it was challenging to keep the Las Vegas rule; many of them recognized (and I saw this repeated in their final evaluations) that it was "easier" to complain/gossip outside the class than to stay in the discussion (deep listening) and see the person talking as someone in community with them.

In part because of discussions like these, over the years I have become more intentional about talking to students about the necessary labor of classroom community: that is, what do we, as a collective, need to do to be constituted as a gathering where we can all be vulnerable and take risks? Setting up a classroom contract at the outset of class is insufficient, because it ignores the intimate difficulties of committing to classroom discussions that offer not just intellectual challenges but emotional ones as well.

Even as the conversation in that class turned out to be formative and productive for those particular students, in general I have struggled with how to help students engage the "Las Vegas" rule with its central goal at heart: treat every person in the room as someone with whom you are building a learning community. Spending time on what each rule in a contract really demands from us helps, but I've also found that recognizing that we are all imperfect members of the classroom space can build spaces of vulnerability. In another class, during a "meta" discussion of how to discuss topics that were deeply personal to most of us, I said, off-handedly, "we are all problematic," only intending to remind the students that no one was immune from criticism and that none of us should assume we knew how to "be woke" and do cultural criticism. My words came up in about a fourth of the final evaluations for the class, reminding me that students listen hard to us when we try to help them listen to each other.

Bridges invite the self-reflection necessary for emotional pedagogies, but they cannot force it. As teachers, we can and must be role models for what it means—what it feels like—to stay in conversation, stay in relationship, and keep looking even when it pains us:

> [Staying in] means each participant needs to seek to understand what other folks are saying and not to assume that they know in advance what someone means. Staying in the conversation involves giving of self; it involves listening with the heart and being fully present. White students often find this difficult since they tend to characterize courses and conversations that center on race as acts of violence.[25]

On the day after the 2016 elections, I had to teach. But I also needed to be real and recognize that I had been attached to narratives of progress and equity that now felt more distant and impossible than ever before in my life. I also knew, however, that I did not know all my students. The ideals to which they were attached were unknown to me; I needed to make space for all of those possible emotions that were going to shape our conversation. The air caught in my throat as I let them know that I was raw, that our discussion of US politics would feel weighty for me today; as our conversation began to swirl, students shared their own emotional states and what they were learning by taking the time to recognize them.

The bodies of American Studies stand as the bloodied legacies of a settler colonial, imperial nation. But in my classroom, the bodies of American Studies are also my students; they are the most recent inheritors and constructors of the cruel optimism of our American dream.[26] We must recognize that studying our history, culture, and society challenges students to reframe how they see this country, to wake up to the cruelty, to not look away. But unless we provide them with the emotional tools to do so, chances are that they will look away, because looking at these bodies that are our bodies and our legacy and our future *me raja me raja*, and, well, if they are not split and in pain, then probably they haven't learned what I wanted them to.

APPENDIX: COMMUNICATION COMPETENCE ASSIGNMENT

Done over the course of a term.

Parts/Schedule:

I. Initial Communicative Competence Check-In

A pre-generated list helps students see the embedded skills involved in listening, speaking, reading, and writing and make choices about what to tackle as a goal and why.

II. Daily Participation Rubric

Requires them to keep their goals in mind and consider what progress they are making (or not) with concrete examples.

III. Midterm Communicative Competence Reflective Assignment

Invites them to review their progress towards their goals so far, with attention to precise reflection using the participation rubric. Gives the teacher a chance to respond, reinforce, and/or recalibrate.

IV. Final Communicative Competence Reflective Assignment

A final chance to reflect on their progress and to give positive feedback to the classmates who have helped them learn. [Alternatively to the rubric-based assignment described here, one could ask for a brief reflective essay that addresses the same questions.]

Rationale and Process:

Designed to help students gain metacognitive skills in the areas of communication and learning, it has also helped students become attuned to their fellow students' contributions and to their own complicated and inevitably emotional approach to listening and learning.

Note:

Ideally, each of these assignments offers considerable blank space so that students see the possible scope their answers might take.

INDIVIDUAL ASSIGNMENTS

Initial Communicative Competence Check-In

Header language:

Please use this initial communicative competence reflection form as a way to shape your participation journal. Check off which speaking, listening, reading, and writing skills you would like to work on this term and which ones you think are strengths for you (feel free to add your own goals). Choose *at least two skills in each area and no more than four* that you will work to improve this term. At midterm, I will ask you to revisit your goals and see if they are still the goals you're working on. At the end of the course, you will use your reflection in this area and your participation journal to write a brief reflective assignment. Your final grade will be based on the depth and precision of your self-reflection as well as my assessment of your efforts at improving your communication skills.

Possible Skills to list:
Speaking: Speak less (I tend to speak too much), Speak more often (I tend to speak too little), Take risks with my contributions, Use concrete evidence when I contribute comments, Build on classmates' statements, Ask questions that generate conversation, Be concise, Use my classmates' names when I respond to them, Use eye contact with the whole class when I speak
Listening: Use body language and eye contact to indicate active listening, Allow myself to learn from classmates, Listen for connections to readings and previous comments, Take effective notes on classroom discussion, Listen fully, without thinking about what I'm going to say, Listen to build on others' comments directly, Keep listening, even when I disagree
Reading: Make time for reading and re-reading, Slow down for deliberative reading, Connect a particular reading to previous readings, Read for evidence used by author, Read for ideas that excite me, Take useful notes on readings, Read for the scholarly conversation (who is the author "responding" to and why), Read for method (how the author does their work), Bring quotes from the reading to class, Read for which perspectives are included and which relevant perspectives are missing, Read for main ideas and arguments
Writing: Paper organization, Strong, defensible claims, Effective and clear analysis of evidence, Appropriate evidence for claims, Clear and coherent prose, Time management, Writing rough drafts and editing,

Effective and clear transitions between ideas and paragraphs, Developing my argument

Daily/Weekly Participation Rubric
Organized as a check-in assignment with three open-ended questions at the end.

Items for checks and notes:

- Came prepared for class--completed assigned reading and any other assignments
- Asked for help when needed and encouraged others to do the same
- Shared my thoughts, reflections, and questions about the topics/readings
- Engaged classmates' ideas fully

The following should be filled out by students with their individual goals ready for checks and notes:

- My listening goals:
- My speaking goals:
- My reading goals:

Open-ended questions:

- Three things I learned today:
- Two questions raised for me in class today:
- One thing I found intriguing in our readings today:

Midterm Communicative Competence Reflective Assignment
Header language:

> This assignment is connected to the goals you have chosen from the initial CC checklist. Please review your participation rubric for your speaking, listening, and reading goals and your notes on progress/obstacles/strategies. Tell me—*with examples and dates*—how you see your work in these areas. If you need to switch goals, explain why. Detail what you will continue to work on, why, and what strategies you have to reach these goals.

Areas for response:

- Speaking
- Listening
- Reading
- Writing

- Tell me a few things you've learned—with dates, please:
- What are some questions raised for you in class?—with dates, of course
- Who are some classmates who were especially helpful to you—and why? (dates!)

Communicative Competence Final Assignment

Header language:

Please have your participation rubric and your midterm communicative competence assignment at the ready when you fill out this form--my principal expectation is that you explore, with *concrete evidence*, what progress you've made toward your goals. With each area, please (1) name your goal(s); (2) *with examples and dates*, give some detail about your strategies, obstacles, and successes toward them; (3) sum up—how do you feel about your work this term in each area? (About 5-6 sentences per area.)

Areas for response:

- Speaking
- Listening
- Reading
- Writing
- Looking at your participation rubric as a whole--the things you've learned, the questions that were raised for you, the classmates who have helped you learn, what are highlights for you? what would you do differently? Please give me a brief, concrete overview of what you've accomplished and what you're still working on (five–six sentences, with at least three dates/examples).
- Finally, please shout out to any/all the classmates you want, with any brief detail that will help them see why you're indebted to them. (As soon as I'm able, I'll distribute these shout outs by email.)

NOTES

1. Ta-Nehisi Coates, *Between the World and Me* (New York: Spiegel & Grau, 2015), 10.

2. Sociologist Eduardo Bonilla-Silva uses HWCU to name and categorize the composition and history of the institutions in which many of us do our work. Eduardo Bonilla-Silva, "The Invisible Weight of Whiteness: The Racial Grammar of Everyday Life in Contemporary America," *Ethnic and Racial Studies* 35, no. 2 (2012): 173–194.

3. Becky Supiano, "Traditional Teaching May Deepen Inequality: Can a Different Approach Fix It?," *Chronicle of Higher Education*, May 6 2018, https://www.chronicle.com/article/Traditional-Teaching-May/243339.

4. Donna Kate Rushin, "The Bridge Poem," in *This Bridge Called My Back; Writings By Radical Women of Color*, ed. Cherríe Moraga and Gloria Anzaldúa (New York: Kitchen Table Press, 1981), xxii.

5. Indeed, I would argue that in urging them to take on, thoughtfully, academic emotional labor, I am actively discouraging them from depending on me, their Latina professor, to do so for them, pushing back in this way against stereotypes of Latinas as hyperemotional and/or naturally maternal.

6. Michael Mark Cohen and Grace Wang, "Teaching the Introduction to American Studies Course: A Dialogue," *American Quarterly* 68, no. 2 (2016): 348.

7. Cohen and Wang, "Teaching the Introduction," 353.

8. Cohen and Wang, 347.

9. George Yancy, "Introduction: White Crisis and the Value of Losing One's Way," in *Exploring Race in Predominantly White Classrooms: Scholars of Color Reflect*, ed. George Yancy and María del Guadalupe Davidson (New York: Routledge, 2014), 2, Kindle ed.

10. Dian Million, "Felt Theory: An Indigenous Feminist Approach to Affect and History," *Wicazo Sa Review* 24, no. 2 (2009): 54.

11. Pedro Pietri, "Puerto Rican Obituary," in *Puerto Rican Obituary* (New York: Monthly Review, 1973).

12. It's worth noting, too, that ethnic studies has long fought against perceptions that identity-based disciplines fail to provide rigorous, "rational" learning. It is important to me that students understand emotional learning as challenging and necessary to achieve full comprehension.

13. Rebecca Hill, "What Is This Thing Called Interdisciplinarity?: Teaching Interdisciplinary Methods Courses in American Studies," *American Quarterly* 68, no. 2 (2016): 363.

14. Lauren Berlant, interview by David K. Seitz, "On Citizenship and Optimism," *Society and Space*, March 23, 2013, https://www.societyandspace.org/articles/on-citizenship-and-optimism.

15. Joseph Nevins, *Operation Gatekeeper: The War on "Illegals" and the Remaking of the U.S.–Mexico Boundary*, 2nd ed. (New York: Routledge, 2010).

16. Joanna Simpson, "Everyone Belongs: A Toolkit for Applying Intersectionality," CRIAW/ICREF, June 2009, accessed July 18, 2017, http://also-chicago.org/also_site/wp-content/uploads/2017/03/Everyone_Belongs-A-toolkit-for-applying-intersectionality.pdf.

17. Karen Cardozo, "When History Hurts: Racial Identity Development in the American Studies Classroom," *America Studies* 47, no. 3/4 (2006): 174.

18. Cardozo, "When History Hurts," 174.

19. For a fuller overview and sample assignments, see here: Melissa Eblen-Zayas, "Communicative Competence Checklist," Learning and Teaching Center Blog, January 3, 2017, https://www.carleton.edu/ltc/ltc-blog/news/communicative-competence-checklist/.

20. Lisa Feldman Barrett, *How Emotions Are Made: The Secret Life of the Brain* (Boston: Houghton Mifflin Harcourt, 2017), Kindle ed.

21. Barrett, *How Emotions Are Made*, location 5296.

22. Barrett, location 2319.

23. Michel-Rolph Trouillot, "Silencing the Past: Power and the Production of History," in *American Studies: An Anthology*, ed. Janice Radway, Kevin Gaines, Barry Shank, and Penny Von Eschen (Malden, MA: Wiley-Blackwell, 2009), 558–566.

24. For student perspectives on how social media and online youth culture can produce a toxic call-out culture, see Conor Friedersdorf, "The Destructiveness of Call-Out Culture on Campus: Reflections from Undergraduates," *Atlantic*, May 8, 2017, https://www.theatlantic.com/politics/archive/2017/05/call-out-culture-is-stressing-out-college-students/524679/.

25. Dyan Watson, "Staying in the Conversation: Having Difficult Conversations about Race in Teaching Education," in *Exploring Race in Predominantly White Classrooms*, 41.

26. Lauren Berlant, *Cruel Optimism* (Durham, NC: Duke University Press, 2011).

15

Making American Studies Great Again?

Teaching the Nation under Trumpism

MEGAN BAYLES AND JULIE SZE

As a field, American Studies engages histories of US nationalism, nativism, empire, neoliberalism, racism, and white supremacy. However, these topics are not what many students typically anticipate our classes—in particular, Introduction to American Studies ("Intro")—to be about when they first encounter them. This gap between the reality of the field and the perception of our classes informs the two key questions that structure the Intro class. How can American Studies be taught when there is a lack of shared expectations of what the class is about? How do contemporary politics, specifically Trumpism, exacerbate the difficulties of these divergent expectations? This chapter addresses the implications of teaching Introduction to American Studies in the context of Trumpism, to make sense of the intellectual and political history of the field during and after the dawn of "post-truth" politics that promises to "Make America Great Again." Although there are different elements to Trumpism, we focus on its two key features: aversion to facts and knowledge, and explicit racism. Many students have responded to renewed national(ist) rhetoric with anger and fear, while others echo it in the classroom—emboldened, perhaps, by the culture of feelings-based racial grievance over evidence-based discourse. Reactions to American Studies are strongly determined by perceptions of what "America" means. This essay addresses our anticipation, incorporation, and management of divergent preconceptions of what American Studies classes are, ranging from "Patriotism 101" to an embedded social/racial justice critique.

The demographics and title of this course make it ripe for unveiling how students respond to and utilize different modes of argumentation and evidence, the need to explain and defend "facts," and how we as educators select course content, produce assignments, and facilitate classroom discussion in the "post-fact" classroom. Following Charles Hale's collection on the theory, practice, and methods of activist scholarship and knowledge production, we position our analysis within the praxis of teaching critical thinking and destabilizing hegemonic ideologies as a political project.[1] We argue that only by understanding both the broader national political conversation and the function of classroom spaces (especially for large general education courses) can scholars and teachers in American Studies respond to internal and external political and scholarly debates about "America." Using the undergraduate classroom as a case study, we suggest that *America*, like *American Studies*, can best be understood as a contested concept based in political/intellectual haven and political/cultural critique. In other words, the struggles of *how* to teach the Intro class (pedagogy) are as important to unveil as *what* to teach (content). These lessons have broader implications outside the particular classrooms that form the basis of our analysis. One of our roles as American Studies scholars and teachers is to understand how the current moment has historical roots yet is also distinct in its formation. Another is to better communicate the analytic within our field, a role that, however personally fraught and difficult, is essential to cultivating an increasingly frayed and distracted landscape. Although we wrote this piece just after the 2016 election, and edited it on the precipice of the 2020 election, we anticipate that our experiences and findings about haven and critique will continue to be relevant.

INSTITUTIONAL AND THEMATIC CONTEXTS

The UC Davis American Studies department is the only freestanding one of its kind at the University of California and is over fifty years old. The Intro course has 150 students, many of whom are first-year students, as it satisfies a number of general education requirements. A vast majority of students are from STEM majors, fewer from the social sciences, and only a handful from the humanities (with even fewer ending up as American Studies majors). Over the past six years, a significant percentage have been international students, overwhelmingly from East Asia.[2] Two faculty have taught this class for over a decade, and they have produced related scholarship that discusses the challenges of how the class is structured, considering how the Intro class is envisioned in the curriculum and what the course is and does.[3]

The overarching pedagogical goal of the course is to teach skills and concepts that a broad range of students can take with them throughout their educational career and beyond.[4] Important threads in the Intro class throughout the years have been the concept of the American Dream and the necessary tension between unity and dissent in democracy. Both of these are consistent with the field of American Studies and specifically attach to critical issues that overwhelm the present. Related, but somewhat distinct, is the notion of American exceptionalism. In political terms, the concept that the United States is unique in the world because of its historical foundation in independence, democracy, and justice remains a deeply resonant political ideal and cultural discourse (though we find that this resonance has become less automatic for some students). In the Intro, the American Dream has been the concept most difficult to get students to engage with critically and analytically. As a central ideology of the US nation, the American Dream remains a source of deep student attachment for many and is one salient example of how student belief before entering the Intro class can impact responses to the class. The justifiable assumption we make is that our students occupy a range of positions along the spectrum of political beliefs. This single assumption was perhaps the most prominent factor in negotiating the Intro class over the course of the time period covered in this chapter.

PLANNING UNDER TRUMPISM

Our thinking about and planning for this course began to shift in the time leading up to the 2016 election, in the context of a contentious national election season marked by virulent nationalism(s), attacks on science and truth, and deep racial unrest. As we each planned and prepared the class, questions about the purpose of the field and the function of this course in the context of a large public university drew into sharp focus. We shaped the class in response to contentious political realities, our responsibilities as educators, and the charged environment of the university. We both struggled with how best to address the political moment in the United States. The class has traditionally historicized the present, posing questions and drawing connections between different historical moments to interrogate and critique. While we thought this approach was still useful—even crucial—we worried, too, that drawing historical parallels would normalize the present.

Some of the changes made to the class were general, as some readings no longer seemed analytically relevant. For example, Sze had been teaching sociologist Eduardo Bonilla-Silva's notion of "colorblind racism," which he developed alongside President Obama's presidential tenure.[5] The 2016 election challenged the notion of colorblind racism, as explicit and overt racism resurged. Sze added new readings from legal scholar Ian Haney-López, first *Dog-Whistle Politics*, and more recently, *White by Law*.[6] Haney-López's work historicizes race and racism. The former explains how race functioned in national politics, and his account of racism as a structural/historical force in the United States provided an invaluable historical and analytic account that moves students away from assuming race and racism to be biological and individual.

Trumpism makes some of the critical work in American Studies more salient than ever. For example, Sze has long taught Patricia Turner's *I Heard It through the Grapevine*, on rumors in African American culture, in the context of *The Birth of a Nation*, race riots, and the KKK. In the past, she occasionally got pushback about why she teaches this material in light of racial progress (student evaluations pre-Trump regularly asked, "Why teach about the KKK?" or "Why teach about white supremacy?"). Under Trumpism, students again accept white supremacy and the KKK as contemporary, not historical, realities. Trump's campaign slogan, "Make America Great Again," is a response to and product of a crisis of the American Dream, particularly as it is perceived by white Americans. The romantic nostalgia of the slogan asserts that there was a "great" moment in US history that has been subverted. Bayles tackles this notion of "greatness" head on by structuring the course around the assertion that this has never been true for many people/communities, as the American Dream is a white, heteronormative, middle class, capitalist ideal—one that relies not just on normative models of family, ability, gender, and sexuality, but explicitly on race.

The core questions of the class are: Who is an American? Where do the boundaries of the nation begin and end? What metaphors, images, sounds, and materials have been used to envision the nation? How have and do Americans conceive of national belonging and citizenship through culture, broadly defined? How is the United States related to the world? Taking the first question historically, through the different case studies in the class, Sze talks about how the "self-evident" question of "who belongs" and "who is an American" was deeply contested, for example, during the Los Angeles Zoot Suit Riots.[7] Through analysis rooted in the course's key questions, the attacks by US military personnel and the broader public on Chicano Angelenos comes to be understood, simultaneously, as historical fact, individual opinion (both in the older white Angelenos' explicitly racist comments and in students' personal reactions to the violence), and a set of political/cultural arguments about the policing of racialized bodies during World War II. While Sze did not explicitly talk about the 2016 election in this context, the racialized attacks on Mexicans during the election cycle came up as an explicit point of comparison during discussions led by graduate teaching assistants and in students' online group discussions.

ARGUMENTS AND EVIDENCE

The production of argument, and the distinction between argument and ideology (and personal opinion), has always been central to this course, but the need for such a framework became accentuated in this context, where it served both structural/rhetorical and emotional functions. In particular, we seek to dislodge the notion of ideology from a left/right political party context and instead use a Gramscian notion of the "common-sense," its consolidation, and also its disruption through counterhegemony. The question of what role American Studies could or should play in participating in and facilitating conversations about national division, increasingly polarized politics and ideological rhetoric, echo chambers, and separate sets of media, facts, and truth was central to our planning concerns for this course. That division does exist, and conversations between people who disagree vehemently with each other are necessary. At the same time, students—particularly students of color, queer students, trans students, students with disabilities, and undocumented students—need safe havens on campus.

The persistence of "post-truth politics" signaled a need for a way to balance the desire and demand for academic debate with the need to make those discussions tenable for students. With that in mind, we set forth the expectation that students frame their classroom discussions in the same way that we, as professors, do: as arguments supported by credible evidence. One of the most important skills in a Gen Ed course is to *teach* and *reinforce* the differences between facts, opinions, and arguments. In general, most students echo the general population in understanding the difference between facts and opinions (though as we see in the next section, "facts" themselves are increasingly under attack). In recent years, we have emphasized understanding, analyzing, and making cultural arguments and utilizing evidence, especially for students who are not familiar with humanistic questions and methodologies.[8]

This focus on facts, opinions, and arguments helps orient the contested politics in the class. We frequently invoke the framework of argument supported by evidence, most often to prevent classroom discussion from devolving into ideological banter and sound bites. We rely on this model, too, to moderate our own strong emotional responses to national and international politics, often echoed in our students' language.

SKILLS-BASED ASSIGNMENTS

Part of the work of teaching first-year students is to facilitate their self-conception as scholars and people in the world—critical thinkers rather than correct-answerers. To do so, we emphasize skills development (e.g., the function of and need to come to office hours, an emphasis on asking questions to increase understanding of concepts, complex forms of assessment).[9] Our persistence and insistence on structuring both discussion and writing in relation to facts, opinions, argument, and evidence laid bare some of the various ideological investments that shape them, as well as critical skill sets our students bring to the classroom. While we understand thoughtful deployment of facts, opinions, and argument to be fundamental to classroom engagement and necessary elements of debate, not all our students come to the classroom with those variegated skills at hand, let alone developed capacities to deploy them. Further, the state of national rhetoric has clear impacts on student thought and classroom discussion.

This observation is most apparent in relation to issues of media literacy. Drawing on current events, students in the Intro course read news stories and watch news clips in class. When asked to think critically about not just the *content*, but also the *context* of news media, students have often echoed Trump's vocal criticisms of "mainstream media." For example, when asked to assess whether or not CNN was dealing in facts, opinions, or arguments, many students identified it as a "left-wing" news source after Trump called it "fake news" at a press conference on January 11, 2017. It became clear to us that this course needed to address media literacy more directly and in a more sustained fashion in order to develop and utilize the framework of fact/opinion/argument in a meaningful way. In fighting the tide of ideologically charged, emotionally based rhetoric, this becomes not just an important analytical skill but also a crucial political project.

We have taken multiple tacks to address media and information literacy. Sze began using a media literacy quiz of the week's major news events written by a colleague who teaches journalism. Students self-grade their quiz and are given full credit for taking the quizzes. The quizzes—a mix of international and national news, civics, and popular culture—reveal a significant ignorance of both international/national news and history. These quizzes then prompt a conversation about epistemology and the ideological production of ignorance. The purpose of the quiz is not to "make people feel stupid" but to talk about gaps and patterns of information literacy—US isolationism, technology (i.e., reliance on social media for "news"), and the dominance of popular culture in their "hearts and minds." Bayles asks her students to complete a media annotation to think critically about evidentiary sources. Students select a news story, briefly summarize it, then go point by point through the article noting what kinds of evidence are used and where that evidence comes from—noting, too, when there are no explicit sources. Students then research the sources and assess their reliability. Finally, students are asked to consider the claims asserted in the article and to analyze them ideologically (in the Gramscian sense).

The emphasis of the second half of the course is students making connections between the course concepts and the world around them. The connections that they make effectively illustrate how they can apply the concepts from different historical contexts to the moment in which they live. For the students' major writing assignment, we ask them to consider their own definition of, and investment in, the American Dream, as well as how their narratives of their families and life trajectories fit alongside or in tension with this cultural narrative, utilizing the following prompt:

> This class has been structured on two key elements that help tell the story of the US nation—the tensions between unity and dissent, and cultural conflict—within the broader theme of the American Dream. One of the tasks of American Studies is to analyze whether there is, or has ever been, a representative American narrative. In our course, we have encountered many narratives of the nation, drawing on various experiences, people,

> texts, and objects. This paper assignment asks you to consider your own personal story in relation to these narratives we have encountered in this class. Whether or not you, yourself, are "American" (whatever that means), your story—your presence in the nation—is connected to the framework of the American Dream and its constituent parts (citizenship, freedom, security, education, class mobility, home, and family). Utilizing evidence to support your argument, write a clear, analytical paper in which you put your story in relation to others in the nation. How and why does your story—your notion of the American Dream, the ways you have come to understand it, and how you envision living it or not living it in your future—fit alongside or in tension with the cultural narrative of the American Dream?

This essay is used to assess their ability to connect the course's critique and their own lives, considering their personal histories in connection with the broader formations of the nation. Many students remain attached to the American Dream, though others come to articulate their understanding of those attachments—intergenerational, tied to their familial immigration narrative, or rooted in understandings of their privilege and broader historical, legal, economic, or political forces.

TEACHING AS TRANSFORMATION

As we stated at the beginning of this piece, ideological and experiential divergence shapes how students perceive both the nation and the field of American Studies. This perception is especially true for the lower-division classes in the department, which, again, draw students from all across the campus, who bring their own assumptions regarding course content. One (highly flawed) metric for assessing the successes and failures of the course is student evaluations at the end of the term.

Evaluations give students who stay in the course a chance to respond to its content and style. In past years, it has not been uncommon for students to write that the course is "too focused on race" or is about "making white people feel bad," though that critique has occurred less frequently with the rise of Trumpism. We understand that to be directly related to the racial and gender identities of the two faculty who have most frequently taught the class, both of whom are women of color (Sze, as well as another faculty member in the department).[10] In fall 2016, for example, Sze received an email complaint that the class was "ruined" by its focus on race.[11] Notably, Bayles, who is white, received only one evaluation comment that mentioned race in winter 2017, despite the course beginning with a discussion of privilege and white fragility and a sustained focus on anti-Black racism and nativism/anti-immigrant sentiment throughout the quarter.[12]

Another source of feedback is student writing and in-class discussion. One of the striking points that emerged is that not all our students believe in working toward an equitable future. Further, those who do are not, in general, optimistic about this possibility. For example, when Bayles asked if journalist Ta-Nehisi Coates makes a sufficient case for reparations for African Americans,[13] students responded almost unanimously that he had, and yet did not think reparations could or should be paid. The most cited reason was that it was not practical. Finally, a student asked, "Why are we talking about this if there's no way it could ever happen?" This failure of intellectual and political imagination was a telling disappointment, as American Studies is a field that invites critical interrogation of the past and the present with an eye on a more just future.

At the time of this chapter revision, the context of Trumpism expands and looms longer in the face of a global pandemic and its wide-ranging impacts and illustrations of class disparities, disability and health vulnerabilities, the failures of capitalism, the threat of martial law, and the question of the 2020 US election. That is the "what," inextricably linked to the "how," or pedagogical function of the class. For both, the ability to think analytically is key. These imperatives are now, more than ever, under political attack.

In this heightened political and historical era, we raise the question of what a large general education lecture in American Studies at a public university *should* be, in a prescriptive sense. Should the classroom be a political safe haven for progressive thought and vulnerable students or a site of critique and debate? Ultimately, this binary is false; the answer is both/and. We believe that the tools of American Studies help us to understand the roots of Trumpism. American Studies focuses on the voices and perspectives of those most marginalized by nationalist and racist ideologies. Teaching and scholarship on American Studies offers a core analytic that is particularly valuable now, whether the focus on the Zoot Suit lends itself to understanding DACA and the struggles of undocumented students, or teaching about the Chinese Exclusion Act connects to how Trump names COVID-19 a "Chinese virus," leading to increased acts of overt and covert anti-Asian violence and rhetoric.

The Intro class both posits a critique of the nation that is rooted in American Studies scholarship and thought, responding specifically and directly to the needs of vulnerable student populations such as undocumented students, *and* strengthens the tools and skills for intellectual debate. We understand this to be teaching as transformation. By *transformation,* we mean not that everyone's beliefs align but that all of the students in the class can analyze the world ideologically and see themselves as members of an intellectual community as engaged citizens in the world (and in fact, that "citizen" is a complex concept itself, despite the overly simplified conflation of citizen with legal status).[14] We believe that to mean that learning skills such as respectful engagement with crucial ideas in American Studies *is* to understand concepts like dissent and consensus and to engage with dialogue and difference. Our practices as American Studies teachers and scholars are essential, now more than ever.

NOTES

1. Charles Hale, ed., *Engaging Contradictions: Theory, Politics, and Methods of Activist Scholarship* (Berkeley: University of California Press, 2008).

2. Our rough estimate is about 15–20 percent in the period under discussion, although these numbers have dropped quickly in the last two years. See also Christina Owens and Abbie Boggs, "The Global American Studies Classroom: International Students and Critical Pedagogy," *American Quarterly* 68, no. 2 (2016): 379–385.

3. Michael Mark Cohen and Grace Wang, "Teaching the Introduction to American Studies Course: A Dialogue," *American Quarterly* 68, no. 2 (2016): 347–354.

4. Julie Sze, "Exploratory Concepts, Case Studies and Keywords for Teaching Environmental Justice and Climate Change from the Humanities," in *Teaching Climate Change in the Humanities*, ed. Stephen Siperstein, Shane Hall, Stephanie LeMenager (New York: Routledge, 2016), 184–190.

5. Eduardo Bonilla-Silva, *Racism without Racists and the Persistence of Racial Inequality in America*, 3rd ed. (Lanhman: Rowman & Littlefield, 2009).

6. Ian Haney-Lopéz, *Dog Whistle Politics: How Coded Racial Appeals Have Wrecked the Middle Class* (Oxford: Oxford University Press, 2014).

7. "Zoot Suit Riots," *American Experience*, directed and written by Joseph Tovares, aired February 10, 2002, on PBS) https://www.pbs.org/wgbh/americanexperience/films/zoot/.

8. We both simplify and make complex these distinctions with concrete examples. To illustrate the messiness of the categories, historical facts, e.g., the 1882 Chinese Exclusion Act, are obviously a product of cultural and political arguments, such as the impossibility of incorporation of Chinese bodies in the United States.

9. We use Paul Robbins's *Lawn People: How Grasses, Weeds, and Chemicals Make Us Who We Are* (Philadelphia: Temple University Press, 2007) to teach ideology.

In it, he explores how lawns came to dominate in US society, using Gramsci's notion of hegemony to illustrate how multiple institutions and processes work together to garner consent, and the possibilities for transformation. For Gramsci, hegemony is the process by which social forces continually interact and change one another, and which show change over time (in what he writes as the "sedimented" deposits of society). What is "common sense" becomes naturalized and is actually a product of institutional and historical forces that are complex and contradictory (see Sze, "Exploratory Concepts").

10. A significant literature on negative student evaluations, specifically for women and/or people of color, has documented how race/gender bias impacts student opinion of instructor competency. See Eva Lilienfeld, "How Student Evaluations Are Skewed against Women and Minority Professors," Century Foundation, June 10, 2016, https://tcf.org/content/commentary/student-evaluations-skewed-women-minority-professors/, and Colleen Flaherty, "Bias against Female Instructors," Inside Higher Ed, January 11, 2016, https://www.insidehighered.com/news/2016/01/11/new-analysis-offers-more-evidence-against-student-evaluations-teaching. For an overview of other issues related to race/gender and universities, please see Gabriella Gutiérrez y Muhs, *Presumed Incompetent: The Intersections of Race and Class for Women in Academia* (Boulder: University Press of Colorado, 2012).

11. This student was negatively responding to a postelection article about the election written by Toni Morrison: "Mourning for Whiteness," *New Yorker*, November 14, 2016, https://www.newyorker.com/magazine/2016/11/21/aftermath-sixteen-writers-on-trumps-america#anchor-morrison. The essay was not a required reading. Rather, the prompt in which it appeared asked students to choose one of the sixteen pieces in the *New Yorker* to respond to in this way: (1) Pick and describe one of these pieces; (2) Connect a keyword/concept and image/reading in the class to the pieces; (3) Make an argument about how what or how you learned from this class (either history or methodology) will help you understand the cultural moment, and a question you have going forward about America (or the United States and its relationship to the world).

12. Robin DiAngelo, "White Fragility," *International Journal of Critical Pedagogy* 3, no. 3 (2011): 54–70.

13. Ta-Nehisi Coates, "The Case for Reparations," *Atlantic*, August 23, 2014, https://www.theatlantic.com/projects/reparations/.

14. Lauren Berlant, "Citizenship," *Keywords for American Cultural Studies*, ed. Bruce Burgett and Glenn Hendler (New York: New York University Press, 2007).

16

#BlackLivesMatter and Feminist Pedagogy

Teaching a Movement Unfolding

AIMEE BAHNG AND REENA GOLDTHREE

> The classroom remains the most radical space of possibility in the academy.
> —bell hooks, *Teaching to Transgress*

In November 2015, student activists at Dartmouth College garnered national media attention following a Black Lives Matter demonstration in the main library of campus. Initially organized in response to the vandalism of a campus exhibit on police brutality, the events at Dartmouth were also part of the national #CollegeBlackout mobilizations in solidarity with student activists at the University of Missouri and Yale University. On Thursday, November 12, the Afro-American Society and the campus chapter of the National Association for the Advancement of Colored People (NAACP) urged students to wear black to show support for Black Lives Matter and hosted an open meeting to discuss racism on campus.[1] That evening, more than 150 people gathered in front of Dartmouth Hall for a moment of silence and a group photo.[2]

Following these planned events, approximately thirty to forty people continued the demonstration in nearby Baker-Berry Library. The group marched through several floors of the library, chanting "Black Lives Matter"; "If we don't get it, shut it down"; and "If we can't study, you can't study."[3] Fueled by an initial report in the *Dartmouth Review,* the conservative student newspaper, and a cell phone video of the library demonstration that went viral, conservative media outlets published sensationalized accounts of the protest in Baker-Berry, accusing students of assaulting bystanders and fomenting "race hatred."[4] Investigations conducted by Dartmouth College officials in the aftermath of the protests found no evidence of violence.

Just six months later, student activists at Dartmouth captured the attention of the national media once again for their activism in support of Black Lives Matter. On May 13, 2016, a group of students removed a controversial billboard created by the College Republicans for National Police Week from the student center. Protesting the billboard's use of the slogan "Blue Lives Matter," activists replaced the display with dozens of posters that proclaimed: "You cannot co-opt the movement against state violence to memorialize its perpetrators. #blacklivesmatter."[5] Reports condemning the student activists appeared in several conservative media outlets, and Dartmouth's senior administrators characterized the protest as "an unacceptable violation of freedom of expression" in a campus-wide email.[6] In the weeks following the controversy, students who participated in the protest faced widespread harassment, including death threats on social media.[7]

Located in the affluent rural town of Hanover, New Hampshire, Dartmouth College is a seemingly unlikely site for Black Lives Matter mobilizations. Here is a snapshot of the context in 2016: There are no #BlackLivesMatter chapters in New Hampshire, and the state's major Black civic organizations are headquartered far from campus in the cities of Manchester, Nashua, and Portsmouth. African Americans comprise just 2 percent of the population in Hanover and less than 7 percent of the undergraduate student body at Dartmouth.[8] Among its counterparts in the Ivy League, the college has the lowest percentage of faculty of color.[9] Furthermore, Dartmouth has "earned a reputation as one of the more conservative institutions in the nation when it comes to race," due to several dramatic and highly publicized acts of intolerance targeting students and faculty of color since the 1980s.[10]

The emergence of the Black Lives Matter movement—following the killings of Trayvon Martin in 2013 and of Eric Garner and Michael Brown in 2014—provided a language for progressive students and their allies at Dartmouth to link campus activism to national struggles against state violence, white supremacy, capitalism, and homophobia. The #BlackLivesMatter course at Dartmouth emerged as educators across the country experimented with new ways to learn from and teach with a rapidly unfolding, multisited movement. Significantly, many of these efforts utilized or emerged from digital media. On Twitter, Georgetown University professor Marcia Chatelain launched the #FergusonSyllabus, a crowdsourced list of books, articles, films, and primary sources that provide context for the 2014 uprisings. The collective Sociologists for Justice also used Twitter to organize a crowdsourced bibliography through the #socforjustice hashtag. Librarians and faculty members at Washington University in St. Louis created Documenting Ferguson, an open-access digital repository that "seeks to preserve and make accessible the digital media captured and created by community members following the shooting death of Michael Brown."[11] And in 2015, Frank Leon Roberts, a professor at NYU, taught the nation's first Black Lives Matter course accompanied by a multimedia digital syllabus.[12] Subsequently, courses on the movement have been taught at Emory University, Wake Forest University, the University of Florida, the University of Michigan, and Mount St. Mary's University.

We offer up this reflection piece as a means of interrogating both the possibilities and the limitations of teaching #BlackLivesMatter at an institution of higher education during a media-saturated moment. What does it even mean to teach a hashtag? For, while one of our aims was to provide history and context for the social movement that accompanies the hashtag, we also wanted to consider the particular interface with social media and digital community making for contemporary organizing. In this essay, we move from a brief narrative overview of how and why the course became a reality on to a discussion of its second run, the adjustments we made, the structural shifts that enabled these changes, and what remained central to the course all along: a commitment to feminist pedagogy. Ultimately, this discussion will bring us to a reflection on the course itself as a curricular intervention and as intellectual labor designed to push the conventions of what counts as academic rigor at an Ivy League institution.

In the two years since the uprising in Ferguson, educators and activists have explored different strategies for bringing Black Lives Matter from the streets into the classroom. Much of the existing literature about teaching Black Lives Matter has focused on incorporating lessons about police brutality and racial discrimination into preexisting courses or designing cocurricular workshops for K–12 students. Absent from this growing literature, however, are the firsthand accounts of educators who have taught courses on the movement at colleges and universities. Our reflection piece seeks to address this lacuna while also foregrounding the classroom as a vital site for movement building and feminist praxis in the age of Black Lives Matter.

BRINGING #BLACKLIVESMATTER INTO AN IVY LEAGUE CLASSROOM

The grand jury decision not to indict Darren Wilson was announced on November 24, 2014, as Dartmouth students were finishing up their fall quarter exams and checking out of campus. Over the following weeks and months, #BlackLivesMatter would galvanize a movement taken to the streets as well as to social media while most of northern New England was preparing for hibernation. Though there would be two die-ins organized in Hanover—one by faculty and staff (including Reena) on December 4 and the other by Dartmouth medical students on December 10—it would be many weeks before the main pulse of campus returned.[13] Would the community bring the exigencies of Ferguson and Staten Island back with them?

On January 16, 2015, the Dartmouth Center for the Advancement of Learning invited Reverend Starsky Wilson (president of the Deaconess Foundation in St. Louis, Missouri, and cochair of the Ferguson Commission), first, to talk about Ferguson and his work in St. Louis and, second, to lead a discussion with faculty about the implications of Ferguson for teaching. It was at this meeting that Dartmouth's #BlackLivesMatter course was first conceived. As Reverend Wilson called on everyone in the room to bring Ferguson into our classrooms, Aimee and our colleague, feminist geographer Abby Neely, set to immediate work figuring out how to get a #BlackLivesMatter course onto the books for spring quarter. It was helpful that the provost was also in the room at the time and told us her office would support whatever we cooked up. Over the subsequent forty-eight hours, Professors Bahng and Neely, while reaching out to department chairs, faculty, and staff who had expressed an interest in getting involved, pulled together and submitted *in three days* the necessary materials for the registrar to include the course in the Spring 2015 catalog.

The logistical obstacles were many, and we met those challenges with the strength that a sense of urgency and commitment to a burgeoning national movement can bring. We would not have time to send a new course proposal through the conventional review process, nor would the course be taught by instructors getting teaching credit for their labor. Instead, we found a willing and generous department in Geography to host the pedagogical experiment as a special topics course, which provided the curricular placeholder we needed to push the class through an otherwise sticky institutional wicket. With a shared grounding in feminist labor studies, the lead instructors took care to anticipate and address how the labor for this course would largely have to be volunteered on top of already full workloads. We kept at the forefront of our brainstorming the need to distribute the work of in-the-classroom teaching, grading, and course development and maintenance as evenly as possible across the two dozen or so faculty and staff who had stepped forward to form the Ferguson Teaching Collective. Along with an indispensable team of instructional designers, librarians, and media learning technologists, faculty from across the disciplines came together over the course before the start of spring quarter in March to develop a syllabus that could work for students with a wide range of familiarity with critical discussions about race and gender. We worked collaboratively through documents shared online and small task forces, as well as in meetings of the whole collective in one room, wherein we designed course assignments, discussed course goals, and strategized the means of assessment.

To respond to the exigencies of the moment, we had little time for new research to develop an ideal curriculum; the preliminary run of the course (aka #BLM 1.0) necessitated pooling the parts of courses already on the books, drawing on people's teaching comfort zones and areas of specialization to piece together a syllabus.[14] In other words, we had to draw on the longer struggles of primarily faculty of color to build an antiracist curriculum at Dartmouth, where various departments do offer courses about structural racism, intersectional feminist analysis, queer notions of family, race in media and performance, histories of social injustice, protest literature, and theoretical engagements with human rights discourse. Though members of the Teaching Collective shared a desire to bring the discussion of racialized police violence to campus, we had different relationships to civic engagement, to practices of activist organizing, and to experiences of discrimination. Comprising administrators, staff, adjunct instructors, tenured and untenured faculty, as well as undergraduate students, the collective included members situated across a range of relationships to institutional power and cultural privilege. One of the first adjustments we would have to make in order to work together was to teach/model/practice a mode of feminist collaboration and to grow a modicum of trust in one another.

GROWING COLLECTIVITY AT THE CORPORATE UNIVERSITY

The Ferguson Teaching Collective was formed in solidarity with experimental practices of living, working, and/or thinking in common that take place among grassroots organizers, artists, environmentalists, DIY communities, radical open source movements, and even some academics who dare to flout demands for more quantifiable outcomes for tenure and promotion in an increasingly corporatized university. In this context, the Combahee River Collective grounded our endeavor in Black feminist praxis. In part, the collective as a formation allowed for reflection on the "thousands upon thousands of unknown" agents of social change across political scales and platforms.[15]

Black feminist collectives are tricky to enact, though, especially at predominantly white institutions. Every collective will experience a tension between its democratic ideals and its will to action. Democracy, after all, is not efficient. Its virtue is complexity, multiplicity, and even disagreement. In order for social movements to move, room for discussion and debate is as crucial as political organizing. The space for dissent, or at least "dissensus," must remain sacrosanct and prioritized over consensus. We disagreed often—about capping the course at a certain number, the syllabus, the assignments, the budget, the guest speaker list, and more. However, what Ewa Ziarek calls an "ethics of dissensus" constituted the engine that kept the movement moving.[16] Indeed, we would revisit this question in the second iteration of the course when students joined us in reading Cathy Cohen's foundational essay on the radical potential of queer politics "Punks, Bulldaggers, and Welfare Queens." Citing Joshua Gamson's "Must Identity Movements Self-Destruct? A Queer Dilemma," Cohen directs our attention to how "the *destabilization* of collective identity is itself a goal and accomplishment of collective action."[17]

When news broke that Dartmouth was to offer a Black Lives Matter course, we had to weather not only the unsurprising conservative media backlash but also the understandable request from #BlackLivesMatter organizers to speak with us about our intentions for the course. On the one hand, Fox Business News's audacity to question the intellectual value of a course on Black Lives Matter before we had even held our first class should be fairly obvious.[18] It should have been just as obvious to us that including #BlackLivesMatter organizers in the shaping of this course would be a good idea and that a conservative Ivy League institution might be considered an unlikely place to find allies, given the intertwined histories of higher education and slavery.[19] Much more likely to expect a more appropriative move from a college that raised its founding funds on the notion that it could help bring enlightenment to American Indians "*in deserto*," even though the college would primarily serve the aspiring clergymen offspring of the landed gentry. A skeptic might have called this a branding issue. At the end of the day, perhaps part of the goal of creating the course was to make #BlackLivesMatter and #Dartmouth feel less incongruous—to affirm the value of Black lives on our campus as well as in Ferguson, Staten Island, Baltimore, and elsewhere. Seeing those hashtags placed directly adjacent to one another in Twitter feeds across the nation confirmed the reach of Black Lives Matter, suggesting that college campuses could be an important staging ground for the burgeoning movement.[20]

Questions about the course's relationship to political engagement and academic rigor highlight the stakes of Black feminist scholarship on the racialized and gendered politics of knowledge production itself. Our course description frames this performative intervention of syllabus-creation-as-political-act from the outset: "Though the academy can never lay claim to social movements, this course seeks in part to answer the call of students and activists around the country to take the opportunity to raise questions about, offer studied reflection upon, and allocate dedicated institutional space to the failures of democracy, capitalism, and leadership and to make #BlackLivesMatter." Even if the course was taking up not only classroom but also curricular space at the institution, was it an occupation staged by an undercommons? Or, as an official course students could take for class credit, did it become part of the established university with all its limitations on more radical approaches to learning? Grades, for example, would be required, as would concrete evidence of deliverable and quantifiable outcomes. The registrar would demand at least one instructor of record, despite our attempt to decentralize authority in the Teaching Collective. When presented with press requests, we would consult the legal team about whether journalists would be allowed into the classroom. In retrospect, some of us may have longed to have proceeded more along the lines of what Fred Moten and Stefano Harney call "fugitive planning," carving out a space "to be in but not of" the university.[21] But in the push to make #BlackLivesMatter a credit-bearing course for students, we were rather quickly folded into an institutional framework and narrative.[22]

As we moved through the term, it was not only the structures of institutionalized learning that made us question what we were doing but also the struggle, even within the parameters of a higher education institutional model, to get the students engaged with the broader movement, especially when our other teaching commitments, service obligations, and research pressures constantly pulled our focus from cultivating a daily classroom environment built on trust and open-mindedness. This was no doubt also a problem of labor. In its first iteration, class met every Monday afternoon in a three-hour-long seminar format. Each week, and therefore each class, featured a new team of instructors, who may or may not have been able to sustain the class discussion from the previous week or pass the conversational baton to the following week. While the hope was to allow the students and student teaching assistants to take on this work, the structure of the course was also designed as a labor-saving strategy. In addition, student-led courses necessitate training we didn't give them and couldn't model on a week-to-week basis. The student feedback would reveal that the course not only felt disjointed from one week to the next but also felt disconnected from the movement on the ground elsewhere. It felt as though every session was the first day of class, as though we were "starting over" again each week with a new set of instructors, methodologies, and dynamics. Instead of "spiraling in and getting deeper and deeper," it felt more like "a mini lecture series."[23] Yet, students also stated that the Teaching Collective offered a powerful example of solidarity for budding activists on campus and urged us to continue to offer the course. So we decided to change things up, starting with figuring out how to run the course again but with two significant adjustments. First, we wanted to address the continuity issue. Second, we wanted to revamp the readings and assignments to reflect a more direct engagement with the #BlackLivesMatter movement. Both concerns required a different structural base.

In February 2015, just shortly after the initial sprint to get the course listed in the spring catalog, the college circulated a call to apply for "reallocation fund" opportunities to support innovative teaching. If selected for funding, our proposal would grant teaching credit for the course as well as $2,000 to assist with programmatic costs. Because Abby would be spending much of the following year conducting research abroad, Reena stepped up to coteach. In May 2015, we heard that we had won the innovative course grant and set to work thinking about how to deepen the course's engagement with the movement across all aspects of the course. We were keen to make some significant changes and faced some immediate questions.

Though there were some consistencies across the two versions of the course worth noting—in both instances, the course largely relied on the labor of untenured women—the second iteration witnessed some significant changes. If two of us were receiving teaching credit, what would happen to the collective? While people's enthusiasm for the course remained strong, it no longer seemed fair to call upon them to sustain the same level of responsibility to the course as in previous years. We began to reformulate the collective as a supplement to the course—for organizing, circulating information, and continuing a practice of ongoing study—study that would become the ever-evolving heart of our practice. To that end, we hoped to kickstart that initiative by purchasing all the required books for the second run of the course for all Teaching Collective members. Ultimately, the collective did become a locus of organizing—composing and distributing an open letter of support for student protesters, for example—as well as a resource for ongoing news gathering of more incidents of police violence as well as Black Lives Matter actions.

As we were preparing to launch the "#BLM 2.0" course, we received a major grant from Dartmouth's new Experiential Learning Initiative, a campus-wide effort to promote intentional, reflective, and community-engaged learning within and beyond the classroom. This grant money would give legs to the public outreach project assignment and our attempts to connect with the Black Lives Matter movement from the first iteration of the course. Students had responded enthusiastically both to the call to public engagement, which resulted in the proliferation of student-led teach-ins, op-eds, and social media conversations, and our Skype session with Grand Rapids #BLM chapter founder Anita Moore. (In fact, one of our students is now the chair of that chapter!) Even as our $45,000 Experiential Learning Initiative grant became a necessary windfall for facilitating more engagement with the Black Lives Matter movement, we were wary of using this money to supply a temporary experience for students—the kind of problematic, drop-in activism model that would leave students feeling good about themselves and the little they had done to make an effort without developing a lasting relationship and impact more directly channeled to grassroots organizations. At Dartmouth, with Ivy League money, it is all too easy to reproduce "the very power inequalities that feminists have worked so diligently to expose and challenge."[24]

Seeking to craft a feminist alternative to "voluntourism" and service learning, we designed the new experiential learning components of the course to foster three outcomes: critical awareness, sustained dialogue, and personal reflection. We drew inspiration in this effort from the writings of Brazilian educator Paulo Freire as well as the work of women of color feminists who have long argued for, and modeled, forms of "community accountable scholarship."[25] We extended the ethos of public engagement from our first iteration of the course, designed to encourage students to "reclaim learning as a popular and democratic activity that resists the hierarchies and exploitative social relations fostered by education as we know it."[26] Our four core books for the course—written by Keeanga-Yamahtta Taylor, Michelle Alexander, Angela Y. Davis, and Ta-Nehisi Coates—provided necessary context for both the current crisis of state violence and the powerful surge in grassroots resistance.[27] (See appendix.) By combining interdisciplinary inquiry with experiential learning, we prompted students to relate scholarly research and theory to the pressing social problems of our contemporary moment.

We also viewed experiential learning as a vehicle for students to enact a feminist political praxis as they collaborated with community organizers, activist media makers, and artists—both on and off campus. While on campus, students participated in discussion-based workshops with community organizers Osagyefo Sekou, Jay-Marie Hill, Darnell Moore, and Pete White. The workshops, in large part made possible by the grant money, examined the process of movement building—through media, music, and community campaigns—in the era of Black Lives Matter. Each visiting speaker also enacted for our students what "theory as liberatory practice" looks like at its best.[28] Following each workshop, we invited students to join the visiting organizer(s) for a free-flowing conversation session, where they often posed questions about building a progressive movement culture at Dartmouth. Reflecting on their engagement with organizers in the classroom, students commented that the experience helped them to gain a deeper understanding of the "tangible impacts and work of the movement."[29] With a classroom comprising about 75 percent students of color (around 66 percent in the first iteration), these Black Lives Matter organizers offered students a language, a set of tactics, and a broader conversation in which to participate. For some, these direct confabulations with more experienced organizers constituted the first time they could speak with someone in the classroom environment about how to address long-standing grievances. Arguably the most diverse classroom on campus, the course included students majoring in social sciences and natural sciences, documented and undocumented students, first-generation and legacy admits, queer and environmental activists, athletes and members of performing arts groups. They would bring these varied connections and affiliations to all aspects of their work, demonstrating the ways in which intellectual production emerges from what Donna Haraway would call "situated knowledges."[30]

Beyond campus, students conducted short-term fieldwork with #BlackLivesMatter chapters and other community-based activist organizations across the nation. Given Dartmouth's geographical distance from the epicenters of Black Lives Matter mobilizations, we thought it was crucial that our course allocate significant time for students to observe, document, and study the work of activists "on the ground." To facilitate sustained engagement with local movements beyond the end of the term, we encouraged students to collaborate with a #BlackLivesMatter chapter or an allied organization either in their hometown or in another locale where they had preexisting ties to the community. Students selected a variety of sites for their fieldwork, including chapters of #BlackLivesMatter and BYP 100, cooperative urban farms in upstate New York, and a spoken word youth organization in Philadelphia. Significantly, four students traveled to California to conduct fieldwork with the Los Angeles Community Action Network (LA CAN) after meeting Pete White, the organization's founder and executive director, during one of the campus workshops.

The culminating assignment for the course prompted students to design multimedia projects that engaged with Black Lives Matter. In these projects, media served as a vehicle for research-based public scholarship on the movement and as a means to stand in solidarity with the movement. Working collaboratively in groups of two or three, students addressed the reverberations of Black Lives Matter on college campuses as well as the movement's ongoing impact on the national stage. Their projects featured several different media formats—from documentary films, podcasts, and music videos to Facebook pages, digital archives, and zines—and highlighted the potential and challenges of documenting a movement as it unfolds. In keeping with the aims of the course, the students presented their projects at a public event attended by local community members as well as Dartmouth students, staff, and faculty.

These group media projects required a collaborative ethos we had been cultivating through our readings and daily practice over the course of the term. Most days we met in a special active learning space that did the physical work of distributing attention around the room.[31] Students often worked in "pods" gathered around six multimedia stations equipped with a projector and wireless connection to their laptops. We used this configuration often for small-group exercises, including on-the-spot, real-time synthesis of a group's responses to a critical passage or media clip. Students could collaborate even in their notetaking, thinking together on a shared screen, where they could collect their questions and comments for presenting to the larger group later. As this was our default set-up, we enjoyed seeing how our various guest speakers used the space, crisscrossing the center of the room, writing notes on all four walls of whiteboard, becoming a moving cursor, hovering over a different group of students at various moments of the discussion. Some days, though, required steadier communing. Midway through the term, students had formed such an intense and trusting community in that room that they started to construct the space themselves, asking if we could sit all at one big seminar table one day, or in a big free-floating circle "so we could all face each other" the next. Students brought in their organizing from beyond the classroom, too, often opening and closing class sharing with their peers what projects they were working on elsewhere on campus and how to get involved. In part, the gathering inward and the attention outward became a routine ebb and flow of the class. This telescoping movement was, in fact, part of the goal of the course, threaded through the kinds of work they were being asked to do for class: writing op-eds, listening to professor-curated playlists of the movement, and creating Instagram essays (one of which would earn its place in an arty publication called *Documentum* in an issue guest-edited by Teju Cole and Teaching Collective member Jeff Sharlet). For all the money and structural orchestration of this course, ultimately, these remarkable students took the reins of the experiment. Without their trust and willingness to participate, none of it would have worked.

Having now taught two iterations of the #BlackLivesMatter course, we are faced with the task of assessing the course's impact and future. In the spring of 2015, Teaching Collective member and history professor Derrick White was denied tenure, and one year later Aimee's tenure bid was also denied. What does it mean that Dartmouth's administration generously funded the #BlackLivesMatter course but refused to acknowledge the very scholars whose intellectual and organizational labor made the course possible? What are the possibilities of sustaining the Ferguson Teaching Collective when "Black and Brown scholarly bodies (student, staff, and professorial)" are "churned up by Dartmouth and other elite spaces"?[32] We pose these questions with the knowledge that the pedagogical work of teaching #BlackLivesMatter will be borne disproportionately by people by color.

And how do we even get to the part of the tale where we must face our classroom, full of Black and Brown faces, on the days when another police shooting of an unarmed Black person has occurred? How do we write the part where we stop in our tracks and remember all the lives cut short and all the families who will likely never receive any justice? Dedicated teachers often talk about extending conversations beyond the classroom. In this case, though we include a link to our publicly available syllabus, some of the most important lessons cannot be represented on those pages. What did it mean to lie ourselves down on the pavement, to embody and reenact the position of the unarmed victims of these police shootings? How do you show up for school every day when you feel the "between the world and me" gap that Ta-Nehisi Coates attempts to set down in words? As we collabo-write this piece in a shared document online, with media feeds running in adjacent tabs, two more stories of audacious police shootings of Black men—one in need of roadside assistance and another reading in his car waiting to pick up his kid—demand our attention. In addition to the stories of Terence Crutcher and Keith Lamont Scott, we have also learned that the Baltimore County officer who fatally shot Korryn Gaines and wounded her five-year-old son would not face criminal charges. And consequently we witness many of our friends needing to take a break from social media, needing to close the tabs, needing to carve out some space to respond to an unrelenting stream of deaths caught on video—to respond on their own terms, where their own words and silences can surface at their own pace.

Ultimately, we wanted to carve out such a space at our institution: a space for the acknowledgment of pain, for the expression of anger at injustice, and for the seemingly insurmountable amount of healing we were hearing the demands for from our students. We also wanted a space where we could help one another shuttle between media-saturated life online and the all-too-quiet Ivory Tower in the so-called Hanover bubble. bell hooks writes that "the classroom remains the most radical space of possibility in the academy."[33] The possibilities we glimpsed at many moments over the two years teaching the #BlackLivesMatter course have moved us and made us grateful to our students, who will maybe grow similar spaces beyond the academy. This chapter is dedicated to them, the ones who hold the key to a movement still unfolding.

CODA: JANUARY 2021

It has been a harrowing five years since teaching the second iteration of our #BLM course. The first month of 2021 has borne witness to the startling contrast between police handling of a predominantly white mob that breached the Capitol building in Washington, DC, on January 6 and the excessive use of force used six months earlier against people protesting structural racism and ongoing police violence in the summer of 2020. Responding in part to the murder of George Floyd, who was aggressively pinned to the ground and asphyxiated by officer Derek Chauvin, the protests of summer 2020 peaked on June 6 in the midst of the coronavirus pandemic. An estimated 15 million to 26 million people risked their lives to fight for their lives in the months following Floyd's death, making the demonstrations and the broader Movement for Black Lives the largest recorded in history.[34]

While we wrote the original version of this article just prior to the 2016 election, we write this coda near the conclusion of Donald Trump's term occupying the office of the president of the United States. Using the authority of the presidency, Trump has issued a series of executive orders that have consistently prioritized corporate interests over the lives and livelihoods of poor people, those of color in particular. While critical geographer Ruth Wilson Gilmore argues that racism can be defined as the "state-sanctioned or extralegal production and exploitation of group-differentiated vulnerability to premature death," Trump's policy actions arguably escalate such exploitation from state-sanctioned or extralegal structures to legally encoded racism.[35]

Trump's Executive Order on Combating Race and Sex Stereotyping, for example, bans the teaching of critical race theory in federal agencies. The order takes specific aim at diversity training in the federal workforce and prohibits granting funds for such purposes, suggesting that efforts to address institutional racial and gender disparities "could promote division and inefficiency."[36] Federal contractors who use "any training, workshop, or similar programming having to do with diversity and inclusion" risk sanctions and/or contract termination. Twisting the language of federal antidiscrimination laws and even manipulating the significance of the Black freedom struggle through misleading gestures to the Montgomery bus boycott and Dr. Martin Luther King Jr.'s "I Have a Dream" speech, EO 13950 makes a slippery, nefarious turn to banning the teaching of ideas such as white privilege and structural racism. "Today, however," it reads, "many people are pushing a different vision of America . . . that some people, simply on account of their race or sex, are oppressors." The executive order is audacious, considering that similar efforts to shut down ethnic studies programs in Arizona, for example, have been overturned and found to be unconstitutional.[37] Even though it is likely that the Biden administration will reverse most of Trump's executive orders, the assault on critical race theory has made its way into the federal register in unprecedented ways. "Teaching a movement unfolding" thus entails reigniting the struggle—in many ways continued from the ethnic studies movements of the 1960s and 1970s—to fight for a foothold in university curricula, all the while remaining alert to the tendency for institutions of higher education to fold courses, students, and professors from underrepresented groups into placating structures of representation without access to substantive change.

In the introduction to *The Reorder of Things: The University and Its Pedagogies of Minority Difference,* Roderick A. Ferguson quotes at length from a letter that Black conceptual artist Adrian Piper wrote to the president of Wellesley College. In the letter, which appears as part of Piper's collage, *Self-Portrait 2000*, the artist articulates and protests the bind of being hired as the only tenured Black woman at Wellesley because of her high-profile antiracism work and the failure of the institution to support her work, even as the college profited from the visibility Piper's work lent to *"its multicultured public image while in reality actively preventing [her] from doing the multicultural work it publicly claims to welcome."* Ferguson takes interest in "how state, capital, and academy saw minority insurgence as a site of calculation and strategy, how those institutions began to see minority difference and culture as positivities that could be part of their own 'series of aims and objectives.'"[38] Although the #BlackLivesMatter course garnered some of the best media coverage Dartmouth could muster amid a spate of more scandalous news headlines, it's important to note that Reena and Aimee, along with several other key members of the Ferguson Teaching Collective, including Treva Ellison and Derrick White, have since left Dartmouth to teach at other institutions, not because there was necessarily a utopia to be found elsewhere, but because we were in search of institutions further along in their commitments to support antiracist work. Among the many letters circulated in the fall of 2020 declaring departmental and institutional support for Black Lives Matter, the ones that stood out were the ones that reckoned with their own participation in and association with white supremacist legacies and ongoing liberal platitudes; the ones that pledged specifically to recruit, hire, retain, and promote scholars of color whose work addresses racialized and gendered systems of power; the ones committing to bringing activists to campus and acknowledging the value of learning and listening to front-line communities; and the ones vowing to hold the police and others accountable for killing people of color. The actions promised in these letters for Black lives fly in the face of Trump's Executive Order on Combating Race and Sex Stereotyping. Our hope is that these declared commitments will stay sharp and urgent; that Black lives will continue to matter; and that teaching #BlackLivesMatter will remain grounded in practices of care and community that emerge out of Black, Indigenous, and woman-of-color feminisms that understand that "freedom is a constant struggle."

APPENDIX: #BLACKLIVESMATTER COURSE SYLLABUS

#BlackLivesMatter
Dartmouth College
Spring 2016

INSTRUCTORS

Prof. Aimee Bahng and Prof. Reena Goldthree, as well as members of the Ferguson Teaching Collective at Dartmouth

COURSE DESCRIPTION

Though the academy can never lay claim to social movements, this course seeks in part to answer the call of students and activists around the country to take the opportunity to raise questions about, offer studied reflection upon, and allocate dedicated institutional space to the failures of democracy, capitalism, and leadership and to make #BlackLivesMatter. Developed through a group effort, this course brings to bear collective thinking, teaching, research, and focus on questions around race, structural inequality, and violence. Through this course, we examine the particular historical, geographical, cultural, social, and political ways in which race is configured and deployed in the United States and beyond in the past and present. The course offers a context, both past and present, for the events in Ferguson, Missouri in 2014. It places those events in a broader context of race and racism in the United States. It examines the entanglements of trauma and violence for individuals, communities, and society as a whole. Finally, by beginning our analysis in Ferguson and moving out from there, this course also offers a way to place these very important current events in broader national and international contexts. Guest speakers will include Black Lives Matter activists who engage social movements in a variety of ways (i.e., through policy, music, or visual culture) as well as members of the Ferguson Teaching Collective at Dartmouth who can share their particular training and expertise in different methodological approaches to the problem of systemic racialized violence. Striking a balance between this complexity and the need for collective inquiry and action is what this course is designed to do. Your participation as students is central to this collective endeavor as we read, think, and learn together.

This second iteration of the #BlackLivesMatter course is supported by funding from an Innovative Course Grant from the Dean of Faculty Office as well as an Experiential Learning Initiative grant through the Dartmouth Center for the Advancement of Learning (DCAL). By combining interdisciplinary inquiry with experiential learning initiatives, this course seeks to connect scholarly research and theory to the urgent social problems that inform the Black Lives Matter movement. To guide our efforts, the course will feature training workshops on public engagement, multimedia production, community organizing, and policy making. Students will conduct short-term fieldwork with a community-based organization of their choosing and produce group media projects to be showcased at the end of term.

LEARNING OBJECTIVES

During this course, students will:

- enact and participate in a learning collective;
- develop critical thinking skills with which to understand important current events;
- think across a number of disciplines;
- interact directly with a community-based organization or activist group;
- communicate important, difficult topics to a broad audience.

REQUIRED TEXTS

- Michelle Alexander, *The New Jim Crow: Mass Incarceration in the Age of Colorblindness* (The New Press, 2012), ISBN: 978-1595586438
- Ta-Nehisi Coates, *Between the World and Me* (Spiegel & Grau, 2015), ISBN: 978-0812993547
- Angela Y. Davis, *Freedom Is a Constant Struggle: Ferguson, Palestine, and the Foundations of a Movement* (Haymarket Books, 2016) ISBN: 978-1608465644
- Keeanga-Yamahtta Taylor, *From #BlackLivesMatter to Black Liberation* (Haymarket Books, 2016) ISBN: 978-1608465620

ASSIGNMENTS

Your achievement of these learning objectives will be assessed through:

- Attendance and Participation (20%)
- Fieldwork and a reflection piece (25%)
    - This assignment is designed to give you the opportunity to be-

come more publicly engaged with Black Lives Matter and related movements. We envision you working in small groups of 2–3. Together, you will work to research and identify an organization where you can observe how community activists pursue social change at the grassroots level. Because you need to respect your other course obligations, many of you may need to stay fairly local. Boston or NYC-based organizations might be your best bet. Others of you may have ties to a group already in your hometown or another meaningful geographical context. Because we also want to facilitate your sustained engagement with a group beyond the scope of this class, we will do our best to support you if you can find a way to make a trip happen that does not conflict with your other schoolwork. To ensure best practices, we require that you develop a formal proposal that outlines concretely how you will cultivate respectful and informed engagement with your organization.

- Op-ed pieces (30%)
    - You will write three op-ed pieces over the course of the term. Each op-ed should be 1,000–1,200 words and must be informed by the assigned readings and central questions of this course. We encourage you to respond directly to Black Lives Matter current events as they unfold over the course of the term. You will be asked to revise at least one of the pieces and submit it for publication online.
- and a group media project (25%)
    - For this culminating assignment, you will work in small groups of 3 to create a multimedia project (documentary film, slideshow with voiceover, video log, recording of a performance) that showcases original research and composition as well as a thoughtful, theoretical framework. This assignment will allow you to use media to intervene in public debates about the Black Lives Matter movement, building on the public engagement workshops that you have completed throughout the term. It will also allow you to develop proficiency in the composition and production of various media forms. Final projects will be shared in a public reception at the end of the term.

NOTES

An earlier version of this essay appeared in *Radical Teacher* 106 (Fall 2016): 20–28. We would like to thank all the members of the Ferguson Teaching Collective at

Dartmouth for their collaborative spirit and material contributions to the making of these courses. We also thank the anonymous reviewers of the original article for their feedback and support. Most of all, we thank and would like to dedicate this piece to the students.

1. For the initial announcement about the protests on Facebook, see https://www.facebook.com/events/984278961637079/.

2. To view a photograph of the demonstrators in front of Dartmouth Hall, go to: http://www.thedartmouth.com/multimedia/1624.

3. Briana Tang, "Students Stage a Protest in Solidarity with Missouri and Yale, Drawing Both Support and Controversy," *Dartmouth*, November 12, 2015, http://www.thedartmouth.com/article/2015/11/students-stage-a-protest-in-solidarity-with-missouri-and-yale-drawing-both-support-and-controversy.

4. "Eyes Wide Open at the Protest," *Dartmouth Review*, November 14, 2015, http://www.dartreview.com/eyes-wide-open-at-the-protest/; a cell phone video of the protest was posted on the YouTube page of Campus Review on November 14, 2015. As of September 18, 2016, it has amassed 1,045,348 views. To view the video, go to: https://www.youtube.com/watch?v=OJAuVQlLxDo.

For examples of the coverage of the protests in the national conservative media, see "Dartmouth Protesters Assault Students While Screaming Racial Threats," Fox News, November 16, 2015, http://nation.foxnews.com/2015/11/16/dartmouth-protesters-assault-students-while-screaming-racial-threats; Jessica Chasmar, "Black Lives Matter Protesters Berate White Students Studying at Dartmouth Library," *Washington Times*, November 16, 2015, http://www.washingtontimes.com/news/2015/nov/16/black-lives-matter-protesters-berate-white-student/.

5. Zachary Benjamin and Michael Qian, "Campus Reacts To Blue Lives Matter Display Replaced by #Blacklivesmatter Posters," *Dartmouth*, May 13, 2016, http://www.thedartmouth.com/article/2016/05/display-removed-in-collis-replaced-with-blacklivesmatter-posters. For a public statement on the protest from student activists who participated, see "Official Statement Regarding Friday's Events," Dartmouth Action Collective, May 18, 2016, http://dac.citizenmodern.org/2016/05/18/official-statement-regarding-fridays-events/.

6. For coverage of the protest in the national media, see "'Blue Lives Matter' Display Vandalized by BLM Supporters at Dartmouth," Campus Reform, May 14, 2016, http://www.campusreform.org/?ID=7591; Jerome Hudson, "Black Lives Matter Activists Destroy 'Blue Lives Matter' Display at Dartmouth College," Breitbart, May 16, 2016, http://www.breitbart.com/big-government/2016/05/16/black-lives-matter-activists-destroy-blue-lives-matter-display-dartmouth-college/; "'Blue Lives Matter' Display Defaced at Dartmouth, College Republicans Say," Fox News, May 17, 2016, http://www.foxnews.com/us/2016/05/17/blue-lives-matter-display-defaced-at-dartmouth-college-republicans-say.html. See also email from Phil Hanlon, Carolyn Dever, Rebecca Biron, and Inge-Lise Ameer to the undergraduate student body at Dartmouth, May 15, 2016, reblogged at http://www.dartblog.com/data/2016/05/012664.php.

7. "A Statement by Mikala Williams," Dartmouth Action Collective, May 18, 2016, http://dac.citizenmodern.org/2016/05/18/a-statement-by-mikala-williams/.

8. For enrollment figures for the 2015–2016 AY, see Dartmouth College Fact Book (2015), https://www.dartmouth.edu/~oir/data-reporting/factbook/enrollment.html.

9. Alexa Green, "College Faculty Are Least Diverse in Ivy League," *Dartmouth*, April 25, 2016, http://www.thedartmouth.com/article/2016/04/college-faculty-are-least-diverse-in-ivy-league/.

10. Stefan M. Bradley, "Black Power and the Big Green: Dartmouth College and the Black Freedom Movement, 1945–75," *Journal of Civil and Human Rights* 1, no. 1 (2015): 25.

11. Documenting Ferguson project is available online at http://digital.wustl.edu/ferguson/.

12. To view the digital Black Lives Matter syllabus created by Frank Leon Roberts, go to http://www.blacklivesmattersyllabus.com/

13. Brady Carlson, "Police Violence against Black Americans Inspires Hanover 'Die In' Protest," New Hampshire Public Radio, December 5, 2015, http://nhpr.org/post/police-violence-against-black-americans-inspires-hanover-die-protest; Annie Ma, "Community Protests Police Brutality," *Dartmouth*, January 5, 2015, http://www.thedartmouth.com/article/2015/01/community-protests-policy-brutality/.

14. The syllabus for the spring 2015 #BlackLivesMatter course at Dartmouth College is available at https://www.academia.edu/12277372/_BlackLivesMatter_Syllabus. This version of the syllabus does not include the more developed assignment descriptions.

15. "The Combahee River Collective Statement," accessed February 6, 2021, http://circuitous.org/scraps/combahee.html.

16. Ewa Płonowska Ziarek, *An Ethics of Dissensus: Postmodernity, Feminism, and the Politics of Radical Democracy* (Stanford, CA: Stanford University Press, 2001).

17. Cathy J. Cohen, "Punks, Bulldaggers, and Welfare Queens: The Radical Potential of Queer Politics?," *GLQ: Gay and Lesbian Quarterly* 3, no. 4 (1997): 439.

18. "Dartmouth Is Offering 'Black Lives Matter' Class?," February 5, 2016, http://video.foxbusiness.com/v/4034458965001/dartmouth-is-offering-black-lives-matter-class/.

19. See Craig Steven Wilder, *Ebony and Ivy: Race, Slavery, and the Troubled History of America's Universities* (New York: Bloomsbury, 2013).

20. For an insightful assessment of the Black Lives Matter movement and the path toward achieving "a mass struggle for our time," see Russell Rickford, "Black Lives Matter: Toward a Modern Practice of Mass Struggle," *New Labor Forum* 25, no. 1 (2016): 34–42.

21. Stefano Harney and Fred Moten, *The Undercommons: Fugitive Planning and Black Study* (New York: Minor Compositions, 2013), 26.

22. For the official institutional narrative about the course, see "Dartmouth to Offer a New Course: '#BlackLivesMatter,'" Dartmouth News, February 10, 2015, https://news.dartmouth.edu/news/2015/02/dartmouth-offer-new-course-blacklivesmatter.

23. Student feedback from #BlackLivesMatter course listening session, May 14, 2015, Dartmouth College, meeting minutes in possession of the authors.

24. Leeray M. Costa and Karen J. Leong, "Introduction Critical Community Engagement: Feminist Pedagogy Meets Civic Engagement," *Feminist Teacher* 22, no. 3 (2012): 171.

25. The term "community accountable scholarship" was coined by black feminist theorist Alexis Pauline Gumbs. On the importance of dialogue and reflection in education, see Paulo Freire, *Pedagogy of the Oppressed* (New York: Bloombury Academic, 2000); bell hooks, *Teaching to Transgress: Education as the Practice of Freedom* (New York: Routledge,1994), 13–22. See also Jasmine Mina and Annemarie Vaccaro, "Role Modeling Community Engagement for College Students: Narratives from Women Faculty and Staff of Color," in *Feminist Community Engagement: Achieving Praxis*, ed. Susan Iverson and Jennifer James (New York: Palgrave MacMillan, 2014), 53–74; Melanie Brazzell, "Community Accountable Scholarship within a Participatory Action Research Model," January 14, 2016, https://www.academia.edu/24561176/Community_Accountable_Scholarship_within_a_Participatory_Action_Research_Model.

26. Gargi Battacharyya, "How Can We Live with Ourselves? Universities and the Attempt to Reconcile Learning and Doing," in "Race Critical Public Scholarship," ed. Gargi Battacharyya and Karim Murji, special issue, *Ethnic and Racial Studies* 36, no. 9 (2013): 1411–1428. Special thanks to Ferguson Teaching Collective member Patricia Lopez, who crafted the language for the public outreach project assignment and did the research to situate public engagement in feminist, decolonial praxis.

27. Keeanga-Yamahtta Taylor, *From #BlackLivesMatter to Black Liberation* (Chicago: Haymarket, 2016); Michelle Alexander, *The New Jim Crow: Mass Incarceration in the Age of Colorblindness* (New York: New Press, 2010); Angela Y. Davis, *Freedom Is a Constant Struggle: Ferguson, Palestine, and the Foundations of a Movement* (Chicago: Haymarket, 2016); Ta-Nehisi Coates, *Between the World and Me* (New York: Spiegel & Grau, 2015).

28. hooks, *Teaching to Transgress.*

29. Online Student Course Assessment Report, #BlackLivesMatter, Dartmouth College, Spring 2016.

30. Donna Haraway, "Situated Knowledges: The Science Question in Feminism and the Privilege of Partial Perspective," *Feminist Studies* 14, no. 3 (1988): 575–599.

31. "Dartmouth Active Learning Classrooms," Learning Design at Dartmouth, accessed December 17, 2020, https://sites.dartmouth.edu/edtech/projects/active-learning-space-incubator-program/.

32. Derrick White, "Black Intellectual Lives Matter," March 17, 2015, unpublished document in possession of the authors.

33. hooks, *Teaching to Transgress*, 12.

34. Larry Buchanan, Quoctrung Bui, and Jugal K. Patel, "Black Lives Matter May Be the Largest Movement in U.S. History," *New York Times*, July 3, 2020, https://www.nytimes.com/interactive/2020/07/03/us/george-floyd-protests-crowd-size.html.

35. Ruth Wilson Gilmore, *The Golden Gulag: Prisons, Surplus, Crisis, and Opposition in Globalizing California* (Berkeley: University of California Press, 2007), 28.

36. United States, Executive Office of the President [Donald Trump], Execu-

tive order 13950: Combating Race and Sex Stereotyping, September 22, 2020, *Federal Register* 85: 60683, https://www.federalregister.gov/documents/2020/09/28/2020-21534/combating-race-and-sex-stereotyping.

37. In 2017, US district judge A. Wallace Tashima permanently blocked Arizona's 2010 state law HB 2281, which prohibited any class that "advocates ethnic solidarity." Characterizing HB 2281 as "invidious discriminatory racial" and "politically partisan" in purpose, Judge Tashima also pointed to a 2012 study that found the Mexican American studies program under attack by HB 2281 "helped improve the graduation rates and test scores of some of the district's worst-performing students." See Associated Press, "Arizona Judge Declares Ban on Ethnic Studies Unconstitutional," December 28, 2017, https://www.nbcnews.com/news/latino/arizona-judge-declares-ban-ethnic-studies-unconstitutional-n833126. See also Taylor Harris, "Arizona Ban on Ethnic Studies Unconstitutional: U.S. Judge," *Reuters*, August 23, 2017, https://www.reuters.com/article/us-arizona-education/arizona-ban-on-ethnic-studies-unconstitutional-u-s-judge-idUSKCN1B32DE.

38. Roderick A. Ferguson, *The Reorder of Things: The University and Its Pedagogies of Minority Difference* (Minneapolis: University of Minnesota Press, 2012), 6.

PART V

American Studies Outside

Rethinking the Classroom and Sites of Learning

17

Obama Loves Sweet Potato Pie

American Studies at a Food Service Training Academy

DORIS FRIEDENSOHN

I'm standing in front of forty-five adult students, several slumped in plastic chairs, in a classroom without a blackboard, desk, or podium. The room is enormous but shallow—about twenty feet from front to back—and wide enough to accommodate another one hundred people. Hardly a conventional teaching space, or for me a conventional teaching situation. On this March (2009) morning at 9:30 a.m., I'm talking about eating grasshoppers, *chapulines* in Spanish. The idea is so bizarre to my audience of cooks-in-training (and to most First World people) that even those eager to grab a quick nap—before they have to perform in the kitchen—have perked up. These Mexican bugs, I explain, "are salty, spicy and crunchy—like crispy fried onions with a bite." Everyone is paying attention. At least six hands are up. Some students are poking their neighbors, and several are grimacing like twelve-year-olds. Soon enough I'll hear that "Mexicans have gotta be crazy if that's what they like." What's more, I must be wacko, too (maybe because I'm white and one of those college professors) for putting bugs in my mouth and not throwing up.

What a telling story—especially for someone devoted, as I am, to anecdotal accounts of teaching American Studies! The forty-five students I'm pleased to provoke—with this detail from across the border—are enrolled in the Food Service Training Academy (FSTA) of the Community FoodBank of New Jersey. The FSTA provides a route into the workforce for low-income people, mostly African American, from the Greater Newark area; its target audience from the school's beginning in 2000 has been ex-offenders and recovering addicts.

I first visited the FoodBank in the spring of 2002. Retired and nearing the end of a food memoir, I was itching for an escape from my desk. "Be prepared," a friend and FoodBank staff member commented wryly. "You'll see the Other America taking home our leftovers. We feed almost 900,000 New Jersey residents a year and let the government off the hook."

My tour of the FSTA began in the main kitchen: sunny and stainless steel modern, with workstations for grilling, frying, baking, slow cooking, and pizza making. Students in jeans and T-shirts, most wearing hairnets (as the industry requires), were chopping salad greens, grilling chicken thighs, and plating freshly baked brownies. It was the fourth week of their twelve-week course, and most seemed attentive to their tasks.

The executive chef was eager to chat. "Here's where it all happens," he began, "if the students show up, pay attention, and master the critical skills." His program was only two years old and still finding its way. Perhaps a writer (and retired college professor) might help explain their mission to the public; perhaps an experienced teacher might be a sounding board for pedagogical concerns he couldn't fully articulate. "Our work is job training," he said. "I know what we need to do in the kitchen; but so much else happens here and could happen—eight hours a day, five days a week." The focus of each school day, he explained, was preparing a full-scale cafeteria lunch. The students learn to cook for one hundred FoodBank workers, the school staff, and themselves: thick soups, hearty stews, vegetables more or less al dente, grains, muffins, and hard-to-resist fruit pies and pastries.

It wasn't the cooking (pleasant, mainstream American fare—with occasional disasters) that kept me attached to the FSTA for almost a decade. What seduced me was the larger project, which I came to identify as "Cooking for Change": the personal transformations required of (most) students to graduate and become certified as cooks. Self-discipline for students was the heart of the matter: following endless rules, obeying instructions, absorbing new terminology, preparing for frequent tests, and staying "clean." Watching the staff struggle to hone students' skills to workplace standards and keep students motivated (for a future job paying a poverty wage of nine to fifteen dollars an hour), I wondered if I could be useful.

But how? I'm not a trained cook. My American Studies background doesn't include studying food, job training, or motivational psychology. I'd have to bide my time, observe, schmooze, and watch for an opening. For more than three years of three or four visits a week, I relished hours of ethnographic snooping: in the kitchen, the lunchroom, the chef's office, and the FoodBank warehouse where students "shopped" for ingredients to cook with. I joined luncheon celebrations whenever a student was released from a halfway house. I gossiped in the women's rest room. Best of all, students (and some staff members) spilled out tales of "changin' my life," which I promptly wrote up. My notebooks bulged with descriptions of classroom and kitchen doings as well as portraits of the actors.

After a long apprenticeship on the sidelines, I finally stumbled on an opportunity. One morning I noticed a couple of unlikely guests—two white guys wearing high rubber boots and heavy hunting jackets—chatting with the chef. His hunter friends, as it turned out, had arrived with twenty pounds of freshly killed deer. "We've got a venison treat coming up!" Chef Jimmy bellowed. After a moment of silence, Roseann screeched, "What? Eat Bambi?" Others echoed her disgust. Ninety minutes later, when Jimmy passed around samples of the perfectly charred, pan-roasted meat, only eight out of twenty students accepted a forkful. What myths and prejudices had made them so closed to experience? Jimmy's cooked deer looked and smelled quite like beef. Yet most students couldn't say more than "No way!," "Revolting," or "That's how I feel."

The Bambi Incident haunted me. Why are some childhood tales so powerful? How is it that beef in clean plastic wrap, slaughtered in factories far from home, seems more palatable than a freshly killed rabbit or deer? Is it okay to eat the animal you kill with your own gun? And most critically: Why are these future cooks so closed to unfamiliar foods? Shouldn't a food service program address such questions?

The chefs, I understood, were doing what they were trained to do and what the certifying "Serv-Safe" exam required. Still, they were mindful of the students' limited culinary experience and their habitual resistance to unfamiliar foods. When I approached them about food as a subject—for example, what grows in the Garden State? How are immigrants changing our foodways? What does the supermarket teach us about agribusiness?—they agreed to make time for me, but just a bit. Maybe once a week.

Ten-minute talks, I promised. And another ten afterward for Q&A. "I'll be entertaining," I assured them. I wasn't proposing a course or expecting students to read handouts. (Homework was not routinely assigned.) I wasn't concerned about sequence or sources or theories of culture. I was thinking anecdotally, as is my habit, about details like the absence of supermarkets in central Newark and the omnipresence of McDonald's and Domino's Pizza. People growing up in a "food desert" like Newark (and with little disposable income) aren't fretting—as visitors to Newark's famous Ironbound (neighborhood) might be—about whether to eat Portuguese, Brazilian, Spanish, or Sicilian. In fact, they're not likely to know what distinguishes one cuisine from the other.

I'm partial to American Studies as a big tent and catchall—especially for general audiences. I'm partial to investigations of everyday life from everyday sources: neighborhood demographics, newspaper and TV reports, photographs, conversations overheard in a bus, family history, oral interviews, and autobiography. I'm partial to telling Black students who live in the ghetto about a Black urban gardening pioneer and a Black minister who built a track around his church to help his parishioners fight obesity. The half dozen sessions described below suggest a range of subject matter, perspective, and sources.

1. SWEET POTATO PIE IS POLITICAL

At a rally on the outskirts of Philadelphia, Barack Obama addressed a mostly Black audience. As an article in the *New York Times* indicated, it was a gorgeous fall morning in 2008, and his presidential campaign was almost over. Obama mentioned that the day before, he and the governor of Ohio had stopped at a small-town diner for coffee and pie. "How's business?" Obama reported asking the guy behind the counter, knowing that in Ohio it had to be terrible. The candidate was getting to his point. "We stopped at the diner because I love pie." The audience cheered. "I'll make you pie, baby," several women called out. "You gonna make me sweet potato pie?" Obama responded. The audience went wild. "We're gonna have a sweet potato pie contest," he continued, "and I'll be the judge. I know sweet potato pie."

In this Black audience were many who doubted that Barack Obama was one of them. After all, he was raised by a white mother and white grandparents, mostly in exotic Hawaii, where there were flowers everywhere but no ghettos in sight. Then he went to Columbia College and Harvard Law School before turning to community organizing. Obama's mention of sweet potato pie was no accident. Food defines family; food creates community; food announces who we are. The call and response on sweet potato pie turned a friendly rally into a love fest between the candidate and his people.

Would apple pie have worked for Obama, I ask? "Sure," Jannetta says. "With white folks. That's what they know." What message would pizza (pie) send? An argument ensues about whether pizza is too Italian. "No," Roberto insists. "The guys in my neighborhood makin' pizza, they're all from Colombia." Do you have to be Black to love this "sweet potato" story? "It's a story about a savvy politician," Ishmael says. "You gotta be smart to enjoy it, to appreciate him."

2. PITA, PIZZA, PEPPERCORNS, AND ICE CREAM, TOO: PHOTOS FROM NEW JERSEY'S ETHNIC FOOD ESTABLISHMENTS

Behind me, leaning against the long classroom wall, are a dozen twenty-by-thirty-inch color photos by food photographer Carol Kitman. From an exhibit I curated entitled *Eat! Eat! Food as Family and Cultural History*, the photos show ethnic shop windows, small eateries, and no-frills markets, all within a half hour of Newark. Dominating the first photo is a mostly empty space, with a ladderlike construction in the center and an escalator-like floor; we see a Latino guy who appears to be flinging a discus upward. "What's happening here?" I ask, rhetorically. We're glimpsing a moment in Toufayan's, a pita bread factory; the pale object in motion is a flawed pita that—with luck—will reemerge from the bottom of the machine in perfect disc form. "The Egyptian owner of this business," I continue, "once manufactured bread in Cairo for use by the airlines. Like many immigrants, he fled instability at home for a fresh start in the US. His pita, in many flavors, can be found in chain supermarkets and high-end shops. He's even got a line for a kosher Jewish clientele. Only in America!" "You need money to make money," Donell says. I smile. What else is new?

"Try this for novelty," I continue. The second photo shows a dark, underdecorated grocery store window. "We're on Newark Avenue, in Jersey City, in the heart of Little India." Through the window, half a dozen beige sacks can be seen on the floor: doubtless for grain, dried beans, spices, and other culinary basics. The real news, I say, is the sign: "Indo-Pak." "On the Asian subcontinent, Indian Hindus and Pakistani Muslims are killing one another. But here in New Jersey, they do business together. How come?" "We don' know the difference between them," Alissa says, "just that they ain't like us. Maybe that's what makes it work."

Many students have a sentimental favorite among the photographs: a small, brown-skinned girl of seven or eight—is she Latina or Asian or mixed?—licking an ice cream cone in a crowded supermarket. "She looks happy," LaDonna says. "The ice cream's good; no one's hasslin' her, telling her she doesn't belong. We all have a right to be in the supermarket, if we got the money and the time."

3. AFRICAN AMERICAN CULTURAL HISTORY

Foodways are changing in the Mississippi Delta, I announce. The *New York Times* reports that a sign in the kitchen of the (African American) First Baptist Church reads "No Fry Zone." At the nearby Seek Baptist Church, the minister presides over a community garden that provides fresh vegetables for parishioners. Members of the Oak Hill Baptist Church, egged on by their leader, have helped build a track on the property, and a majority of members now sign up for organized walks.

What's going on here? Mississippi, it turns out, ranks first in the nation in heart disease, second in adult diabetes, and second in obesity. (Many African Americans in the North belong to this cohort—including a good number at the FSTA.) Even when confronted by data about a health catastrophe that's killing their relatives, Black Mississippians resist changing their diet. It's our culture, they argue. Yes. But the culture has changed, a group of health gospel pastors insist. Today, no physical effort (neither raising the animals nor farming the land) is required to bring pork chops and potatoes to the table. Only a trip to the supermarket.

"Who's ready to give up fried chicken," I ask? "Is a vegetarian diet the answer to this Black health crisis?" "Yeh, we gotta deal with it," Jamal says. But I don't hear energy in his voice. "Who's got time to walk?" he adds. I want to say, "make time," but I hold my tongue. Would I make time with a night job after school, 6 p.m. to midnight, like Jamal has, and three little kids wanting attention? "Salads are okay," Sara-Ann says, "especially for white folks. The greens are pretty, but too much for my budget."

4. *FOOD, INC.*, OR HOW INDUSTRIAL AGRICULTURE RULES OUR EATING

Chef Ron wants to show *Food, Inc.*, the brilliant full-length muckraking film about industrial agriculture, during class time. I offer to lead the discussion, indicating that we'll need two sessions—with more than an hour for each. "Take as much time as you need," he says. As the film gets underway, Eric Schlosser and Michael Pollen, both celebrated critics, hold forth on the evils of Big Agriculture and lament the passing of the family farm. Two smart white guys, in work shirts and jeans, drone on—not connecting with this audience. After a while, the scene shifts to vast, industrialized chicken farms where Mr. Perdue and his investors make millions. We watch overfed chickens waddle around on weakened legs, ankle deep in their own shit. Why are these chickens so misshapen? "To give customers more white meat," LeBron says. The students squirm in their seats; clearly, the helpless chickens are another powerful illustration of the bond between racism and profit.

Unlike Pollen and other featured talking heads, FSTA students don't lament the loss of the family farm; few of their ancestors were owners. But they react to the exploitation of immigrant farm workers—picking vegetables without union support or running water in their shacks or schooling for their kids. "Not fair, not any of it," Jamal says. "Corn investors get rich while everyone else gets robbed or gets sick." "I'll cook those chickens," Adrienne adds, "if that's what I gotta do, but nobody can force me to eat 'em."

5. GLOBAL PERSPECTIVES: EATING BUGS

"Today's story is from Southern Mexico," I announce. A few years ago, in the main square of Oaxaca, I was approached by a woman in a traditional long skirt and white lacy blouse selling bright red grasshoppers, *chapulines* in Spanish. Buy from me, senora, she pleaded. The first time I encountered chapulines, maybe forty years earlier, I couldn't imagine putting a bug in my mouth—not to mention a handful of bugs. But since that time, I'd learned more about grasshoppers. The bugs, which are collected in cornfields during the summer months, are then killed in scalding water, fried in lard, and seasoned with garlic, chili pepper, and lime juice. Delicious. My kind of snack. So I gave the woman a dollar for a small bag of chapulines and took them back to my hotel room.

Later, as I poured a glass of wine, I imagined the woman's unwashed hands on my bugs and what other "bug" she might pass along to me. I dropped the snack in the trash. The next evening, at an upscale restaurant with white tablecloths and formally attired waiters, I noticed chapulines on the menu, served with warm tortillas and guacamole. At last! I remember my excitement as I smeared the tortilla with guacamole, sprinkled a few chapulines on top, folded it in half, and took a tentative bite. Amazing! Like a great BLT!

"What's the point of this story, you want to know?" Two points, actually: First, all over the world people eat bugs because they are local, cheap, and rich in protein. Second, Mexicans eat chapulines because their grandparents did and their neighbors do—and because they are passionately attached to the texture and flavor. Is there a lesson for us? Shall I find out who is selling grasshoppers in New Jersey and bring some to class? We'll have a tasting. Who's signing up? Only two students raise their hands. No matter. I'm guessing that the other twenty-two people in the room will remember my story and repeat it to their friends. Maybe that's how people start rethinking their views.

6. ACTION FOR (SMALL) CHANGE

Everyone wants change or claims to. But few people are prepared to seize a modest opportunity without a guaranteed payoff. In class, I read an offer by the City of Newark to provide small garden plots to residents for ten dollars a year. I might as well be speaking Chinese. Twenty-six of the thirty students in the room remain slumped in their seats. "Here's the name of the contact person," I say, "and here's her phone number. Who's going to check this out?" Four women raise their hands, three who have children and the fourth who helps care for her grandchildren. "My daughter's school is doing this, and we can follow up," Alicia says. "I want my kids to know fresh lettuce, not that wilted stuff from the bodega," Letitia adds. Jasmine, sitting in the front row next to Alicia and Letitia, nods. "Unless we show the way, it'll just be more of the same for the kids: hangin' out, lookin' for trouble."

The four women who respond know that a tiny garden plot isn't going to put money in their pockets; at best, it might produce fresh tomato sauce for an occasional pasta dinner. Still, the Newark garden project allows them to say to themselves and their kids, "Yes, I can." Gestures, they understand, make a difference. Doing beats bitching. While most students and all the males in the group fixate on the high cost of hours in the sun and hands in the dirt, these women believe that their kids need them to model hope: to be urban gardeners regardless of whatever else is happening in the ghetto.

SOME NUTS AND BOLTS

The ten-minute talk proved ridiculously demanding. I spent hours editing and reediting each one. I honed my delivery—going for the theatrical, the humorous, and the self-revealing. I had to grab the students' attention. I also had to be clear enough for those few who had not graduated from high school and for others with limited English. And one additional challenge: I had to vary the approach and materials to keep my audience from grabbing a nap at no risk to their record.

The presentations described above—my favorites among a dozen or so—were given many times over a five-year period (the FSTA runs a new class every fifteen weeks). All elicited lively responses from students—perhaps none more so than the Mexican chapulines tale. Among other effective sessions were: The Marketing of Bottled Water; Bear Stew and Bambi; Newark as a Food Desert; What's Authentic?—Or, Consider Dog (a Chinese and Korean Favorite); An African American Urban Gardening Pioneer; Mud Cookies in Haiti; Real Food According to Michael Pollan; and Couscous, Samosas, and Arepas at Whole Foods.

While I never mentioned to students that what we were doing was "American Studies," most of them understood that we were sampling from a vast cornucopia called Eating in America: Who wants to eat what? How are our "choices," if we have them, shaped? What are our neighbors making for dinner? How is food connected to poverty and politics? to health and education? to opportunity and pleasure?

CONCLUSION

I'm delighted to celebrate the enhanced position of food in American Studies. Once an outlier subject, food studies allows twenty-first-century Americanists to look freshly at a wide range of concerns: from diversity and industrial agriculture to poverty, health, child development, and urban planning. At the FSTA, I created food-centered minilectures built around anecdotes and drawing on a variety of fields—from demography and electoral politics to consumer culture and religion—and a range of materials from film and photographs to newspaper articles, TV reports, and personal narrative. This eclectic version of American Studies suited the teaching challenge at hand. It engaged students where they were, used a language they comprehended, and addressed recognizable social, political, and personal issues. In each class, a fair number of students relished my provocations and the chance to connect cooking to concerns beyond the kitchen.

Teaching American Studies (or any other liberal arts subject) to future cooks who will work in supermarkets, chain restaurants, and the kitchens of schools, hospitals, and retirements centers isn't a goal of PhD training in our field. It helped that I was retired, restless, and eager for a new project. After an initial year at the FSTA, with my food memoir, *Eating as I Go: Tales from America and Abroad,* still unfinished, I wrote a chapter for the book about memorable moments and personalities at the school: about their hopes for a fresh start but also the impediments, including racism and poverty-fed rage waiting to explode. This backlog of experiences—along with thirty prior years of innovative teaching—made a difference when I began my talks. I knew the value of listening closely, encouraging students' self-expression, and acknowledging my mistakes when challenged. Or without being challenged.

More than six years have passed since I published *Cooking for Change: Tales from a Food Service Training Academy* (with photos by Steve Riskind), which treats many of these matters. Now, as I think back on my potpourri of talks, I see them as part of a larger project on "The Joys of Being an American Studies Generalist." I can imagine an analogous hodgepodge of lectures given by Americanists to home-health-care aides, construction and hotel workers, bus drivers and security guards: about American people and places, social arrangements, values, and questions of power.

The Americanist who plays this game, as I have, takes pleasure in making unexpected connections—interdisciplinary or other. How many meanings—about advertising, consumption, and the exploitation of animals—attach to the vogue for chicken breasts? How many issues open up—concerning diet, sociability, and the power of religion (for starters)—when a minister imposes a "no fry zone" on his parishioners? We all learn on the job—especially in nontraditional classrooms. We come to know ourselves better, our (race- and class-related) advantages and fears—such as those that allow some of us to enjoy eating bugs and Bambi. In addition, we discover that seeing America through the eyes of our students is educational for us, often packed with surprises. They know what it's like to cope in a calamitous time, without enough money, food, or reliable shelter. They know the barriers created by capitalism to "cooking for change." They also know the seductions of sweet potato pie—and its limits.

A NOTE ON MY SOURCES

National news articles and features from the *New York Times* offered timely and culturally provocative material for many of my talks. My food memoir, *Eating as I Go: Tales from America and Abroad* (Lexington: University Press of Kentucky, 2005), was a useful source of both global and ethnic New Jersey food narratives. Carol Kitman's photos were part of a 1985 photo history traveling exhibit that I directed, funded by the State of New Jersey, and entitled *Eat! Eat! Food as Family and Cultural History*. Finally, my book *Cooking for Change: Tales from a Food Service Training Academy*, with photos by Steve Riskind (Englewood Cliffs, NJ: Full Court Press, 2011), offers portraits of students and staff and an extended discussion of the program described in this essay.

18

Ruined for Life

Cocreation, Service-Learning, and Taking American Studies Scholarship Seriously in an American Studies Intro Course

ELIZABETH DUCLOS-ORSELLO, KRISTIN ANDERSON, JAKE LEFKER, AND ROSARIO UBIERA-MINAYA

> Wow. For a "land of opportunities" we do make it hard for people to get opportunities.
> —Student

❖ ❖ ❖ ❖ ❖ ❖ ❖ ❖ ❖ ❖ ❖ ❖ ❖ ❖ ❖

INTRODUCTION

Liz: "My goal is to ensure that this course ruins you for life," I announce at the beginning of each semester teaching American Identities, the gateway course for American Studies concentrators and minors, and a course that fills various general education boxes (including one that addresses diversity, social justice, and power dynamics) at the regional public university where I teach. The muffled giggles and audible gasps have become commonplace. "Yes," I say, "my goal is to try to ensure that something in this course—a text, a discussion, an assignment—so profoundly unsettles you or challenges your current understanding of the world that for the rest of your life, when you encounter a similar situation or topic you will curse me . . . because you can't think about it the same way again."[1] Although I first encountered this notion in a social justice volunteer program when I was twenty-one, in a deep way this is what American Studies as a "field" is about and why I boldly claim it as my intellectual home.

And in the years that I have been teaching American Identities at Salem State University (SSU), the assignment that has arguably done the most "ruining" is a voter education and poll monitoring service-learning and blog project I call American Studies in the Real World, cocreated and co-recreated over nearly a decade in partnership with my three coauthors, all former staff members at the Northshore Community Development Coalition (NSCDC).[2] At its heart is my desire to try to put into practice the theoretical and political positions that often shape American Studies rhetoric. Together, we have all been ruined for life. We have transformed not only our students but also the NSCDC, my approach to teaching, and, crucially, what American Studies *is* at Salem State and in our community. Here, collectively, we share the successes, struggles, and lessons learned from our specific take on an American Studies–community partnership: specifically that a shared authority model must be the driver, that overcoming the established narratives of university and "community partner" is hard but critical work, and that ambiguity is necessary if we are to challenge power dynamics and structural inequality—within as well as outside of higher education.

2011: SETTING THE SCENE

Kristin, Rosario, Jake: The Northshore Community Development Coalition is a regional affordable housing and social impact organization located in the Point Neighborhood of Salem, Massachusetts, a neighborhood characterized by its Dominican, Puerto Rican, and Albanian families. In 2011, NSCDC was a newly formed organization, having been created out of the merger of two long-standing organizations in the region. NSCDC was entering into the community development space in Salem after a dormant period of relationship building and neighborhood engagement, but with a strong vision about approaching the work of neighborhood revitalization through comprehensive planning, engagement, and collaboration. Short on resources and staffing, NSCDC was turning toward community leaders and institutions, such as SSU, to build capacity and foster long-term partnerships that would help achieve the new organization's mission and help NSCDC grow.

Liz: Salem State University is the most diverse regional public comprehensive university in Massachusetts: 40–50 percent of students are Pell grant eligible, and a significant percentage of students are first-generation, BIPOC, nonnative English speakers, and/or immigrants or the children thereof.[3] Our American Studies courses attract students majoring in business, human services, STEM, or health care who are aiming to fulfill a general education requirement with no sense that there is a connection between this discipline and the world at large. At SSU, where "civic engagement" has been a core value and strategic goal since the early 2000s, they are also seeking relevance and applicability. And so, in 2011, hoping to revamp the American Studies program and its introductory course, I set my sights on a specific goal: to find new ways to demonstrate what so many of us in the field know to be true: that the skills, methods, approaches, and materials of American Studies are applicable to recognizing and addressing structural inequality and injustice. But I also hoped to address two other issues. First, students were not really "getting" some of the concepts in the course (such as Du Bois's double consciousness, or the difference between assimilation and cultural pluralism). More reading and more class time weren't going to get us there. I saw the limits of what could happen in my classroom—no matter the amount of innovative pedagogy I tried—and so I reached out to the NSCDC, whose staff I had collaborated with on other projects over a few years. Driving my outreach was my second, most pressing concern: my interest in pushing the boundaries of what "social justice" pedagogy might look like if I took to heart the words of Karen Halttunen, that as academics, "we [must] divest ourselves of the special authority sometimes granted to us" and "enter democratic partnerships with other members of our communities."[4] This mantra, reinforced by many other American Studies scholars, has driven much of what we, the authors here, have cocreated since 2012.[5] Further, from the beginning, our partnership was built on a model of collaboration informed by Jacques Rancière's notion of "*equality of intelligence*": "where those who know something engage with those who know something else."[6] This final principle has kept us honest and proven essential to our collaboration's longevity and impact.

2012–2014: LAYING THE FOUNDATION FOR A NEW WAY OF PARTNERSHIP

Kristin: The Point neighborhood of Salem, Massachusetts, has been historically underrepresented in elections and its voters regularly disenfranchised. The heart of our project aimed to change that fact while educating students about the complex factors that have led to this voter disenfranchisement. As Liz and I worked on developing the project, the idea was to have the service serve as a critical text in the course. It would be compared/contrasted with other course texts to explore civic and personal "American" narratives of "newness," "belonging," and "opportunity."

The student engagement was to include three key parts on three days over three months: (1) time learning about the NSCDC; (2) time learning about and addressing perceptions and realities of life in the Point neighborhood; and (3) formal training in the mechanics of voter registration followed by the work itself, including knocking on doors and registering voters. On Day 1, members of the NSCDC staff visited Liz's class for a workshop about our work and the issues of inequality and access to political power in the city. On Day 2, I developed and led a neighborhood walk to help students begin to think about the links between access to voting/voice in electoral politics and the services and care offered to some neighborhoods but not others in our historic city. For many of the students in the class, this was their first time in the Point neighborhood. The final phase was a four-hour session on a Saturday in April 2012, during which students were trained in the basics of canvassing and voter registration and then in small groups were paired with a neighborhood resident leader who guided them and assisted them in their canvassing and registration work.

To ensure equity and accountability all around, we took the step to develop a memorandum of understanding (MOU). This MOU laid out three sets of goals: for the American Studies students and program, for the NSCDC, and for the partnership itself. We identified outcomes, deliverables, and timelines to meet them all. And we signed it, formally, before beginning. It was a roadmap for a way to do engaged American Studies that did not center the university or the faculty member. Students, faculty, and community leads were named as cocreators and coequal here. (See appendix A for the 2018 version of our MOU.)

Liz: A critical element of the assignment that has accompanied the NSCDC project work from the beginning is that no credit is given for just "serving." Rather, as with any text assigned in a class, learning is demonstrated through a student's ability to extract meaning from it and make new connections. And so three times during the semester, at appointed times keyed to each phase of the collaboration, students would write a blog entry (about three hundred words) following a modified "critical incident" model.[7] They would first describe a specific experience they had during the engagement with the NSCDC, then offer a connection to a particular topic in the course (from the unit that paralleled the service they discussed), and finally put their service "text" in conversation with another assigned cultural product from the unit in which the service had taken place. They also had to read and respond to one another's posts. (See appendix B for blog assignment sheet.)

That first year, student responses indicated that the project achieved many of the goals we set regarding collaborative learning. The role of one of the neighborhood's resident leaders in this success was particularly clear. Lucy was the city's first Latinx city councilor, a Point resident and head of the neighborhood association. As one student wrote of their experience door knocking and registering voters, "Honestly, I was way outside my comfort zone . . . [but] somehow we were placed with Lucy . . . and this worked in our favor because she knew everybody [and] we confidently knocked on doors under her lead." Another student underscored the value of having a Spanish-English mentor as they carried out their work. It was only because of this neighborhood leader's expertise that Anglophone students were able to overcome what would have been paralyzing communication barriers. Regarding the ways in which the service assisted students in making sense of other class materials, a number of students were also able to point out connections to assigned texts. One honed in on narratives of opportunity, writing:

> In regards to the US being a "Land of Opportunity," while we walked through the Point and listened to what [the NSCDC staff] and the other group leaders had to say, the opportunities available to many of the Point's residents challenged the stories of "self-made men" like Andrew Carnegie who, in *How I Served My Apprenticeship*, wrote, "from ranks of the poor so many strong, eminent, self-reliant men have sprung and must continue to spring," mainly due to perseverance or strong work ethics. . . . The ideas proposed by Carnegie (and Franklin) that hard work is all it takes to achieve success don't consider other obstacles that may appear, such as language barriers or poverty.

Figure 18.1. Students door knocking under the guidance of experienced neighborhood leaders, year one of partnership. Photo Credit: Elizabeth Duclos-Orsello.

Another student quoted Alaine Locke's 1925 essay *Enter the New Negro* in a post commenting on the dissonance between a past they thought was past and the service text that challenged this. And, in what was a powerful recognition of the problematic model of liberal white "helper" or "savior," a third student reflected on the lessons to be drawn from W. E. B. Du Bois's work.

Despite the successes of this first year, the project's limitations also came into sharp focus. Although students could articulate some of the course's most challenging themes and concepts more clearly than before, they didn't seem to be able to make all the links hoped for. An additional challenge was the inherent privileging of the university calendar and the alignment of project activities with formal course deadlines and "outcomes." It also became clear that to sustain the effort, NSCDC staff would have to be willing to prioritize this project for the long term. And, finally, while the NSCDC was the lead on the project, my role in coordinating and leading key segments of the work had been significant.

Kristin and Liz: And so we made some changes for year two. The most notable was to formally add the following into the goals for the project as a whole: *"To help students begin to understand the historical and contemporary structural issues involved in voter disenfranchisement (particularly tied to race, ethnicity, language, ability, economic status, education, and immigrant status) and to understand mechanisms by which individuals can effect change in this area and pursue social justice for all."* This allowed us to direct student learning toward structural issues and agency more directly. It also meant that more authority had to be ceded to the NSCDC staff and neighborhood residents and that the blog assignment needed to encourage reflection in these areas. In addition, we embarked on very fruitful conversations with the staff at the NSCDC to determine what was the best way to work within or push back against the limitations imposed by the university calendar as well as how the project could be refined to fit more centrally into the strategic priorities of the NSCDC. In the end, we felt that we had created something new and exciting and that students and the work of the NSCDC had been transformed by it. So our refined project continued for two more years. But by the end of 2015, the NSCDC had a new chief program officer (CPO), and both the NSCDC and SSU had new needs and new opportunities.

2016: POLL MONITORING BEGINS AND AUTHORITY SHIFTS

Rosario: I had come on board as CPO in 2015, and by the spring/summer of 2016, with the presidential election looming, I had some new ideas about what we needed to do in our community engagement work. Canvassing and voter registration were not enough. Troubling anecdotal evidence of the challenges that non–English speaking and nonwhite residents had been having at the polls in Salem meant that our community-based work needed to investigate and respond. If the partnership with SSU was to be successful, students needed to better understand the mechanisms of voting and voter protection and needed to be mobilized to help us address potential voter suppression. At the same time, the NSCDC's fledgling public arts and mural program in the Point neighborhood offered a new opportunity to use the physical location of our work to new ends. Because I am Dominican, immigrated to Salem, and came of age in the Point, when I became CPO, it was an opportunity for students to learn from someone who was an authority on the neighborhood and on the Dominican immigrant experience, but who also held official authority within the organization. Liz and I wanted to see whether or not we could move the work in a new direction and have the students see themselves *as students of the NSCDC*, learning from us and becoming more fully part of our activist work around voting rights.

Liz: While students had largely been enthusiastic about the project to date, I began to realize that managing student expectations was critical. There had been a sense among some students that the work had not really been "impactful"; students wanted to be "change makers," and the behind-the-scenes work of voter engagement and registration was not as dramatic as they would have liked. The blog posts showed me that some students were still struggling to find a way to make concrete links between the service experience and texts about inequality and opportunity that I had hoped would emerge organically. I also felt that I still needed to find a better way to formally honor and recognize the expertise and lived experiences of those students whose lives were situated in and around the neighborhood with which we were engaging without burdening them. This latter point was essential. Too much civic engagement scholarship and work assumes a distance between those who are serving and the people/neighborhoods where service is being performed. At institutions like SSU, the "us" and "them" is blurry at best. I now knew that I had more than a handful of students whose families lived in our focus neighborhood and/or were clients of the NSCDC. Many others lived in similar neighborhoods in nearby cities. Taking to heart the reality that students in their situations often feel that they are asked to "represent" or "teach" other students, even as they are also engaging in significant "service" in their daily lives, meant that a more conscious approach was needed.[8]

Finally, I needed to get much more comfortable than I usually am with ambiguity, especially in the classroom. And I needed to help the students do so as well. Part of this important work was to actively disengage from the structures of the current neoliberal university and educational models that focus on "outcomes" and even "backward design," which assume that logic models and reporting/gathering data are the most useful frames for learning and transformation. Pushing back against the rhetoric of my own university, I had to work at better engaging a model of reciprocity that centered the process more than the end product. More practically, as a magnet in my office reminded me, I needed to channel Gilda Radner's proclamation to embrace the "delicious ambiguity" of life.[9]

Figure 18.2. 2017: Students headed out to begin poll monitoring; reviewing observations recorded by classmates at voting sites earlier in the day. Photo Credit: Elizabeth Duclos-Orsello.

Rosario and Liz: Thinking this through together led to some additional changes in the structure of the project, including highlighting Rosario's expert status, changing the blog assignment slightly, and using an even more explicitly assets-based model in all aspects of the project.[10] We determined that we needed to center the particular MOU goal that had been added in 2014 (regarding *"understand[ing] the historical and contemporary structural issues involved in voter disenfranchisement . . . "*), which meant it was critical for students to understand voting and election day as a key part of the larger project of enfranchising wider groups of residents to effect change. To this end, we amended the project to include poll monitoring as part of the work the students did. Each student continued to participate in some form of preelection voter engagement but was also trained as a nonpartisan poll observer and spent a few hours on election day monitoring polling sites across the city, taking notes and reporting back on any possible infringements of voting rights.

We also changed the location of the initial class/NSCDC meeting. The first day of training now happened on site at the NSCDC, thereby clearly establishing the NSCDC as *the classroom* for this portion of the course and Rosario as the expert and faculty. In this way we highlighted the authority and expertise of those who lived in the neighborhood, both staff and students. Their voices were given more weight in discussions and activities for the duration of the project. Additionally, we added to the neighborhood walk to explore an earlier period of immigration and exclusion in the neighborhood, when between the 1880s and 1950s it was home to thousands of poor, non-Anglophone (but white) immigrants who found themselves marginalized and without access to centers of Anglophone power or influence.[11]

Finally, Liz refined the student questionnaire completed prior to our first joint meeting to better assess and surface student expertise and experience vis-à-vis both the Point neighborhood and voting itself, and she began sharing all the student project-related writing with the NSCDC staff. This allowed NSCDC staff to more fully access the students in the way an instructor would. For coinstructors, this was essential. She also tinkered with the blog assignment, allowing more flexibility in student connections between the course and the world at large, and carved out more time for postservice reflection.

The addition of poll monitoring had immediate real-world impacts, helping produce a data set that led to an investigation of infringements on voter rights in Salem, especially among BIPOC and nonnative English speakers. And we found that the students, in blogs and end-of-semester reflections, in addition to seeing themselves as being agents of change, were transformed in four key ways: recognizing a shifted locus of authority; identifying the quiet but powerful ways that lack of access to democratic processes is built and maintained; the difficulty inherent in work for change; and the ways in which central narratives of opportunity, in particular, fail to account for the lived experiences of people whose lives often look like theirs. So, our collaboration continued.

2018: DECENTERING EVEN MORE—POWER DYNAMICS AND SOCIAL JUSTICE

Liz: By the summer of 2018, I knew SSU students would be returning to an institution that had been marked the previous year by the brave activism of Black, Brown and Proud, a student group formed in response to both growing microaggressions and racist graffiti that had appeared more than once on our campus. I also anticipated new student expectations for courses that purported to address issues of social justice or inequality as mine did.

In addition, I wanted to find a way to more fully celebrate and lift up the linguistic diversity and multilingualism of my students. How, in a tangible way, could this project and assignment challenge commonly held beliefs (even among my own multilingual students) that English monolingualism was what marked someone as "American"? And I was concerned about the requirement of class work on election day, knowing my students' complicated work, home, and educational commitments. Finally, I hoped to explore more fully what it would mean for students to take on additional responsibility for writing the project text with my newest NSCDC cocreator.

Jake: I had been the project's day-to-day NSCDC contact for fall 2017, and in May 2018, I was promoted to director of community engagement. My tenure was shaped by growing resident concerns about access to critical information in Spanish, a desire at the NSCDC to more fully engage with SSU, and the NSCDC's newly launched Punto Urban Art Museum, consisting of murals by world-class artists on NSCDC-owned buildings.[12] So, I realized that in addition to the existing MOU goals we needed to make sure (1) that resident needs regarding access to voting information in Spanish were met; (2) that students understood the service-learning project as one led by the partner organization rather than the university or the professor; (3) that El Punto was a more central part of this partnership; and (4) that the students fully comprehended the possible legislative impacts of the 2018 Massachusetts ballot questions.

Liz and Jake: Six years into this partnership we began to reimagine it once more in response to our new opportunities and challenges. First, Liz altered her course's objectives to align with a new general education category tied to diversity, power dynamics, and social justice.[13] This allowed us to make even more explicit the authority of Point residents on their neighborhood and to decenter the authority of universities. To ensure this, we altered the final joint goal of the MOU to read: "To break down some barriers between campus and the broader community and help students understand that learning happens in many places, that many people are teachers, *community members are experts of their community* and we are all learners." Then, to ensure that students were more fully invested in the work of the NSCDC while being sensitive to the timing concerns of election day, we altered the project so that all students had an option to do two volunteer sessions at the NSCDC outside of election day, rather than requiring one preelection date and election day itself.

Finally, we also bulked up the neighborhood walk to include key murals that highlight the Dominican and Puerto Rican cultures of many of the neighborhood's residents. Jake also included Espacio, NSCDC's multiuse community space, on the tour and spent time exploring the remodeled Mary Jane Lee Park—a public park in the center of the neighborhood. He emphasized the grassroots advocacy work carried out by the Point Neighborhood Association, the Latino Leadership Coalition, and other key players in the Point, including NSCDC, to advocate for public moneys to fund the remodeling of the park, which converted neglected parking spaces into a community gathering space. Attention to Espacio, the murals, and the park served as crucial impetus for postwalk conversations, as students were asked to recount their observations of the assets and challenges visually present in the neighborhood. By emphasizing the Point neighborhood's assets first and then discussing the challenges inherent in a high-density, low-income neighborhood, Jake effectively set the stage for how the students would learn during the voter engagement program. We found this approach quite successful in decentering the university in the minds of the students and centering the residents of the Point neighborhood as the experts on the neighborhood and the main drivers of positive change therein, and Jake as the expert on community engagement.

Figure 18.3. 2018: Neighborhood walk during first class meeting on site at NSCDC. Jake Lefker standing in front of murals in the Punto Urban Art Museum, discussing the neighborhood's history and present and the art. Photo Credit: Elizabeth Duclos-Orsello.

Jake: In addition to my efforts developing our initial group tour, as I thought about how to best leverage the skills and time of the SSU students, as well as to ensure that they were prepared to do the sort of high-quality work that our community engagement team was known for, I realized that I needed to increase the time and energy of my team for this project and consider more centrally the students' work schedules and skills (especially language skills). So, I built in more direct training and reconceptualized how I prepared the students for each phase of our work. As I planned and trained students for both door knocking/voter registration and phone banking efforts, I made bilingualism a key feature, provided calling scripts in English and Spanish, emphasizing the value of being bilingual (I am bilingual and Latinx), and helping all of the students to practice their opening statements until they felt comfortable enough to call or knock on a door on their own.

My goal for the phone banking, door knocking, and ballot question sessions was to ensure that students were all knowledgeable about the election process and the specific 2018 questions and that they had both context and experience to understand the *why* behind the final component of the voter engagement program: poll monitoring. To this end, even more than in the past, my student training from our first meeting sought to provide important context from recent years in Salem where poll workers violated, whether intentionally or not, the rights of voters, especially those who were new voters or those with language barriers. It was through the efforts of previous years of SSU poll monitors that some real changes had come about in the election practices in Salem, and I brought this to the fore.

Jake and Liz: At the NSCDC, the community engagement staff noted that the students' expanded commitment and greater staff control over the framing of the project increased the NSCDC's capacity to fulfill its own goals to expand responsive programming in the Point neighborhood. Students came away from the 2018 version of our project knowing more than ever about the scope and impact of the NSCDC's work and having grappled in exciting new ways with issues of where authority lies in the United States, how cultural production and the circulation of certain narratives and not others can frame "Americanness," how language functions as a barrier and a tool of access, and their own capacity to effect structural change. In blog posts and pre/post reflections, every student recognized the authority of Jake and his team for the full run of our collaboration. And, importantly, from the first visit to the NSCDC on, students could explain the long-standing structural barriers to full municipal support for the residents of the Point neighborhood as well as the work of the organization. Also, Jake's addition of a full-fledged discussion of the El Punto murals as part of the neighborhood walk made clear to students the ways in which (re)presentation of an area of a city can enhance or limit leaders' care and concern for the residents therein. More than one student reflected on the ways in which the narratives of "Americanness" portrayed by the art in El Punto challenged a nineteenth-century Salem-produced painting we had examined, which depicted America as a place of belonging for whites of European descent.

And crucially, many multilingual students were empowered when they found their Spanish language skills to be a valuable asset in our work. Time and again, native Spanish speakers noted something akin to one student's pronouncement that the challenges of phone banking were reduced for them because "most of the people that were answering were Hispanic so I had to speak Spanish which wasn't a challenge for me." Finally, more so than in prior years, students found creative synergies between our work with the NSCDC and the other course texts, and they were able to articulate in deeper ways the link between this course, issues of power dynamics, and their own lived experiences and trajectories. They made links to the racial hypocrisy on display in Margaret Bourke White's famous 1937 photo "The Louisville Flood" and to the continuation of slavery despite the rhetoric of many founding documents. The words of a Black student sum up a pattern engaging the theme of opportunity: "The service supported the materials in the class in the sense that it shows who America really helps and that we can choose to use our voices because we are fortunate to have voices, to raise awareness of the issue." And, as another student put it in their final self-reflection for the course: "I was ignorant to the fact that still today [2018] we still have people who have the right to vote being denied. . . . The most powerful part of my whole experience was learning the truth and watching myself change."

Liz: Our continued decentering of me and my voice was essential to the outcomes. At the end of 2018, I realized how much I relished being the nonexpert, but more importantly how much it mattered to my students that I was explicitly a nonexpert—that, for this portion of our course, I was a student in many of the same ways they were. And I realized that stepping back allowed me to play a different and equally critical role: as supporter, as fellow traveler, as partner in the messy and often personally uncomfortable work of becoming vulnerable and becoming hyperaware of my places of comfort and discomfort. In this way, I was able to not only create space but to hold space in the classroom and in my interactions with students to witness their struggles, their learning, their new observations about inequality, power dynamics, and their place in all of it. At the same time, by the end of 2018, it was clear that American Studies at Salem State had been irrevocably changed by the long-term partnership with the NSCDC. The election-based work tied to learning about structural injustice had become not only a centerpiece of this one introductory class but also something that students, faculty, and staff at SSU had come to recognize as being central to what American Studies itself was and should be at SSU. Students have increasingly come to the course with stories of friends who have done this work and are eager for this learning themselves. And course completers who are American Studies majors or minors often refer back to and draw upon this project as they progress in the program. There is no turning back.

CONCLUSION

Kristin, Rosario, Jake: The NSCDC has been transformed by this project. The process of developing this work thoughtfully from the beginning allowed it to become deeply imbedded into the culture and values of NSCDC over the past eight years. Partnership development, MOUs, and multiyear service-learning projects (with SSU and others) have become fully integrated across NSCDC programming. The organization has adopted the value that it is a "learning institution," and this project became a model for expanding capacity without traditional program development and staffing. This approach has garnered significant interest and goodwill from the community as it found project-based ways to bridge the town-gown divide, helping the organization to be nimble in adopting new opportunities that aligned with our core mission.

This integration of a service-learning project also had a positive impact on staff. Employees at the NSCDC feel increasingly empowered by the opportunity to work with students and faculty as educators and experts, and it has provided an opportunity for learning and growth within the organization. These impacts on staff further deepened the priorities of NSCDC to partner with universities by invigorating a sense of life-long learning and collaboration across programs.

Liz: My approach to teaching and learning has been permanently reoriented. I've come to even more fully embody the idea of "generative-oriented reciprocity" in which the focus of partnership is on "making space," that is, it is less about what we *do* together but how we *are* together.[14] Unlike in a class where I am the only instructor, or even in a coteaching model with another university-based educator, in this partnership I am not in control of the variables in the moment, nor do I get to control how we change things the next time I teach the course. Social justice and attention to power dynamics means decentering that which normally has been centered. What might seem obvious to a faculty member—pick a different text, tweak assignments, manage my time better, reorganize the sequence of materials and topics in the course—are not all within my control. I have ceased to see myself as the author of this learning experience. The work is hard and complex and always challenging. And the outcomes have been fabulous. From an American Studies classroom standpoint, the development of this portion of the course and its metamorphoses over the past eight years have made clear to students that much of what they know to be American Studies is made and remade not in the pages of books but in the "texts" written and rewritten and unpacked with and by classmates and community-based cocreators. Within my own department (Interdisciplinary Studies), this work laid the groundwork for a reframing of department-level outcomes around social justice and equity. And, critically, the success of this partnership has become a valuable model for ethical, sustainable civic learning at SSU as we move ahead into a new era of operationalizing "civic engagement" institution-wide through a frame of critically engaged civic learning that centers cocreation between students, faculty, the university, and community-based organizations, modeled on the work of the collaboration described here.[15]

Kristin, Rosario, Jake, and Liz: In the end, although job titles and personnel at the NSCDC have changed again and there are ever new pressures on the "outcomes" and "assessment" of American Identities at SSU, we (and our organizations) remain committed to this project because we have all been ruined for life. Both the NSCDC and American Studies at SSU are changing and morphing because of this partnership. So here we are, in the blush of another fall in New England with a new collaboration for this year taking shape: one that, like all the others, is a variation on our basic model in response to current needs. In 2020, the linked traumas of COVID, economic devastation, and a public reckoning with racial injustice mark our students, our clients, and our work. Public health and safety mandates have moved the class online and require physically distanced civic engagement work. Liz and the current

NSCDC leadership have made many adjustments, and anticipate new challenges, but carry on confident that by sharing authority and being committed to writing texts in real time on the landscapes of everyday life, they may well be able to ruin more students for life. We haven't cracked the code or developed the one "correct" path to the public-centered teaching and learning that is possible in an American Studies context. Rather, we are following in the footsteps of the likes of American Studies greats like bell hooks, Gloria Anzaldúa, and Ruth Gilmore who call on us to transgress, embrace life at borders, center those at the margins, never be too comfortable, and listen to and learn from the deep and abiding dissonance around us.

APPENDIX A: MEMORANDUM OF UNDERSTANDING (MOU)

"American Identities" Service-Learning Project FALL 2018 // Course: IDS 232 "American Identities"
Voter Education/Registration and Poll Observing in Salem, MA
Partnership: North Shore CDC & Prof. Elizabeth Duclos-Orsello, Salem State University

Brief Description/Overview of the Project/Partnership

The project and the need it meets: Throughout the fall semester, 2018, up to 25 students (and 1 instructor) enrolled in course IDS 232 "American Identities" will work in a collaborative and ongoing manner with staff at the North Shore Community Development Coalition (NSCDC) to assist in voter education and registration activities in The Point neighborhood in Salem and its vicinity during the months of September and October 2018 and serve as trained poll observers and in other election-day volunteer roles as needed by the NSCDC in Salem on Election Day: November 6, 2018. (Students will complete two volunteer sessions: either one pre-election day and one on election day or two prior to election day: details below.)

This project is designed to assist the NSCDC with their ongoing work to increase civic education and voter empowerment in The Point neighborhood, to help educate Salem residents on the value of voting, and to ensure fair and legal elections in Salem. The context for these activities is as follows: 1) The continued existence of the Electoral College and a FPTP (first past the post), two-party political system has created an environment around the country in which people believe their vote doesn't count. Salem, MA, is not immune to this sentiment. The danger herein is an apathy that leads to low voter turnout, especially in marginalized communities and neighborhoods. 2) The Point neighborhood has historically been underrepresented in elections and its voters regularly disenfranchised. This project aims to help students understand the factors that influence voter turnout and how to improve voter turnout, to help students gain knowledge about the process of and challenges of electoral politics, and to educate students about the complex historical and structural factors that have led to voter disenfranchisement in Salem and elsewhere. The service will serve as a critical text in IDS 232 and will be compared/contrasted with other course texts to explore civic and personal "American" narratives of "newness," "belonging," and "opportunity." Students enrolled in IDS 232 must complete this service project to be able to complete and earn credit for the related assignments in the course. It is the student's responsibility to find a time/way/method to complete at least 6–8 hours of related service that is needed by the NSCDC. We will work with your schedules and needs.

The goals of this service-learning partnership are

- To further the mission of the NSCDC, an organization focused on community and economic development in Salem, MA, and the surrounding communities. In particular to provide human capacity so that the NSCDC may continue the voter empowerment, registration, and poll monitoring work begun in 2012 in partnership with SSU.
- To achieve the academic learning goals of students enrolled in IDS 232. In particular to use the text of service to explore, engage, and critique American narratives of "newness," "belonging," and "opportunity" as these are expressed in other textual, visual, and material sources in the course.
- To help students begin to understand the historical and contemporary structural issues involved in voter disenfranchisement (particularly tied to race, ethnicity, language ability, economic status, education, and immigration status) and to understand the mechanisms by which individuals and groups can effect change in this area and pursue social justice for all.
- To break down some barriers between campus and the broader community and help students understand that learning happens in many places, that many people are teachers, community members are experts of their community, and we are all learners.

The partnership will include the following components:

- Approximately 25 students and Prof. Duclos-Orsello will train for and assist in **EITHER** **<u>A *or* B</u>:** (totaling between 6–8 hours of activity for each student).
    - **A.** One 2–4 hour shift assisting with a number of voter education and registration activities in The Point neighborhood of Salem, MA, between October 2 and November 7. (There will be options for door knocking, voting education, phone banking etc.) AND one 2–4 hour shift assisting with the Why Your Vote Counts event on October 10th at Espacio (105 Congress Street).
    - **B.** One 2–4 hour shift assisting with a number of voter education and registration activities in The Point neighborhood of Salem, MA, between October 2 and November 6. (There will be options for door knocking, voting education, phone banking, etc.) AND a 4-hour shift as a poll monitor or one of a number of other Election Day volunteer tasks on Election Day, November 6, 2018.

The work will be coordinated by the NSCDC. The service may be completed at any of the times/days offered by the NSCDC. More information to be made available to students on the day we visit the NSCDC on October 1st. Since this assigned activity is equivalent to "homework" and "reading a text," the 6–8 hours required is comparable to other class/course work.

- Staff at the NSCDC will serve as IDS 232 guest lecturers for students enrolled in IDS 232. They will teach about the work of the NSCDC, the demographic and sociocultural makeup of Salem, the NSCDC's work in shaping/responding to social inequality and the issue of voting, representation, and the like. These guest lectures will also prepare students for their service. The first of these class sessions will take place at the NSCDC during class time on October 1st, 2018.
- Prof. Duclos-Orsello will prepare students for service and will devote appropriate class time and course assignments to helping students link service to/with course materials.
- Staff and volunteers at NSCDC will provide the prerequisite reading to Prof. Duclos-Orsello prior to the October 1st class at North Shore CDC and NSCDC staff will coordinate students on day(s) of service.
- Staff and volunteers will help students learn about "American" identity and culture in and through their partnership with students on day(s) of service.
- Students will complete intentional written reflections related to service and connected to course material via three blog assignments.

SSU Faculty (Duclos-Orsello) will:

- Introduce students to service-learning and the partnership prior to October 1st and accompany them to the NSCDC on October 1st during class time. (1:10–3:50 pm [students requested to arrive by 1:00 and be able to stay until 4:00])
- Assist NSCDC partners in preparing students for service and participate in each of the following (depending on student choice) A. one voter registration/education event; B. at least 4 hours of service on November 6, 2018.
- Assess students' completion of and work on service activities [with input of NSCDC staff]. Include three specific reflection activities for students throughout semester.
- Provide students with academic support, skills, and knowledge to ensure the completion of the service.
- Provide NSCDC with syllabi for the course.
- Be available to meet with/speak with NSCDC staff, volunteers, others, throughout semester re: issues related to course, SSU etc.
- Agree to one mid-term meeting (prior to the start of the service) on September 27th, 1–2pm and one "midterm" meeting on October 18th, 10:45–11:45am with NSCDC to review partnership and project. December 3rd, 9–10am will be the end-of-term meeting. These meetings will be held at SSU.

NSCDC Staff will:

- Coordinate necessary logistics for service work including training.
- Introduce SSU students to NSCDC's mission and issues of Salem demographics and voting on October 1st, 2018.
- Track students' completion of and work on service activities and offer assessment of it [with input from Prof. Duclos-Orsello
- Agree to one midterm meeting (prior to the start of the service) on September 27th, 1–2pm and one midterm meeting on October 18th, 10:45–11:45am with NSCDC to review partnership and project. December 3rd, 9–10am will be the end-of-term meeting. All meetings will be at SSU.
- Train students for poll monitoring on October 29th at SSU during class time [2:45pm–3:45pm]

SSU Students will:

- Participate in all pre-service lectures and training in September and October 2018 during class time. This includes the training on October

1st at the NSCDC during class time and poll monitoring training on October 29th during class time at SSU.

- Sign up for, show up for, and complete at least two sessions of service from among the options presented by the NSCDC. Each student MUST complete at least 6 hours made up of:
  A 2–4 hour shift volunteering in pre-election day activities between October 1st, 2018, and November 6th, 2018.
  AND 1 of the FOLLOWING 2 OPTIONS:
  A 2–4 hour shift assisting with the Why Your Vote Counts event on October 10th, 2018, from 6–8pm at Espacio (105 Congress Street).
  A 4 hour shift volunteering on Elections Day (includes a range of possible activities) on November 6th, 2018.
- Follow all rules and protocols as instructed by NSCDC staff.
- Complete all required surveys and reflection assignments associated with the service-learning project.

SIGNATURES/ DATE

North Shore CDC: **Elizabeth Duclos-Orsello**
CPO SSU: **Student:**

APPENDIX B: BLOG ASSIGNMENT

BLOG ASSIGNMENT
Tied to COMMUNITY-BASED SERVICE-LEARNING WORK

Blog: 15% of grade **Course Objectives Met: 2, 4, 6, 7, 9, 10**
DUE: 3 Dates throughout Semester, noted on syllabus and in Canvas

ASSIGNMENT EXPLAINED: "America: A View from Salem"
Rationale and Overview: Major goals of this course include engaging with the ongoing work of scholars to define or explain "America" and "American" identities, learning from our place-based civic/service-learning project, and deepening our understanding of how American Studies theories, approaches, and concerns play out in and can shape our own communities. To this end, you will all contribute to a class blog that links our civic/service-learning texts to other course materials and connects American Studies to the "real world." This blog will focus on the images of "America" and "Americans" **that emerge from your civic/service-learning activities with the NSCDC.** You will post

3 times during the semester, making links between knowledge gained/ experiences had during our NSCDC project and knowledge gained via other course materials.

Each post **must** reference some aspect of our civic/service-learning work and consider the degree to which the information you are blogging about extends, contradicts, challenges, or supports other images/ ideas of "America" or "Americans" you have encountered in class. You will need to be specific with your descriptions and you will need to discuss/reference a specific part/ element/experience of the NSCDC project since your last post. To be clear:

- First post should refer to the **class sessions** with the NSCDC staff
- Second post should refer to your individual service with the NSCDC **prior to** election day
- Third post will reference **election day** work

Your posts must be 250–300 words each.
You must also respond at least 2x to your classmates' posts.

EACH "BLOG" POST MUST

- DISCUSS a SPECIFIC experience/insight you had during our service-learning work. Describe what happened in detail. What you saw, heard, felt, experienced. Paint a word picture for your reader. You are not summarizing your whole experience, rather you are describing some smaller portion of it that engaged you in a powerful way.
- Make a link to A SPECIFC COURSE TOPIC (see syllabus for these—they are labeled "TOPIC," such as "Women and Opportunity" or "Race and Belonging") from Unit III onward.
- Make a link to at least one specific cultural product explored in class (a specific document, image, etc. that we have analyzed). What, specifically, is the link or tension between your engagement work and this cultural product. Use your skills of close reading/ looking to unpack and offer a tight link.

Note: each blog post must link to a different topic and cultural product.

ASSESSMENT

Blog posts will be evaluated based on:

1. the thoroughness of your discussion/analysis of the civic/service-

learning material, event, encounter, or conversation you are posting about

2. the degree to which you relate what you see/hear/learn in your engaged work to our class discussions, materials, and themes in a ***specific and detailed*** **way.**
   - "specific and detailed" means the following (to earn full credit):
     - Mentions a course theme or topic specifically and makes a comparison/link.
     - Mentions at least one course cultural product by title/author/creator, discusses specific aspects of it (passages, visual elements, etc.), and makes a comparison/link that extends class discussion.

NOTES

1. "Ruined for Life" is the unofficial motto of the Jesuit Volunteer Corps (JVC), a sixty-plus-year-old US-based nonprofit that aims to effect structural change and transform lives through the placement of full-time volunteers living and working with those fighting injustice and poverty. It was an early model for both the Peace Corps and Americorps/VISTA. I was a JVC volunteer in 1995–1996 in Kansas City, Missouri. "Dare to Change," Jesuit Volunteer Corps, accessed June 26, 2020, https://www.jesuitvolunteers.org.

2. We use the term "service-learning" here as it is still commonplace in many universities. However, at many places—including at Salem State University—it is being replaced by language that decenters "service" as a frame. The project we discuss here, and the formal model we developed for it, was instrumental in making this shift at Salem State. The term for what we do is now "community engaged civic learning."

3. Enrollment data from the Salem State University public Factbook and Common Data Set can be found here: "Strategic Planning and Decision Support," Salem State University, accessed January 14, 2020, https://www.salemstate.edu/salem-state-difference/facts-and-figures/strategic-planning-and-decision-support. In fall of 2018 (last available data), 50 percent of students were Pell Grant eligible and 39 percent of our undergraduate students identified as BIPOC. Of this 39 percent, the majority identify as Latinx, followed by Black or African American.

4. "Presidential Address to the American Studies Association, November 4, 2005," *American Quarterly* 58, no. 1 (March 2006): 12. Liz's engagement with these issues and frames in American Studies, specifically, began in 2002 during her first encounter with Julie Ellison of Imagining America.

5. Most recently by Scott Kurashige in "'Unruly Subjects': American Studies from Antidiscipline to Revolutionary Praxis," *American Quarterly* 72, no. 2 (June 2020): 307–336.

6. This particular turn of phrase ("where those who know something . . . ") is borrowed from Anthony Huberman's articulation of Rancière's concept. See Huberman, "Take Care," The Showroom, accessed December 3, 2020, https://www.theshowroom.org/library/take-care, originally in Mai Abu ElDahab, Binna Choi, and Emily Pethick, eds., *Circular Facts* (Cambridge, MA: MIT Press, 2011). Drawn from Jacques Rancière, *The Ignorant Schoolmaster: Five Lessons in Intellectual Emancipation*, trans. with intro. Kristin Ross (Stanford, CA: Stanford University Press 1991), 32 and ch. 3, especially 66–73. In "'Unruly Subjects,'" Kurashige reinforced equality of intelligence as a key frame for our work, reminding us that "the ASA . . . [is] a site that recognizes the critical role that artists and public scholars play in the production of knowledge," 314.

7. The critical incident method (or Technique) is frequently used by researchers in social service, education, and health-care arenas. Participants offer direct observations (usually from memory) of an incident that impacted them (either positively or negatively) in relation to an outcome under investigation. The foundational text is J. C. Flanagan, J. C. "The Critical Incident Technique," *Psychological Bulletin* 51, no. 4 (July 1954): 327–358.

8. See T. D. Mitchell and D. M. Donahue, "'I do more service in this class than I ever do at my site': Paying Attention to the Reflections of Students of Color in Service-Learning," in *The Future of Service-Learning: New Solutions for Sustaining and Improving Practice*, ed. J. Strait and M. Lima, 172–190 (Sterling, VA: Stylus Publishing, 2009); Robert T. Teranishi, Margary D. Martin, and Carolo Suárez-Orozco, "Engaging Immigrant-Origin Students in Higher Education," *Diversity and Democracy* 16, no. 2 (Spring 2013), https://www.aacu.org/publications-research/periodicals/engaging-immigrant-origin-students-higher-education.

9. K. S. Yep, and T. D. Mitchell, "Decolonizing Community Engagement; Reimagining Service Learning through an Ethnic Studies Lens," *The Cambridge Handbook of Service Leaning and Community Engagement* (Cambridge: Cambridge University Press, 2017), 294–303; Lina D. Dostillo, Sarah M. Brackmann, Kathleen E. Edwards, Barbara Harrison, Brandon W. Kliewer, and Patti H. Clayton, "Reciprocity: Saying What We Mean and Meaning What We Say," *Michigan Journal of Community Service Learning* 19, no. 1 (Fall 2012): 25. On making space, see E. Steinman (2011) "'Making Space': Lessons from Collaborations with Tribal Nations." *Michigan Journal of Community Service Learning* 18, no. 1 (Fall 2011): 5–18.

10. An asset-based approach views diversity of experience, thought, etc., as an asset in a classroom or community and builds from what students (or others) bring with them. This is in opposition to a model premised on "deficits." It builds on the work of Friere, Giroux, and others and is part of both pedagogical and community development discourses.

11. The NSCDC headquarters had moved into an historic building that had served as a meeting space for this earlier French-speaking immigrant community from Quebec for generations. For more on this earlier history of the neighborhood see "French-Canadian and Franco-American Heritage in Salem, Massachusetss,"Salem State University, accessed June 26, 2020, http://di.salemstate.edu/fasalem.

12. See Punto Urban Art Museum, accessed July 26, 2020, http://puntourbanartmuseum.org.

13. Liz's course was among the first on campus to align in this way, and although the content did not change, what this meant, practically, was that students were engaging in explicit dialogues and discussions throughout the semester regarding the ways in which structures of oppression and discrimination are built and maintained in the cultural, social, and political realms in the United States. Because the text of our service project fit right into this model, she spoke regularly with students about how to ensure their blog posts engaged these links. For more on the requirements of DPDS courses, see "2020–2021 Undergraduate Catalog," Salem State University, accessed July 26, 2020, https://catalog.salemstate.edu/content.php?catoid=47&navoid=12071&print#General_Education_Requirements.

14. On generative-oriented reciprocity, see Dostillo et al., "Reciprocity," 25. On making space, see Steinman, "'Making Space," 5–18. Also see Leanne Betasamosake Simpson, *As We Have Always Done: Indigenous Freedom through Radical Resistance* (Minneapolis: University of Minnesota Press, 2017), 19.

15. For a description of this model, see "CECL Inventory for Social Change," Salem State University, accessed June 26, 2020, https://www.salemstate.edu/academics/centers/center-civic-engagement/civic-learning.

19

Monumental Protest; or, Remaking Places through AR

INGRID GESSNER

> Something profound has happened to your camera. Its very purpose—capturing images—has expanded to include a new role: creating a bridge between our physical and digital worlds. . . . The camera can become a window into a world enhanced with digital information—adding a piece of sculpture to your bedroom or a car to your driveway. Neither actually there, but appearing to be and believably so.
> —Graham Roberts, "Augmented Reality: How We'll Bring the News into Your Home," *New York Times*, February 1, 2018

❖ ❖ ❖ ❖ ❖ ❖ ❖ ❖ ❖ ❖ ❖ ❖ ❖ ❖ ❖

The technology referred to in this *New York Times* article is called augmented reality (AR) and presents digital objects that are directly registered in the real world. This means that virtual information and the physical world are aligned to each other in a coordinate system, so that the virtual content appears to be located in the real world, as seen through the displays of mobile devices. As an art practice, AR provides new avenues to knowledge production, commemorative practices, historical education, and cultural heritage awareness. In this sense, it comes close to political activist art and public pedagogy and is indeed already being used in video art and museum education.[1] It is here that I see the connection between AR artists and practitioners of American Studies, namely, in fostering political activism (innate to American Studies as a discipline) and a renewed appreciation of the social function of artistic creation. One aim of this chapter is to use the existing connections between AR, media education, and American cultural studies to make the technology accessible, experienceable, and usable for a broad public.

My experiences stem from an American Studies course that I have taught (with slight adaptations) in two different countries (Germany and Austria): at the University of Erlangen-Nuremberg, the University of Regensburg, and the University of Education Vorarlberg. Course titles have varied from American Cultures of Memory and American Spaces: Building Many Americas or Uniting the States to American Public Art and Contested Memory, but the basic goal has been the same. The discussion- and case-studies-based seminar has in all three instances introduced students to the field of cultural memory studies. For this purpose, students examined how American history is preserved, sanitized, or contested through monuments, memorial sites, forms of public art, and museum exhibitions, while other events and experiences fall into oblivion. For me, as someone who has studied the cultural epidemiology of infectious diseases in the eighteenth, nineteenth, and early twentieth century, one such void or blank space stands out: the 1918 influenza pandemic that killed at least 50 million people worldwide (with about 675,000 deaths occurring in the United States) has seen close to nil public memorials or commemorative markers, neither to those who perished nor to those who literally fought this battle as doctors and nurses and who would have been natural recipients of public gratification and heroization through memorials in any comparable deathly event of similar magnitude. With the COVID-19 pandemic we are witnessing a different, much more memory-conscious approach: archives and museums started collecting artifacts when the first repercussions of the outbreak were being felt, and the *New York Times* commemorated the then 100,000 lives lost to the pandemic on Memorial Day 2020 by collecting obituaries from across the United States while drawing attention to racial disparities of the pandemic due to health inequities.[2] However, listing the names of those killed through racist violence, from Native genocide to slavery to the killings of countless people under police custody, would not only inflate the pages of the newspaper but also ignite a long outstanding debate about America's past. These events and individual experiences are indeed more seldom the subject of public naming and commemoration, not because they have fallen into oblivion but because no public consensus has been reached.

An important goal of the course is to help students understand that memorials and monuments always tell us more about the time they were erected than about the events or people they commemorate. In this sense, they are more about forgetting and the forging of new myths. This is particularly relevant as debates about the future of southern Confederate memorials have turned violent. Protesters against the monuments' removals have argued that their preservation is necessary in order to remember the past. Yet the public acts of commemoration and protest celebrate a particular (hi)story and conceal or even erase that of slavery and continued violence against Black people. I believe that it is our responsibility as teachers and as American Studies practitioners to recast these monumental narratives in order not to sweep aside the uncomfortable histories of colonialism and racial injustice. Two promising attempts at telling counterhistories are the unveiling of Kehinde Wiley's equestrian statue *Rumors of War* at the Virginia Museum of Fine Arts in Richmond, Virginia, in December 2019, and the opening of the National Memorial for Peace and Justice and the Legacy Museum in Montgomery, Alabama, in April 2018.[3] Wiley's young African American astride the horse has dreadlocks, a hoodie, and ripped jeans and confronts the Confederate statues and their evocation of Lost Cause ideology on Richmond's Monument Avenue.[4] At the National Memorial for Peace and Justice, eight hundred suspended steel slabs honor the victims of lynching in eight hundred counties. Corresponding identical markers of each steel column are lined up in rows like coffins, intended to be installed in each county, when local officials and citizens are ready to address racial and economic injustice in their communities.[5] In the long run, we need more memorials like these and more than website statements pledging future change from directors and boards of trustees of predominantly white-identified museums. Museums will get new audiences only if they showcase Black artists, Indigenous artists, and artists of color and rewrite the stories they tell and are open to rewrite them again in the future. Young people who have attended the course I am describing know a lot about being cool with change. Attending the seminar also gave them a deeper understanding of the function, relevance, and role of sites of memory in relation to questions of identity, ethnicity, and belonging.

In two of my courses, I focused on American cultures of memory and commemorative processes not only on a theoretical level, but also on a practical level. I introduced students to AR art projects, and we explored—and eventually tried out ourselves—how AR can be used to engage in questions of exclusion, classism, and racism, all of which concerned us in this seminar. Memorials, statues, and historically relevant buildings—as well as their absences—are ideal test cases for such a practice of digital augmentation. I presented various AR media art projects to the students, and we explored how the different artistic approaches make visible issues of exclusion and belonging. Finally, we tried out this media practice for ourselves, using memorials, historical sites, statues, and commemorative plaques—or the absence of them—as projection surfaces for our own AR projects.

Additionally, experiencing AR encourages us to occupy two locations at once—to think of ourselves as both "here and there"—situated in our immediate physical and cultural location as well as in the digitally augmented world. In this chapter, I show how the students' AR projects, which ask them to combine the critical analysis of an object with a creative idea, acquired technical competence, and factual knowledge and historical source material, offer an ideal way to engage with questions of our past, present, and future. I call this assignment and the AR experiences that the students create "MemorARy" or "MemorARies" (in the plural). My goal is to enable fellow American Studies practitioners to follow in my footsteps when they are teaching critical concepts of our discipline, such as memory, place, identity, and ethnicity, and to show their students how to create their own works of academically informed art.

While I believe that my findings regarding this AR project are applicable to contexts beyond central Europe, where I am based, I want readers to be aware of the special circumstances in which my insights were first generated. I taught the described courses between 2016 and 2020 in the institutional and social context of the German University and the Austrian University of Education. The course language was English, while the native language of the students was mostly German, occasionally Turkish or another European language. Groups ranged from fifteen to twenty students, of whom one or two were international students (mostly through the Erasmus Program[6]), two to three second-generation migrants, and three to five students who were the first in their families to pursue an academic education. Faced with a multilingual, socioeconomically diverse, and international student body, I looked for ways to meet the needs of students (as nonnative speakers, migrants, and prospective teachers). What I present in the following is a way to deal with these challenges that has worked well for the students and for me.

A major push to develop MemorARy came from conversations with colleagues and students, all of whom were frustrated about how the humanities in most European countries currently did not utilize e-learning and digital tools in ways that fully realize the technology's potential. An important difference between the United States and Europe that stands out is digital infrastructure, with an infrastructural head start enjoyed by most US institutions of higher education. Likewise, digital innovations in the classroom seem to have been implemented in the United States more easily. However, some colleagues have pointed out that a digital divide between smaller and less-well-funded US institutions and big(ger) research universities continues to exist. It is here that I see the beauty and applicability of MemorARy, which is based on the free HP Reveal app (alternatively the BlippAR app) and runs on mobile devices (smartphones) that the students already own. It does not require any additional budget or even the acquisition of third-party funds, nor are there any overhead costs. Even without AR, smartphones already enable socioeconomically disadvantaged students to access higher education more easily by making literature and research results available anywhere with internet access and allowing students to use the possibilities of electronic course platforms without additional costs. Raquel Kennon's argument on behalf of mobile phones is worth reiterating here, because smartphones may indeed enable disadvantaged students to participate in class discussions by providing easier access to readings, research, and course activities.[7] Within the MemorARy project, smartphones become effective pedagogical tools that enhance student participation and engagement in the socioeconomically diverse transnational classroom of many European countries (and beyond).

As a learning experience for preservice teachers, the MemorARy digital project also entails the core methods of American cultural studies, such as critical reading, reflection, and one's own (creative) text production. It is a form of self-determined, student-centered learning.[8] The MemorARy seminar and digital project is thus suited for preservice teachers, as well as more generally for any BA program in American Studies as well as ethnic, interdisciplinary, gender, and women's studies. Students develop a range of skills and competencies that are often implicit in the curricula anyway:

- critical reading and digital literacy skills; media literacy and methods of knowledge acquisition;[9]

- research, organization, and evaluation of information;[10]
- the ability to effectively communicate the findings of one's reading (including readings of inanimate objects);
- critical awareness and appreciation of the place(es) we inhabit once students uncover and reflect their palimpsestic, multidimensional structure(s) and communicate their findings back to the involved communities.

Learning with AR also has a positive effect on the motivation of learners and promotes the acquisition of specialized knowledge and technical skills and abilities.[11] This, in turn, increases the chance that students who have already gained experience with AR will integrate this format into secondary school education as future teachers.

In the first part of the course, we work together at the intersection of the concepts of memory, space, and place. Erika Doss's *Memorial Mania* (especially her introduction) has proven to be an excellent opening text and discussion starter. Doss explains the omnipresence of memorials by what she calls "memorial mania: an obsession with issues of memory and history and urgent desire to express and claim those issues in visibly public context." She posits that "today's growing numbers of memorials represent heightened anxieties about who and what should be remembered in America."[12] Students mostly agree with Doss and point out that her hypothesis is also applicable to a European context, or—more specifically—to the country or region they hail from. We also read Pierre Nora's seminal essay "Between Memory and History: Les Lieux de Mémoire," and students work in an in-class group activity to identify Nora's understanding of "memory," "history," and "lieux de mémoire/sites of memory."[13] I assign the individual concepts to different groups, provide them with Sharpie pens and large sheets of paper, and ask them to present their results to the entire class. I make their posters available on the course's e-learning platform for further reference and to ensure learning success.

Over the next few weeks, students explore how unity and belonging are negotiated versus difference and otherness through artistic creation and the appropriation of landscapes and cityscapes. One goal is to examine political and cultural tensions that are part of every memory process. In most cases, those involved in a memorial project try to reach a consensus on what should be remembered. It is often more problematic when it comes to giving a voice to formerly marginalized groups who rightfully demand a rewriting of the national narrative. A vivid example of this is the redesign of Philadelphia's Liberty Bell Center, which today serves as a place of remembrance of the Enlightenment ideal of freedom and as a memorial to the atrocities of slavery.[14] The museum shares its foundations with the part of the former house of President George Washington that was reserved for his slaves, and it deals openly with this violence-ridden history. Another example is the changing face of the National Mall in Washington, DC, which has always been a place of national remembrance with its numerous museums, memorials, and monuments. With the addition of the National Museum of the American Indian (2004) and the National Museum of African American History and Culture (2016), a more differentiated version of American history has since been on display. As a result of the protests against racial injustice following the killings of George Floyd, Tony McDade, Breonna Taylor, and Ahmaud Arbery by police, the Museum of Natural History has taken down an equestrian statue of Theodore Roosevelt that emanated a clearly imperialist vision with an African American man and a Native American man standing alongside him.

Seventy-five years (as of 2020) after the end of World War II, the seminar also pays particular attention to how the war's celebratory US-American narrative of national unity and democratic triumph is being challenged and augmented by counterhistories and experiences of diverse American publics—just at the moment as the last eyewitnesses are dying.[15] We specifically turn our attention to the lesser-known war experiences of formerly marginalized groups, such as the Navajo Code Talkers, whose encryption method was used in the Pacific War;[16] the segregated flight unit of the Tuskegee Airmen;[17] and the Japanese American soldiers who, while their own families were interned in camps on the American West Coast, were among those involved in the liberation of the Dachau concentration camp.[18] Besides generational change, there seems to be something about round numbers that makes events worth remembering. In this vein, we examine efforts to commemorate key figures in the June 1969 Stonewall Uprising on Christopher Street, New York City. In fact, statues of LGBTQ individuals are virtually nonexistent among the city's and nation's monuments.

Non-US-based students, like those who are attending my seminars in Austria and Germany, might have heard of some of these sites but certainly not all of them. The challenge is to familiarize the course participants with different places of remembrance (from mourning, trauma, and gratitude to hero worship) as early as possible in the semester. I have found it most effective to take students on a visual lecture tour at our first meeting of the term. First, I use photographs and short video clips (embedded in a regular presentation) to introduce students to as many commemorative sites as possible; second, I encourage them to think in as many directions as possible before they choose a topic that they want to explore. Eventually, each student becomes an expert for one commemorative place; if more students are interested in the same example, I let them explore different aspects of it. The above list can be easily adapted to the different needs and interests of teachers and students. In fact, students often have their own topic suggestions, which I then incorporate into the course. For example, in order to bring World War II experiences closer to my European students, I ask them about traces of that war in their own communities. Quite often, we start talking about war memorials and the fact that even the tiniest villages have them. However, they date to World War I and earlier wars of the nineteenth century. If there is any reference to World War II at all, it is usually in an attenuated form that simply lists the names of the dead (which is the case for most war memorials in Austria and Germany). The situation is different in Croatia, as a naturalized Austrian student from this former Yugoslavian republic has pointed out in one of my classes. Croatian partisans (heroes of the resistance) are revered and commemorated (e.g., in the Monument to the Detachment in Brezovica Forest). I am convinced that the World War II approach to the course works equally well in Asia and the Americas. In fact, a student from mainland China who attended my class at Erlangen-Nuremberg took our discussion on World War II as an opportunity to write a research paper commemorating the massacre in Nanjing, in which she discusses the depiction of atrocities in current and historical US-American and Chinese sources.[19] The prompt to contemplate traces of World War II in their communities always brings us to discuss the Holocaust and its commemoration; if not, I draw attention to it.[20] Most European students know the locations of former concentration camps, and many have visited at least one camp as part of their secondary school education. Other low-threshold signs of Holocaust commemoration are *Stolpersteine*, "stumbling stones" or metaphorically stumbling blocks.[21] Each stone commemorates a victim outside their last-known freely chosen residence. There are now more than 70,000 of these stones laid in more than 1,200 cities and towns and more than 20 countries, including Argentina, Austria, Belgium, France, Germany, Hungary, the Netherlands, Russia, Slovenia, and Ukraine. Together, they constitute the world's largest decentralized memorial.

The method of openness means that the syllabus is different every time I teach the course. Once students have picked their memorial, monument, or museum exhibition, I ask them to inform themselves about the site and develop a critique of it, so that they can serve as experts for the session in which we discuss their topic. Questions may include, but are not limited to, the following: What is the political, social, and cultural context of what is being remembered? Do you see any political or cultural tensions in this site? Who has decided what is worth remembering? How did the people and groups involved agree on the respective form of commemoration? Have some voices been heard, and others silenced? Is everybody represented accordingly? Are there any gaps?

As Elizabeth Duclos-Orsello, one of the editors of this volume, has pointed out, "American Studies scholars such as Karen Halttunen, Robert Hayden, Shelley Fisher Fishkin, and Robert Warrior have long explored the ways in which attending to place and place-making can center or de-center power and privilege and have mapped ways that places are made/re-made through activities in the political, legal and cultural realms."[22] These "places" inform both our and our students' lives, and a place-based approach to learning seems the inevitable consequence. With the AR assignment MemorARy, I apply Duclos-Orsello's prompt in order to locate American Studies practice in the specific geographical locations in which it occurs.

MemorARy is based on HP Reveal, and the following is the procedure I used with this software; it can be adapted to whatever platform you use.[23] Because of the accessibility and simplicity of the free app HP Reveal (formerly "Aurasma") or the BlippAR app, students and instructors do not need to be coding geniuses or computer wizards to create an augmented reality experience. Students may either use their own mobile devices or borrow university tablets. I instruct students to create an account in HP Reveal and log in to their account. All they have to do is click on "Create New Aura"[24] in Reveal Studio or Blippbuilder and select a trigger image by uploading an image file or by choosing an existing file.[25] I advise students to have a high-resolution picture with ample details of the object they want to augment. When users later try to unlock the AR experience, they have to point their mobile devices at exactly this "image" in the real world.[26] The next step is to select an overlay, such as a video or an image. The overlay can take any shape they want, including a carefully animated video or a simple text-based information card. I advise students to preview the "Aura," that is, their augmented experience, and to save it. If they do not want to share their first saved creation yet or ever, they need to navigate to the "Library" to make it private, that is, invisible for others. In most cases, however, students are eager to launch the Aura by opening the HP Reveal app on their mobile devices and logging in, using the same username and password they created for their HP Reveal Studio account earlier.[27] By using the "Auras" tab in the "Explore" section, they drag the page downward to refresh the Aura. At this point, everybody with a mobile device and the HP Reveal or BlippAR app may select the app's viewfinder and point their device at the trigger image to view the newly created Aura.

Students may work alone, in pairs, or in a group to create an AR experience. The main objective is to communicate their take on a particular site of memory in an engaging manner for an audience of their peers. I would advise against a grade-relevant evaluation of the MemorARy project. MemorARies are not assessed on the basis of their technical implementation (i.e., students do not get extra points if the final product is visually impressive), but the entire group actively interacts with each finished creation, so that we arrive at a kind of impact factor based on the exchanges and comments that each project triggers. Throughout the design process, I encourage students to create their own resources, their own drawings, pictures, music, animations, filmed scenes, or interviews, and they have to submit a written documentation of these steps. The project takes place in three separate stages:

1. **Planning**. This is the phase where students envision how their MemorARy will look and sound.
2. **Production**. This means creating, collecting, recording, and/or filming all the artifacts (e.g., images, videos, sounds, narration) they will need for their MemorARy. The principle of learning by design (LBD), or, more precisely, "learning about technology by using it to design something," has proven helpful for this kind of media production.[28] In this form of interaction, you learn about design by "doing design," thereby relying less on overt lecturing and traditional teaching. Design is learned by becoming a practitioner, not merely by learning about practice.
3. **Editing**. This stage is done using video-editing software such as Power Point, iMovie, or Movie Maker, where students can stitch the artifacts together that they will use to create their overlay in HP Reveal or Blipp AR.

It is helpful for students to be introduced to a model of what they are to produce themselves. For this purpose, the cultural heritage and preservation project *Mi querido barrio* (My Beloved Neighborhood) has worked best in inspiring students' imagination.[29] *Mi querido barrio* was commissioned by the Caribbean Cultural Center African Diaspora Institute (CCCADI) in East Harlem, New York City, and combines questions of past, present, and future with issues of social, racial, and gender justice.[30] As gentrification threatened the neighborhood's sense of place and high-rises replaced brownstones, Marta Moreno Vega, the founder of the institute, turned to AR technology to preserve the cultural landmarks of East Harlem. In order to make the unseen visible, several local artists and activists used images of people and places that have vanished and overlaid these stories onto the neighborhood. By pointing a mobile device at location markers, anyone can unlock augments—artworks, photographs, former buildings, and interactive features—that bring the past to life.

I have found it useful to break up the class into smaller groups and have them explore the individual creations of several participating artists on the CCCADI website. One such artist is Oliver Rios, a Puerto Rican American muralist who grew up in East Harlem. Rios's artworks, which have long vanished from the streets, get a second life through AR. By unlocking his murals on their mobile devices, people can experience them like in the 1980s; they can now even enlarge Rios's paintings or walk around them. Users are prompted to add their own responses by uploading screenshots or audio files and thus cocreate an affective crowd-sourced archive by entering into a dialogue between an AR object, the site, and their own particular gaze.[31] Rios believes that AR technology can strengthen his community: "It is a great way to not only educate but preserve and connect. I think that the more people start using it, especially the younger generation, the more they are going to open their eyes and want to reinvent."[32] Another group of students looks at Tamiko Thiel's "El Barrio Is Home," in which residents share with others what their community means to them. When the augment is activated, viewers are surrounded by golden-lettered words from residents of the community. After their explorations, the individual student groups present their observations, findings, and insights to the entire group.

Before students start conceptualizing and developing their individual ideas, I take them on a renegade tour to a random place of controversial representation; this may be a museum exhibition or a monument. The goal is to "hack" the place by asking what can be seen and what cannot be seen and then changing it. We may begin by uncovering gender or race codifications and then develop ideas to alter the exhibition by including new questions, texts, or artefacts to disrupt the normative gendered or discriminatory statements. A simple intervention might include putting a cardboard sign on a string around a statue's neck. Even if the sign is removed on the next day, it might start a conversation in the community. The students' ideas will ideally turn into mini research projects: for example, bringing to life a person who is not part of the discourse. The ultimate aim is to visually create a patchwork of stories, images, and questions in digital MemorARies. An example for a "hack," or intervention, from outside the MemorARy project is how Americans are exploring new ways to deal with Confederate monuments, which in many states still stand as troubling testaments to the country's racist past and have led to horrible incidents of violence. Cities such as Atlanta, Savannah, and Decatur, Georgia, as well as Richmond, Virginia, and Franklin, Tennessee, have placed explanatory panels on or alongside the statues detailing the real history behind them.[33] Far from proposing this rather simple practice as a remedy, I believe it is one way to start and continue an important conversation.

Students in Regensburg, whose old town is a UNESCO World Heritage Site, have chosen the Walhalla Memorial for their MemorARy creations. The Walhalla Memorial is a hall of fame that honors distinguished people in German history. The Walhalla itself is a neoclassical Parthenon-style building above the Danube river, which was conceived in 1807 by Crown Prince Ludwig. Inside the temple, 65 plaques and 130 busts are displayed that cover two thousand years of history. It is quite a transnational and illustrious collection of people, including Dutch painter Jan van Eyck, Desiderius Erasmus of Rotterdam, and Austrian composer Wolfgang Amadeus Mozart—all of whom are clearly not Germans from today's point of view. It usually does not take long until students start to come up with questions of their own. If not, and in light of the absences and sometimes completely unknown presences, I ask: Who is there? Who is not there? Who is this person? Who was added at which time? Where are the women? A group of students formulated this last question as a MemorARy inside Walhalla, so that in the future every visitor with a smartphone can read and ponder it. Another group of students enhanced the bust of anti-Nazi political activist Sophie Scholl by adding more faces of people from the resistance movement and by producing a short video about her and the nonviolent, intellectual resistance group the White Rose (*Die Weiße Rose*). Scholl and the other members of the group had mounted an anonymous leaflet and graffiti campaign against the Nazi regime before they were discovered and executed. At Walhalla today, everybody who points their mobile device at Sophie Scholl's bust with HP Reveal running on it may unlock this AR experience.[34]

One American place that would work well in a course like this is the

Figure 19.1. ***Where Are the Women? MemorARy inside Walhalla (near Regensburg).*** **Photograph by Markus Gloede, October 28, 2019.**

NYU Hall of Fame of Great Americans. The semicircular neoclassical arc that originated in 1900 includes 102 bronze portrait busts from Alexander Graham Bell to Eli Whitney. Another one is the National Statuary Hall in the United States Capitol. But in fact, any local history museum, memorial or monument, art or gallery exhibit that invites us to enter into a dialogue is a place to start a public pedagogy project.

The University of Education Vorarlberg Feldkirch is situated on the border between Austria, Switzerland, and Liechtenstein (not far from Germany to the north and Italy to the south). When it celebrated its eight hundredth anniversary recently, I asked my students who was part of the city's narrative and who was not, and, who, do we think, should be part of the story? Feldkirch has been a contact zone and a crossroads throughout its history and continues to be one until this day.[35] The aim is to enable Austrian and international students from diverse migratory backgrounds to make this visible by using the idea of the crossroads as well as that of the contact zone. For example, we know of one border experience that was recorded by James Joyce, who had traveled through Feldkirch by train in 1915, in the middle of World War I. He was considered an "enemy alien" in his then hometown of Trieste (a part of Austria-Hungary) and wanted to travel to Zurich. During border control checks at Feldkirch, the train on which Joyce and his partner Nora Barnacle were traveling was boarded, and passengers were inspected by officials; Joyce escaped arrest by a whisker. The episode is commemorated with a quotation by Joyce displayed at the Feldkirch rail station. If Joyce had been arrested then, he would have been unable to write *Ulysses* in its present form. An additional AR-plug could pick up the historical background of this episode and link it to the many other unknown people who had to flee their home countries and seek asylum in Switzerland, many of whom fled Nazi Germany during the interwar years. I am imagining AR shadow figures on our smartphones that invite us to explore the (his)stories of those who fled Nazi terror before and during World War II along this route, but also the many untold stories of war and climate refugees of the twenty-first century.

The AR memory projects, MemorARies, that emerged so far are an addition to the manifold archival, public, and oral history projects that often exist in the form of websites that have evolved out of the collaboration between students and teachers and that preserve previously silenced experiences and present neglected (hi)stories for a wide audience. But contrary to websites that cannot be experienced at the actual sites they refer to, the "cultural work" of the created AR experiences remains in place even if the generations of students who created them have moved on. They have permanently left their marks in the form of augmentations to the real world. Where students have placed them, others can access their creations, stories, images, and film clips.

Finally, I do not want to shy away from addressing arguments against digital technologies in teaching and learning. Critics have noted that they have not proven to be superior to traditional methods and that they require more time to develop, implement, and evaluate.[36] In fact, judging from my own experience, teaching and learning digitally depends on careful time-consuming preparation by instructors as well as targeted study questions and streamlined and carefully monitored assignments. I addressed this challenge by using the time I saved through being freed from traditional classroom instruction and the time-consuming mentoring and grading of research papers to develop guidelines and conduct workshops. In the end, the MemorARy project creates additional ways for the students to read, think, and communicate newly acquired knowledge. The digital assignment challenges them to think outside the box and make decisions about how to communicate what they have found in their readings.

With this project and my description of it, I hope to have started a broader conversation on how e-learning and, even more so, critical digital practice can help advance skill sets that are crucial to American Studies but that are often only implied or suggested but rarely carried out. MemorARy breaks down the walls of the university by enabling students to share their findings and engage in a dialogue with a wider public. It is these dialogical possibilities of the AR installation that may transform places. The practice also exemplifies the role the reading- and text-oriented humanities play in this particular moment. The students' reading practice can be experienced in their MemorARies and invite dialogue and contestation as a strategy of social change.

NOTES

1. Ingrid Gessner, "Tamiko Thiel's Virtual Reality Installations as Sites of Learning in and beyond the Museum," *Studies in the Education of Adults* 48, no. 2 (July 2, 2016): 155–176, https://doi.org/10.1080/02660830.2016.1229849.

2. Dan Barry et al., "Remembering the 100,000 Lives Lost to Coronavirus in America," *New York Times*, updated May 27, 2020, https://www.nytimes.com/interactive/2020/05/24/us/us-coronavirus-deaths-100000.html.

3. Campbell Robertson, "A Lynching Memorial Is Opening: The Country Has Never Seen Anything Like It," *New York Times*, April 25, 2018, https://www.nytimes.com/2018/04/25/us/lynching-memorial-alabama.html.

4. Reggie Ugwu, "Kehinde Wiley's Times Square Monument: That's No Robert E. Lee," *New York Times*, September 27, 2019, https://www.nytimes.com/2019/09/27/arts/design/kehinde-wiley-times-square-statue.html.

5. See the Equal Justice Initiative (EJI) projects at https://museumandmemorial.eji.org/.

6. The Erasmus Plus Program (EuRopean Action Scheme for the Mobility of University Students) is a European Union (EU) student exchange program that since 2014 includes all the EU programs for education, training, youth, and sport, including the Lifelong Learning Program. The original Erasmus university student exchange program was established in 1987.

7. Werner Sollors et al., "Reckoning by Cyphers, Laughing with Robots: New Technologies in Research and Teaching," *Amerikastudien/American Studies* 64, no. 1 (2019): 22–23, https://doi.org/10.33675/AMST/2019/1/5.

8. M. Dunleavy and C. Dede, "Augmented Reality Teaching and Learning," in *Handbook of Research on Educational Communications and Technology*, 4th ed., ed. J. Michael Spector, M. David Merrill, Jan Elen, and M. J. Bishop (New York: Springer, 2014), 735–745.

9. Neven A. M. El Sayed, Hala H. Zayed, and Mohamed I. Sharawy, "ARSC: Augmented Reality Student Card—An Augmented Reality Solution for the Education Field," *Computers & Education* 56, no. 4 (May 2011): 1045–1061, https://doi.org/10.1016/j.compedu.2010.10.019; James M. Mathews, "Using a Studio-

Based Pedagogy to Engage Students in the Design of Mobile-Based Media," *English Teaching: Practice and Critique* 9, no. 1 (May 2010): 87–102.

10. Eric Klopfer and Josh Sheldon, "Augmenting Your Own Reality: Student Authoring of Science-Based Augmented Reality Games," *New Directions for Youth Development* 2010, no. 128 (2010): 85–94, https://doi.org/10.1002/yd.378.

11. Josef Buchner, "Augmented Reality in der Hochschullehre: Einfluss auf Motivation und Lernerfolg," in *Hochschule digital.innovativ #digiPH: Tagungsband zur 1. Online-Tagung*, ed. Marlene Miglbauer, Lene Kieberl, and Stefan Schmid (N.p.: Books on Demand, 2018), 143–156.

12. Erika Lee Doss, *Memorial Mania: Public Feeling in America* (Chicago: University of Chicago Press, 2010), 1.

13. Pierre Nora, "Between Memory and History: Les Lieux de Mémoire," *Representations* 26 (1989): 7–24.

14. Ingrid Gessner, "Must-See Sights: The Politics of Representing U.S.-American History," in *Pictorial Cultures and Political Iconographies*, ed. Udo J. Hebel and Christoph Wagner (Berlin: Walter de Gruyter, 2011), 377–400, http://dx.doi.org/10.1515/9783110237863.377.

15. Birgit Däwes and Ingrid Gessner, "Commemorating World War II at 70: Ethnic and Transnational Perspectives—An Introduction," *American Studies Journal* 59 (May 6, 2015), https://doi.org/DOI 10.18422/59-01.

16. Birgit Däwes, "Transnational Debts: The Cultural Memory of Navajo Code Talkers in World War II," *American Studies Journal* 59 (2015), https://doi.org/DOI 10.18422/59-04.

17. Renée Ater, "Commemoration, Race, and World War II: History and Civil Rights at the Tuskegee Airmen National Historic Site," *American Studies Journal* 59 (May 3, 2015), https://doi.org/DOI 10.18422/59-05.

18. Ingrid Gessner, "Liberating Dachau: Transnational Discourses of Holocaust Memory," in *Transnational American Memories*, ed. Udo J. Hebel (Berlin: Walter de Gruyter, 2009), 243–265.

19. Caitlin Liu, "New Monument Recalls Veterans' Valor in War, Struggles at Home," *Los Angeles Times*, June 6, 1999; Megan Liu, "Can the Past Serve the Present? The Nanjing Massacre Memorial Hall," *Journal of Chinese Humanities* 3, no. 2 (2017): 203–218, https://doi.org/10.1163/23521341-12340050; Zhang Sheng, "The Nanjing Massacre as Recorded in American Sources," in "Nanjing Massacre: Eightieth Anniversary, 1937–2017," *Chinese Studies in History* 50, no. 4 (2017): 279–298, https://doi.org/10.1080/00094633.2017.1425039.

20. I recommend working with Henderson and Lange's collection of essays: Marius Henderson and Julia Lange, eds., *Entangled Memories: Remembering the Holocaust in a Global Age* (Heidelberg: Winter, 2017).

21. Laura Katzman and Gabriella Paulix, "The Fine Art of Memorialization: A Conversation with Gunter Demnig," in *Entangled Memories*, 39–68.

22. Elizabeth Duclos-Orsello, introductory remarks, panel, "Place, Protest, and Pedagogy: A Roundtable on Teaching in Place" (EBAAS, London, 2018).

23. Unfortunately, HP Reveal is no longer available since January 2020. An open source alternative is ARpoise (http://arpoise.com/). Together with the AR-vos app it allows you to create and view location-based augmented reality. On

iOS it uses Apple's ARKit and on Android it uses Google's ARCore to provide image triggered augmented reality (https://ar-vos.com). Another alternative is the BlippAR solution, which is free of charge for educators and students for three months, which is usually enough to run the AR project (https://www.blippar.com/ar-studio). The BlippAR app to view location-based augmented reality is available free of charge from the Apple App Store and the Google Play Store.

24. The name "auras" for the experience users are creating comes from the earlier provider of the software, which was called Aurasma.

25. A good description of this process is provided by Buchner, "Augmented Reality in der Hochschullehre," 149.

26. This functions much like a QR code that leads you to a website. Yet, in the case of an AR experience, the Aura is visible in the real world.

27. To see the AR experience they have created, they need the HP Reveal app from the App Store or Google Play.

28. M. J. Koehler and P. Mishra, "Teachers Learning Technology by Design," *Journal of Computing in Teacher Education* 21, no. 3 (2005): 94–102.

29. Several of Tamiko Thiel's AR artworks also lend themselves as models for students (http://www.tamikothiel.com/). For a discussion of her art as well as the *Mi querido barrio* project, see Ingrid Gessner, "Digital Modernities: Augmented and Virtual Reality Art as Affective Archive," in *Modernities and Modernization in North America*, ed. Ilka Brasch and Ruth Mayer (Heidelberg: Universitätsverlag Winter, 2018), 449–471.

30. The project was part of the *Home, Memory and Future* exhibition that celebrated the Caribbean Cultural Center's grand reopening in its new location in 2017 (https://cccadi.org/miqueridobarrio).

31. Gessner, "Digital Modernities," 464.

32. Quoted in Beverly Bryan, "How Augmented Reality Is Fighting Cultural Erasure in East Harlem," *Creators* (blog), October 23, 2016, https://creators.vice.com/en_us/article/wnpmpm/augmented-reality-east-harlem-cultural-diaspora.

33. Hannah Natanson, "Two Women Lead a Free Tour of Charlottesville's Confederate Monuments Each Month: A New Website Lets Everyone Listen," *Washington Times*, August 20, 2019, https://www.washingtonpost.com/lifestyle/2019/08/20/two-women-lead-free-tour-charlottesvilles-confederate-monuments-each-month-new-website-lets-everyone-listen/.

34. Katie Rickard, "Memorializing the White Rose Resistance Group in Post-War Germany," in *Memorialization in Germany since 1945*, ed. B. Niven and C. Paver (London: Palgrave, 2010), 157–167.

35. Mary Louise Pratt, "Arts of the Contact Zone," *Profession*, 1991, 33–40.

36. John Traxler and Agnes Kukulska-Hulme, "Conclusion: Contextual Challenges for the Next Generation," in *Mobile Learning: The Next Generation*, ed. John Traxler and Agnes Kukulska-Hulme (New York: Taylor & Francis, 2015), 215.

20

"The Walk of Memory"

An Excursion into Race, Place, and History in the (Southern) American Studies Classroom

KENDRA HAMILTON

I teach at Presbyterian College, a small liberal arts college with origins as a school for orphans of the War of Rebellion. Our founder, William Plumer Jacobs, figures in our founding myth as a "gentle warrior" of a Presbyterian minister who had, before accepting the Lord's call, worked in the trusted position of clerk to the proceedings of the South Carolina secession convention. Though he never served in the military, plunging instead into mission work in upper South Carolina, his diary documents another sort of battle: his ceaseless efforts to build his church, then his orphanage, and finally his college. Alongside charming details from his personal life—his determined courtship of the woman who was to become his wife, his unintentionally comic efforts to stamp out dancing among "the young people"—the diary documents his single-minded pursuit of a vision of service and servant leadership extending across the Piedmont region, embracing the "New South Creed" and expressed in the school motto *"Dum vivimus servimus"*: "While we live, we serve."

Our institution in 2020 is not as pious as in, say, 1920, but it's no stretch to say that we—and the town and region—have supped so deeply here on the myth of good Christian virtue and innocence that to confront any other version of the story would be a bit more than just a "difficult conversation." From our motto to our mascot (a zany fighting Scot in blue tartan and hose) to cherished rituals such as the physical signing of the honor code during fall convocation, we have fashioned ourselves here as a community of servant leaders for whom honor, faith, and a certain Scots tenacity are guiding virtues. The entirety of this community's knowledge of itself is of an idyllic existence in a timeless and eternal past.

Of course, to learn otherwise, one would need look no further than Jacobs's aforementioned diary. For he writes, too, of the terror and violence of Reconstruction, of seeing friends arrested, of testifying in the Ku Klux Klan trials. He seems shocked to his soul when sixteen "Negroes" are taken from a neighboring county's jail and lynched. He's confused and dismayed by pitched gun battles between Black people and white people during Reconstruction-era elections. Confusion, however, is mingled with complicity. He's unable to imagine friends and parishioners participating in Ku Klux outrages and mounts a vigorous defense. And there's a grim justice to his tone when he recounts the attempted assassination of Joe Crews, a prominent Scalawag: "Was there ever a man so hated in Laurens County as he! He has been its terror. Now that he lies at the point of death there are none who wish his recovery."[1] These events, too, are part of our institutional history, though constituting an alternative narrative heretofore consigned to the scrap heap of historical amnesia.

The conflict between the events I've just recounted and the vision of our town and region celebrated at, for example, college Homecoming games and town Christmas parades is never far from my thoughts and praxis. As an African American faculty member in English and Southern studies with responsibilities that include directing a Mellon-funded research initiative on our city's past as a (segregated) mill town, I have commitments both to maintaining and growing my minor and to communicating our mission and values to town and gown stakeholders. The fact that these stakeholder communities have so little knowledge of their own collective history complicates my task even as it attests to the power of the mechanisms that white supremacy has used to protect itself. Rhetorics of colorblindness and postracialism, among other strategies of historical erasure,[2] are deployed defensively—and usually quite unconsciously—to justify, vindicate, and recenter whiteness whenever racial inequity or often even the *presence* of race is about to be noted.

The flourishing over the long twentieth century of Lost Cause narrative framing and cultural practices and the contemporary conflict over the memory and meaning of Confederate statues and symbols represents only one category of response in this ongoing project of deflection and defense.

So how, against this backdrop, do I, as an African American faculty member working primarily with students from privileged white Southern backgrounds, historicize and contextualize the cultures and histories of white supremacy for them? I start . . . by taking them for a walk, one in which we explore the meaning of history, memory, and gestures of mourning. I invite you to journey with me as I recount our mutual process of discovery with this method.

The "walk" is a Walk of Memory, connecting *lieux de memoire* with *milieux de memoire*[3]—that is to say, connecting marked sites of civic memory that celebrate occasions and persons important to this former mill town's ruling class with unmarked sites of lived social memory, whose meaning is kept alive by word of mouth, even if of necessity, only in whispers. These sites include but are not limited to:

. . . A tasteful marble sarcophagus, placed at the heart of
Clinton Cemetery, behind the soaring Gothic spires of the First
Presbyterian Church. The dedication reads
"Rev. William Plumer Jacobs
D.D., L.L.D.
Born
Mar. 15, 1842
Died
Sept. 10, 1917
Founder of the
Thornwell Orphanage"
. . . Another marker that "everyone" knows about but few
will speak of. Half covered by sand and weeds at the farthest
corner of the First Presbyterian Church cemetery, it's about
the size of a composition notebook, this dark slate plaque that
bears a haunting inscription:
"In Memory Of
Our Colored Friends
Who Were Buried Here
1855—1869"
. . . Crossing the railroad tracks, a towering obelisk, at the
crossroads at the center of town. Hyper-visible in the civic

> landscape, this monument to the War of Rebellion is so common, so everyday, a sight that most passersby fail to register it. Dedicated in 1911, and rising to the height of the roof of the adjacent train depot, it shouts its message, "lest we forget" . . . in a town whose population was at the time 55 percent African American.[4]
>
> . . . Nearly invisible in the landscape, a substantial two-story home, across the street from First Presbyterian and just two long city blocks from the war memorial. This was the home of contractor Norris Dendy, youngest son of the most successful Black businessman in town, who on the Fourth of July, 1933, became the "last man lynched in Laurens County" for the crime of building his family home on the "white" side of the tracks.

Over the course of the walk, students several times cross the iconic "train tracks" of Southern myth and memory—a line of physical demarcation that in Clinton, as in so many other cities and towns, served to segregate by race (the all-white textile "mill hills" from the historic African American Bell Street neighborhood) and also by class (both of these working-class communities from the wealth, prestige, and prosperity of the town's founders and elites, who lived to the south and east). These are divisions that linger—particularly as, with the demise of the mills and the failure of any other source of employment to replace them, racial lines of demarcation have dissolved and the working-class sections of town have devolved to a state of desperate poverty. The walk makes visible, in ways that take students unawares and invite them to make connections with the landscapes of their own lived memory, the mechanisms of power white supremacy has at its command: mechanisms that extend to the reshaping of the landscape itself.

THE POWER OF PLACE, MEMORY, AND AN INCLUSIVE THEORY OF RACIAL HARMS

The efforts of New Southern studies scholars to decenter and dethrone these notions notwithstanding, the South remains defined in the popular imagination (including that of my students) by a set of antimodernist tropes memorably summarized by Barbara Ladd in her 2005 essay, "Literary Studies: The Southern United States." To be sure, Ladd is careful to complicate and update the baseline picture she draws, but the general outlines of her account would generate little controversy in my undergraduate classrooms.

Southern literature, Ladd says, is characterized by and reflective of a culture with "a strong sense of place, based on memory, insularity, and a tragic history of defeat in the Civil War" along with "the 'universal' values of honor, chivalry toward women, gentleness with subordinates." Southern literature is, indeed, a "concrete" literature, "enmeshed in all the particularities of place and lived history . . . reflect[ing] the southern belief in evil, in the Fall, and in the limited efficacy of any progressivist or reform agenda." Finally, it is "shaped by oral traditions . . . [and] the social categories [of] family, community, place."[5]

It should escape no one's attention (though it often escapes that of my students) that the imagined community invoked by this definition is centered in masculinity, privilege, and white identity—and indeed this observation has inspired generations of scholars to undertake the work of complicating the terms of the debate, subjecting "honor," "faith," "family," and especially "community" to extended critique and reinterpretation.[6] I have chosen in my writing and work in the classroom to engage with the vaunted Southern "sense of place," following the lead of feminist geographers from Delores Hayden's enabling work on the "power of place" to Katherine McKittrick's stunningly evocative work on Black women's "cartographies of struggle" to complicate my students' notions of space and place and their own positions therein.[7] At the same time, I've found historian Michael Kammen's eight propositions for studying the past offer an essential, accessible framework for helping students at the undergraduate level to separate the categories of history and memory and to understand the role of collective memory in their own lives. Indeed, so important are the propositions to this assignment in particular and to the work I do in the Southern studies classroom more generally that they bear repetition in full.

Kammen begins, "Indeed, if collective memory (usually a code phrase for what is remembered by the dominant civic culture) and popular memory (usually referring to ordinary folks) are both abstractions that have to be handled with care, what (if anything) can we assert with assurance" about them?[8] This is how he answers:[9]

1. That public interest in the past pulses; it comes and goes.
2. That we have highly selective memories of what we have been taught about the past.
3. That the past may be mobilized to serve partisan purposes.

4. That the past is commercialized for the sake of tourism and related enterprises.
5. That invocations of the past (as tradition) may occur as a means of resisting change *or* of achieving innovations [emphasis in original].
6. That history is an essential ingredient in defining nation, group, and personal identity.
7. That the past and its sustaining evidence may give pleasure for purely aesthetic and nonutilitarian reasons.
8. And finally, that individuals and small groups who are strongly tradition-oriented commonly seek to stimulate a shared sense of the past within their region . . . , their social class . . . , their ethnic group . . . , or even their entire nation.[10]

So, these are the most important of my inspirations. But a third idea, with a genealogy extending from Thomas Jefferson to Benjamin E. Mays, is also foundational: that of an inclusive idea of racial harms. Whites are not just perpetrators of racialized violence; they are also victims of it. Indeed, being forced in childhood to witness and learning eventually to accept—and even celebrate—racialized violence is one of the key mechanisms by which white supremacy reproduces itself.[11] The Walk of Memory assignment is an attempt to build a scaffold for students whose identities are anchored in the "branches without roots"[12] of settler-colonial whiteness to knowledge that they critically lack and without which they cannot grow: that is to say, an understanding of history that helps them to grasp, without undue violence, that everything they think they know about who they are is no more than, as David Blight put the matter, "a set of beliefs in search of a history"[13] rather than an actual history. My students—a group that is mostly Southern, sheltered, religious, certain—are so accustomed to being centered, as Joe Feagin states the case in *The White Racial Frame*, as the "protagonists" of history that they see this as their right.[14] They are so confident in their roles within history, identity, literature, as both innocent and heroic that the work of coming to a new understanding of their role within the drama of race is not just a "difficult conversation"—*it, in fact, represents a spiritual and existential crisis.*

What students face, often for the first time, in classes like mine is a confrontation with "the trauma of whiteness": "an image and knowledge of themselves" not as heroes and saviors but "as violent aggressors, morally destitute, even barbaric."[15] The encounter with the pathology of the Southern racial regime is pedagogically necessary, essential to their moral and intellectual development, but it is also dangerous: dan-

Figure 20.1. This modest slate plaque outside the fence line of Clinton Cemetery reads "In Memory of Our Colored Friends Who Were Buried Here, 1855–1869." As of 2020, it is the only physical evidence within the city limits of the existence of Clinton's enslaved community.

Figure 20.2. Consider the contrast between the "colored friends" plaque and the prominent placement of the sarcophagus of civic leader Rev. William Plumer Jacobs, founder of the three most important institutions in the city: the First Presbyterian Church, the Thornwell Orphanage for war orphans, and Presbyterian College.

Figure 20.3. This towering monument to "Confederate heroes" was placed at the city's "five points" intersection in 1911 by the United Daughters of the Confederacy.

Figure 20.4. This substantial two-story house was built by the Dendy family, which operated highly successful contracting, laundry, and truck-farming operations in Clinton. Norris, the youngest son, was baited into a fistfight with a white business rival on the Fourth of July, 1933, and became "the last man lynched in Laurens County" on the morning of the fifth, purportedly because of the fight. But an NAACP investigation and national news coverage following the event revealed that the family—and Norris specifically—started receiving death threats in concert with the construction of this house on the "white" side of the railroad tracks. The house is unmarked and its role in Clinton's history is unacknowledged.

gerous for students who may find defense mechanisms of denial, evasion, even attack triggered, hindering their learning; but especially so for faculty, particularly vulnerable junior faculty, who may find themselves on the receiving end of backlash—and not just from students, but from parents, administration, even other faculty—that can threaten not just their effectiveness but also their jobs.

THE JOURNEY: THE ASSIGNMENT

The Walk of Memory, first introduced in 2018, constitutes the culminating assignment in the first unit of SOST 205, Introduction to Southern Studies, the anchor course for the interdisciplinary Southern studies minor. The design of the course has evolved substantially since my arrival at Presbyterian College in 2014, as I shall describe; but historically, since its introduction to the college curriculum a little more than a decade and a half ago, SOST 205 had been structured thematically, with the appeal of certain of those elements—for example, the Southern storytelling tradition, Southern humor, Southern food, Southern music—so well-established that the class had come to be viewed as a "gut": a fun "celebration" of Southern culture, popular particularly among students active in the Greek system. This of course much against its original intent.

My decision to depart from the syllabus I had inherited in order to introduce more rigor in the number and sophistication of the readings and to press students to confront more directly the raced and gendered inequalities baked into their assumptions about Southern history and identity was met with initial surprise—as students found their expectations of the class violated—followed by polite but stony resistance. In other words, things did not go well. I kvetched to colleagues that students were not meeting my expectations for reading comprehension and class discussion. And while student evaluations made clear their dissatisfactions with the readings and the reading load, other interactions—memorably, a student research presentation and paper on Southern "honor" traditions and the Kappa Alpha Order—clearly seemed intended to provoke a fight. Most disappointingly, after I dutifully took the feedback into account and redesigned the course, enrollment plummeted by two-thirds the following academic year and took several more years to recover, potentially jeopardizing the continued existence of the minor. It was, ironically, a decision to "lean in" to what was most emotionally charged and challenging in the course material that led to the current design of the class and a subsequent recovery in enrollments with a different and more engaged generation of students.

The precipitating event for the change was a fall 2017 campus "teach-in" following the "Unite the Right" rally in Charlottesville, Virginia, earlier that summer. You may recall the indelible images of a ragtag band of University of Virginia students confronting a torch-bearing mob at the feet of the Thomas Jefferson statue by night, while the following morning Proud Boys, militias, neo-Nazis, and neo-Confederates slugged it out with Antifa on the streets of the city amid rumors of a "stand down" order to police forces. Due to my nearly twenty years of residence in Charlottesville[16] and my deep connections among the university and religious communities that had been active in the "resistance" to Donald Trump's policies, I was able to share my preferential access to videos and social media content and give a first-person perspective on the events while colleagues from other departments discussed the relevant historical and political contexts.

The catharsis produced by the event was quite powerful for our campus. With a standing-room-only audience, a historic convergence of African American faculty,[17] and a broad coalition of support across disciplines and from administration, including the college's president, the teach-in had the makings of an epoch-making event. And in the wake of it, it occurred to me that perhaps what had been most missing from my American Studies classroom . . . had been me.

Here was an irony. I had for so long been an advocate for the power of the standpoint in the production and promulgation of knowledge, and yet, inexplicably, my own intimate connections to two of the worst acts of racial terrorism of the decade had not made their way into my classroom praxis, in a context in which inclusion might have been not just relevant but also efficacious. I am, after all, a native of Charleston, South Carolina, a woman of Gullah-Geechee cultural descent, with a personal connection not just to all of the relevant histories—enslavement, Reconstruction, Jim Crow, integration—but to the victims of the Emanuel AME Church massacre as well. Similarly, my connection to Charlottesville runs through all of its elite institutions—the University of Virginia, Monticello, the Charlottesville City Council—and through its religious activist communities as well. On August 12, professors who are personal friends interposed their bodies between students and neo-Nazis. Members of my church, the Episcopal church, were on the front lines as well. All were witnesses who gave poignant testimony to the indifference of authority, unexpected acts of grace and heroism, and sharing both in texts and videos and Facebook posts.

Had I been afraid to make these sources of knowledge available to my students? I had to admit to myself the answer was yes. Could I see a path forward, using my standpoint to illuminate other relevant standpoints—for example, the United Daughters of the Confederacy, the Ku Klux Klan, and the many ordinary men and women standing in between? The answer here also was yes. And thus was a fourth (and one hopes final) iteration of SOST 205 born, one that foregrounds the history and memory of monuments and the central nature of the dilemma they present for our democracy. The first unit of that new course is titled: "History and Memory: Charleston, Charlottesville . . . and Clinton."

The initial meeting of the unit convenes in the college archives, both to introduce students to the research resources of which they will be expected to avail themselves in the coming weeks and months and also as an object lesson in the first of the key concepts: Michael Kammen's propositions. After a framing discussion on "how we remember the past," students are paired off and given the opportunity to explore two permanent exhibits: the first, a replica of the Founder's Library, with books, furnishings, and artifacts (including a copy of the S.C. Ordinance of Secession) associated with Jacobs's life and legacy; and second, a re-creation of Stonewall Jackson's bedroom, with furnishings donated by a collector and library donor. What ensues is a pair-and-share activity, as students work through the propositions then reconvene as a class to discuss which propositions are the most relevant to the exhibits and which of the exhibits is most appropriate to the college setting.

The other class sessions in the unit introduce the collective memory of the Lost Cause myth and connect them to a submerged American history of racist oppression and violence by weaving together readings (e.g., chapters from Mitch Landrieu's 2018 *In the Shadow of Statues* and Ethan Kytle and Blain Roberts's 2018 *Denmark Vesey's Garden*); visits to the college archives to explore primary source materials on the Dendy lynching; and personal experience—personal memories of and responses to acts of mass racial violence from their own lifetimes (specifically, the Charleston massacre and the Charlottesville race riot). Class discussion generally reveals a surprising fact: that, without a context in which to understand and assimilate events like Charleston and Charlottesville, a sort of historical amnesia has *already* begun to set in for these students. "I just didn't know what it was all about, so I never thought too much about it" was a common response to the Charlottesville riot. Discussion of the Charleston massacre, on the other hand, tends to evoke much clearer moral condemnation—"I just figured he was crazy—or a monster"—but the desire to look away seems even more intense. Students have to be actively prodded to discuss the killer's emotionally bereft childhood, his gradual radicalization process. The questions his life and fate raise appear to be very close to the bone for this generation.

The unit ends with class presentations from the Walk of Memory assignment, and here it becomes very clear which students have begun to make the essential connections and which have not. Students who are resistant or unaware emphasize Southern ideals—for example, the beauty of elite homes or the beauty of the walk itself (note: only one of the neighborhoods can be said to be "beautiful"). Similarly, they may attempt a sort of "both sides" equivalency to balance out their discomfort. One example from fall 2019 was rather ironically telling. "Even though not everyone agrees with the Confederacy morals, the town still appreciates them because they helped this town flourish and withhold [*sic*] their own morals." Students willing to dig deeper, however, were able to share powerful insights with their classmates. These observations, from a student who appeared to have spent a great deal of time pondering a textile mill exhibit inside Clinton's city hall, were exemplary. She wrote:

> There were no observations of any blacks as having even an ounce of status or power within the Mills. Everyone with status was white and mostly male. Thus, a clear bias within the company.
>
> I also saw a picture that displayed the various positions within the Mills. The only black individuals who were listed were two black men. And, they were janitors.
>
> Again, the history seems to have been manipulated into how those with wealth want their legacy to be remembered.
>
> Lastly, there were also pictures of children working in the Mills. I was saddened when I saw those images. I felt those children's potential had been miserably squandered. There was nothing self-sacrificing and noble about children like that. I understand the time period was different and children had to work too. But, the injustice still troubled me.

The Walk of Memory is an assignment designed to do a difficult thing: it attempts to pierce the veil of invisibility surrounding whiteness and white identity and to highlight the alternate facts white supremacy has used to fictionalize its operations. The assignment lays bare the tensions with which my students contend: their embodied "knowing" that things they have witnessed or experienced are not right—are, in fact, desperately wrong; their sense that racism is not natural or inevitable; their fear of acknowledging or cluelessness as to how to atone for the social norms created and maintained at great cost in their name. The assignment is my attempt to acknowledge the role we scholars can play at a critical juncture for the young people we teach. How do we help them suture the gaping holes in their critical awareness that their parents and their culture have torn and papered over? The assignment is an early hurdle in a semester-long process, one that attempts to discompose their complacency without tripping their defense mechanisms.

What I have learned from this assignment is twofold: that, on the one hand, the defenses in the edifice of white supremacy are crumbling. There is great power in watching students make that leap of apprehension—suddenly grasping the enormity of the omissions and elisions in their worldview and setting out eagerly to do the work of filling the gaps. On the other hand, engagement can flip into defensiveness on a dime. Too much too fast can sap their creative energy as the internal focus turns to survival; noise and distraction may be seized upon to prevent true reflection; feelings of persecution are the ultimate refuge.[18] While constant vigilance against the old paradigm's death throes is required, it is undeniable that Blackness and Otherness are entering academic and communal discourses in the American Studies classroom in ways they never have before. The questions that linger are how long faculty doing this work will remain the "disagreeable mirrors" of James Baldwin's phrase—or at what point the news we bring will constitute a great getting-up morning for our classrooms and the culture at large.

NOTES

1. William Plumer Jacobs, *The Diary of William Plumer Jacobs*, ed. Thornwell Jacobs (Atlanta: Oglethorpe University Press, 1937), 136, 141, 145–147, 176.

2. Thandeka, *Learning to Be White: Money, Race, and God in America* (New York: Continuum International, 1999).

3. Adapted from Pierre Nora's "Between History and Memory," in "Memory and CounterMemory," special issue, *Representations*, no. 26 (Spring 1989): 7–24.

4. South Carolina was still a majority Black state in 1910, with African Americans comprising 55 percent of the population. It's interesting to note that while the state's population increased 13 percent since the 1900 census, the African American population actually shrunk. In Laurens, African American presence fell from 59.3 percent to 54.8 in 1910. Bureau of the Census, "Population: South Carolina: Composition and Characteristics of the Population," *Thirteenth Census of the United States: 1910* (Washington: Department of Commerce and Labor, 1910), 7, 12.

5. Barbara Ladd, "Literary Studies: The Southern United States," *PMLA* 120, no. 5 (October 2005): 1629.

6. Thomas F. Haddox, "Southern Literature," in *Keywords for Southern Studies*, ed. Scott Romine and Jennifer Rae Greeson (Athens: University of Georgia Press, 2016): 254–256.

7. Delores Hayden, *The Power of Place: Urban Landscapes as Public History* (Cambridge, MA: MIT Press, 1997); Katherine McKittrick, *Demonic Grounds: Black Women and the Cartographies of Struggle* (Minneapolis: University of Minnesota Press, 2006).

8. Please note that Kammen's division of collective memory maps rather neatly upon Nora's *lieux de memoire* and *milieux de memoire.*

9. The numbers are not original; they have been added for ease of reference.

10. Michael Kammen, *Mystic Chords of Memory: The Transformation of Tradition in American Culture* (New York: Vintage, 1993), 9–10.

11. This is, indeed, the central thesis of the theologian Thandeka's *Learning to Be White* (1999).

12. A memorable phrase Zora Neale Hurston uses in quite a different context in *Their Eyes Were Watching God* (1937; New York: HarperPerennial, 2006), 16.

13. Quoted in Christopher Wilson, "We Legitimize the So-Called 'Confederacy' with our Vocabulary, and That's a Problem," *Smithsonian*, September 12, 2017, https://www.smithsonianmag.com/smithsonian-institution/we-legitimize-so-called-confederacy-vocabulary-thats-problem-180964830/.

14. Joe Feagin, *The White Racial Frame: Centuries of Racial Framing and Counter-Framing*, 2nd ed. (New York: Routledge, 2013).

15. Veronica T. Watson and Becky Thompson, "Theorizing White Racial Trauma and its Remedies," in *The Construction of Whiteness: An Interdisciplinary Analysis of Race Formation and the Meaning of White Identity*, ed. Stephen Middleton, David R. Roediger, and Donald M. Shaffer (Jackson: University Press of Mississippi, 2016), 247–266.

16. Including serving, while still a graduate student, on Charlottesville City Council 2003–2008.

17. We have recently reached an all-time high of three tenured African American faculty members on a roughly eighty-member roster. This figure might sound shockingly low, but at 6.2 percent, it is actually higher than the national average of 5.4 percent cited by the *Journal of Blacks in Higher Education.* "The Snail-like Progress of Blacks in Faculty Ranks of Higher Education," *Journal of Blacks in Higher Education*, no. 62 (2009), http://www.jbhe.com/news_views/62_blackfaculty.html.

18. Watson and Thompson, "Theorizing," label hypervigilance, a sense of persecution, dissociation, and diminished creativity as the four signs of racialized white trauma, or in their phrase "white schizophrenic subjectivity." These, they say, are the chief among "the myriad of ways an investment in whiteness can distort how people think, act, and perceive reality. This form of subjectivity . . . amplifies white fear . . . and disconnection between people . . . and stifles the ability to discern the real from the imagined," 249.

Afterword

KANDICE CHUH

❖ ❖ ❖ ❖ ❖ ❖ ❖

In her chapter in this volume, Sarah Hentges explains, "I teach [Octavia] Butler's work like she lived and wrote—with a 'positive obsession.'" Hentges notes, "I am a fan because everything I love about American Studies—namely, the way in which it challenges the 'truths' of our country—is reflected in Butler's stories." The phrase "positive obsession" comes from Butler, who writes of it as a kind of navigational drive, a force that overwrites choice and prompts us to think in terms of teaching's intimacy to desire: "Positive obsession is about not being able to stop just because you're afraid and full of doubts. Positive obsession is dangerous. It's about not being able to stop at all." Persistence and pleasure in the face of uncertainty and doubt hold Butler and American Studies in common for Hentges and serves as a resonant description of the state of the field as illuminated by the American Studies classroom, the explicit aim of this volume.

American Studies is, the essays gathered here attest, something of a collective positive obsession, and one that, variously, occasions risk taking for the sake of truth and in the address of power, acceptance of discomfort as a condition of un/learning, and a critical understanding of both the potency and limitations of teaching as a world-making activity. What is the state of the field from the perspective of the classroom? It is vibrant, worldly, immensely heterogeneous, and altogether vital in the fullest senses of the term. Through the classroom, American Studies gives students and faculty the resources and skills necessary to apprehend and remake the world; and through the classroom students and faculty provide American Studies specificity and groundedness in the material lives of ideas. We see that it is with a certain obsessiveness that courses are designed, assignments derived and modified and modified again, texts and objects selected and changed, and lectures and discussions crafted.

This collective obsession is not positive in a celebratory sense so much as it connotes being oriented toward something: greater understanding, more knowledge, the securing of social justice, the remediation of racism in all its intersectionality, more community, more consideration, more life. American Studies is very much a "big tent," to borrow a phrase from Doris Friedensohn's essay, and its teachers are less interested in defining its boundaries than in figuring out how to translate the resources attached to the rubric into these positivities. (Such disinterest if not wariness seems exactly appropriate for a field whose thematics include sustained study of the necropolitics of the US nation's historic and ongoing regulation of its borders.) This volume invites us to think of that process of resource translation as one of the *mattering* of American Studies—of the materials that anchor us as well as their significance; of the effort to materialize the positivities of the field; and, decidedly, of how the idea of mattering keys into historic and present conditions as articulated and figured by the Black Lives Matter movement and American Studies' attunement to the urgent necessity of their address.

Indeed, key among the capacities provided by the American Studies classroom as represented in this collection is apprehension of the foundational role of racial, gender, ethnic, bodily, and class differentiation, together with settler colonialism, in the production and sustenance of the US nation as constituted by the differential mattering of some lives over others. Migration and migrant histories and experiences, the representational politics of popular culture, US interventionism, slavery and revolutionary movements—these name only some of the curricular focuses identified in these essays. While several of the pieces observe resistance to student acknowledgment of these aspects of US history and culture that belie its exceptionalism, these "alternative ways of knowing," as Paul Croce puts it, clearly comprise the primary fabric of American Studies pedagogy. Arguably no longer "alternative" to the field, one way in which teaching American Studies matters is by (sometimes obsessively) acting as a conduit for knowledge unaligned with power and the powerful.

Note, too, the resonance with Butler's framing of positive obsession as describing movement in the face of fear and doubt. There is no small amount of courage expressed in these chapters, on the part of both teachers and students and often their subjects of study. Vulnerability, discomfort, difficulty, and doubt all find presence in the teaching of American Studies, and understandably so given how these qualities also accompany the lived experience of the US nation. Unsurprisingly but importantly, the overrepresentation of whiteness and cis-hetero-masculinity in the academy means that these particular qualities are differentially distributed and experienced among the teachers writing these essays as well as the students appearing in them. Subject position still matters, and sometimes in pronounced ways, depending on student demographics and institutional locations. Students catalyze the un/learning of teachers at times because of these contingencies (Rodriguez, Stock), bringing to bear their own embodied knowledges in their encounters with American Studies teachers, texts, and objects.

The classroom precipitates different kinds and scales of fear and doubt; the American Studies pedagogy elaborated through this volume is infused by such signs of openness to becoming more knowledgeable, more attuned to shifting historical conditions, more attuned to self in relation to other and to the complex personhood of the other. Institutional context likewise compels training and retraining—cycles of undisciplining and redisciplining, as Nihad Farooq sketches in her contribution. The deep heterogeneity of classroom spaces—from those located in a Georgia engineering college to the verdant New Hampshire setting of Dartmouth, to a small Presbyterian college and big public universities, and from high school to a food services training academy, and encompassing the variegated sites of service learning among them—thrillingly speak to the everywhereness of American Studies. Such diversity of locations also excitingly mirrors the range of administrative rubrics under which American Studies operates: Asian American studies, media studies, ethnic studies, Latinx studies, African American studies, religious studies, sociology, popular culture studies—the list goes on. Each of the contributors here has in one form or another moved with the question Paul Lauter poses: "Why this thing, in this way, at this time?" Why this field, this class, this assignment, at this time, in this place? Discomfort and doubt—or the discomfort of doubt—entails courage in the address of such questions.

Crucially, this is not a collection of stories featuring heroic teachers overcoming obstacles in noble pursuit of the truth! Instead, we are witness to the matter-of-factness of confronting resistance, encountering ignorance, and working under sometimes the narrowest or persistently excoriating of constraints and conditions. To be sure, considerable emotional labor and even psychic distress explicitly but also tacitly characterize the work we see sketched here. If Adriana Estill's call to elaborate *emotional pedagogies* is this volume's most overt example of such, Reena Goldthree and Aimee Bahng's and Kendra Hamilton's chapters also describe attenuating conditions as they name the difficulty, the impossibility, and, simultaneously, the necessity of teaching American Studies in and at their respective locations. What we learn is not that the distress of some is "worth it" in the vein of a rationalist cost-benefit analysis, nor is teaching American Studies to be lauded as an expression of virtue. Rather, we come to understand that these are pedagogies of discomfort that correlate with full and critical engagement with the realities of America. The contradictions that inhere in such engagement—of reveling in the aesthetics that take flight from the awfulness of racism, of the creatively critical acts that repurpose objects (photographs, monuments) toward unaligned aims—induce analysis rather than reaction, study and reflection in place of drama, in short, teaching instead of heroism. The imparted lesson is simple and powerful: what is needed is not individual sacrifice or genius but collective work.

That collective work is decidedly and resoundingly multilateral. Not only is knowledge and un/learning reciprocal between students and teachers in the American Studies classroom, but they are also vertical affordances. Elizabeth Duclos-Orsello, Kristin Anderson, Jake Lefker, and Rosario Ubiera-Minaya identify bell hooks, Gloria Anzaldúa, and Ruth Wilson Gilmore as part of the intellectual genealogies they draw on and extend; the traditions of women of color feminism and theorization of intersectionality find strong presence in Richard Rodríguez's piece among others; American Studies disciplinary history itself serves as point of departure in Paul Lauter's essay; and, notably reminding us of intergenerationality as an important conduit, Stanley Thangaraj's father makes an appearance as a source of pedagogical insight. Moreover, the breadth of disciplinary and interdisciplinary training invoked here—including media studies, anthropology, cultural studies, history, ethnic studies, and literary studies—bespeaks forms of institutionally legitimated knowledge that are also part of the American Studies project. So, too, are present the lived and living knowledges of the bodies of the students and teachers and the subjects of history and poetry, of politics and art and film, that constitute the American Studies classroom. All this is to note that the metaphysics of the American Studies classroom defy conventional time and space and teem with all manner of knowledge and insight. Such multivocality generatively antagonizes the gatekeeping function of the academy and is realized through pedagogical practices like the walking tour and experiential learning in addition to textual assignment and thematic focus. Given the intellectual traditions and genealogies that have been so formative for contemporary American Studies, that classroom practices define the field in terms of collectivity and community across time and space makes all good sense. There is something radically democratic conveyed by this sense of openness—of American Studies as a big tent—that is both the ground and horizon of understanding that our classrooms are spaces of unlimited possibility.

It is, finally, this expansive and vibrant sense of possibility, attached to an equally vital sense of urgency, that comes to define American Studies through the classroom in this volume. A field comprising teachers who intend to bother students (Croce) and to ruin the fantasy of America (Duclos-Orsello), to produce cognitive dissonance (Estill), and to insist that a given American Studies class act as a point of departure and not arrival ("let this seminar be a starting point," Kabria Baumgartner proposes), American Studies thwarts whatever expectations might attach to the rubric prior to engagement with it, as it creates space for collective hard thinking about issues that matter. It is no wonder that the field has been a lightning rod, provoking as it does those inured and willfully attached to the produced ignorance that is American exceptionalism. As the volume's editors observe, it is a field among those regularly accused of inculcating students with radical politics. The essays here neither affirm nor in fact deny such a charge. Instead, they demonstrate that American Studies' overweening pedagogical interest is in enhancing and expanding all our intellectual capacity writ large. (As an aside, I cannot but note that those who would collapse getting smarter with radical politics might do well to consider the implications of such an elision—namely, the intimacy of the status quo with an attachment to ignorance.)

Expanding our sense of what is possible is an appropriate description of at least part of what Octavia Butler gives us through her writings. As Hentges suggests, Butler's ability to imagine worlds that at once resonate with and depart from historic conditions and present realities catalyzes recognition of teaching as the creative act of world making. Labor and brilliance simultaneously subtend what it means to envision and enact radical possibility in and through teaching. Against the scene of the severe contraction in public support for education and educators that has for some decades now pervaded the contemporary US cultural and political economic landscape, the creativity, labor, and intellection of Black and Brown women like Butler, Gloria Anzaldúa, Ruth Wilson Gilmore, Katherine McKittrick, and bell hooks invoked in this collection, sharply emerges as the luminous condition of possibility for American Studies as a world-making project. Following their lead, we understand difficulty and discomfort to be less obstacles than terms referring to conditions of work; following their lead, we understand teaching American Studies to be less an option than a necessity—to be, indeed, a positive obsession.

Contributors

❖ ❖ ❖ ❖ ❖ ❖ ❖

Kristin Anderson served as the chief program officer at the North Shore Community Development Coalition from 2009 to 2015 and is currently the development project manager at The Community Builders, Inc. in Connecticut.

Guillermo Avila-Saavedra is professor and chair of media and communications studies at Salem State University.

Aimee Bahng is associate professor of gender and women's studies at Pomona College, author of *Migrant Futures: Decolonizing Speculation in Financial Times* (2018), and has another book project underway tentatively titled "Transpacific Ecologies."

Kabria Baumgartner is associate professor of American Studies and core faculty in women's and gender studies at the University of New Hampshire, and author of the award-winning book *In Pursuit of Knowledge: Black Women and Educational Activism in Antebellum America* (2019).

Megan Bayles is lecturer in American Studies at the University of California, Davis. She coedited, with Achy Obejas, *Immigrant Voices: 21st Century Stories* (2014).

Kandice Chuh is professor of English American Studies and critical social psychology at the Graduate Center, City University of New York, and a former president of the American Studies Association. She is the author of *The Difference Aesthetics Makes: On the Humanities "After Man"* (2019) and *Imagine Otherwise: On Asian Americanist Critique* (2003), and the coeditor, with Karen Shimakawa, of *Orientations: Mapping Studies in the Asian Diaspora* (2001).

Paul J. Croce is professor of history and director of American Studies at

Stetson University, and author of *Science and Religion in the Era of William James: The Eclipse of Certainty* (1995) and *Young William James Thinking* (2018) and creator of The Public Classroom, https://pubclassroom.com/.

Dave DiPietro teaches at Somerville High School in Somerville, Massachusetts. He holds an MA in American Studies from UMass-Boston and an MA in teaching from Tufts University.

Elizabeth Duclos-Orsello is professor and chair of the Department of Interdisciplinary Studies and coordinator of American Studies at Salem State University, and the author of *Modern Bonds: Redefining Community in Early Twentieth-Century St. Paul* (2018).

Joseph Entin is professor of English and American Studies at Brooklyn College, City University of New York, the author of *Sensational Modernism: Experimental Fiction and Photography in Thirties America* (2007), coeditor, with Sara Blair and Franny Nudelman, of *Remaking Reality: U.S. Documentary Culture after 1945* (2018), and coeditor, with Robert Rosen and Leonard Vogt, of *Controversies in the Classroom: A Radical Teacher Reader* (2008).

Adriana Estill is professor of English and American Studies and director of American Studies at Carleton College. She is currently at work on a book about the telenovela's traits and meanings in US media spaces.

Nihad M. Farooq is associate professor in the School of Literature, Media, and Communication at Georgia Tech, and the author of *Undisciplined: Science, Ethnography, and Personhood in the Americas, 1830–1940* (2016).

Roderick A. Ferguson is professor of Women's, Gender, and Sexuality Studies at Yale University and a former president of the American Studies Association. He is the author of *One Dimensional Queer* (2019), *We Demand: The University and Student Protests* (2017), *The Reorder of Things: The University and Its Pedagogies of Minority Difference* (2012), and *Aberrations in Black: Toward a Queer of Color Critique* (2004). He is coeditor, with Grace Hong, of *Strange Affinities: The Gender and Sexual Politics of Comparative Racialization* (2011).

Doris Friedensohn is professor emerita of women's studies at New Jersey City University, and the author of *Eating as I Go: Scenes from America and Abroad* (2006), *Cooking for Change: Tales from a Food Service Training Academy* with photos by Steve Riskind (2011), and *Airports Are for Waiting and Other Travelers' Tales* (2019).

Ingrid Gessner is professor of English and American Studies at Vorarlberg University of Education in Feldkirch, Austria, and the author of *Yellow Fever Years: An Epidemiology of Nineteenth-Century Literature and Culture* (2016), *Collective Memory as Catharsis? The Vietnam Veterans Memorial in Public Controversy* (2000), and *From Sites of Memory to Cybersights: (Re)Framing Japanese American Experiences* (2007).

Reena Goldthree is assistant professor of African American studies at Princeton University.

Kendra Hamilton is associate professor of English and Southern studies at Presbyterian College.

Sarah Hentges is associate professor of American Studies at the University of Maine at Augusta, and the author of *Girls on Fire: Transformative Heroines in Young Adult Dystopian Literature* (2018), *Women and Fitness in American Culture* (2014), and *Pictures of Girlhood: Modern Female Adolescence on Film* (2006).

Rebecca Hill is professor of American Studies at Kennesaw State University, and the author of *Men, Mobs and Law: Anti-Lynching and Labor Defense in US Radical History* (2009).

Wendy Kozol is professor of Comparative American Studies at Oberlin College, and the author of *Distant Wars Visible: The Ambivalence of Witnessing* (2014) and *Life's America: Family and Nation in Postwar Photojournalism* (1994).

Paul Lauter is Allan K. and Gwendolyn Miles Smith Professor of Literature, Emeritus, at Trinity College in Hartford, Connecticut, and a former president of the American Studies Association. He is the author of several books, including, most recently, *Our Sixties: An Activist's History* (2020), and *From Walden Pond to Jurassic Park: Activism, Culture, and American Studies* (2001). He is also the general editor of *The Heath Anthology of American Literature.*

Jake Lefker is the former director of community engagement at the

North Shore Community Development Coalition. He is currently an MBA candidate, consortium fellow, and Toigo Foundation Fellow at the University of Southern California Marshall School of Business.

Richard T. Rodríguez is associate professor of media and cultural studies at the University of California, Riverside, and the author of *Next of Kin: The Family in Chicano/a Cultural Politics* (2009).

Linda Stewart is the director for graduate student support at the Center for Excellence in Teaching and Learning (CETL) and associate professor in the Department of English at Kennesaw State University. She is a coeditor, with Laura R. Davis, of *Teachers as Avatars: English Studies in the Digital Age (2011)*. Her research on the scholarship of teaching and learning focuses on narrative studies and contemplative pedagogies.

Catherine McNicol Stock is the Barbara Zaccheo Kohn '72 professor of history and American Studies at Connecticut College, and the author of *Nuclear Country: The Origins of the Rural New Right* (2020), *Rural Radicals: Righteous Rage in the American Grain* (2017), and *Main Street in Crisis: The Great Depression and the Old Middle Class on the Northern Plains* (1992), and coeditor, with Jon Lauck, of *The Conservative Heartland: A Political History of the Postwar American Midwest* (2020).

Julie Sze is professor of American Studies at the University of California, Davis, and the author of *Noxious New York: The Racial Politics of Urban Health and Environmental Justice* (2007), *Fantasy Islands: Chinese Dreams and Ecological Fears in an Age of Climate Crisis* (2015), and *Environmental Justice Movement in a Moment of Danger* (2020), and the editor of *Sustainability: Approaches to Environmental Justice and Social Power* (2018).

Stanley Thangaraj is associate professor of anthropology, gender studies, and international studies at City College, City University of New York, author of *Desi Hoop Dreams: Pickup Basketball and the Making of Asian American Masculinity* (2015), and coeditor, with Constancio Arnaldo and Christina B. Chin, of *Asian American Sporting Cultures* (2016). He won the American Studies Association's 2015 Comparative Ethnic Studies Award for his newest project on Kurdish America.

Rosario Ubiera-Minaya served as chief program officer at the North Shore Community Development Coalition from 2015 to 2018 and currently is executive director of Amplify Latinx in Boston, Massachusetts.

Index

Numbers in italics refer to pages with figures.